WINNING BY PROCESS

WINNING BY PROCESS

The State and Neutralization
of Ethnic Minorities in Myanmar

Jacques Bertrand,
Alexandre Pelletier,
and Ardeth Maung Thawnghmung

SOUTHEAST ASIA PROGRAM PUBLICATIONS
AN IMPRINT OF CORNELL UNIVERSITY PRESS   ITHACA AND LONDON

Copyright © 2022 by Cornell University

All rights reserved. Except for brief quotations in a review, this book, or parts thereof, must not be reproduced in any form without permission in writing from the publisher. For information, address Cornell University Press, Sage House, 512 East State Street, Ithaca, New York 14850. Visit our website at cornellpress.cornell.edu.

First published 2022 by Cornell University Press

Library of Congress Cataloging-in-Publication Data

Names: Bertrand, Jacques, 1965- author. | Pelletier, Alexandre, author. | Thawnghmung, Ardeth Maung, author.
Title: Winning by process : the state and neutralization of ethnic minorities in Myanmar / Jacques Bertrand, Alexandre Pelletier, and Ardeth Maung Thawnghmung.
Description: Ithaca [New York] : Southeast Asia Program Publications, an imprint of Cornell University Press, 2022. | Includes bibliographical references and index.
Identifiers: LCCN 2021051812 (print) | LCCN 2021051813 (ebook) | ISBN 9781501764530 (hardcover) | ISBN 9781501764684 (paperback) | ISBN 9781501764547 (epub) | ISBN 9781501764554 (pdf)
Subjects: LCSH: Minorities—Government policy—Burma. | Minorities—Political aspects—Burma. | Burma—Politics and government—21st century. | Ethnic conflict—Burma. | Burma—Ethnic relations—Political aspects.
Classification: LCC JQ751.A38 M544 2022 (print) | LCC JQ751.A38 (ebook) | DDC 320.9591—dc23/eng/20220213
LC record available at https://lccn.loc.gov/2021051812
LC ebook record available at https://lccn.loc.gov/2021051813

To all the peoples of Myanmar

Contents

List of Figures, Maps, and Tables	ix
Preface and Acknowledgments	xi
List of Abbreviations	xvii
Note on Terminology	xix
Introduction	1
1. Winning by Process: Leveraging Formal Negotiation, State Institutions, and War	19
2. The Failure to Win by War: The Limits of Bamar Dominance and Ethnic Minority Repression	39
3. Democratization: Layering and Sequencing in the State Institutional Arena	61
4. Process over War: From Ceasefire to Political Dialogue	82
5. Normalizing Weak Ethnic States: Constitutional Lock-In and Implementing Layers	110
6. Outflanking and the Erosion of De Facto Autonomy	131
7. Fragmentation, Marginalization, and Subjugation: Layering and Locking In Ethnic Recognition	149
Conclusion	174
Notes	191
Bibliography	215
Index	237

Figures, Maps, and Tables

Figures

1. Myanmar's peace process — 98
2. In- and out-migration in Myanmar's ethnic states — 169

Maps

1. Map of Myanmar — 7
2. Proposed self-administered zones, National Convention (1994) — 155

Tables

1. Number of interviews (and focus groups) in Myanmar by year — 16
2. Number of interviews by category (excluding focus groups) — 17
3. Negotiation process: Three key arenas — 23
4. Winning by process: Five key strategies — 26
5. Distribution of powers, 2008 constitution (summary) — 57
6. Bilateral ceasefires (2011–12) — 89
7. Agreements reached at the 21st Century Panglong Conference, 2016–20 — 103
8. Layers of ethnic representation in the 2008 constitution — 152
9. Ethnic political parties, 1990 and 2015 elections — 159
10. Mother tongue use in four states/regions of Myanmar — 172
11. Mother tongue and social promotion in Myanmar — 172

Preface and Acknowledgments

This book's cover photo was taken on our way to Hakha, Chin State's remote capital, in the early days of the 2015 rainy season. This picture captures not only the beauty of Chin's rugged landscape but also the essence of our argument. When not interrupted by landslides, as in the picture, our seventeen-hour journey from Mandalay was long, steep, tortuous, slippery, and perilous, like Myanmar's own road to peace and federalism. By any standard, this journey was challenging, yet we were told that the road to Hakha used to take several days by lorry, so this was a vast improvement. As we publish this book, a new airport in Falam connects Hakha to Yangon and Mandalay within a few hours. But there is nothing like the road to understand Myanmar's size and diversity, inequalities and contradictions, as well as its people's strength and resilience. The improbable road to Hakha opened up to vibrant communities, eager to survive and promote their identities. At the same time, it ironically showed how resolute the state is at expanding its clout over the whole territory, integrating and taming its "unruly" periphery. We hope this book captures this fundamental tension.

This book changed with the rapid and enthralling evolution of events over the course of the last decade. We came together initially as a team with very modest aims. When the regime opened up in 2011, there was tremendous excitement and exhilaration at the possibilities ahead. Burmese abroad returned to Myanmar with new optimism regarding how they could participate in rebuilding the country. So did numerous international organizations, international nongovernmental organizations (INGOs) foreign scholars, and many other interested parties. Some new, exciting local NGOs and research organizations were created, and all offered new ways of channeling this energy. After decades in the United States, Ardeth Thawnghmung was one such scholar who returned to participate in many new events, and she helped several new organizations to think about research and policy approaches. In 2012, she invited Alexandre Pelletier, at the time a PhD student at the University of Toronto, to use his knowledge, particularly on federalism, in a couple of early workshops looking into possible solutions to the long-standing civil war with ethnic minorities. Jacques Bertrand joined the conversation soon thereafter, having worked extensively over the previous years on secessionist and autonomist conflicts in Indonesia, the Philippines, and Thailand.

What initially began as an initiative to jointly organize a workshop in Yangon soon developed into an exciting joint book project, and several years of fieldwork in various ethnic states and regions. Already in 2013, we were collectively ambivalent about the depth and significance of the explosion of workshops sponsored by numerous foreign countries and organizations, and sought to deepen the analysis. There was no substitute for digging into the empirical reality, engaging armed groups, government officials, ethnic political parties, and civil society organizations not only in Yangon but in Chin, Kachin, Kayin, and Shan States and in other regions where we could go. Rakhine became off-limits but we could mostly travel throughout Myanmar for the following seven years. We were able to organize very productive trips all together in 2015 and 2016, and several follow-up trips thereafter, with many others on our individual schedules. Cumulatively, we are grateful for the hundreds of people we were able to interview, and the months of fieldwork that form the basis of much of this collective effort.

At the substantive level, we also kept rethinking the scope and emphasis of the book. Working on evolving events is always a challenge. While our starting point was clear, its end was open. Our initial research traced deeply the evolution of state policies toward ethnic minority groups under the Union Solidarity and Development Party (USDP) government, and the rapid changes being implemented not only in peace negotiations but also in state governments. We were able to capture, with generous funding from the United States Institute of Peace, the evolving pace of state institutions and their impact on peace negotiations during this transitional period. We initially thought that the book would conclude with the 2015 elections, but we were too curious as researchers, and ultimately too excited to end our journey at that point. Our field trips were beginning to capture some of the most interesting points in our book in the early year or two of Aung San Suu Kyi's government, and so we could not resist continuing to track the change under the National League for Democracy (NLD) government, returning to several ethnic states to assess differences and continuity between the two governments. We are grateful that funding from the International Development Research Centre and other sources allowed us to return up to the end of the NLD's mandate. Our collective analysis evolved, the manuscript was rewritten numerous times, and we finally agreed on its angle and thrust when the coup occurred.

The coup ended up not changing our analysis. The alternative book would have assessed the state of the political dialogue, civil war, and state policies toward ethnic minority groups up to the end of the NLD's first mandate. This book frames the whole decade of peace negotiations and institutional change that ended with the coup. In many ways, the coup sealed our analysis and gave us confidence that what we had tracked and analyzed over the previous decade was crucial for understanding how ethnic relations with the Bamar majority would continue to evolve, irrespective of whether the Tatmadaw succeeded in its plans, or whether a broader democratic movement won out.

Our view that the state was "winning by process" showed the strong historical continuity, the risks, and even the missed possibilities that the decade of change revealed. While, like many others, we were all excited and optimistic about the rapid changes set in motion in 2011, we nevertheless remained skeptical of the Tatmadaw's intentions and, over time, came to more sobering conclusions. Our disappointment was strongest that the democratic aura surrounding Aung San Suu Kyi and the NLD soon revealed much more continuity with the past, and the USDP in particular, rather than a new horizon for ethnic minority groups. While colleagues, Myanmar specialists, and activists might disagree with our arguments, we certainly invite debate over the interpretation of the evidence. It became clear to us, however, that little progress was achieved for ethnic minority groups, whether in the political dialogue or in state institutions, and the NLD, not only the Tatmadaw, certainly shared a large portion of responsibility. While we agree that the state became two-pronged, and that the NLD and Tatmadaw were at loggerheads with each other, we found surprising convergence in their views with respect to offering genuine federalism to ethnic minority groups. Instead, our evidence showed continued centralization and numerous attempts to thwart and dilute concessions in the political dialogue, as well as to severely restrict the power allocated to ethnic minority groups through the 2008 constitution, even after its very modest amendments.

What might be seen as a pessimistic outlook is, in fact, an analysis of the outcome and the factors leading to it, with a view to reveal some significant dynamic processes involved when negotiating at the same time as participating in democratizing state institutions. Our hope is that, rather than conclude that there is no path to peace, our book can demonstrate to future negotiators and their advisers how to take stock of the complexity of interrelated processes and better position themselves for more open and productive bargaining.

We were deeply alarmed at how rapidly the political situation deteriorated after February 2021. Not only were many of the people who helped us suddenly silenced, but their lives were also threatened. We continue to share much grief for the losses that the population in Myanmar suffered once again. In order to ensure that we put no one at risk, we decided to anonymize all of the interviewees in our references. Similarly, while there are many people we would like to thank for their help during these past years, it is unfortunate that we can name only a few.

We would like to thank individuals and organizations who shared with us their experience, information, and interpretations through individual interviews and focus group discussions across different parts of the country. These include members of the Karen, Chin, Kachin, Shan, Mon, Kayah, Pa'O, and Rakhine communities. We are grateful for the time and help of these representatives of political parties; civil society organizations; community-based, nonprofit international, or local organizations; religious organizations; ethnic armed groups; think tanks; private businesses; activist organizations; and ethnic culture and literature organizations. Some of them are ethnic affairs ministers, state/regional ministers, and elected members of national or local parliaments. We are also grateful to a few high-level officials in Naypyidaw who agreed to meet and discuss openly some controversial issues. We also thank those from several ethnic minority regions and Yangon who participated in the initial workshops that began our journey in Yangon and Bago. Their insights convinced us to push beyond the very superficial surface that we had scratched in those initial discussions, and triggered our scholarly curiosity to probe deeper and further during the following years.

A few individuals deserve our strongest gratitude. Among the few that we are permitted to mention, Dr. Cin Khan Lian (Ar Yone Oo) stands out, for helping in so many ways, including with an initial trip to Chin State, where the realities of ethnic minority states, and the very challenging trip we experienced amid landslides, allowed us to capture the essence of our argument in the photo that we chose for our book cover. Along with Saw Eh Htoo (Kaw Lah Foundation), and Myat The Thitsar (Enlightened Myanmar Research Foundation, or EMReF), he also helped to arrange workshops, focus group discussions, and individual meetings for us in 2015 and 2016 in Yangon and Bago Regions and Kayin and Chin States and he kindly granted us the permission to publicly acknowledge them. A few locally based individuals were tremendously helpful in assisting us with making contacts and organizing interviews in Kachin, Kayin, and Shan States. We wish we were able to name them here. Finally, many thanks to Khun Noah (not his real name) for collecting some very useful data from official sources and for cross-checking details for us.

A few foreign specialists and experts on Myanmar shared their insights: Richard Horsey (International Crisis Group), SuiSue Mark, Jeremy Liebowitz (Myanmar Multiparty Democracy Program and International Republican Institute), Matthew Arnold (the Asia Foundation), and senior consultants and directors of INGOs on peace issues. The following individuals offered feedback and helped with specific details throughout our research period, up until the manuscript was published: Su Mon Thazin Aung (Institute for Strategy and Policy-Myanmar), Padoh Ta Doh Moo (KNU), Padoh Steve (KNU), Ashley South, and Myat The Thitsar (EMReF). Mark McDowell was helpful in a variety of ways, as was Patrick Kum Ja Lee (International Development Research Centre). We thank Mi Joo for her excellent logistical support on two of our trips.

We are very grateful to anonymous reviewers who provided some incisive and extremely valuable and constructive comments. We took up some of the challenges they presented, and launched into revisions that went much further than merely responding to them would have required. But we are grateful for their initial spark that made us rethink a few important points and allowed us to redraft parts of what we believe is now a better book as a result.

At the University of Toronto, we would like to thank the doctoral students who provided enormously useful research assistance. In particular, Jae Park did superb work in helping us prepare the final manuscript. Justinas Stankus was very helpful during one of our trips to Shan State. We are also very grateful for colleagues and students who provided useful comments on parts of the theoretical work at the Comparative Politics Workshop. A special thanks to Nina Boric (Asian Institute), as well as Julie Guzzo and Michael Li (Political Science), who helped us navigate the intricacies of funding agencies and university bureaucracy that enabled our work.

We are grateful to our spouses for their support, patience, and understanding during our long travels and absences.

We were very fortunate to receive grants from several funding organizations. We are grateful for generous support from the United States Institute of Peace and the International Development Research Centre. The findings and conclusions expressed in this book are ours only and do not necessarily reflect the views of either of those organizations.

Finally, we invite the reader back on the road to Hakha. As we stopped for several hours, one of our travel companions told us, "We, ethnic people, have waited more than sixty years for peace and federalism—another landslide won't make a difference." As we finish this book, the latest coup is yet another landslide, but we hope that Myanmar will find itself on a new, better road soon.

Toronto, Québec, Lowell—June 2021

Abbreviations

AA	Arakan Army
BGFs	Border Guard Forces
BSPP	Burma Socialist Program Party
CEFU	Committee for the Emergence of a Federal Union
CNF	Chin National Front
CPB	Communist Party of Burma
CSO	civil society organization
DKBA	Democratic Karen Buddhist Army
DKBA-5	Democratic Karen Buddhist Army–Brigade 5/Democratic Benevolent Army
EAM	ethnic affairs minister
EAO	ethnic armed organization
FPTP	first-past-the-post
GAD	General Administration Department
IDP	internally displaced person
INGO	international nongovernmental organization
KIO	Kachin Independence Organization
KNPP	Karenni National Progressive Party
KNU	Karen National Union
LDU	Lahu Democratic Union
MNDAA	Myanmar National Democratic Alliance Army
MoE	Ministry of Education
MP	member of parliament
MPC	Myanmar Peace Center
MTB MLE	mother tongue–based multilingual education
NC	National Convention
NCA	Nationwide Ceasefire Agreement
NCCT	Nationwide Ceasefire Coordinating Team
NDF	National Democratic Front
NDSC	National Defense and Security Council
NGO	nongovernmental organization
NLD	National League for Democracy
NMSP	New Mon State Party
NUG	National Unity Government

PM	People's Militia
RCSS	Restoration Council of Shan State
SAD	self-administered division
SAZ	self-administered zone
SLORC	State Law and Order Restoration Council
SPDC	State Peace and Development Council
SSPP	Shan State Progressive Party
TNLA	Ta'ang National Liberation Army
UNFC	United Nationalities Federal Council
UPC	Union Peace Conference
UPDJC	Union Peace Dialogue Joint Committee
USDP	Union Solidarity and Development Party
UWSA	United Wa State Army
WGEC	Working Group on Ethnic Coordination

Note on Terminology

In 1989, the Myanmar military replaced existing English names for the country and its divisions, townships, cities, streets, citizens, and ethnic groups with what it considered to be more authentic Myanmar names. In this book, we use the pre-1989 names when discussing events that took place before 1989 and the newer names when discussing events that happened after that. One exception is our use of the term "Karen"/"Kayin." We use "Karen" rather than "Kayin" to refer to the people, their culture, and their language even after the changes made in 1989. "Karen" has remained the common terminology to refer to the group in English-language scholarship, as well as among Karen themselves. We nevertheless use "Kayin" to refer to the state, the political and geographical subdivision of the Myanmar state. We use the Myanmarized term for the other ethnic minority groups, as they either remained the same as before 1989 or became more commonly used.

PRE-1989 NAMES	POST-1989 NAMES
Rangoon	Yangon
Moulmein	Mawlamyine
Pegu	Bago
Irrawaddy	Ayeyarwady
Pegu	Bago
Magwe	Magway
Tenasserim	Tanintharyi
Arakan	Rakhine
Karen State	Kayin State
Karenni	Kayah

In this book, we also generally use the names of the political wings of ethnic armed organizations (e.g., Karen National Union, Kachin Independence Organization) instead of their armed wings (e.g., Karen National Liberation Army, Kachin Independence Army), except for some that are more widely known through their armed wing's name (e.g., United Wa State Army, Ta'ang National Liberation Army, Arakan Army). The list below clarifies which terms we use in this book.

NAME USED IN THIS BOOK	OTHER KNOWN NAMES
All Burma Students' Democratic Front	none
Arakan Army (AA)	Union League of Arakan
Chin National Front (CNF)	Chin National Army
Democratic Karen Buddhist Army (DKBA)	none
Democratic Karen Benevolent Army–Brigade 5 (DKBA-5)	none
Kachin Independence Organization (KIO)	Kachin Independence Army
Karen National Union (KNU)	Karen National Liberation Army
Karen National Union/Peace Council	none
Karenni National Progressive Party (KNPP)	Karenni Army
Lahu Democratic Union	none
Myanmar National Democratic Alliance Army (MNDAA)	Myanmar National Truth and Justice Party
National Democratic Alliance Army	none
National Socialist Council of Nagaland (Khaplang)	none
New Mon State Party (NMSP)	Mon National Liberation Army
Pa'O National Liberation Organization (PNLO)	Pa'O National Liberation Army
Pa'O National Organization (PNO)	Pa'O National Army
Restoration Council of Shan State (RCSS)	Shan State Army–South
Shan State Progressive Party (SSPP)	Shan State Army–North
Ta'ang National Liberation Army (TNLA)	Palaung State Liberation Front
Wa National Organization	Wa National Army

WINNING BY PROCESS

INTRODUCTION

Civil war has ravaged Myanmar for over sixty years. From its creation, the independent Burmese state established a fragile relationship between its majority population of Bamar and a number of smaller ethnic minorities. These tensions were partly responsible for the collapse of Myanmar's initial democratic order and the rise of several insurgencies in various areas of the country.[1] During those years, recognition and self-determination were at the core of ethnic demands. Ethnic minority groups clung to what they perceived as Aung San's initial conception of the Burmese state as enshrined in the historic Panglong agreement of February 1947.[2] While largely reinterpreted, it nevertheless became a symbolic document that ethnic leaders repeatedly hailed as the promise of Bamar nationalists, and Aung San in particular, for a federal state. Meanwhile, the central state and its military reinforced centralization while pursuing a steady policy of "Burmanization."

In 2011, however, Myanmar came close to changing that path toward peace. After several decades of military rule, the regime began to liberalize, first transitioning to a civilian government and then in 2015 to Myanmar's first free and fair election since the 1950s. With this transition, both the Myanmar state, particularly reformists from the former regime, and ethnic armed organizations (EAOs) saw opportunities to seek a peaceful resolution to war. After sixty years, the army and the EAOs shared war fatigue. For the first time, they met in formal negotiations, reached a national ceasefire, and began a broader political dialogue. In 2015, the National League for Democracy (NLD), under its leader, Aung San Suu Kyi, was elected with high hopes that it would craft a path to peace, particularly since Aung San Suu Kyi had obtained strong support from ethnic minorities. Once again, in 2020, the NLD won a landslide victory that included broad support in ethnic minority areas. By February 2021, those hopes vanished after the Tatmadaw launched a coup that prevented the NLD from beginning its second mandate. The coup marked a sudden end to the ten years of negotiations involving the Tatmadaw, the civilian government, and ethnic minority groups.

In this book, we examine this decade of missed opportunity. We analyze why progress toward a peace agreement remained elusive, despite all parties suffering from war fatigue and wanting civil war to end. For most of the decade, the peace process appeared stalled. By "stalled," we mean that the conflict remained neither resolved nor in a full state of warfare. Some groups had signed ceasefires and were negotiating a peace agreement that was producing few results. Others maintained territorial control without active civil war. Violent conflict involved only a handful of EAOs against the state and occasional skirmishes with others, including those that signed ceasefire agreements. This state of affairs remained relatively constant throughout much of the NLD's five-year mandate. Why, despite strong initial conditions that favored conflict resolution, was so little accomplished toward a peace agreement?

While the 2021 coup might suggest that the previous decade was merely a sham, we disagree with such an interpretation. Before the transition to civilian rule in 2011, the Tatmadaw had attempted divide-and-rule strategies to weaken the possibility of alliance among EAOs and reduce the number of fronts in the civil war. But after 2011, it launched a decade of attempted negotiations as part of its so-called "road map to democracy," not only to reintroduce a form of civilian government but also to end the civil war. The military launched a coup neither to suspend the peace process nor to end a failed strategy toward ethnic minority groups. The coup was aimed mainly at dislodging Aung San Suu Kyi and her NLD in order to regain control over civilian rule. That it backfired miserably and created a downward spiral of violence is a topic for another book. For our purposes, the sudden end to the peace process was a by-product of the coup, not one of the Tatmadaw's goals.

As we show, the state—whether the Tatmadaw or the civilian government—was gaining from the existing process as EAOs were losing some of their leverage while the state institutions and practices spread to previously untapped areas of control. The coup was actually costly to the Tatmadaw's goals of reducing ethnic minority gains toward a federal state, ensuring a more centralized Myanmar and reducing the costs of civil war. It shifted Bamar and even NLD sympathies in favor of EAOs. It allowed new, if perhaps fleeting, alliances to emerge between Bamar and EAOs to resist the Tatmadaw, whereas the armed groups had come to distance themselves and even dismiss the NLD as a possible political partner. But again, this was an unexpected outcome of the coup, not its initial intention.

This book shows that exploiting a stalled conflict can be a winning strategy, particularly for the state. While the peace process and the broader conflict appeared stalled in Myanmar, the state actually gained, reaching its goals better than ever before. It was able to reduce the costs of war while avoiding extensive political and economic concessions to ethnic groups. While some armed groups gained as well, mostly from pursuing business interests in the resource sector, the Myanmar state was able to increasingly neutralize its former opponents without much compromise or costly war. Meanwhile, ethnic minority groups remained as distant as ever from reaching the goals that brought them to war in the first place.

In broader comparative terms, our analysis of Myanmar suggests the need to understand better how warring parties sometimes use process to make strategic gains where war has failed. Scholarship on civil wars and peace negotiations views stalled conflict as inherently temporary, and likely to move either to a negotiated agreement or to more intensive violent conflict. Protracted civil wars and stalled peace processes are generally seen as wars in which no party can successfully win against the other. Forces on the ground are relatively balanced, or, at least, neither side can crush its opponents and have the incentive to surrender. Conflicts are also seen as stalled when bargaining fails, when commitment problems and information asymmetries prevent peaceful settlements, or when rebellion becomes a business and all or some of the parties benefit from its continuation. Yet, in all of these cases, the literature suggests, the equilibrium can be tilted at any time. We contend instead that a stalled conflict can reveal a hidden process in which parties continue to make gains through a more subtle mix of continued warfare, negotiation, and strategizing within existing institutions.

The Argument

This book argues that, on the eve of the Tatmadaw launching a coup in 2021, the Myanmar state had been "winning by process" rather than by war or by negotiated agreement. The apparently stalled conflict served the state's interests, even if not fully by design. While conflicting parties can win a war or reach peace agreements, we rarely view any point on the continuum in between as a winning outcome. Yet, as we show, "process" is key to understanding how stalled conflicts benefit some actors, particularly states.

We frequently refer to the Myanmar "state" for shorthand, but we recognize that the reality of Myanmar's complex state structure and the historical dominance of its military (the Tatmadaw) require much more nuance. Furthermore, with partial democratization after 2011, more groups were able to access and participate in state institutions.

The "state" represents the ruling elite's preferences and its control over its executive and legislative branches as well as the military's control of key areas of governance. Nevertheless, within state institutions, mostly at the regional and local branches of the state and in the national parliament, there are representative and governance opportunities for ethnic minority groups to gain access to new but limited opportunities within the state. We use "the state" when referring to the ruling elite—whether civilian or military—that represents one side of negotiations writ large with ethnic minority groups. We use "state institutional arena" to refer to the broader set of institutions that include within the state some spaces for ethnic minority groups to carve out new powers and obtain resources from the central government.

The Myanmar state is defined by the historically strong control that the military has held. As Callahan argues, the origins of the Myanmar state were intrinsically tied to war during the colonial and early postcolonial periods, thereby creating a strong political imbalance between the military and civilian sectors in society. The subsequent dominance and autonomy of the military that also permeated the decade of quasi-democracy created a relatively unique type of state that would more adequately require an analysis of a two-pronged state structure, particularly after the election of the NLD.[3] Where relevant, we discuss the Tatmadaw and the civilian government's role separately. But, in essence, our analysis shows that there was a convergence of interests, including the Bamar majority's dominance, which permeated both the Tatmadaw and the civilian "side" of the Myanmar state.[4]

Winning by process entails that one or more actors in a conflict—in this case, the Myanmar state—manage to exploit a stalled conflict or peace negotiations by neutralizing their opponents through strategies designed to limit those opponents' abilities to make gains. The state was said to be "winning" because it was able to maximize political stability and make progress toward achieving its goals, while minimizing or avoiding altogether political concessions and the use of force. Winning by process means reaching stability by manipulating the web of rules, institutions, and norms of engagement through which conflicting groups interact in three arenas—namely, formal negotiations, state institutions, and war. Winning by process can be a subtle, often underhanded, but no less efficient way to make gains in a long-standing conflict.

In its simplest form, "process" can be defined as a series of steps to reach specific goals, in this case a resolution of conflict. In the chapters that follow, we expand on a set of strategies that the state, and sometimes other actors, deploys to seize control of the process and steer it to its advantage. We identify five such strategies. First, *locking in* rules of engagement, bargaining, and institutional parameters within which to negotiate power allows certain actors to control the agenda and the degree of inclusion of negotiating parties, and to define rules that promise outcomes from which they can benefit. Second, *sequencing* can greatly advantage one party over another, through determining steps in the negotiation and the order of institutional changes, such as constitution making or amending prior to other changes, when to hold elections, or when armed groups are expected to disarm or disband. Third, *layering* adds sites of negotiating power and resource allocation, which includes the expansion of state institutions to members of opposing groups, such as representation in local government that then competes for representation. But it also includes the pluralization and fragmentation of state opponents, through the multiplication of organizations such as political parties and civil society organizations (CSOs). Fourth, *outflanking* is used to circumvent or bypass negotiating partners by accessing their supporters directly. Fifth, an *outgunning* strategy uses violence with the specific aim of making gains at the bargaining table.

Together, these strategies are used to control process and make gains across three arenas. First, the *formal negotiating arena* captures institutions specifically created to bring conflicting parties to the bargaining table. Second, the *state institutional arena* refers to institutions where groups obtain representation and powers beyond those of armed groups, which generally seek to monopolize these roles during a civil war. In a democratic setting, groups can negotiate gains for themselves beyond what is being negotiated in the formal bargaining arena. Third, the *theater of war*, largely analyzed in the literature on alliance-making, lies beyond formal negotiations and state institutions but influences them in many ways. In this arena, bargaining strategies reflect the resource and power differential of conflicting parties, without rules or procedures.

An attention to process shows how actors become entangled in a series of commitments, rules, and institutions that constrain or empower their ability to reach their goals. In many cases, nonstate armed groups become most constrained, and their goals more elusive, as negotiations drag on or a conflict remains stalled. Given highly asymmetric power in most civil war contexts, particularly in the presence of multiple armed groups, the state is usually in the best position to gain the upper hand and use process to its advantage.

We show that, from 2011 to 2021, the Myanmar state was slowly entrenching its particular framework for representing ethnic minorities while appearing to negotiate with them. EAOs continued to aspire to an elusive goal of "federalism," and some to self-determination, but other ethnic minority leaders' day-to-day participation in national politics and the running of their ethnic state contributed to legitimizing, or at least consolidating, the 2008 constitution. The process of establishing a new web of institutions and rules of the game had unwittingly altered the power balance between ethnic minority groups and the state. It shaped the transitional government's implementation of the 2008 constitution, the negotiating framework leading up to the "nationwide" ceasefire and, after that, the slow-moving 21st Century Panglong Conference. Whether by design or by a series of more or less coordinated interactions and interventions, the state largely controlled how this process unfolded. The path created by this institutional environment, and the stalled nature of the conflict, entrenched interests and expectations that highly constrained future options for a federal state, at least one close to ethnic groups' goals.

The Myanmar State and the Politicization of Ethnicity: From Civil War to Winning by Process

Ethnicity has been a core principle of territorial organization in Myanmar, but its definition and scope remain contested. "Ethnic minorities" include groups defined in terms of ascriptive criteria such as language, religion, color, and territory.[5] But there are few, if any, objective means by which ethnic groups can be identified. In Myanmar, the state officially recognizes 135 "ethnic nationalities,"[6] but they are subject to debate due to their ambiguous nature. The Bamar constitute the largest ethnic group.[7] Shan, Kachin, Karen, Kayah, Mon, Rakhine, and Chin have been recognized and provided with their own states, but they are mostly umbrella identities that are often divided into multiple different ethnic groups.[8] Several groups, such as the Chin, are further divided along sub-ethnic lines and mainly come together as one group in response to the political incentives created by territorial recognition. Others, such as the Wa, Pa'O, Danu, Palaung (Ta'ang), Kokang, and Naga, were given special self-autonomous administrative status in 2008, but not their own state. Rohingya constitute a minority that is territorially concentrated in northern Rakhine State but is perceived as an illegal "migrant" group from Bangladesh.[9] The state refers to them as "Bengali" and does not recognize the "Rohingya" group among the 135 official categories.

While ethnicity has long been accepted as a core principle of representation, its form and empowerment have been highly contested as well. From the outset, the first constitution of Burma in 1947 enshrined the ambiguity by creating a number of ethnic minority states, and even recognizing a right to secession for some of them. The 1947 constitution created the Kachin, Shan, and Karenni (now Kayah) States, but proclaimed a "Union" of Burma, rather than a federal

MAP 1. Map of Myanmar.

state as promised during the Panglong Conference.[10] Arakan (now Rakhine), Chin, and Karen (now Kayin) were made into special divisions, with few of the political rights of the Shan and Kachin States, and Mon were not recognized at all. Many articles of this initial constitution enabled the centralization of power at the expense of Burmese states and regions. The Burmese national government eventually used these powers to circumvent state power and increasingly "Burmanize" the country even under the first decade of democratic rule.[11] Subsequent constitutions, including the latest adopted a few years before liberalization, provided greater protection for the central government's prerogatives and overriding powers than it did for constituent states.

In the years following independence, state weakness and a growing split among the Bamar elite contributed to the rapid erosion of democracy and descent into civil war. Supporters of communism left the political system and organized a revolutionary insurgency. Meanwhile, ethnic minorities became quickly disillusioned by the state's failure to abide by promises to create more inclusive and representative institutions. This led to one of the longest civil wars of the twentieth and twenty-first centuries. The Karen launched a first insurgency in 1949, in response to disagreements over the boundaries that made up the Karen state. With an increasingly centralizing Burmese state, and policies designed to promote the Bamar language, customs, and (Buddhist) religion, ethnic minorities felt increasingly betrayed and resentful at what they perceived to be the broken promises of the Panglong Agreement. The 1947 constitution failed to deliver meaningful fiscal and administrative powers to the federated states, while ethnic minorities felt overwhelmed by the policies designed primarily to serve the large Bamar majority.[12]

After the 1962 coup, the recognition of ethnic minorities was surprisingly maintained. The regime even brought to seven the total number of ethnic states by creating a new state for Mon and converting Rakhine and Chin special divisions into states.[13] These states were devoid of any meaningful powers, but they preserved the ethnically based conception of the Burmese territorial state. At the same time, the military regime embarked on a long campaign to crush the rising insurgencies over the next several decades. No political solution was found, nor did the civil war end. Some armed groups were defeated or found accommodations with the central state, while new ones arose or groups splintered.[14] There were still more than a dozen main insurgent groups by the end of the military regime in 2011.

The transition to civilian rule and electoral democracy was truly unprecedented in Myanmar's recent history. It offered new opportunities to negotiate and genuinely increased confidence in reducing past arbitrariness in policies toward ethnic minorities. The military-supported Union Solidarity and

Development Party (USDP), under U Thein Sein, a former military official, won a landslide victory in the 2010 elections. Thein Sein then began more systematic negotiations for ceasefires, with the ultimate goal of reaching a nationwide ceasefire agreement. Negotiating frameworks and procedures were a novelty in Myanmar, where past ceasefire agreements between the military regime and insurgent groups were primarily informal and unwritten. For groups that both proposed and participated in ceasefire negotiations after 2011, there was increased confidence that the negotiating process and signed documents would be respected and implemented. The political dialogue began with the Union Peace Conference in the last few months of Thein Sein's administration, and continued under the Aung San Suu Kyi government. Not surprisingly, Aung San Suu Kyi, the daughter of Aung San and Myanmar's first post-2011 democratically elected leader of Myanmar,[15] appropriated the symbolism by renaming the political dialogue with ethnic minority groups the 21st Century Panglong Conference. The NLD government followed a similar negotiating framework that both sides had adopted with the expectation that, under democratic rule, the process's outcomes would be respected and binding.

Nevertheless, as this book shows, the process itself constrained EAOs and frustrated their hopes for self-determination, which has become widely known in the public discourse as federalism. While strategic maneuvering is expected during any negotiation, EAOs likely failed to envision at the outset how they might be outmaneuvered under rules that they themselves agreed to, and even proposed, but that the state ultimately controlled. As a consequence, as their incentives for peace increased, they nevertheless engaged in a process with an uncertain outcome, in which their ultimate goals appeared elusive.

The transition to civilian rule and democratization entailed significant state-led transformations in the administration of states and regions. The military regime adopted a new constitution in 2008 that Thein Sein's transitional government began to implement. Many of its clauses significantly transformed states and regions' powers and resources. For ethnic minority states, new parliaments were created, and chief ministers obtained greater budgetary allocations and more authority than they had in the past, even though they remained presidential nominations with relatively little formal independence from the central government. New positions of ethnic affairs ministers were created in states and regions where a significant concentration of ethnic minorities resided, outside of their "home" states. They were tasked with representing the interests of the ethnic minorities, particularly on cultural affairs.

The new democratic environment, ironically, contributed to creating more trust while also giving leverage to the state to funnel ethnic minority groups toward its goals. Although highly imperfect, as we will show, democratic institutions and procedures provided a measure of predictability and rules on which negotiations could build and the management of ethnic minority regions could proceed. The unintended consequence, however, was that ethnic minority groups found themselves highly constrained by the negotiating process that they had suggested at the outset. The differences and division among a myriad of ethnic minorities also made it difficult for them to reach consensus among themselves. The divisions occurred between EAOs that fought for autonomy and those that were content with business opportunities or that were allied with Myanmar's military. These divisions were also visibly present between EAOs that employed violence and ethnicity-based political parties that used nonviolent approaches to reach their goals. These groups disagreed over the extent to which they should compromise with the Burmese state and what exactly the future federal state should look like. Furthermore, while the central government implemented the 2008 constitution during the transitional phase, it created a whole new layer of administration and governance, devolving powers and providing some fiscal resources to all states and regions, including ethnic minority ones.

Moreover, ethnic minority states began to administer their affairs on a number of issues during the first few years after the return to civilian rule. Procedures retained strong centralizing tendencies, but nevertheless allowed for more initiative on the part of legislatures and executives. State governments, mostly with the strong backing of the central government, undertook new infrastructural and development programs that, in some regions, contributed to significant improvements from decades of authoritarian rule. They also provided new services, such as the expansion of education and access to health care. Although still very poor, they nevertheless rose above their dismal state under the previous regime. Finally, as the private sector began to expand, although still at a very small scale, state officials, ethnic minority leaders, and even EAO leaders gained access to profitable ventures.

Therefore, the Myanmar state was winning by process, as its own vision of a very limited federal state was promoted in the 21st Century Panglong Conference and implemented through the 2008 constitution. Beyond the imbalance of forces favoring the state, we contend that the process of negotiation and the institutions put into place in ethnic minority states created a web of constraints that significantly increased the costs of crafting a decentralized federal state and funneled ethnic minority groups (including armed groups) into the state's preferred model. This plan did not significantly change from the USDP-led government in alliance with the Tatmadaw to the NLD government when the Myanmar state increasingly appeared two pronged, with divisions growing between Aung San Suu Kyi's government and the Tatmadaw. On the question of compromise and negotiation with ethnic minority groups, we maintain that there was little difference: the NLD made few attempts to offer greater concessions, continued to implement the 2008 constitution, and generally favored a strong, centralized state. While the NLD sought constitutional change to reduce the political role of the Tatmadaw, it eschewed demands for a more genuinely federal state. Meanwhile, the federal ideal broadly espoused by EAOs, often ill defined but deep in its goals, seemed increasingly unattainable.

Situating the Argument

Winning by process contrasts with its two well-known and well-theorized alternatives: winning by war and winning by agreement. In winning by war, one of the sides defeats its opponent, either by crushing it or by taking over the state.[16] In winning by agreement, actors achieve a negotiated peace settlement, which generally includes a reconfiguration of the postwar political institutions through guaranteed representation, legislative vetoes, power sharing, or territorial autonomy. What is missing is greater attention to how process produces and shapes a whole set of outcomes that fall in between. Commonly referred to as "stalemates" or "protracted conflicts," these outcomes are often ignored as transient points on a trajectory toward peace or losing in war.

Studies of civil war show the difficulties of ending war through military means, particularly when multiple armed groups are present.[17] They focus on shifts in alliance making or strategic positioning of civil war actors in the face of ceasefire agreements or bargains with the state. The analysis is centered on understanding the factors that prevent the state or armed actors from reaching decisive victories.[18]

Conversely, studies of bargaining and negotiation emphasize factors that lead to, or prevent, agreements between warring parties.[19] Some scholars focus on the bargaining process itself and the conditions that lead to compromise or concessions in formal negotiation.[20] Others debate the relative merits of alternative institutions to offer templates that can allow reaching compromises and agreements that remain stable. They have considered extensively the merits of federalism, territorial autonomy, and power sharing, among others. The endpoint is the main focus while negotiation is viewed through the lens of confidence building between parties, compromise in the crafting of new institutional solutions, or conditions of stable agreements between parties.[21]

Our argument refocuses the attention on the broader process itself and stalled conflict as foci for analysis. Stalled conflicts are more than temporary pauses in violence between warring parties. Instead they involve webs of engagement, rules, and institutions that parties use to gain leverage outside the theater of war, bind other parties, or increase their ability to seek concessions, side deals, or greater gains in peace agreements. The process we analyze expands beyond formal negotiations as well. It encompasses parallel engagements that occur within existing states structures, such as the role of nonarmed actors in political parties, local parliaments, and CSOs.[22] We suggest that analyzing this broader "process" helps explain why certain paths are taken or compromises made while others appear impossible to achieve. Behind stalled conflicts, there are always actors and strategies, and, in the end, one actor such as the state can be said to be "winning" if it seizes control of the process and exploits it to make significant gains. By bridging the analysis of how aggrieved groups use or resist existing institutions with negotiations involving armed groups, we can better understand why stalled conflict can sometimes persist. It can become itself a negotiation strategy if its lengthy nature shifts the balance of power between armed actors while reducing the costs of war.

Overall, our focus lays out an analytical terrain rather than a set of correlational propositions. We zone in on the sequences of negotiated steps, the power relations that determine the rules and procedures of negotiations, and the interconnected arenas of negotiation in which power is deployed and strategies developed to make relative gains in the broader bargain between the state and ethnic groups. By analyzing how various ethnic groups engaged the state from formal negotiations to state institutions and war, we can better understand how interactions in one arena influence and impact the others.

This book, therefore, places at the center of its analysis the decade of Myanmar's stalled conflict and process of negotiation between armed groups and the state from 2011 to 2021. It shows how the Tatmadaw and the civilian government used negotiations to make gains toward its shared vision of a mostly centralized Myanmar state. By doing so, it complements what we see as two groups of studies: a first that has emphasized the dominance of the Tatmadaw throughout Myanmar's postindependence history, including the quasi-democratic period, with consequences for our understanding of relations with ethnic minority groups; and a second that has viewed optimistically the changes brought about by the more open political environment and the liberalizing features of the 2008 constitution, thereby allowing ethnic minority groups to make some important gains.

Understanding the state's strategy is crucial for interpreting how it approached negotiations with EAOs. Mary Callahan's seminal contribution to the study of the Burmese military, counterinsurgency, and state making in postcolonial Burma helps us to better understand the militaristic evolution of the Burmese state and the path that led to a transition where the military remained dominant.[23] The evolution of democratic institutions, as well as various negotiating forums, requires an analysis of the Tatmadaw's broader strategies of state domination, as well as its strategic reliance historically on centralization and assimilation alongside violent repression, with its deeply held belief in their necessity to maintain the state's integrity.

For the first few decades of the civil war, much of the analysis focused on the relative power of EAOs against the Tatmadaw. Martin Smith's *Burma: Insurgency and the Politics of Ethnicity* was for a long time the only book that provided a broad overview of the conflicts.[24] It focused mainly on the armed groups themselves, their ideological affiliations, and the ebb and flow of various alliances and divisions that repeatedly prevented ethnic minority groups from reaching their goals. Its fine-grained analysis helped to illuminate the intricacies of the insurgencies and various groups. It was focused on the pre-1990 period of violent clashes between the Tatmadaw and EAOs, however, while the subsequent decade revealed significant developments in the regime's multipronged strategy, with an attempt to use increased military force against insurgents as well as to entice them through bilateral ceasefires and the National Convention with promises of negotiating a peaceful outcome. While the accommodation of EAOs by General Khin Nyunt in the 1990s appeared to be a shift in approach, the Tatmadaw accepted ceasefires and discussions of institutional changes as long as they did not significantly challenge the premises on which it had built the state.[25] Ashley South's *Ethnic Politics in Burma: States of Conflict* extended the analysis of ethnic armed conflicts up to 2008.[26]

From this perspective, state power remained dominant throughout the post-2011 period and was consolidated primarily in the Tatmadaw, but also in the increasing attempt to rebuild state institutions after passing the 2008 constitution. The transition to civilian rule was accompanied by the creation of new state structures, such as local parliaments, and greater institutionalization of past state practices and process, including the role of chief ministers. But as Melissa Crouch argues, the 2008 constitution kept traces of previous constitutions and ensured that the military maintained its influence in the posttransition period.[27] Nick Cheesman goes further, as he emphasizes how the whole apparatus of law, from the authoritarian to the contemporary period, was designed to reinforce the primacy of "law and order" and state coercive power with as few limitations as possible, and certainly with little regard in the end for a rule of law.[28] The state, therefore, projected power in the transition period through new institutions and laws, but against the backdrop of formal military dominance and continued seepage of past practices, links to local illicit economies, and authoritarian norms.

Our analysis of the negotiation process, the implementation of the 2008 constitution, and relations between the state and EAOs takes this broader context into account. The coup of 2021 was not surprising, given the Myanmar state's past character and the continuity of the Tatmadaw's dominance. But it does not take away the significant decade of strategic attempts by the Tatmadaw to empower a civilian government within particular bounds, and to seek a new pathway out of civil war. It certainly did loosen up some control over the process, as we show in subsequent chapters, particularly in the early stages, where we claim that it arguably allowed greater space for negotiation to open up real opportunities for compromise and change. But overall, and over time, it was able to influence the agenda and pace of negotiations, while supporting the civilian government's implementation of the 2008 constitution with decreasing returns for ethnic minority groups.

A second group of studies, by contrast, view with an overly optimistic lens the changes that the implementation of the 2008 constitution brought about, as well as the USDP's and NLD's policies toward ethnic minorities. Some emphasize the unprecedented nature of the Nationwide Ceasefire Agreement or of the Karen National Union (KNU)'s first-ever ceasefire, or specific state policies such as education that allowed ethnic minority groups more space for local education or cultural preservation.[29] Several nonacademic publications by insiders in the peace process (high-ranking officials and advisers) within the government or government negotiation teams offer descriptive, mostly positive accounts of steps toward peace negotiations.[30] Reports by local think tanks and international organizations focus on aspects of decentralization under the 2008 constitution. Some even argue that the constitution was "quasi-federal" and that the federal character and governance of Myanmar could be strengthened or deepened within the current constitution.[31] Ironically, most of these organizations viewed the 2008 constitution as undemocratic and unfederal only a few years earlier. Yet several subsequently accepted that incremental reforms were a pragmatic second best, showing just how the state, and the military in particular, had managed to force its framework as a *sine qua non* for negotiating future institutional change.

While the coup of 2021 would appear to give credence to the first group over the second, the changes that were put into place over the previous decade were significant, and certainly a departure from the past. There were some important changes that the 2008 constitution introduced, and that allowed many new actors to claim representation of ethnic minorities alongside EAOs. The Nationwide Ceasefire Agreement, the political dialogue, and the changes within the state—whether in education or in even more decentralized governance—did constitute significantly different approaches to the management of ethnic relations in Myanmar. It would be an exaggeration to view the decade simply as evidence of continued dominance by the Tatmadaw, with its endgame being a given. Similarly, it would be too optimistic to see those changes as having constituted significantly large gains for ethnic minorities toward their broader goal of federalism. Instead, as we contend, the process itself of widening the scope of negotiation and crafting a broader web of engagement could well have led to significant concessions and perhaps even substantive agreements. With hindsight, it revealed instead the ability of the Tatmadaw and the civilian government to use the process to their advantage and make gains toward their own vision for the Myanmar state, where it had failed through war. As a result, the coup interrupted what was actually a winning strategy, rather than being evidence of the Tatmadaw's view of a failed process with respect to the management of ethnic relations.

Finally, our book places the study of ethnic conflict and civil war in Myanmar within a broader comparative context, while acknowledging the work that has emphasized the specific, and sometimes unique, conflicts involving particular ethnic groups. Ardeth Maung Thawnghmung's work on the Karen, for example, draws our attention to members of ethnic minorities outside of ethnic states and the control of EAOs.[32] More recent studies shed light on several armed groups' governing structures and service delivery roles (Karen, Kachin, Mon, Pa'O) and their varying relationships with their respective constituents and state authorities during the peace process.[33] But with a focus on the Karen or a limited number of ethnic minorities, one is left without the analysis of how broad this phenomenon became and how it spread to other ethnic groups, with important implications for negotiations focusing on ethnic states as the basic unit of organization. We extend this analysis and show that the more widespread presence of minorities outside their states and the institutionalization of alternative forms of ethnic representation created a tension with aspirations for a federal state. In this way, the book complements more focused studies that have usefully analyzed how particular ethnic groups navigated changes in state institutions and practices.[34] But its scope also excludes engagement with some important dimensions of conflict, in particular religiously motivated mobilization and the Rohingya conflict. Following the conflict in Rakhine, numerous studies looked at nationalism among the Buddhist majority and its relation to citizenship and exclusion.[35] In many ways this aspect of conflict is quite different, and almost separate, from the conflict involving all other ethnic minority groups. Therefore, we engage it mostly in relation to some of the consequences of the constitution of 2008 for the mobilization of ethnic nationalities and the modalities that explain aspects of Rakhine nationalists' resentment of the Rohingya.

A Note on Methodology

This book builds on research in various regions and ethnic states in Myanmar from 2014 to 2019. We took several trips each year, some as a team and others individually, during this period that covered both the transitional government under the USDP and that of Aung San Suu Kyi's NLD after 2015. We conducted 174 interviews and eight focus group discussions with EAO leaders, government officials, religious leaders, nongovernmental organizations (NGOs), and others in Chin, Shan, Mon, Kachin, Kayah, and Kayin States; the Bago and Sagaing Regions, and Yangon and Naypyidaw.

In 2014, a member of our team conducted initial fieldwork in the Yangon Region, meeting Karen and Kachin leaders and politicians (see table 1). As a team, we started fieldwork in 2015. We conducted three focus group discussions: a first in Yangon, for three days, with representatives from ethnic political parties and CSOs from Chin, Kachin, Kayin, Naga, Mon, and Rakhine States; a second with religious leaders from Kachin, Chin, and Kayin States at the Myanmar Institute of Theology in Yangon; and a third, a two-day discussion in Bago with the Karen ethnic affairs minister, and representatives mostly from Literature and Culture Committees, and from political parties. We also traveled to Mon State, and conducted interviews with CSOs, the New Mon State Party, and NLD rank-and-file activists, as well as Muslim and Buddhist leaders.

In June 2016, amid the rainy season, and after a thirty-hour drive in the mountains and several landslides (pictured on the book's cover), we attended the preparatory meeting of the Chin National Conference in Hakha, Chin State. In Hakha, we also conducted several interviews with representatives from political parties, CSOs, and the Chin National Front, as well as religious and state officials. On our way back, we did several interviews in the Sagaing Region, and then we headed to Kayin State, where we met with the KNU. In 2016, a member of the research team also attended the Union Peace Conference's deliberations and preparatory meetings.

In 2018 and 2019, we went twice to Kachin State to meet with the Kachin Independence Organization and local CSOs and visited several camps for internally displaced persons (IDPs). During the second trip, we also met with representatives

TABLE 1 Number of interviews (and focus groups) in Myanmar by year

	2014	2015	2016	2018	2019	2020	TOTAL
Chin			6 (1)		12		18 (1)
Kachin			7		8	2	17
Shan					9		9
Kayin					13		13
Mon	3	6 (1)	1				10 (1)
Yangon	7	38 (3)	37 (1)	1	9		92 (4)
Kayah						2	2
Bago		1 (1)					1 (1)
Sagaing						5 (1)	5 (1)
Naypyidaw					7		7
Total	10	45 (5)	44 (2)	8	58	9 (1)	174 (8)

of the Lisu and Shanni communities. In 2019, we went back to Chin State to conduct additional interviews, focusing this time on state officials. We also went back to Kayin State, where we interviewed state education and health care officials, members of the KNU health and education departments, and several members of the Joint Monitoring Committee, both from the government and from the KNU side. Finally, in 2019, we went to Shan State, where we met with Pa'O representatives, including the Pa'O National Liberation Organization, and the Restoration Council of Shan State. These added to several interviews over the five years with local experts, members and leaders of CSOs, political party representatives, and state officials in Yangon and Naypyidaw.

Table 2 shows a breakdown of our work in Myanmar. Over five years, we met with thirty-four homegrown NGOs or CSO representatives from a wide array of groups, such as women's organizations, development organizations, and cultural promotion organizations. CSOs and NGOs are often very well positioned to discuss the state of the peace process in their area and achievements and challenges when dealing with EAOs, political parties, and state officials. We also met with a total of sixteen religious leaders, by which me mean only non-lay religious representatives: Buddhist monks, Christian ministers and pastors, and imams and ulama. The largest category is the nexus directly involved in the peace process—namely, ethnic leaders, politicians, armed group representatives, and peace-related organizations such as the former Myanmar Peace Center. The category of local experts includes local academics and local journalists, while the category of international experts is composed mainly of international nongovernmental organization (INGO) representatives from groups such as the World Bank and the International Crisis Group. Then we met mostly state-level officials to ask about decentralization and interactions with Naypyidaw. Access in Naypyidaw is always a challenge, and that is true for most foreign researchers. Still, in 2019 we were able to access high-level officials in health and education to get a sense

TABLE 2 Number of interviews by category (excluding focus groups)

NGO and CSO representatives	30
Muslim leaders	3
Christian leaders	9
Buddhist leaders	6
Peace-related organizations	16
Ethnic leaders	15
Ethnic armed organizations	22
Political parties and politicians	12
Local experts	21
International experts	10
State officials	20
Other	10
Total	174

of decentralization from the Union level. Finally, the category "other" includes mostly interviews with everyday people—for example, interviews with IDPs in Kachin State and displaced Muslims in Mawlamyine.

Throughout the book, we have anonymized most of the interviews cited or quoted. In post-2011 Myanmar, many leaders and actors—government officials, political parties, CSOs, and EAOs—were more than willing to explain their causes and concerns publicly. But the coup completely changed the threat for our informants, and we prefer not to take any risks. In other cases, our informants themselves were not comfortable with being named, so we removed their names from this book at their request.

The following chapters develop our analysis of how the Myanmar state has opened up to an unprecedented level while still molding the outcomes of the process to meet its preferred goals. It shows how, prior to the coup, the state was able to essentially neutralize ethnic groups without the cost of war or significant political concessions. Chapter 1 frames our analysis by defining what we mean by "process." We do so by identifying three key arenas (formal negotiations, state institutions, and war) in which the process unfolds, and five key mechanisms (locking in, sequencing, layering, outflanking, and outgunning) through which one party, in this case the state, can steer the process in its favor.

Chapters 2 and 3 develop the context against which the current negotiations and implementation of the 2008 constitution have occurred. The former explains the path of Bamar dominance through successive regimes and, while pointing to the novelty of the transitional period (2011–21), shows how the junta was able to lock in a new constitution in 2008, a crucial building block of the sequence to come. Chapter 3 acknowledges that democratization, even partial, layered new state institutions that expanded the number of actors claiming representation, and created new allocations of power that favored some degree of decentralization.

The next four chapters develop our analysis of the three negotiation arenas. Chapter 4 examines the formal process of negotiation leading to the Nationwide Ceasefire Agreement and subsequent political dialogue. Chapter 5 discusses how the 2008 constitution's implementation created a new model of decentralization that ultimately strengthened the state's position toward ethnic minority groups. Chapter 6 explains the state's outflanking strategy through its expansion into gray areas after reaching ceasefire agreements, and the way in which it was eroding the previous de facto autonomy that ethnic minority groups held in some areas. Finally, chapter 7 shows that the layering of new representative institutions during that period increasingly fragmented ethnic groups and contributed to neutralizing them.

1

WINNING BY PROCESS

Leveraging Formal Negotiation,
State Institutions, and War

Myanmar constitutes a key case to understand how process can shift the balance of power in negotiations to end civil wars. The state was able to make gains at the expense of ethnic armed organizations (EAOs) by manipulating rules of formal negotiation and state institutions to its advantage, while weakening its opponents in the theater of war. The conflict appeared "stalled," but the state could increasingly exploit it to its advantage.

This chapter presents a framework that places process at the center of the analysis. Negotiations to end conflict occur not only in formal peace forums but also indirectly through existing state institutions as well as the theater of war. The process by which the state and armed insurgents engage one another in these different arenas creates a web of constraints, rules of engagement, and interactions that modify power relations beyond the brute dynamics that war entails. It helps explain, in this case, why "stalled conflict" contributes to the state's advantage, which we refer to as "winning by process." Winning by process is a dynamic outcome that is neither final nor irreversible but that clearly gives a firm advantage to one side in a conflict, in this case the state.

Myanmar's decade of reform (2011–21) changed the calculus by which ethnic minority groups and the state approached negotiations. First, it raised expectations that peaceful outcomes, and a negotiated agreement, were much more likely than in the past. Second, it expanded the number of actors involved in negotiations. In the state, an elected, civilian government became a player in parallel to the Tatmadaw; among ethnic minority groups, ethnic political parties, ethnic representatives in local and national parliaments, and community leaders grew more significant alongside EAOs that had previously claimed exclusive leadership and representation of their respective groups. Third, it expanded the relevant arenas of negotiation beyond formal talks and the theater of war. By crafting and implementing new democratic institutions at the national and state/regional level, and by implementing the 2008 constitution, the state created a new space where power and resources for ethnic minorities became negotiated within representative and governance institutions.

This chapter argues that carefully analyzing how these aspects interact with each other allows us to better understand state strategies to manipulate process to its advantage, and how its opponents find themselves entangled in webs of constraints that they fail to foresee. First, it develops a conceptual framework to analyze how process is an important yet often neglected aspect of understanding conflict outcomes. Second, it contends that steps in negotiations involve more than the formal strategies, rules, and deliberations that shape actors' goals and determine areas of common ground. It includes the interplay of actors in settings outside of negotiations that have those actors' own set of rules, constraints, and incentives that ultimately contribute to shaping conflict outcomes. Third, it suggests five key mechanisms through which the state can win by process: locking in, sequencing, layering, outflanking, and outgunning.

While this chapter emphasizes the importance of process, it falls short of offering predictive propositions regarding exact sequences, pathways, or mechanisms that yield a set outcome. Instead it shows its relevance as a field of analysis to better understand conflict outcomes, while acknowledging that the particular process leading to such outcomes varies by context.

Why Process Matters

Most civil wars end though military victory.[1] *Winning by war* involves one side defeating the other, and imposing its conditions unilaterally. For insurgent forces, victory means seizing control of the state or seceding. For government forces, victory means crushing, disarming, or suppressing insurgent forces for good. One side's victory is thus another's defeat. Military victory, when decisive, is often the most durable way of resolving civil wars. In "Causes of Peace," Robert H. Wagner argues that military victories produce more stable outcomes than negotiated settlements because they destroy the losers' capacity to reignite the war.[2] More recently, Monica Toft has shown that military victories were indeed less likely to relapse and, more controversially, also less deadly over time.[3] Although winning by war may prove surprisingly durable, Roy Licklider nevertheless reconfirms a long-standing view that negotiated settlements were the best way to avoid mass violence, either genocide or politicide, in the aftermath of a conflict.[4]

Winning by agreement, the alternative to war, resolves conflict by finding an acceptable compromise or negotiated solution. In this scenario, according to I. William Zartman, "the key to a successful resolution of conflict lies in the substance of the proposals."[5] As in Myanmar, "ethnic civil wars" constitute a very large proportion of civil wars more broadly.[6] For these cases, scholars of ethnic conflict have long debated whether centripetal or centrifugal solutions were most efficient and durable.[7] For some, providing territorial autonomy, veto power, and separating ethnic groups along several institutional dimensions, such as "consociational" types of arrangements, are the best configuration to ensure ethnic peace.[8] Yet others have argued that by sealing ethnic identities and providing them with fixed institutions, the state in fact creates incentives to perpetuate and sometimes exacerbate ethnic divisions.[9] If autonomy may successfully address one type of conflict (territorialized minorities), it may leave unaddressed other conflicts stemming from minorities that are nested within autonomous territories. Instead, as Donald Horowitz argues, durable solutions include incentives to create interethnic coalitions, such as electoral systems, or disincentives to play the ethnic card, such as a ban on ethnic parties.[10] This debate has pitted the two camps against each other for decades, with little consensus. Part of its limitation lies in the difficulties inherent in comparing institutional templates without taking into account specific paths leading to institutional choices and the way in which alternative institutional solutions are received in particular historical contexts.

New institutions are never created ex nihilo or negotiated as clean templates. Institutionalists have not sufficiently emphasized how they are the outcome of a negotiation *process*, one that involves a sequence of responses and strategic decisions. The possibility of reaching an agreement, and its substance, is always influenced by existing institutional and constitutional structures, past and current aspirations, the number of parties involved, the length of time in negotiation, and the recurrence of violent outbreaks. As Horowitz notes, institutional and constitutional solutions, if ever adopted, are unlikely to resemble their originally intended form. The determination of a particular institutional "model" is highly improbable where there is a clear majority and a strong asymmetry of preferences, and where there is a "multiplicity of participants and a multiplicity of objectives." Bargaining involves the exchange of preferences, and that exchange is inimical to the realization of a single constitutional design. "Tidy constitutional designs," Horowitz writes, "have generally been propounded without regard to untidy processes of adoption."[11]

Static comparisons of institutional and constitutional solutions therefore miss the point that a "menu choice" approach is never possible. Particular types of institutional solutions, such as federalism, are embedded in historical paths of ethnic identity formation and institutionalization, war, and state making that make particular choices politically explosive, or are imbued with layers of implied connotations that render their adoption almost impossible. For instance, in Indonesia, because of its association with the divide-and-conquer strategies of the late period of Dutch colonial rule, the mere mention of federalism became associated with secession and the breakup of the Indonesian state, making it impossible to use as a conceptual framework at various points of constitutional negotiation and amendment.[12] In Myanmar, federalism has also become loaded with context-specific connotations, with the Tatmadaw equating it with the EAOs' aspirations for independence, and ethnic minority groups raising it to the status of symbolic aspiration based on a preconceived idea of historical commitment (the Panglong agreement), but with little notion of its potential substance.

An analytical emphasis on process refocuses attention on how negotiations are shaped by such historical constraints. The sequences of cycles of civil war, institutional change, and past negotiations all feed into the bargaining process, and ultimately influence the array of possibilities in first reaching agreements and then with regard to what types of solutions may be possible.

A focus on process also traces and explains why and how lags in negotiation, bargaining tactics, sequences of agreements on rules and norms, and various points of deploying bargaining power feed into the potential for an agreement to be reached, as well as ultimately shape civil war outcomes. Existing constitutions, for example, may constrain how any agreement will subsequently be ratified. In other contexts, agreement on rules of negotiation may limit some actors from participating, and potentially create incentives to derail the negotiations. Finally, the pace and substance of discussions may be highly influenced by side payments, attempts to co-opt actors, or the tactical use of violence to create pressure on opponents. Even a unilateral provision of certain powers and resources can aim at attenuating demands in formal negotiation. These dimensions require attention to how the process of negotiation unfolds, and to points of engagement between opposing parties.

We posit that tactics and the deployment of bargaining power are cast much more broadly than only in the sphere of formal negotiations. As aptly captured by the literature on civil war and bargaining, tactics oftentimes involve the use of war, not necessarily to win but to raise the costs of failing to agree. But they can also leverage existing state institutions.

Three arenas create interrelated points of engagement for civil war opponents to exert power and shape the outcomes of discussions. The first is the *formal negotiation arena*, the most visible and well understood, where negotiations proceed according to previously agreed-on rules and procedures (see table 3).[13] In this arena, negotiations involve high-level talks in visible and mediatized forums, with the frequent presence of national and international observers and

TABLE 3 Negotiation process: Three key arenas

Formal arena	• Negotiations through stages, regulated by rules and procedures • High- and low-level talks, with top-level politicians, military elites, and community leaders
State institutional arena	• Day-to-day politics in the legislative, executive, and judiciary branches, at the national and regional levels
War arena	• Leveraging brute force as a negotiation strategy • Balancing, bandwagoning, alliance shifting, and spoiling

third-party mediators. These negotiations often involve lower-level talks among community leaders (e.g., ethnic and religious leaders and intellectuals), and a host of problem-solving workshops, training sessions, and peace commissions.[14] In this setting, we are likely to see the strongest attempt to adopt rules that even out the playing field between opposing groups and the state. Since formal negotiations rely on the willing participation of various parties in a conflict, even the weakest actor holds great leverage over the procedures and rules to enlist that actor's participation and secure a measure of influence that is usually much greater than its actual power.[15]

In Myanmar, bilateral ceasefires in 2011 and 2012 between the Tatmadaw and EAOs set the stage for negotiating the Nationwide Ceasefire Agreement (NCA) in 2015. The NCA, adopted after nine rounds of high-level negotiations and five EAO leaders' summits, jump-started several postagreement mechanisms related to ceasefire monitoring as well as a larger political dialogue. The first round of the national dialogue, called the Union Peace Conference, was held in January 2016. After some initial uncertainty, the newly elected Aung San Suu Kyi government upheld the NCA and tried to convince other groups to sign. The government mostly preserved the broad framework for political dialogue, while making minor modifications and renaming it the "21st Century Panglong Conference." This framework included a series of steps, or stages, and bargaining institutions (regional dialogues, steering committees, joint committees, union conference, ratification process), which included both higher- and lower-level talks.

A second arena is the *theater of war*. As the bargaining literature has shown, the negotiation process also occurs outside formal bargaining settings, where power is much less constrained. The state and ethnic minority groups interact in the theater of war without the restraints of rules, formal negotiation, or state institutions. Instead, they deploy brute power in the interaction with their opponent, often to make gains in other negotiation arenas. A return to war, or its threat, is a negotiation tool, used to increase leverage at the formal bargaining table. For insurgent groups, flexing muscles is often the only way to maintain such leverage. For an incumbent state, a threat of violence may attempt to rebalance negotiation and force concessions. Violence by spoilers, often breakaway or disgruntled insurgent factions, if not meant to sabotage the peace, seeks to gain those actors a seat at the formal bargaining table or discredit insurgent representatives.

In the case of Myanmar, the relatively unconstrained role of the Tatmadaw loomed large. Under the new democratic rules, the Tatmadaw preserved its independence, particularly on security matters. But it also continued to use violent repression against ethnic minority groups, while maintaining some informal arrangements with former insurgent groups that were transformed into Border Guard Forces or People's Militias under the Tatmadaw's command. Several EAOs continued to wage war as part of their tactics to either disregard or create pressure on the formal negotiations. War continued with the Kachin Independence Organization (KIO), the Arakan Army (AA), the Ta'ang National Liberation Army (TNLA), the Myanmar National Democratic Alliance Army (MNDAA), and the Shan State Progressive Party (SSPP). There were also skirmishes between the Tatmadaw and ceasefire groups such as the Karen National Union (KNU) and the Restoration Council of Shan State. Direct military intervention shaped the negotiations' parameters as well as the crafting of the new democratic institutions, while the Tatmadaw's continued independence and decades of military rule created patterns of governance that persisted.

A third arena, the *state institutional arena*, is often overlooked in the literature on negotiation. In authoritarian settings, negotiations occur essentially in the formal negotiation arena and the theater of war. But in more democratic contexts, with some freedom of expression, negotiations invariably spill over into the state arena. By "state institutional arena," we mean state institutions such as the legislative, executive, and judiciary branches of government, at the national and subnational levels, as defined by the constitution. Ethnic minority groups participate to some degree in governance at the same time that negotiations are occurring. While in some cases war may have rendered such institutions almost irrelevant, in others they regulate the territorial representation of ethnic minorities, their existing powers, and access to state resources. While state institutions are being renegotiated in the formal negotiation arena, they nevertheless regulate relations between the state and ethnic minorities and have an impact on policy outcomes. Most importantly, they entrench new interests as they modify previous patterns of distributing power and resources, particularly when they are also newly established, as is the case during a democratic transition. The consequence is that previously perceived "ethnic minority" interests become much more diverse and complex due to the expanded political space.

An important consideration is the distinction between the "state" as one side in a civil war, and the "state institutional arena" as inclusive of different levels of government and its various branches. When referring to the state in opposition to armed groups, or in negotiations, it is usually conceptualized as a unitary actor because the executive controls both war and formal negotiations with its warring opponents. The state in its broader sense, what we call the state institutional arena, includes a number of distinct actors with different interests within its institutional apparatus, where conflict is regulated, constrained, and often resolved by its institutional mechanisms. The state institutional arena becomes most significant during periods of democratic opening or full democracy, where it incorporates such disparate interests.

In Myanmar, negotiations took place alongside a decade of democratic reforms. The 2008 constitution expanded the relevant arenas of negotiation beyond formal talks and the theater of war. By crafting and implementing new democratic institutions at the national and state/regional levels, and by implementing the 2008 constitution that served as the basis for the military regime's democratization plan, the state became a new space where powers and resources for ethnic minorities became negotiated. Developments in the state arena influenced formal talks and the theater of war, and the latter shaped the constraints on and opportunities arising for ethnic minority groups within new state institutions. The 2021 coup significantly closed off the state arena.

Winning by Process

The broader process that bargaining entails spans not only three arenas but also a significant time period when victory in war or peace are nowhere in sight. It is possible to exploit and make gains in this interstitial space, even if it appears to be a temporary lull or a quasi-equilibrium point, a pause toward either victory in war or a breakthrough agreement.

Negotiations often fail to produce change and, instead, drag on for years.[16] They tend to stall when forces on the ground are relatively balanced, when alliances among insurgent organizations shift, or when one "spoils" peace efforts.[17] Sometimes they are used as "tactical interludes," a time to rest, regroup, and rearm, or as a concession to external pressures.[18] At other times, rebellion becomes a business, or some parties benefit from its continuation.[19] But such equilibrium can be broken. Zartman argues that interest in peace emerges when stalemates become "mutually hurting," generating a sentiment that conflicts cannot be escalated to victory and that the deadlock is painful and costly to all.[20] In such cases, other hurdles may also need to be overcome. Negotiations move ahead only when commitment problems are solved through credible guarantees, such as third-party involvement, or with security assurances for warring parties in the postwar period.[21]

We contend that stalled conflicts are more than pauses and that they can be exploited to make significant gains. Process creates certain pathways that largely constrain possible outcomes in negotiating an end to civil war. Actors engaged in this process can use it to their advantage, even if no actual agreement is reached through bargaining. Winning by process, while not a final and static outcome, captures this. It usually occurs in the context of an apparently stalled conflict, where neither party is winning the war and no agreement is reached, yet there is evidence that one actor is de facto reaching its preferred outcome.

It is the state that most often gains from manipulating process. While it may not win by war, it is usually in a stronger position and has many more instruments to deploy, including access to its institutions and resources. Conversely, one can certainly envision cases where an armed group benefits from manipulating process and a stalled conflict by securing the ability to rearm, strengthen its position, and gain territory. Our focus here mostly relates to how the state can use its asymmetrical advantage over civil war opponents. Winning by process is therefore the state's ability to gain an advantage by manipulating the rules of negotiation, the structures of the bargaining process, and the negotiation of power and resources across the three arenas. It avoids both the cost of war and the cost of significant concessions while still progressing toward the state's goal of ending civil war.

There are several strategies that the state uses to manipulate process. We present five main categories: locking in, sequencing, layering, outflanking, and outgunning. Table 4 provides a summary and brief explanation:

TABLE 4 Winning by process: Five key strategies

Locking in	• Setting the agenda (narrowing, expanding, or postponing issues to be discussed)
	• Agreeing on rules and procedures (constraining negotiations' pace, nature, and content)
	• Including and excluding parties at the table
Sequencing	• Introducing steps in the negotiation and implementation process (creating hurdles, bottlenecks, veto points, coordination problems)
	• Defining an order of institutional change, sometimes with conditional steps
Layering	• Adding sites of negotiation, power, and interests
	• Pluralizing and fragmenting the actors involved
Outflanking	• Engaging the opponent on multiple fronts, bypassing opponents' official representatives
	• Winning people's hearts and minds, weakening opponents' legitimacy
Outgunning	• Leveraging the use of force as a tool of negotiation
	• Defecting from agreed ceasefires or launching targeted attacks as a mode of negotiation pressure

Locking In

The early stages of a negotiation generally have disproportionate importance for the subsequent stages of negotiation and implementation. It is in these early stages that actors agree (or concede) to rules of engagement, the formal process by which the state and armed groups will discuss and attempt to reach an agreement. This first step is crucial as it sets constraints that bind actors to particular rules for how discussions will proceed and how those discussions may lead to consensus points. While agreed on or conceded at the outset, these rules can sometimes serve the interests of one party over the other.

In the presence of multiple armed groups, the state can gain significant advantage in setting the rules. Not only does it often have more negotiation resources, but multiple groups may have more difficulty coordinating and reaching agreement among themselves. The state is less likely to suffer from such coordination problems. The outcome is that these rules then matter disproportionately over time, even though in the short term they may seem like just setting the terrain for bargaining.

More specifically, there are three aspects of the early negotiation phase that have significant effects on the subsequent process of negotiation: (1) agenda setting, (2) actor inclusion and exclusion, and (3) procedures and rules. These early agreements reflect the power balance at the onset of negotiation, but over time they may become disconnected from the actual balance of power on the ground. This type of mismatch creates space for actors to seek an advantage over their adversary.

(1) *Agenda setting.* During the early phases of bargaining, negotiating parties discuss the range of issues where agreement may be possible. This may include items to be discussed, as well as whether the parties are seeking a partial agreement on sets of concerns or a broader one, such as a peace agreement. These prenegotiation talks usually set the boundaries of what will be addressed, and can define a narrow or expanded agenda, sometimes resulting in an agreement to postpone some items as a trade-off for reducing risk and uncertainty and moving the negotiations forward.[22]

(2) *Actor inclusion and exclusion.* There are at least two important aspects of agreeing on which actors will be involved. One of the most important considerations is whether to invite a third-party mediator. The inclusion of third-party mediation increases the credibility of commitments made during negotiations and can therefore create more trust at the outset, with the expectation that other parties will be genuine in their

offers and more likely to implement and preserve the agreements that are reached. Third parties often obtain guarantees that agreements will hold, and monitor their implementation.[23] Another consideration is the range of actors that are included in the negotiations. There are trade-offs between exclusive and inclusive peace negotiations. Exclusive ones tend to involve some armed groups but not all, with the consequence that they can lead to the emergence of "spoilers" who intend to derail the process.[24] Alternatively, more inclusive ones can be helpful to legitimize the negotiations, as they extend to a broader set of insurgent groups or actors. But the outcome is often more diluted and superficial, as agreements require approval from a broader set of groups.[25]

(3) *Procedures and rules of negotiation.* In the prenegotiation phase, there are usually meetings to establish the rules by which discussions will proceed and agreements will be reached. They may include a number of rules that constrain the parties' future ability to make modifications to the structure of negotiations, including a process for ratifying any agreement. While such discussions may well be held in good faith, it is difficult to predict whether they will be favorable to one side or the other. So parties may become locked into a structure of negotiation that eventually they come to regret, if they find that it gives more leverage than expected to their opponent.

Setting the stage for negotiations entails a strategic attempt to draft procedures and rules that will give leverage to negotiating parties. As Joseph Jupille's "influence maximization hypothesis" predicts, actors negotiate and agree to rules that will maximize their influence.[26] Ahead of negotiations, it is difficult to predict what kind of leverage actors will obtain within a particular framework, but certainly the goal is that the rules will likely produce desired outcomes. Strong actors seek to maximize the rules' flexibility and minimize how they might reduce their leverage. Conversely, weaker actors have a strong stake in adopting rules and procedures that give them leverage beyond their perceived relative power.

Once formal negotiations begin, those rules and procedures create constraints but also define the relative power that each party has to present, deliberate on, and agree on proposed settlement points. While it is not possible to define ex ante the full set of strategies that actors will adopt, procedural rules and negotiating frameworks play an intervening role between material power and outcomes. The rules and procedures themselves provide a set of incentives and constraints that define what, how, and when issues can be negotiated.

Yet strategies do not always conform to the rules set out initially, and there is some unpredictability in the path that negotiations will take. As William Riker contends, negotiation is the "art" of manipulation.[27] No sooner are rules in place than political actors seek to use them to outmaneuver their opponent. They may seek to change the rules of the game if the expected outcomes fail to meet their objectives.[28] The most powerful actors can bully or threaten weaker parties. Threats, side payments, or other forms of projecting power outside the negotiating arena all constitute the realm of bargaining.[29]

The bargaining framework reflects both a staged process of negotiation and a multilayered set of negotiations inside and outside the framework itself, which includes leveraging the state institutional arena and the theater of war. While weaker negotiating parties, such as several small-armed groups, may negotiate rules that can increase their leverage, they cannot anticipate how more powerful negotiating parties will use those rules once negotiations reach further stages. Agreeing first on rules of negotiation, then signing a ceasefire, commits the parties to the process and makes defection costly, particularly in the presence of multiple groups. The incentives for any particular group to leave the negotiations are very low, as it would risk losing any say in outcomes while gaining little leverage externally to influence the negotiations. Unless it can launch a powerful threat to resume civil war and derail the negotiations, it risks less by remaining at the negotiating table and seeking to create stronger bargaining power through coalitions with other negotiating parties. As anticipated by the bargaining and alliance literature, the presence of multiple groups significantly raises the risk of failure. Since the state sits on one side of the table, and multiple groups on the other, there is one mostly cohesive negotiating side facing one fragile side, with groups seeking multiple objectives that do not always lead to a strong bargaining position. This opens up more possibilities for the state to exploit weaknesses, divide its opponents, and manipulate the rules to its advantage. Alliance among groups, while a potentially strong source of leverage, can also become a weakness when interests and negotiating objectives among various groups diverge.

As we will see in chapter 4, in Myanmar, the complexity of negotiating in the presence of multiple armed groups was overcome, and a framework was created to negotiate first the Nationwide Ceasefire Agreement and then a political dialogue. The framework, however, which was actually proposed by the armed groups, became constraining as negotiations proceeded. In particular, three factors weakened their negotiating power. First, their own weakness in maintaining a united front in the negotiations opened up opportunities for the state to manipulate the rules and create divisions among the parties. Second, as negotiations moved from ceasefire to political dialogue, the broader inclusion of nonstate actors among ethnic groups with no ties to the armed groups further weakened the groups' ability to confront the state and its strategic maneuvers. Third, power struggles and the rapid transformation of institutions outside the negotiations created interests that repeatedly weakened the bargaining power of groups operating within the framework.

Furthermore, the presence of multiple ethnic armed groups made a common strategy and broad inclusiveness almost impossible. Cunningham emphasizes the role of "last signers" as balancers that hold out against ceasefire agreements to obtain greater leverage for their group interest.[30] Among some of the larger groups, there were incentives to avoid the negotiating table and pursue their objectives in the theater of war in the hope of gaining a better agreement as the last signer.[31] A "last mover advantage" emerges when a growing coalition of actors have committed to an agreement, increasing the transaction cost of abandoning that process. The remaining holdouts can thus expect that, as the breaking point is reached, significant concessions will be incorporated into the framework to secure their participation.[32] As the civil war continued against some groups, such as the AA and the KIO, it became clear that they sought greater leverage to set their conditions on a future bargain and secure gains that could better serve their group's interests.

Sequencing

The sequencing by which formal bargaining and other institutional features are introduced can greatly influence the ability of parties to subsequently make significant gains. As this framework accounts for the introduction of a state institutional arena, how the state arena opens up, under a period of liberalization or democratization, can have an impact on formal negotiations.

As mentioned before, democratization helps to increase the credibility of any commitments made, but the sequence of introduction of peace agreements, new democratic institutions, and elections can very significantly affect the outcome. As part of peace agreements, there will be specific policies to provide new resources, new forms of representation, or new institutions that will be introduced in a particular order. A key component is the time period of demobilization, disarmament, and reintegration, which can be a point of great contention, as the state often demands some degree of demobilization and disarmament prior to negotiation, while insurgent groups often see the ability to return to war as an ultimate resource to achieve their bargaining goals. Other considerations will often include measures to reconstruct infrastructure and the economy, measures to improve reconciliation, or agreements on transitional justice.[33] How and when these are introduced can give considerable leverage to one party over the other. Furthermore, in order to reassure combatants, these measures require credible guarantees. So any agreement on demobilization, disarmament, and reintegration; new institutions; reform of the economy; or other grievances in conflict are superseded by a prior need to design an agreement that gives sufficient guarantees to insurgents that the terms will be respected. These may include joint agreements for monitoring implementation, conditions attached to reaching particular thresholds, or deadlines for implementing certain aspects before moving to other stages.[34]

As part of the negotiation arena, the introduction of steps toward negotiating and implementing a final agreement can multiply the possibilities of derailing it. Such steps oftentimes create veto points where one or more players can halt a process of reaching an agreement or create roadblocks toward its implementation. Whether these involve deadlines to achieve certain negotiated outcomes before moving on to subsequent stages, or establishing certain sequences of concessions, the more steps that are created, the greater the probability of failing to reach the hoped-for, positive outcome.[35]

Beyond the formal negotiating arena itself, the sequence of introducing institutional changes alters the bargaining parameters. Elections, for instance, can dramatically change the outlook of formal negotiations if newly elected leaders have very different inclinations to accommodate insurgent demands or depend on coalitions that include ethnic minority groups involved in an insurgency. Some scholars have argued that early elections might be destabilizing. As Brancati and Snyder have noted, "Holding elections soon after a civil war ends generally increases the likelihood of renewed fighting, but . . . favorable conditions, including decisive victories, demobilization, peacekeeping, power sharing, and strong political, administrative and judicial institutions, can mitigate this risk."[36] Others show that implementing accommodative measures prior to elections can increase the likelihood that the latter will promote peace.[37] So what types of institutions are created, and when they are introduced in relation to negotiations to end civil war, can have a strong impact on the durability of peace.

In the Myanmar case, as we will show, sequencing was important. The military regime adopted the constitution of 2008 and set the institutional parameters to open up the state arena to democratization. A transitional civilian government then led the first round of negotiations that ultimately produced the Nationwide Ceasefire Agreement, which established the framework for subsequent negotiations. This transitional government, under the Union Solidarity and Development Party, attempted to seal a process for political dialogue before the first elections scheduled for 2015. Finally, it convened a first Union Peace Conference immediately after those elections, which created new constraints for the National League for Democracy, which won in 2015 and inherited these changes prior to forming the first democratically elected government. This particular sequence allowed the military civilian government to set the rules of negotiation prior to the election that produced the first elected government. It created strong constraints on the ability to break away from that process, or to consider negotiating outside the parameters of the 2008 constitution. In the same manner, the NLD government attempted to reach agreements at the fourth session of the 21st Panglong Peace Conference after the peace process had stalled for over a year two months prior to the elections in 2020.

Layering

Layering relates to the accumulation of sites of negotiation, from the formal negotiation to the institutions of the state, as well as the theater of war. Layers of process are interconnected between these arenas. With democratization, the state arena expands as new institutions such as regional parliaments, courts, civil society groups, and political parties are established. Aggrieved groups gain greater access to representation or sites of governance, alongside insurgent groups that continue fighting. The resources and powers that are obtained in the state arena create new avenues for negotiation and influence the claims that are subsequently made in formal negotiations. Through the layering of new institutions, armed groups may no longer be the sole representatives of ethnic minorities, but one actor among many others. Layering can substantially alter the political environment and push armed groups to the periphery of the negotiation.

Existing state institutions reflect a particular distribution of power between ethnic minority groups and a majority. They allocate resources, divide jurisdictions among different levels of government, and enshrine rights. Civil war usually arises when state institutions are unable to regulate conflict, as ethnic minority groups resort to violence when alternative strategies fail or the state represses them.[38] Under some circumstances, negotiations proceed while civil war is ongoing, and prior institutions are preserved, but in others, ethnic groups operate in a vacuum of institutional functionality.[39] Since these prior institutions are often part of the initial cause of conflict, and are themselves an object of negotiation, their role as an arena of interaction may remain minimal or have little impact on any reallocation of power between both parties. They often serve as a template against which future changes are compared.

When democratic transition and peace negotiations proceed mostly in parallel with each other, the state institutional arena becomes much more significant. Democratic transition has two important effects. First, it broadens the scope of actors that lay claim to political representation and the design of new institutions, thereby giving ethnic minority groups greater points of engagement with the state. Second, the transitional government begins creating new institutions that alter the prior balance of power, mostly by decentralizing and defusing power where it was once much more concentrated.[40] Democratic institutions by their nature expand the locus of participation and representation, whether this means new political parties accessing parliament and obtaining cabinet positions, second chambers representing regions, more significant local government representation, or many other means of accessing state power and resources. A democratizing state therefore opens up a whole new realm by which ethnic minority groups that might previously have been represented only by armed groups can now access state resources and make claims to representation. Such expanded access does not occur in isolation from more formal bargaining to end civil war or strategies to make gains through war—in particular in civil wars, where armed groups claim to represent an ethnic group.

In the context of parallel negotiations to end civil war, this access therefore creates a new set of political actors that appear alongside armed groups, and whose constituency overlaps. Where the latter might have held a near monopoly over the group they claimed to represent during the civil war, the multiplication of groups and political actors significantly challenges their position. This effect is even more evident in competing claims for ethnic group representation.

Furthermore, as new institutions are established, they create new sites of power and interests. Parliamentary elections enable political parties, and subsequent representatives, to compete directly with armed groups for political representation. They may even seek to displace armed groups, which in prior years might have maintained a monopoly over ethnic representation.[41] Other institutions can also create new interests. In multiethnic societies, measures to implement various forms of territorial decentralization create new positions of power that can also create new positions at the regional level from which ethnic representation can be claimed.[42]

The creation and layering of such institutional structures diversify the interests among ethnic groups, thereby further complicating formal negotiation processes. The case of Myanmar followed this path. First, with the implementation of the constitution of 2008, even if powers assigned to regional governments were weak and could be bypassed, they created new interests and patterns of governance. After transitioning to civilian rule in 2011, the state pursued more actively the implementation of the 2008 constitution, which the junta crafted and passed in anticipation of political liberalization. The constitution not only retained prerogatives for the military, which is a strong point of contention, but also enshrined new structures of governance at the state and regional level. The state presented these changes as a new model of decentralized governance, while ethnic minority groups negotiated what they perceived to be a new federal state.

Second, negotiating jurisdictional powers and fiscal resource allocation unveiled the strong divergence in interests within and among ethnic groups, as shown by strains arising from the ceasefire process. While the negotiation process assumed a symmetric approach toward federalism, by which power would be redistributed equally among states and regions, some groups appeared increasingly content with some decentralized powers while others sought greater ones. Some armed groups retained a strong preference for an idealized version of federalism, but other groups that were given business opportunities and limited autonomy over a narrow patch of territory appeared content with the status quo. Finally, the 2008 constitution already recognized another level of distinct status—self-administered zones—that created a precedent for a strongly asymmetrical distribution of power, and that gave incentives for smaller ethnic groups to seek similar accommodation.

As chapters 4, 5, and 7 show, the implementation of the 2008 constitution, alongside negotiations in the 21st Century Panglong Conference, therefore created a new framework of governance at the local level. The devolution of power, allocation of fiscal resources, creation of parliaments, and extension of local bureaucracies provided a new institutional framework that constrained future options. Negotiations can lead to crafting new institutions, but "clean templates" are rarely possible, even more so when new institutions are created during a period of democratic transition, which infuses the emerging stakeholders with a new sense of legitimacy and representativeness. Discussions and negotiations on modifications to the 2008 constitution, therefore, became highly informed by the unfolding practices and institutions at the state and regional level, which in turn created new interests that were fed back into the negotiation process. These changes included some convergence and even dismantling and replacement of some armed groups' alternative systems of service provision, such as education and health care, as they were integrated into existing state structures.

Outflanking

Outflanking is a strategy by which one of the parties attempts to circumvent and weaken its opponent. Specifically, we refer to a state strategy to build ties to civilian populations that the insurgent groups claim to represent, and thereby create new sources of loyalty or interest that weaken insurgent support. As has been well researched in the literature on civil war, insurgents seek to build constituencies of support, which allows them to sustain themselves and legitimize their opposition to the state.

Scholars have studied extensively the choices that civilian populations make in the context of civil war, and their impact on war duration and insurgency goals. Generally, insurgent groups seek the support of civilians, as they are crucial to their effort. They therefore seek a variety of ways to nurture that support, not only through coercion or financial incentives.[43]

Systems of governance in territory they control can provide a means of spreading insurgent ideologies or cultural beliefs, as well as goods and services that help to build support. These relationships require the right set of institutions, systems of rule, and effective communication, as they may challenge existing authority structures in local communities, and therefore turn civilians against the insurgent groups.[44] When prewar institutions are well established and strong, there tends to be more resistance to alternative systems of governance that insurgents attempt to introduce, and therefore insurgents compete with existing institutions for legitimacy and delivery of services.[45]

Similarly, in some circumstances, when insurgent groups have established governance institutions and deliver services in territory they control, the state may end up competing and attempting to re-create links to civilian populations when it regains access to contested areas. In such disputed areas, the state may use coercion or rely more effectively on building institutional networks and providing economic benefits. Government expenditures are an essential component of attracting greater numbers of people to integrate and become loyal to the state.[46] These may be used to co-opt opponents by buying loyalty with benefits, by doling out patronage targeted at former insurgent and community leaders,[47] or by providing public goods, such as infrastructure, to benefit the broader population.[48]

As chapter 6 shows, although the NCA and political dialogue were more institutionalized and promised greater formal autonomy if conclusive, the uncertainty of the transitional phase opened up opportunities for the state to erode past autonomy. The Myanmar state responded to local ethnic populations' demand for development, social services, and education. By doing so, it undermined the EAOs' capacity to provide services and, by extension, their legitimacy in the eyes of ethnic minority groups. It was able to expand its influence into ethnic states because of a lack of delimited territories in the ceasefire agreements and a lack of interim arrangements for local governance. As a result, the state was able to expand its reach into territory previously at war and to essentially recentralize control over many jurisdictional areas. Health care, education, and land management are three strategic policy areas in which the central government became highly invested.

In chapter 7, we show that the Tatmadaw developed ties to minorities within ethnic minorities. It did so to weaken the major ethnic groups that obtained states and that were most centrally represented in the negotiations. Combined with the layering strategies that gave new recognition and power to these smaller groups, the Tatmadaw's provision of support to these groups aimed at outflanking major ethnic groups that claimed to represent them as well.

Outgunning

Outgunning is, simply put, the old adage that "war is politics by other means." As a strategy, we conceptualize outgunning as leveraging the use of force as a tool of negotiation. While recognizing that the use of force generally entails an attempt to win, there are also instances of defecting from agreed ceasefires or launching targeted attacks in direct response to objectives sought in formal negotiations. Although the theater of war often expresses an absence of alternative means of engagement or negotiation, it is occasionally tied to parallel processes of negotiating ceasefires or peace agreements, as well as changes in the power and resources obtained through the state arena. Outgunning is therefore part of a repertoire of negotiation tools that do not necessarily entail a breakdown of negotiation, but is one of several strategic steps in an overall process of bargaining.

The literature on civil war has identified similar strategies, such as alliance shifting, especially when multiple armed groups are involved. Rebel groups may seize an opportunity to strike a short-term bargain that serves their interests, even if it taxes the chances of reaching a more comprehensive negotiated settlement. Bilateral deals change the number of players and force other rebel groups to rethink their strategies, while making subsequent deals more difficult to reach.[49]

At times of transition, as Snyder has most strongly argued, some groups may have an incentive to mobilize violently to defend or promote nationalist identities in order to win, or retain, control of the state.[50] Launching violent attacks or escalating violent mobilization becomes part of the array of strategies to control the newly democratic institutions. Clearly, if negotiations between the state and armed groups are occurring in parallel to the establishment of democratic institutions, they become part of this calculus.

But even when a large number of armed groups sign on to a ceasefire or join negotiations, there are strong incentives to continue the war. As Cunningham has emphasized, a major group may hold out against ceasefire agreements in order to obtain greater leverage.[51] A "last mover advantage" emerges when a growing coalition of actors have committed to an agreement, increasing the transaction cost of abandoning that process. The remaining holdouts can thus expect that, as the breaking point is reached, significant concessions will be incorporated into the framework to secure their participation.[52]

Smaller, weaker groups tend to bandwagon with major players that can more closely advance their interests, but their behavior can sometimes be difficult to predict. Three factors influence how they align. First, as Fotini Christia observes, the absence of an enforceable commitment on the part of the stronger group can trigger concern and defection on the part of weaker groups in an alliance.[53]

If they are unsure that the larger partners will protect their interests in bargaining, they may break away and side with another major player and balance against their former ally. Second, according to Christia, "each alliance change is a tipping point in the distribution of relative power, with groups updating their probability of expected returns and choosing whether to shift alliances." Bandwagoning among smaller parties often occurs when a victory is in sight.[54] When one major group agrees to negotiate a broader ceasefire, small groups will tend to bandwagon in the fear that they may be left out of an agreement, and lose. Third, spheres of influence are a strong factor influencing smaller groups. Small groups are more likely to bandwagon with, rather than balance, large groups with which they are in close geographical proximity, and benefit from the latter's financial or military backing.[55]

The impact of such shifting coalitions and alliances in bargaining entails that some groups either break away or balance against the negotiation process, or threaten to do so. The continued arena of warfare provides an external bargaining tool as leverage for greater gains, for an alternative process, or as a threat to gain concessions.

The state, on the other hand, sometimes resorts to attacks or intensifying violence as part of its negotiating tool kit. In Myanmar, for instance, the Tatmadaw, by acting somewhat independently from the negotiation process, also used military force to exclude players from bargaining or in attempts to reduce the leverage of some major players, such as the KIO.

The civil war in Myanmar, with its numerous armed groups, is difficult to end through bargaining, in part because of the difficulty of finding common ground to end the violence and enable all groups to participate in negotiations. The dynamic changes of alliances and strategic maneuvering between "ceasefire" and "non-ceasefire" groups illustrate many of the processes observed in the civil war literature. The game is mainly a balancing act among larger and more powerful armed groups, with smaller and weaker ones bandwagoning with other powers to protect their interests, while the Tatmadaw and the state attempt to take advantage of these divisions. As we show, the three main armed groups—the KNU, the KIO, and the United Wa State Army—shifted alliances or broke away from coalitions in a quest to gain the greatest leverage from any settlement. From early bilateral settlements in the late 1980s to signing the first nationwide ceasefire, these shifts occurred in response to each other's positioning, in balancing movements that aimed at securing better deals for their respective groups. As a result, these changes in alignment relative to each other, while occurring in the theater of war, had a direct impact on negotiations, made even a negotiating framework difficult to achieve, and gave the state opportunities to make gains.

This chapter has presented a framework to analyze how actors take advantage of a broader negotiation process, in an apparently stalled conflict, to secure gains previously unattainable through war. Five strategies are deployed across three arenas, with the state institutional arena and the theater of war being intrinsically tied to formal negotiations. This attention to process helps to identify how a powerful actor, such as the state, can be making gains (and be seen as "winning") in situations where the literature might otherwise have seen a conflict as "protracted" or in a stalemate, with no victors in war or any peace agreement in sight. The process that involves a strategic deployment of these strategies becomes itself an equilibrium point, as the resulting stalled conflict yields gains for one side of the negotiations and can be a desired outcome. One side may then want such a state of the conflict to remain, as it can achieve many of its goals by reducing the costs of war and casting a net that ultimately makes a future peace agreement less costly too. As the case of Myanmar shows, this broader process of negotiation ultimately enabled the state to deploy strategies effectively to weaken EAOs, expand the reach of the state, occupy territory that the EAOs previously held, and create increasing division among groups, while making few concessions in formal negotiations.

2

THE FAILURE TO WIN BY WAR

The Limits of Bamar Dominance
and Ethnic Minority Repression

Myanmar's conflict reflects a long-standing pattern of the Bamar-dominated state's attempt to undermine ethnic minority groups. British colonial rule introduced rigid categories of ethnic identities and pursued divide-and-rule policies that favored minority groups at the Bamar majority's expense. It prevented the formation of a nationalist movement that could have united the majority and minority ethnic groups under a pan-Burmese idea of nationhood. Instead the independence movement was largely Bamar led, while ethnic minority groups remained outside of its mobilization. As a result, a profound political gap divided the majority Bamar and ethnic minorities at the time of Myanmar's independence in 1948. This division laid the basis for civil war, subsequent decades of violent conflict, and state policies of assimilation and repression of ethnic minority groups. The 2008 constitution, transition to civilian rule in 2011, and the coup of 2021 all arose out of this long path of Bamar domination, albeit in different forms.

Successive governments have sought a solution to the ethnic "problem" through war and policies designed to repress and ultimately assimilate or emasculate ethnic minority groups. Decades of authoritarian rule perpetuated old conflicts and created new ones. Policies of Burmanization, combined with civil war, produced some assimilation and displacement. State co-optation of some ethnic armed organizations (EAOs) succeeded in reaching temporary agreements that allowed leaders to pursue private gain and interests while failing to address deep grievances. Other strategies sought to divide large ethnic groups in order to weaken their resistance. But overall, these decades mostly pitted the

Tatmadaw against EAOs in a long-lasting conflict where the dominant strategy on both sides was to win by war.

The 2008 constitution emerged out of the post-1988 military junta's first attempts to shift the emphasis away from war. It sought to appease ethnic minority groups through a decade-long National Convention (NC) during which it ostensibly prepared Myanmar for democracy with new institutions that would accommodate ethnic minority demands. The process, however, was so restricted and controlled from above that it differed very little from the previous strategy of winning by war. The NC, although a form of formal negotiation arena, locked in a highly scripted agenda and conditions for participation that severely reduced EAOs' incentives to join wholeheartedly. Alongside the theater of war, therefore, the formal negotiation process lacked any credibility.

Despite the failure of a negotiated agreement, the 2008 constitution nevertheless became the basis of the post-2011 semidemocratic regime that shaped relations between ethnic minority groups and the Bamar majority. Ironically, it still opened up a new political space that marked a clear departure from the previous strategy of winning by war. It expanded and made credible two new arenas: a formal negotiation arena in which EAOs were willing to participate with more optimism, and a state institutional arena where new forms of representation and empowerment were created.

In this chapter, we make three points. First, the Burmese state in its various forms has reflected, and been unable to overcome, a bias toward Bamar-majority dominance. Second, the strategy of attempting to win by war and repression through assimilation ultimately failed. Third, the highly scripted first attempt to develop alternative negotiation strategies was also unsuccessful, but laid the basis of a new institutional framework, the 2008 constitution. The last section reviews the important features of the constitution, which created the first institutional layer shaping the engagement between the state and ethnic minority groups in both the subsequent formal negotiation and the state institutional arenas.

The Origins of Ethnic Conflict in Myanmar

Independence from colonial rule produced many anticolonial nationalist movements that laid the foundation for unity among diverse peoples residing within the administrative boundaries of a colony and living under foreign government dominance. Many postindependence states, such as Indonesia, promoted such "official" or "state" nationalism by further fostering a common culture, core legitimizing principles often enshrined in first constitutions, national ideologies, or sets of policies designed to unite their diverse populations.[1]

In Myanmar, however, British colonial rule (1824–1948) crystallized instead distinct and antagonistic identities, with Bamar on one side and ethnic minorities on the other. "Burmese" nationalism became exclusively Bamar rather than more inclusive of all groups within the territory of Myanmar, and it tended, according to Matthew J. Walton, to "equate elements of Bamar culture and history with a presumably broader 'Burmese' heritage."[2]

Myanmar has a large number of ethnic, cultural, religious, and linguistic groups. No reliable and available data on ethnic groups exist, but the state has officially recognized 135 "national races." While experts have challenged their arbitrary nature, the official identities remain widely cited because of a lack of an alternative classification of groups.[3] Bamar are the majority group and constitute about 68 percent of the population. They are mostly located in the Irrawaddy River basin and the lowlands, and speak the Burmese language. Most of the 135 national races are part of one of seven larger ethnic groups: the Shan (8.5 percent), Karen (6.2 percent), Rakhine (4.5 percent), Mon (2.4 percent), Kachin (1.4 percent), Kayah (2.2 percent), and Chin (0.4 percent).[4] Many of these ethnic groups are located on the periphery of the current Myanmar state in mountainous highland areas. According to the 2014 census, 87.9 percent of the population is Buddhist, mostly among the Bamar, Mon, Rakhine, and Shan peoples. Christians constitute 6.2 percent of the population and Muslims 4.3 percent, respectively.[5] They are mostly ethnic minorities such as Chin, Kachin, some Karen, Rohingya, and descendants of Indian origin.

Before the arrival of the British in 1826, ethnicity and religion were politically trivial in Myanmar.[6] Burmese kingdoms fought over territory, resources, and people rather than ethnicity per se.[7] While valley people, Bamar, Rakhine, and Mon, occasionally fought against each other, they also intermarried and mixed, particularly given their shared Buddhist religion. Loyalties were rooted in clan, kinship, or patron-client relations rather than ethnicity.[8] Burmese kingdoms, based in the valley region, generally ignored minority hill tribe populations, which were considered illiterate and uncivilized. Yet they allowed some groups, such as the Kachin, Shan, and Karenni, to retain their autonomy in exchange for recognizing the monarchy and paying tribute.[9]

British colonialism (1826–1949) helped crystallize and politicize distinct and antagonistic identities by reinforcing geographic and cultural separation between valley and hill peoples. The British ruled Burma through two administrative systems. They used direct rule in lowland Burma, where Bamar mostly lived. "Ministerial Burma," as they called it, was organized into divisions and districts, each placed under a commissioner and deputy commissioner.[10] By contrast, the British adopted indirect rule in upland Burma, mostly populated by ethnic minorities. The "Frontier Areas," included part of today's Kayin, Kayah and Shan States, as well as parts of Rakhine, Chin, and Kachin States, and the Naga Hills. In some of these, such as Shan, Karenni, and Kachin, traditional and hereditary chiefs were granted a large degree of local autonomy in civil, criminal, and financial affairs.

While Burma was considered a province of British India until 1937, the British allowed it to exercise some degree of home rule from 1909 to 1935. But these reforms further institutionalized rather than removed the distinctions between lowland and upland peoples. In lowland Burma, the British introduced a parliament, elections, and a limited form of local democracy.[11] Yet upland Burma remained a distinct administrative region.

In 1935, the British created a new, two-tier administration by dividing the Frontier Areas into "Excluded" and "Partially Excluded" Areas. Some of the Partially Excluded Areas had the right to elect members of parliament, while others did not. Excluded Areas remained entirely outside the authority of the elected legislature and were kept under the authority of a governor or local traditional authorities.

Also, Ministerial Burma included forms of communal representation for some, but not all, ethnic minorities. The Karen and immigrant Chinese, Indians, and Anglo-Burmans gained reserved seats in parliament. Yet the British granted no such seats to Mon, Southern Chin, Rakhine, or the Muslim majority in northern Rakhine, for example. By the end of the colonial regime, as Martin Smith puts it, "the map of Burma [became] a curious patchwork of oddly different administrative islands."[12]

Burmese nationalism emerged in response to the marginalization of the Bamar but also because the colonial regime empowered some ethnic minorities. Burmese developed, as a result, a pattern of "essentialist" nationalism, dominated by Bamar culture and leadership. The British deliberately avoided recruiting from among the native majority and disproportionately enlisted ethnic minorities. There were almost no Bamar in the army and none in the military police. Chin, Kachin, and Karen represented 83 percent of the indigenous portion of the armed forces in 1931, but only 13 percent of the population. After 1935 the British opened the ranks to Bamar, but they remained largely underrepresented. On the brink of World War II, there were only 472 Bamar soldiers (including Mon and Shan, which the British counted as Bamar) in the regular army, compared to 3,365 from ethnic minority groups. The Bamar majority resented the discrimination they felt in the armed forces.[13]

The Bamar also resented colonial migration policies and economic discrimination.[14] Burma was part of British India until 1937 and the colonial authorities allowed Indian migration to Burma. A small minority of Indian merchants, moneylenders, and middlemen came to dominate the economy in the colonial capital, the densely commercialized zone of wet-rice cultivation, and the Irrawaddy delta.[15] After the Great Depression, more than a quarter of rural land changed over to a moneylending Indian caste, the Chettiar, who then brought with them more Indian peasants and repopulated villages. In the cities, Indians occupied positions as administrators and government officials, while low-caste Indians dominated most of the unskilled labor force. More than half of Rangoon's population was Indian in 1931. Resentment fueled a series of anti-Indian and anti-Muslim pogroms and riots in the 1920s, 1930–31, and 1938. The Chinese community, too, was the occasional target of such attacks.

Bamar grew suspicious as well of the close relationship between the British, Christian missionaries, and ethnic minorities. Among some ethnic groups, religion provided a powerful stimulus to the development of broader national identities. Chin, Kachin, and Karen became more consolidated identities in part because of missionization. Kachin, for instance, is a collective category for at least six principal lineage groups, while Karen is a collective name for twenty or so.[16] Yet Christian missionaries fostered institutions that transcended these subgroups. They codified and promoted some ethnic languages, and they created writing systems, translated the Bible, and wrote dictionaries.[17] The development of a literary tradition among hill people helped generate new imagined communities based on the narration of common historical origins, language, national costumes, cultural practices, and moral standards.[18] Christian missionaries also built churches, schools, civil society organizations, and networks. In doing so, they provided institutions that helped local political elites mobilize across local identities and support broader and stronger ones. This was particularly useful among Chin, Karen, and Kachin, three profoundly fragmented tribal societies.[19] Finally, Christian missions and schools created a Western-educated elite that became the key leadership in these nascent ethnic nationalist movements.

While the nationalist forces were overwhelmingly Bamar during the war, most ethnic minorities remained loyal to the British, often fighting against the Bamar. Ethnic minorities saw the British as protectors against the Bamar and the colonial regime as a source of opportunity to accede to the armed forces and the colonial administration. In the 1940s, the "thirty comrades" who formed the anticolonial movement's nucleus were all Bamar except for two Shan. In 1942, the group formed the Burma Independence Army. Most of the ten-thousand-man army, which sided with the Japanese, was composed of Bamar, with some Shan and Mon. Most ethnic minorities, such as the Karen, Lahu, Chin, Naga, Kachin, and Muslims in Rakhine (now identifying as Rohingya) remained loyal to the British and fought against the Burma Independence Army and the Japanese. Therefore, the Bamar viewed the ethnic groups as allies of the colonial power, while the ethnic groups viewed the Bamar as collaborators with an occupying power. Toward the end of the war,

Bamar nationalists turned against the Japanese, but continued to recruit from among the Bamar and regard the ethnic minorities as stooges of the British.[20]

The rift between the majority Bamar and the ethnic minorities prevented the development of a new overarching national identity, inclusive of ethnic minorities. This initial gap proved extremely durable and shaped most of the postindependence political trajectory.

The Failure to Win by War: Bamar Dominance and Ethnic Conflict

The British regained control of the colony in 1945 and reluctantly agreed to negotiate with Aung San and his party, the Anti-fascist People's Freedom League, made up predominantly of Bamar from a wide spectrum of political ideologies, but mostly Communists and Socialists. The most pressing question was whether the Frontier Areas would be associated with Ministerial Burma or remain independent. Initially, the Shan, Karen, Karenni, and Chin asked to remain autonomous under British rule. Ethnic groups legitimized their claim to autonomy by asserting that they had been independent people with unique languages and cultural practices before the arrival of the British colonizers. The Mon and Rakhine people, who lived in the valley region alongside Bamar, also asked for separate states, claiming that they had historical roots prior to the Burmese kings' invasion in the eighteenth century.

The British agreed that they would grant independence by 1948 in the valley areas, or Burma "proper." They promised that the hill areas—that is, Frontier Areas—would continue under British rule until its people agreed to be incorporated into the rest of Burma. The Panglong Conference was organized to secure the hill peoples' support for a unified Burma by promising autonomy and equality. Chin, Kachin, and Shan representatives attended the conference, which took place in February 1947. At the conference, valley representatives promised the Frontier Areas full autonomy in internal administration. On that occasion, Aung San famously promised that "if Burma receives one kyat, you will also get one kyat."[21] This promise would remain ingrained in the ethnic leaders' memory and is repeated to this day.

The agreement secured at Panglong laid the foundation for Myanmar's first constitution in 1947. The constitution did not mention the words "federal" or "federalism," but according to Josef Silverstein, it was clear that it was its "main intention."[22] It created three new states from the former Frontier Areas—the Shan, Karenni, and Kachin States. The Shan States were grouped into a single state with an extraordinary right to secession after ten years. The Karenni States were also joined into a single state with a similar secession right. The Kachin seemingly abandoned this right in exchange for the inclusion of Myitkyina and Bhamo into the Kachin territory. Burma was granted a bicameral legislature with a 125-seat Chamber of Nationalities and a 250-seat Chamber of Deputies.

The agreement, however, failed to be inclusive. At the conference, the Karen, Karenni, Rakhine and Mon were not represented.[23] The agreement basically ignored them. The new constitution reflected these limitations as well. On the one hand, it gave some autonomy to new states. The Kachin, Karenni, and Shan States' elected and hereditary leaders benefited from some degree of executive, judiciary, legislative, and economic authority. State governments, however, remained subordinate both legally and fiscally to the Union government.[24] The status of the Karen state and its political rights were left to be decided only after independence. Karen were dispersed all over the territory, with a majority living outside the Karen state, so issues of status and border were particularly difficult to resolve. They were nevertheless granted some special recognition: they received twenty-two reserved seats in the legislature, a Karen Affairs Council, and a Karen minister.[25] By contrast, Mon and Rakhine received no special recognition. The Bamar considered the two groups part of Burma proper because they were part of the Bamar empire before the arrival of the British and because their racial identity was similar to the Bamar. Even for the Chin, who participated in the conference, the deal was a far cry from federalism. They did not get a state, but a special division, with few of the Shan and Kachin States' political rights.

It also rapidly became clear that independent Burma would not be a multi-ethnic federation. Instead the Bamar elite captured the state and the armed forces and began centralizing the country. The government imposed Burmese as the compulsory language of the administration and the sole language of education after fourth grade. It also established the Ministry of Culture and Mass Education, which, in theory, was meant to promote the values of the indigenous cultures, but which in practice gave primacy to Bamar history and culture.[26] The government also promoted Buddhist missions to the hill regions, especially the Karen, sanctioned and promoted by the Ministry of Religious Affairs and the Buddha Sasana Organization. In the 1950s, the central government, Bamar elites, and military personnel increasingly bypassed traditional rulers in the ethnic minority states and centralized power.[27]

U Nu's government faced rebellion from all sides in the early days of independence. The constitution and the Anti-fascist People's Freedom League government failed to accommodate the demands of most ethnic groups for greater autonomy and independence. As a result, the latter began to use armed resistance. Furthermore, part of the Bamar elite, later joined by dissident members of the army and police, and ex-soldiers from the People's Volunteer Organization, also launched a rebellion under the banner of the Communist Party of Burma (CPB). Around a third of the army joined the Communist insurrection that spread throughout the valley area. The Pa'O, Mon, Rakhine, and Mujahid rebellions in northern Rakhine all broke out around 1948.[28] The Karen insurrection started a year later over a disagreement about the future Karen state's status and boundaries. The constitution initially confined the Karen state only to remote areas where the Karen formed a majority. Karen leaders, however, wanted a large part of the delta region, where Karen and Bamar were intermixed.[29]

A second wave of insurgencies rocked the country in the late 1950s and early 1960s. Initially, Shan, Karenni, and Kachin remained loyal to the Burmese government for about ten years. They were, after all, the only ethnic groups accommodated in the constitution. Tensions were growing, however, as the Union government increasingly became more centralized. The Shan rebellion broke out in 1959, after the invasion of the Kuomintang and the influx of Burmese troops and central government officials into Shan State. In 1961, U Nu made Buddhism the official state religion of Burma. It may have been a strategy to thwart the Communists, but it increased frustrations among the Kachin and Chin, who were mostly Christian. The Kachin began their rebellion in 1961, and the Chin began theirs in 1964, mostly in response to increasing resentment toward the government's failure to accommodate ethnic minorities.[30]

General Ne Win, the armed forces' commander, seized power in 1962 to prevent the country from "disintegrating." Yet the coup merely transferred power from civilians to the military and did nothing to change the ethnic composition of the holders of central state power.[31] Far from offering a solution to Burma's political violence, the coup, as Smith puts it, "poured oil on the flames of the country's ethnic insurgencies."[32]

The Revolutionary Council (1962–74) preferred to deal with ethnic demands through military rather than political means. It initiated peace talks in 1963–64 with various armed groups but quickly rejected their demands for autonomy and offered no political concessions.[33] Ethnic leaders in turn rejected the regime's blatant attempts to co-opt them. The council therefore launched intense military attacks, including scorched-earth campaigns that resulted in the deaths, suffering, and displacement of civil populations in conflict areas. Most importantly, it failed to assuage the ethnic groups' grievances against the military and the government.

Despite military campaigns, insurgent groups continued to control large areas along the border, funded by abundant natural resources, taxes, and opium. The strongest group among them was the CPB, which controlled Pegu Yoma, the Irrawaddy delta (until early 1970s), and much of the remote territory in northeastern Burma. It had also established a presence in western Burma, Central Shan

State, and Kachin State. While Bamar dominated the leadership of the Communist Party, a large majority of rank-and-file soldiers were from ethnic minority groups. The five largest EAOs were the Kachin Independence Organization (KIO), the Karen National Union (KNU), the SSPP, the Shan United Revolutionary Army (also known as the Tai Revolutionary Council), and the New Mon State Party (NMSP). Most of these groups operated like states and provided social services, which ranged from education and health care to dispensing justice to populations under their control. The Burmese territory was therefore divided into government-controlled, rebel-controlled, and contested areas. In the late 1960s, U Nu, the former prime minister of Burma, fled to the border areas in Thailand to join the resistance with the KNU, and established a short-lived alliance of major armed groups in Southeast Burma called the National United Liberation Front. The alliance collapsed mainly because of U Nu's unwillingness to accept the KNU and NMPS' proposal to include a constitutional right of secession in the future Federal Union Republic.[34] Some EAOs formed an alliance with the CPB, but others shunned it for its Bamar-dominated leadership and lack of sensitivity toward minority groups' grievances.

The adoption of a new constitution in 1974 transformed the government into a Socialist one-party state, with basically no new concessions to ethnic minorities. Under the guidance of the new Burma Socialist Program Party (BSPP) (1974–88), the constitution created seven Bamar-dominated divisions and seven non-Bamar ethnic states, which was a symbolic recognition, but other provisions maintained centralization and Bamar domination of these states. Despite its appearance, the constitution was not federal in any way. The states were empty shells; power and resources were strongly centralized in the Union government. The regime also dissolved the parliament; banned associations, unions, and political parties; and suppressed protests and freedom of expression. It created an autarchic system, which included cutting off the country from the outside world; expelling foreign missionaries, scholars, and Western foundations; and nationalizing most of the economy.

The government tried to suppress demands for self-determination by institutionalizing its own watered-down, depoliticized version of culture. The Revolutionary Council removed Buddhism as the state religion and no longer cautioned against proselytizing among non-Buddhist minorities. The regime also allowed ethnic minorities to promote their culture and language as long as doing so did not threaten national unity. It allowed, for instance, the teaching of minority languages in minority areas only up to second grade. During that period, Buddhist monasteries and Christian churches were often used to teach language after school hours or during the summer.[35] Meanwhile, however, Ne Win also attempted to "Burmanize" the entire population by making Burmese the only language of communication in government and schools, and restricting cultural and religious activities.[36] Schools promoted a curriculum that celebrated national unity and the majority group's heritage and traditions while smearing martyrs of minority groups as "rebels" or "collaborators of colonial government."[37] National diversity was celebrated through the Union Day, New Year's, and National Days of several ethnic groups, but they were top-down and strictly monitored to reflect the official version of appropriate cultural representations by different nationalities. Ethnic minorities were also marginalized from positions of power. Decision-making was reserved for Ne Win and his predominantly Bamar-elite group; few ethnic minorities occupied high-profile government offices at the regional and national levels. Finally, the national army was gradually transformed into a Bamar-dominated institution.

The Ne Win regime solidified military dominance and replaced a weak and fragile democratic government, but its approach to ethnic minorities exhibited remarkable continuity. Civil war had begun under the decade of democratic rule, and mainly spread more broadly and deepened under Ne Win's and the BSPP's repressive policies. Small accommodations toward the teaching of ethnic minority languages were dwarfed by the continued assimilationist policies and centralization that had also characterized U Nu's earlier approach, although implemented and expressed differently. In the end, the regime's approach crystallized the war effort on both sides, rather than enabling either side to reach its goals.

The 1988 Uprising and Shifting Strategy

The 1988 prodemocracy uprisings led to the demise of the BSPP and to a shift in the regime's strategy with ethnic minorities. The regime saw an urgent need to minimize internal security threats to avoid a new, bolder uprising. In particular, it wanted to avoid a potential alliance between the Communist Party and EAOs. In addition, it wanted to take back control of the border, reduce black-market activities, and shift trade revenues from armed groups to the state. According to Zaw Oo and Win Min, it concluded that "four decades of war had proven that a total military victory was not realistic."[38] After 1988, the new regime adopted two main strategies. In the theater of war, it started negotiating ceasefires in a classic attempt to close one front in order to succeed in another. In parallel, the state established a formal negotiation arena, meant to prepare a new constitution. But the negotiation arena existed almost in name only, as the government kept it tightly under its control.

The Tatmadaw seized power in September 1988 to crush the popular uprising demanding democracy. The military crackdown on nationwide protests was brutal: thousands were killed, injured, or imprisoned, while others fled into insurgent-controlled areas and joined the armed rebellion. The military formed the State Law and Order Restoration Council (SLORC) and organized a general election in 1990, but repudiated its results after Aung San Suu Kyi of the National League for Democracy (NLD) won a landslide victory. As a consequence of the military's brutal suppression, many student leaders who participated in the 1988 demonstration and elected members of parliament fled to the border areas to join the resistance with EAOs. NLD MPs-elect formed an exile government called the National Coalition Government Union of Burma, and formed an alliance with several EAOs, the National Council of the Union of Burma, to establish a democratic federal system.[39] At least among the broader alliance of the NLD and ethnic minority groups, there was some opportunity to craft a vision of Myanmar that would grant greater representation and power to ethnic states along federal lines.

The change of regime, meanwhile, maintained intact the state's centralization and Burmanization strategies. If anything, the new regime actually committed more resources, political will, and criminal sanctions to back up this agenda after 1990, in what Mary Callahan calls "the most concerted government effort at minority assimilation and disempowerment in the twentieth century."[40] Language became a key tool in the regime's effort to rebuild the state and pacify the population. Thus, the government shifted to a more invasive and assimilationist attitude toward ethnic minorities. For example, it did not hesitate to arrest schoolteachers and monks who were guilty of teaching ethnic languages.[41]

Yet the international outcry against the regime's gross human rights violations, and its persistent incapacity to redress the country's poor economy, called for a change of strategy. The SLORC abandoned its isolationist, quasi-Socialist policies by opening the economy to foreign and local investors, while still maintaining lots of constraints. In 1988 the cash-strapped government legalized the thriving cross-border trade by installing government-controlled checkpoints along its borders with China, Thailand, India, and Bangladesh. It oversaw the implementation of large-scale cross-border logging, mining, and dam building, the construction of oil and gas pipelines, and commercial concessions to foreign and local companies in agriculture, fisheries, and gemstone mining.[42] Both China and Thailand reduced their support to armed groups along the borders and strengthened their ties with Myanmar's central government to secure further access to natural resources and expand cross-border trade. Western economic sanctions against the country's military regime only strengthened the government's dependence on China, which soon became Myanmar's major investor and its leading supplier of arms.[43]

More crucial still was the military's decision that it was time to slowly release its tight grip on power, provided it could maintain control over the process and its outcome.[44] In order to do so, it crafted a path to change that involved reducing the intensity of civil war and drafting a new constitution. It sought bilateral ceasefires with the EAOs and hosted a national convention to discuss its "road map to democracy." This process ultimately led to the adoption in 2008 of a new constitution, which actually maintained a central role for the military as well as a strongly centralized state, rather than addressing the root causes of the conflicts.

Bilateral Ceasefires

After it refused to hand over power to the NLD in 1990, the SLORC attempted to appease ethnic groups. Seeking to open up a new formal negotiation arena alongside the theater of war, it first pursued ceasefire agreements that were mostly informal and involved little prenegotiation discussions. These agreements, in the end, became a Tatmadaw strategic tool to divide EAOs and reduce the number of fronts in its war effort.

A first wave of ceasefires occurred in 1989 with the breakup of the CPB, from which several EAOs emerged. The party collapsed in 1989 after years of declining Chinese financial support under Deng Xiaoping and discontentment with strictly hierarchical structures and patronizing Bamar-dominant leadership by rank-and-file leaders, a majority of whom were ethnic minorities. As its resources dried up, several armed groups had become increasingly involved in the drug trade, which eroded its ideological underpinnings. It also failed to provide a haven and inspiration for antigovernment protests in 1988, while the creation by EAOs of an anti-Communist National Democratic Front (NDF) in 1976 offered an alternative path for uniting ethnic minority armed groups toward a common federal goal without secessionist demands.[45] As a result, some groups began to break away from the CPB. A Kokang group left, followed by a main Wa armed group. The Wa demanded autonomy within their territory. A number of groups in the Shan State soon followed, including the SSPP and the Ta'ang National Liberation Army.

The SLORC took advantage of this situation by reaching ceasefire deals with the four main splinter groups that had formed the core of the CPB. The latter's breakup threatened to reconfigure the theater of war and its alliances, so the military reacted quickly. Long-standing armed groups, mostly located along the Thai border, sought to create alliances with the new breakaway groups. The KNU, which had led the anti-Communist NDF since 1976, made early openings to the

Kokang and Wa. Communication was difficult, however, due to the Tatmadaw's strong offensive strike against NDF groups. The SLORC regime gained the upper hand by reaching out to former CPB members. Khin Nyunt sought to prevent new alliances from being built by brokering deals with the Wa and Kokang. As Smith contends, "It was widely understood that by agreeing to a ceasefire and to supplying the mutineers with goods and fuel, the Tatmadaw, with its many troubles in the cities, was desperate for a break in hostilities."[46] As some reached ceasefires with the Tatmadaw, others, too, became desperate for such a break. A few months later, the military reached additional ceasefires with the Shan State Progressive Party (SSPP, or Shan State Army–North) in the Shan State and the New Democratic Army–Kachin in the Kachin State.

The junta certainly benefited from striking deals with some of the armed groups. These ceasefires were typically simple exchanges, all of them unwritten (with the exception of the Kachin ceasefire). Attacks from both sides would cease, while the state allowed the armed groups to control some territory and even govern it independently, with government authorities requiring permission to enter EAO-controlled territories. Ceasefires also allowed the Tatmadaw to focus more of its resources on weakening other armed groups. They were also a precursor to what would later become a more systematic strategy of outflanking EAOs, in this case by displacing them in the economic realm. According to Smith, "The ceasefires of the SLORC era swiftly surpassed in significance those of Ne Win's days, and this was to be one of the Tatmadaw's most successful moves away from the BSPP past. Scant resources could be conserved and troops redeployed to more troubled regions of the country. Moreover, by vigorously entering the economic field, the Tatmadaw was to have far more success in seizing the local initiative from armed opposition groups than it ever had in 26 years of fighting."[47] In particular, the military intensified its campaigns against the KNU, which had been one of the most powerful groups. The KNU lost control over large portions of its territories, while increasing numbers of Karen civilians were displaced and added to the large refugee flow along the Thailand-Burma border.[48]

These ceasefires led to what Callahan calls "fluid and complex" mosaics of power in Myanmar, with political power in the hands of "either the Tatmadaw, antigovernment armed forces, criminal gangs, or paramilitaries."[49] While these arrangements protected drug barons' and local warlords' interests, other armed groups established social services and supported internally displaced people. The NMSP, for instance, provided services and Mon schooling in the two "special regions" it controlled as a result of the 1995 ceasefire; it also resettled in its own camps Mon refugees that had fled to Thailand and were being pressured to return to Myanmar. The KIO also provided schooling and other social services.[50]

The Tatmadaw reached agreements with about sixteen armed groups between 1989 and 1995. The United Wa State Army and the Pa'O National Organization signed agreements in 1989 and 1991, respectively, and obtained special regions and administrations with some degree of exclusive control. Large armed groups, claiming to represent their large respective ethnic groups, gained some exclusive control over parts of their claimed territory, while many areas remained either at war or controlled by the government. The NMSP, the Democratic Karen Buddhist Army, and the KIO signed agreements during this time period that allowed them to establish some control and even governance over some territory, while other areas with local Mon, Karen, and Kachin were governed by the state or remained at war.

The process involved in reaching ceasefires was more a strategy in the theater of war than a sign of opening up a negotiation process. There were few rules of engagement, and the nature of the agreements was largely informal. So the net result was mostly a brief pause in violence in some areas, and a temporary ability to extend services and governance in a few territories. These ceasefires gave the Tatmadaw new leverage to attempt to win by war against some of the strongest and most persistent armed groups, such as the KNU. But given the clearly informal nature of ceasefire agreements, the lack of subsequent promises of negotiation, and the poor credibility in the first place of a signed agreement with the Tatmadaw, this outcome could be better seen as a temporary lull in the theater of war, rather than as part of a more complex bargaining process.

The National Convention

In parallel with ceasefires, the SLORC announced in 1992 the creation of a national convention to write a new constitution. The convention was a slightly more credible gesture toward formal bargaining, by adding a forum where ethnic minority groups could presumably negotiate new powers under the planned constitution. But it soon became apparent that the process remained completely under the military's control, and there was little pretense of an actual negotiation.

The government initially intended the NC to include the opposition NLD and ethnic minority groups, both armed groups under ceasefire and political parties. In reality, most delegates were township-level officials carefully selected by the SLORC and officially named as representatives of national races, peasants, workers, intellectuals, and public servants.[51] Of the 702 delegates, only ninety-nine were members of parliament. Despite broadening slightly beyond the EAOs to include some new ethnic political parties, the convention became merely a highly choreographed set of meetings intended essentially to rubber-stamp its new constitution.

Consequently, the NC rapidly lost legitimacy shortly after beginning in 1992. After only two days, the government suspended the convention following dissension from the opposition and ethnic delegates. It was suspended once more a few months later, and again after a year. In November 1995, the NLD and several elected ethnic opposition parties left in protest at the heavy-handed and highly centralized decision-making process. One political party representative commented, "We were closely monitored. Military intelligence officers were everywhere in the meeting room. If we gave interviews to foreign media like the BBC, the military intelligence would question us the next day. There were signs that our places were searched, as we found our pillows and blankets shuffled whenever we returned to our rooms."[52] The government adjourned the convention in 1996. It was increasingly clear to everybody that it had been a failure and that the junta had used it to bolster its legitimacy with little intention of introducing a more liberalized environment. The government had apparently drawn up the six objectives and 104 basic principles of the future constitution before the National Convention even started.

Under General Khin Nyunt's initiative, the regime tried to revive the NC in 2003 by first announcing a seven-step "road map to democracy." The government faced most of its opposition from ethnic nationalities, so when the NC finally resumed in 2004, it adopted a new approach focused on attracting the support of ethnic minority groups. Ethnic nationalities, many of which had previously aligned with the NLD, were lured into discussions with the regime. They made up over half of the 1,088 delegates invited and formed a majority in three of the eight category groups.[53] This was quite a change from the previous iteration of the convention. Martin Smith also noted a change in official policies toward former insurgent groups, which were previously referred to as "bandits, saboteurs, racists, or as leftist or rightist extremists." The state-controlled media changed how they described these groups, which became known officially in the NC as "specially invited guests."

Some insurgent groups that had reached ceasefires with the state in the 1990s, such as the Kachin, Shan, Mon, Pa'O, and Wa, were optimistic about reaching a long-lasting settlement. The new NC was a moment that many ethnic parties had long hoped for, as they considered it a potential benchmark for change. Armed opposition groups under ceasefire were unable to stand in the 1990 general election and few were involved in the earlier NC between 1993 and 1996. They saw the start of a face-to-face dialogue in Yangon as the culmination of their ceasefire strategies for reconciliation and the reforms that had begun over a decade earlier.[54]

By all accounts, the new convention led to lively debates. Ethnic nationalities had the right to choose their own delegates, and felt they had the right to raise any issues, which they generally did.⁵⁵ Some EAOs were even able to propose new ideas. Proposals submitted by a three-party grouping (the United Wa State Army, the Myanmar National Democratic Alliance Army, and the National Democratic Alliance Army) representing the Wa, Kokang, and Mongla, and by a thirteen-party alliance composed of some of the major armed opposition groups, including the SSPP, the KIO, and the NMSP, received the most attention.⁵⁶ The Wa-Kokang-Mongla group, for instance, asked for stronger and more autonomous regions within Shan State, which sparked objections from ethnic Shan parties as well as from other local minority groups in Shan State. One delegate who attended the NC as a political party representative recalled that "everyone, including the Tatmadaw and other smaller groups, made proposals and counterproposals for self-autonomous regions. Shanni from Kachin State asked to separate from Kachin State, while Kachin from the Kokang area in Shan State asked to join the Kachin state."⁵⁷

Despite these lively debates, however, the state strictly managed and controlled the content, tone, and direction of the convention's deliberations. Another delegate, who attended as an "intellectual" in the latter part of the NC, said,

> We did not have input in any of the substantive issues nor minor revision of the drafts [of constitutions] even though we were told to provide feedback in our individual groups. For instance, a delegate in our group suggested reconsidering the design of the country's new flag because it looked like Ghana's, but his proposal was rejected. We could not even make minor copyediting suggestions, even though there was a Burmese specialist in our group who pointed out some grammatical errors. A military officer who was assigned to be a minute taker assured us that these are only drafts and they would get fixed, but we didn't get to see what he wrote down.⁵⁸

Federalism was out of the question. On the one hand, a watered-down version of the proposals for self-governance by the Wa, Kokang, and Mongla was incorporated into the constitution by the creation of "self-administered zones" (SAZs). On the other, the proposals by the thirteen-party alliance, what Smith calls "an articulate espousal" of what was essentially federalism, were rejected outright.⁵⁹ Yet even the creation of self-autonomous regions, which according to Smith were carefully crafted to appear "inclusive" and supportive of "autonomy,"⁶⁰ were a facade at best. As a veteran politician from an ethnic minority group with self-autonomous status recalled, "When the BBC asked me if I was happy with the outcome of the NC, I said yes! We provided input to one hundred and four principles that were to serve as a basis of the future constitution. We asked for self-autonomous status and we got it! But we soon realized that we did not have any say over the final wording of the constitution and the autonomy given to SAZs is similar to the size of a small pasture."[61]

The convention thus kept the State Peace and Development Council (SPDC) firmly within the bounds traced by its road map to democracy. It set the pace and it ultimately controlled the convention's outcome as well. The NC led to the writing of the 2008 constitution, which emphasized a more open but "disciplined" democracy with continued military involvement in politics. The junta concluded its road map's fourth stage by holding a popular referendum on the constitution, which was reportedly approved by 92.4 percent of the population.[62]

In the end, the military drafted the constitution it had always dreamed of, but gained little of the legitimacy it was hoping to win. The second NC was a more credible process, but it was also an extreme use of a locking-in strategy, creating rules, setting agenda items, and controlling the deliberations in a way that precluded any outcome other than the Tatmadaw's preferred one. Although delegates went along with the process for some time, most armed groups remained at a distance. Some smaller armed groups or those with potential benefits remained, but they had secured their concessions through the informal ceasefires. That the Tatmadaw won, in this case, was a foregone conclusion.

The 2008 Constitution: Setting the Stage for Subsequent Negotiations

With the 2008 constitution, the NC's main outcome, the state was crafting its strategy for a more significant use of process several years later. The 2021 coup suggests that the regime may have underestimated how democratization could ultimately threaten its interests. But in terms of its relationship with ethnic minorities, the constitution provided the military with sufficient guarantees to open up a formal negotiation arena and allow for more freedom in the state institutional arena.

The constitution of 2008 was never meant to be federal. It enshrined a slightly reformed version of the Union of Myanmar that perpetuated Bamar and military dominance of the central government, which continued to control most powers and resources. As a result, it incorporated a few superficial elements of ethnic minority proposals, while showing little federalist substance.

The constitution divided the territory into seven regions and seven states that were constitutionally equivalent. It maintained the same territorial demarcation created under the 1974 constitution, with half of the states located in Bamar-majority regions and half in ethnic regions. The constitution reintroduced regional governments, headed by a centrally appointed chief minister and a small cabinet of line ministries. Ministers, however, did not have bureaucracies, but supervised and coordinated the activities of certain departments of Union-level line ministries.[63] The constitution also created elected unicameral legislatures (Hluttaw) in each state. State legislatures were composed of two elected MPs per township and a constitutionally guaranteed 25 percent of seats for non-elected members of the military.

Despite the reintroduction of regional governments, the central government retained major decision-making power and authority. The constitution gave the Union-level legislature the sole authority to pass legislation relating to education, health care, defense, security, foreign affairs, judicial matters, and financial powers, including the control of currency and coinage, the central bank, and all taxation matters except for land revenue and excise duties. The constitution also gave the president the power to select the state/regional chief ministers, who then formed a cabinet composed of civilian ministers of specific portfolios, a state/region minister for border and security affairs, a military officer nominated by the commander in chief of Defense Services, and elected ethnic affairs ministers for ethnic groups with 0.1 percent of the population in any given region.[64] The Union government had residual powers, which meant that any powers not specifically granted to states were automatically under the Union's jurisdiction.[65]

The legislative powers of the states/regions were limited and essentially regulatory in nature. For example, Schedule 2 of the constitution granted to regional governments powers relating to "energy, electricity, mining, and forestry." These jurisdictions, however, were limited to power generation that was off the national grid, the regulation of salt products, polishing local gems (but not mining gems), and firewood. Similarly, in the social sector, these powers were limited to managing traditional medicine, welfare, stevedoring, and cultural heritage preservation. In the industrial sector, the constitution gave power to the states in nonstrategic or small-scale activities or "industries other than those prescribed to be undertaken by the Union level," as well as "cottage industries" (see table 5).

The constitution established five new SAZs and one self-administered division for ethnic groups that were a minority in their state but a majority in two adjacent townships. The idea of an additional layer of administration for minorities without states was first proposed during the NC in 1993. SAZs were meant to rationalize the status of ceasefire groups that were granted some territorial autonomy, such as the Wa and the Pa'O. These areas were administered by indirectly elected and appointed "leading bodies" headed by a chairperson, elected MPs, military appointees, and representatives of other minorities. If states had limited powers, these areas had even more insignificant powers. They were responsible for vaguely defined urban and rural projects, development affairs,

TABLE 5 Distribution of powers, 2008 constitution (summary)

SECTORS	UNION (SCHEDULE 1)	REGION/STATE (SCHEDULE 2)
1. Union defense and security	Defense, war and peace, law and order, police	
2. Foreign affairs	Diplomacy, treaties, immigration, extraditions	
3. Finance and planning	Currency, central bank, income tax, commercial tax, duties, loans, lottery	Land revenue, excise duty. municipal taxes, small loans and business; local planning
4. Economy	Economy, commerce, imports/exports, corporations, hotel, tourism, etc.	Economic, commercial, and cooperative matters in accordance with Union laws
5. Agriculture and livestock	Land administration, vacant land, land survey and records, marine fisheries, livestock, dams	Agriculture, plants and crop pests and diseases, chemical fertilizers, agricultural loans and savings, freshwater fisheries, livestock breeding
6. Energy, electricity, mining, and forestry	Petrol, natural gas, and other inflammable liquids; mines; minerals; gems; pearls; forests; environmental protection	Electric power production and distribution (small, medium), cutting and polishing of gemstones, village firewood plantation
7. Industry	Industrial zones, standardization of manufactured products, intellectual property, research	Industries other than those under the jurisdiction of the Union level, cottage industries
8. Transport, communication, and construction	Inland water transport, ports, carriage by sea, air transport, land transport, highways, bridges, television, satellite communication, postal and internet services	Ports, jetties, roads, bridges, and pontoons with the right to be managed by the region
9. Social sector	Education; health care; foodstuff; welfare of children, youths, and women; fire brigades; social security; labor organizations	Traditional medicine, social welfare work within the region, preservation of cultural heritage, museums, theaters, cinemas, photo exhibitions
10. Management	General administration, town and village land, associations, prisons, border areas, census, citizenship	Development matters, towns and housing developments, honorary certificates
11. Judicial	Judiciary, lawyers, criminal law, civil law	

and public health, and the prevention of fire, the maintenance of pasture, water, and electricity, and public roads.

A crucial obstacle to the autonomy of the regional government was the near-total lack of autonomous revenue. The taxation powers of states and regions were, like legislative powers, very restricted (Schedule 5). They included taxes on land, excise, dams, motor vehicles and vessels, local production of minor forest products and salt, various service fees, fines, and tolls, as well as the proceeds from properties and those state economic enterprises that were run by the region or the state. The Union government, on the other hand, retained all lucrative taxes, including commercial, income, and natural-resource-related taxes.

The constitution also ensured that laws and regulations that the Union government had passed remained in place, even if they were under the jurisdiction of states and regional governments, provided that they did not contradict the constitution. Article 446 stated that existing laws were to remain in operation insofar as they were not contrary to the constitution until and unless they were repealed or amended by the Pyidaungsu (Union) Hluttaw. Article 447 specified that existing rules, regulations, bylaws, notifications, orders, directives, and procedures were to remain in place insofar as they were not contrary to the constitution, unless the Union government repealed them. Consequently, state and regional governments were limited by the existing legislative and regulatory framework over all jurisdictions, while only the Union government could act to modify it.

The judiciary was strongly centralized. The president, in consultation with the chief justice of the Union, nominated the state/regional chief justice. All courts were subordinated to the national Supreme Court, which had final appellate authority over other levels, including resolving "disputes, except constitutional problems between the Union Government and the Region or State Governments." The constitution created a Constitutional Tribunal of the Union to resolve constitutional disputes between regions, states, and the Union.

The constitution did not create a separate bureaucracy in states and regions. The government departments at the state level were almost entirely dependent on the General Administration Department, a branch of the military-led Ministry of Home Affairs (until 2018).[66] The General Administration Department controlled the districts and townships, two of the country's core administrative institutions.[67] The vast bulk of government civil servants working in the state and regional governments were from the central government. The local state or regional government did not have its own staff.

The 2008 constitution therefore reproduced many aspects of previous constitutions, but also introduced a new space of indeterminacy. It made important changes to the structure, operation, and power of the Union and state/regional governments, but it was resolutely meant to preserve a strong central government that retained the most significant fiscal and jurisdictional powers. The NC had included ethnic minorities as a legitimation strategy, but ultimately met few of their demands and instead introduced a constitution that was designed to preserve central government power after the transition. The 2008 constitution nevertheless created new layers of institutions, new actors, and new rules of interactions that were different from previous constitutions, and that would become part of a strategic layering that ultimately diffused ethnic minority power.

In this chapter, we have laid the groundwork for our analysis of the state's strategies during the semidemocratic hiatus. We have provided a selective overview of some of the important periods in the evolution of the Burmese postindependence state and its relationship to ethnic minority groups. At the risk of oversimplifying, we make three key analytical points.

First, the colonial administrative structure and the path to independence left a deep divide between ethnic minority groups and the Bamar majority in control of the new state. This divide proved difficult to bridge, as tensions arose out of the first constitution and state policies that increasingly favored the Bamar majority at the expense of accommodating ethnic minorities' demands.

Second, the state's militarization further exacerbated relations, as civil war and violence became further entrenched, EAOs monopolized the nonstate representation of ethnic groups, and the state under Ne Win intensified Burmanization policies. The constitution of 1974 gave token representation to ethnic states, with no significant concessions made to ethnic demands. The main strategy remained war and repression.

Finally, the SLORC/SPDC military-dominated state appeared to have changed direction with new ceasefires and the NC that invited ethnic representatives, but Burmanization and a centralized state remained. But it essentially pursued the same strategy while attempting to reduce the number of fronts it faced. While it tried to lure EAOs into a negotiation process, it was too controlled and choreographed to constitute a credible negotiation arena. The 2008 constitution that came out of the convention preserved a strong central state and enshrined a vision of ethnic minority representation that provided very limited powers to ethnic states.

Throughout the last few decades, the state's interests and approach to ethnic minority groups remained relatively constant. Against the backdrop of civil war, state policies revealed continued Bamar-majority dominance, a tendency to reify Bamar norms and culture to apply them countrywide and make them the "Myanmar" standard, and a preference for strong directives and centralized state management. The extent to which such a state reflected the Tatmadaw's own institutional interests and culture requires little analytical consideration, given the latter's dominance and primary role in building the Burmese state. The state and the Tatmadaw were too blended to be effectively distinguishable.

The post-2011 period remained strongly imbued with the shadows of the past. Beyond the constitutional preservation in 2008 of the Tatmadaw's independence, oversight, and reserved powers, civilian structures also remained informed by the militarized culture of the past. Emerging democratic forces penetrated state institutions, most exemplified by Aung San Suu Kyi and the NLD's victory in the 2015 elections. While the state would increasingly become two pronged, there was nevertheless a convergence with the Tatmadaw around a Bamar-majority set of preferences. These were reflected in the overall state's implementation of the 2008 constitution, continued pockets of civil war, and negotiation strategies that undermined ethnic minority groups, as the following chapters show.

3
DEMOCRATIZATION
Layering and Sequencing in the State Institutional Arena

The junta's decision to open up the political regime and begin a process of democratization had significant impacts on relations between the state and ethnic minority groups. In the past, the regime was fairly monolithic in its approach, except for Khin Nyunt, who appeared for a time to lead a faction of military officers keen on negotiating with ethnic armed organizations (EAOs). For the most part, however, the state appeared to be strongly united in its policies toward ethnic minorities. It confronted a variety of ethnic minority groups that were represented by armed organizations, as other potential representatives were shut out in the post-1990 period. Once the regime began to democratize in 2011, however, the number of actors multiplied. With a more credible parliament and the addition of state/regional parliaments, state institutions reflected more diverse sets of interests and a less monolithic character. Even more so, state leaders themselves became more divided as the military retained seats in parliament and in the cabinet, defending its own views and interests mostly independently from the civilian government. At the same time, EAOs lost their monopoly on representation, as ethnic political parties proliferated alongside a number of ethnically based civil society organizations and community leaders. Ethnic groups also gained positions as leaders and representatives in state governments and legislatures.

Scholars have offered competing explanations of why the military regime, which took power in 1988, decided to undertake political reforms in 2010. Some say the military introduced political reforms to improve its image, which was undermined by persistently slow economic growth, widespread poverty, and finally an economic crisis that mismanagement, economic sanctions, and

Cyclone Nargis in 2008 helped to trigger.[1] Others argue that reforms were the result of the military's attempt to appease the international criticism of the crackdown on popular demonstrations in 1988, and to respond to the opposition movement that had grown since 1990 and whose expression was most vivid in the 2007 Saffron Revolution. Some scholars also contend that the military introduced reforms to reduce Myanmar's overdependence on China, which only intensified due to the West's economic sanctions.[2] In general, however, they all agree that the military initiated reforms in a strategic attempt to secure its interests in any future Myanmar state and to "repackage" itself without a fundamental realignment of political power.[3] This began with carefully monitored elections for national and regional legislatures in 2010 to ensure a landslide victory of the military-supported Union Solidarity and Development Party (USDP). Thirty-seven political parties (over half of which were ethnic minority parties) ran candidates, but the USDP won easily, partly because the National League for Democracy (NLD) boycotted the polls because its conditions for electoral changes were not met.[4] These conditions, contained in the so-called Shwegondaing Declaration of April 2009, included the unconditional release of all political prisoners, a review of the undemocratic principles of the 2008 constitution, and an all-inclusive free and fair election under international supervision.[5]

The Myanmar state's partial democratization nevertheless created greater pluralization of actors and diversified the field of interests. While the core grievances and issues under negotiation remained the same as in the past—namely, ethnic groups' demands for federalism and their resentment toward the Bamar majority's dominance—they became addressed in different arenas of negotiation. Government representatives and leaders worked within the confines of the 2008 constitution to implement new powers and resources provided to ethnic states and ethnic minorities more broadly. The state launched formal negotiations, first with the objective of reaching a broad ceasefire with EAOs, then to engage in a political dialogue with a wider set of ethnic representatives to achieve a final political settlement. Meanwhile, some areas of Myanmar's military and EAOs continued the civil war.

Democratization added a new state institutional arena where powers and resources between ethnic groups and the state would be negotiated and reallocated. This arena was added to the formal negotiation arena, which was given new life with formal ceasefires and an unprecedented political dialogue. The expansion of arenas of negotiation produced outcomes that sometimes appeared contradictory. They created new venues to exert pressure for reform and electoral incentives for state actors to promise policies that would benefit minority populations. But at the same time, they unveiled multiple and conflicting interests and positions that led to deadlock or the lowest common denominator, or that privileged the position of those with the largest numbers (i.e., the Bamar) or favored those with the strongest bargaining powers (i.e., the military). By comparison to the period of so-called negotiation in the National Convention (NC) under the military regime, the democratization period certainly opened up more opportunities for actual negotiation and realignment of power in multiple arenas. Nevertheless, conservative forces within the regime were able to regain control over the process and limit the extent of the reforms.

By focusing on process, which is key to understanding how the state crafted a new web of institutions and interests, we can better understand why the devolution of power created a more decentralized Myanmar but limited the capacity to negotiate and implement a more significant federal state. Sequencing was key, as the adoption of the 2008 constitution prior to democratization laid the basis on which the state institutional arena operated after 2011. The layering of new institutions diffused ethnic minority groups' points of negotiation but gave them new opportunities to make some gains. Some of the pace and degree of reforms did not entirely follow a clear design. There was a general consensus within the regime that a certain amount of decentralization should take place to allow more ethnic peace and stability but that concessions should be limited, reversible, and carefully controlled by a strong and centralized Myanmar state. The reforms went further than the military and conservative forces within the government preferred, but, overall, the state was mostly able to maintain its leverage over ethnic minority groups and funnel them toward its goals. Legacies of authoritarian rule further influenced the nature of the evolving political culture and practices that also supported a more limited set of accommodations. In the end, the Myanmar "state" became increasingly divided into two entities, with the Tatmadaw on one side and the civilian government on the other (particularly after the victory of the NLD in 2015). But the evidence shows that despite this division, state objectives remained relatively continuous and steady, characterized by a high degree of centralization and little appetite for concessions to ethnic minorities' goals of federalism.

In the following sections, we first focus on how new, partially democratic institutions created opportunities for ethnic minority groups to make unexpected gains, mostly due to power struggles among factions within the regime. Second, the transition expanded the number of actors claiming representation and advancing their respective interests. Within the state itself, the creation and allocation of new powers to regional and state parliaments added layers of interests that reduced the government's unity of purpose, while sometimes creating new alliances of convenience for decentralizing power and resources. Ethnic minority groups became more included within some of the new state structures, while new organizations emerged to claim representation of ethnic minorities. As a result, EAOs lost their monopoly on representation. While the unity among

EAOs had been difficult to achieve and remained challenging, the emergence of new groups created ever-greater obstacles to a unified strategy even if they shared common goals of crafting a new federal state. Third, when the NLD gained power, it reacted to the previous cracks in the USDP's ruling elite by ironically centralizing power to avoid diluting its effectiveness and unified objectives. Aung San Suu Kyi maintained tight control over the NLD and the civilian portion of the government. But she failed to capitalize on her strong electoral legitimacy to make significant concessions to ethnic minorities. Instead, she balanced apparent concessions with nurturing the Bamar majority, on whom the NLD depended for electoral support.

Democratic Institutions: Fragmenting Interests and Windows of Opportunity

The new democratic institutions emboldened reformists within and outside the regime. New groups began to create pressures for change, while divisions within the regime began to appear. Much of the reformist push aimed to open up the economy, allow more civil society organizations to form and operate freely, negotiate reductions in the military's control, and shed authoritarian practices. But along with this agenda, there were inevitable spillovers in the thorny issues of ending civil war and negotiating a path to peace with EAOs. First, some important divisions within the state showed that there were some strongly held differences regarding how far to reform the state, particularly in accommodating ethnic groups. Second, moderates seized the opportunity of such divisions to push reforms further than former junta leader Senior General Than Shwe probably intended at the outset. Third, the majority of Bamar also wanted significant reforms, and some of these promised to benefit ethnic minority groups. Together, these changes created a path that offered opportunities to push for significant reforms that did not necessarily reflect a clear design.

While the military likely carefully monitored the reform process, it certainly could not predict how far it would go or, ultimately, its outcome.[6] The political leadership was uncertain about the extent to which Than Shwe would continue to play a role. He had apparently selected as president U Thein Sein, former military general and prime minister in 2007–10, precisely because the latter was perceived as weak, loyal, and therefore uncontroversial. Thein Sein was elected by the national legislature (which nominated three presidential candidates, one by the upper house, one by the lower house, and one by military representatives). But Thein Sein soon surprised everyone by proactively dictating the direction of the reforms, and began to act on his authority.[7]

But changes went even further. While it appeared that the NC and the constitution of 2008 had been well crafted stepping-stones toward the 2010–11 opening, it became increasingly unclear whether the endpoint was well defined or lost in the transition. As a senior analyst of Myanmar's political developments told us in an interview, "The transition took off in a way that even the president couldn't expect. It is only when the transition started that people started to reveal their real position. They realized that resisting would be bad for their interests—they were onboard ideologically from the beginning, they had to move and be onboard pragmatically. That happened when things started to change."[8] As a result, the reforms began to appear fragmented; they advanced at an uneven pace and sometimes were followed by reversals. The latter reflected evolving alliances within the ruling elite and with a growing number and diversity of nonstate actors.[9]

Cracks appeared in the ruling elite despite a broad consensus on the need for reform. No one contested the need for political liberalization or ending the civil war to foster economic development and restore political stability. But there were disagreements over the nature, degree, and pace of democratization. Those who benefited from the previous regime were worried that reforms might affect their interests, while others felt that reforms were not going fast enough.[10] The military remained the most conservative and hard-line faction within the government, even though there were some differences within the leadership. The USDP government held an uneasy balance between hard-liners (mostly in the military), moderates within its ranks, and those in between.

Even among so-called moderates, some divisions appeared. Thura Shwe Mann, who gained the position of Speaker of the lower house and who was known as a moderate within the State Peace and Development Council (SPDC), had served as joint chief of staff of the Tatmadaw under Than Shwe in 1992. He was considered to be the third-most-influential man in the SPDC regime and to have a close relationship with Than Shwe.[11] Shwe Mann apparently resented Than Shwe's choice of Thein Sein as president. Nevertheless, he was given the position of Speaker, from which he could provide a check against executive power. The position also became a podium with which to pursue his personal rivalry with Thein Sein.[12] Aside from these grudges, he challenged the government by openly questioning its policies and practices in the parliament and later began to work closely with Aung San Suu Kyi after she was released from house arrest in late 2010 and her party entered parliament in 2012.[13] As the 2015 elections approached, the competition turned to electoral interest, as both Shwe Mann and Thein Sein sought the USDP's endorsement as presidential candidates.[14] The rivalry between two senior ex-generals of the SPDC era, both of whom were generally seen as part of the moderate group from the military, helped to push reforms further than initially intended.

Overall, the democratic institutions produced electoral incentives for moderate forces within the government to outmaneuver each other to push for further reforms, including toward minority ethnic groups. A prominent member of the government's team negotiating with the nonstate armed groups noted that "the democratic transition was never intended to go this far. When the transition began, new institutions emerged. Even within the military there were diverse interests, no longer just senior generals. Then there were more major actors shaping political change, and no one could monopolize the process. It evolved in a much different way than anticipated with the seven-point road map set by the previous government. We underestimated the reformers, and soon realized that some reformers were going the extra mile."[15]

Thein Sein's and Shwe Mann's positioning for the 2015 elections had spillover effects on the state's approach to ethnic minorities. They sought to gain the support of ethnic minorities, hoping that it would increase their popularity within the USDP and make gains for the party in ethnic minority areas. This competition created some policy reversals and pushed some of the reforms either further or more quickly than anticipated by the hard-liners. Meanwhile, ethnic leaders sought to take advantage of this opportunity. "Ethnic people in parliament," an adviser to one ethnic armed organization, the Chin National Front, told us, "say that Shwe Mann has been very attentive to their demands for decentralization. My feeling is that MPs have a much better rating of Shwe Mann than Thein Sein. Armed groups, on the other hand, have a good view of Thein Sein."[16] Shwe Mann certainly sought to influence MPs (members of parliament) and use legislative power to enhance his status, while Thein Sein invested in the negotiations with EAOs.

Upon becoming president, Thein Sein took several initiatives that were favorable. He assigned one of six advisers in the presidential office (officially known as the minister of the president's office) to work specifically on decentralization. He commissioned a study titled *The Framework on Economic and Social Reform*, which advocated for adding more areas to the initial list of decentralized responsibilities to regional governments.[17] The president's office oversaw the passing of the 2012 Ward and Village Tract Administration Law, which led to indirect elections for village tract and ward administrators.[18] Between 2011 and 2016, the government initiated a majority of the 232 laws that were passed in the national parliament.[19] These included a number of reforms that benefited ethnic minority groups, such as the promotion of the culture and language of "national races," the rights of local populations to be consulted on resource exploitation, and the expansion of regional and state governments' decision-making power and budgets.[20]

One of the government's earliest policy reversals, the Myitsone Dam project's cancelation, shows Thein Sein's attempts to capitalize on the support he gained from ethnic minority groups while sidelining his rival. The SPDC government had signed a contract with China to build the Myitsone hydroelectric plant in Kachin State at the confluence of the Mali and N'Mai Rivers. This $3.6 billion megadam project was located in an area known for its rich biodiversity and cultural heritage, including a number of historical churches and temples. The construction would have displaced thousands of people and adversely affected the country's river system and rice-growing areas. The project began in 2009, and the government continued to support it despite protests by Kachin local leaders, particularly the Kachin Independence Organization, and later pressure from civil society organizations and the general public. In a sudden reversal, however, Thein Sein decided on September 30, 2011, to postpone the project, without consulting with the minister responsible for it, the heads of the two national parliaments, or the two vice presidents. It was perceived partly as an attempt to sideline Shwe Mann from important policy deliberations.[21] The president's decision no doubt increased his popularity and drew much applause from domestic grassroots organizations, including environmental conservation groups, human rights activists, and international communities, which opposed the building of the megadam. But this decision came as a surprise to members of the ruling elite, particularly Shwe Mann, who was sympathetic to the public's concerns and would have benefited politically as well if he had been included in the decision. Shwe Mann was reportedly notified of the president's decision at the last minute and therefore felt that Thein Sein had tried to take all of the credit by excluding him from it.[22] While the decision showed that Thein Sein reacted to new pressures from ethnic groups and anticipated the political capital that could be gained, he was also ensuring that his rival would not move first and play a critical role in the government's reversal. His act ushered in the beginning of the tension between Thein Sein and Shwe Mann, which would later influence the peace negotiation process.

Similarly, Thein Sein also limited Shwe Mann's involvement in the peace process, again to prevent him from making political gains. Initially there were two negotiating teams, one from the government, led by Minister Aung Min, and one from the parliament, led by Brigadier General Thein Zaw, who focused more specifically on EAOs in Shan State. Aung Min's team gradually presided over the entire peace negotiation process, leaving Shwe Mann and the parliamentarians who were members of the Union Peace Working Committee to complain about being entirely excluded from the actual peace negotiations.[23] Aung Min, for instance, reportedly encouraged the Karen National Union (KNU) leader General Mutu Say Poe to meet only with the president, despite the KNU's request to also meet with Shwe Mann and the military chief. Aung Min, according to Su Mon Thazin Aung, reportedly reasoned that "he and the president stood against others during the NDSC [National Defense and Security Council] meeting, projecting that some of the members still held the conventional (military-centre) mind-set."[24]

In response, Shwe Mann openly criticized the government, thereby reinforcing the public display of divisions within the regime. He emphasized the need for MPs to be informed in order to understand the ongoing peace process. He stressed the need for the NDSC to meet regularly, questioned the lack of transparency of the Aung Min–led ceasefire negotiations, and warned that concessions to EAOs might be illegal and unconstitutional. Finally, he was critical of the use of nonauditable foreign grants to finance projects that supported the peace process.[25] His criticism was influential in the NDSC's decision in July 2013 to use public funds instead of international aid for these purposes. The president then requested 7 billion kyats ($7.1 million) of the national budget in fiscal year 2014–15, which required approval from parliament and could be seen as a victory for Shwe Mann's efforts. Nevertheless, the NDSC and the legislature were unable to actually monitor Aung Min's peace process, which continued until the end of the USDP government's mandate.[26] As Su Mon Thazin Aung notes, "In this way, the president and his close allies could exclude his major power rival the lower house chairman from the process while [his team] could earn public and international legitimacy from building peace with [EAOs]."[27]

Shwe Mann also attempted to portray himself as the champion of public interests by forming a Constitutional Amendment Implementation Committee to propose constitutional amendments, which included recognition of greater areas of autonomy for regional governments and legislatures.[28] After review, the committee proposed six amendments, but only one of them (which replaced the word "military" with "defense" as a requirement for president) was passed in the legislature, due mainly to opposition from the military legislators. Proposals that were rejected included lowering the threshold for amending the constitution from 75 percent to 70 percent of the total MPs; the removal of Section 59(f), which prohibited anyone with children or spouses who are foreign citizens from serving as president or vice president. Although his plan backfired and led to his dismissal as the USDP party chairman, Shwe Mann may have brought the amendments up for a vote knowing that they would fail, mainly to improve his chances of being selected as the nation's president in the next electoral cycle.[29]

Beyond the public eye, many reformers working within the government had a sense of urgency to seal certain reforms for fear that the hard-liners would attempt to reverse the concessions that the government had made. These fears related to broader democratic reforms as well, but were particularly strong with respect to ethnic minorities, where commitments to reform appeared to be most ambivalent. As a leading staff member of the Myanmar Peace Center (MPC) observed, "We were trying hard to press for lots of legislation to lock in gains before the election [of 2015], in order to make reforms irreversible."[30] In particular, the MPC and a few prominent EAOs sought to convince both the reformists and the hard-liners within the government and the military to accept the Nationwide Ceasefire Agreement (NCA) and principles of federalism. They emphasized security and political benefits, organized study tours in federal countries to show how federalism was not threatening, and used third-party intervention to apply pressure.[31] These efforts managed to break some of the previous barriers to a more peaceful settlement, including the thorny question of federalism. "It took us two years to make the government understand this point [that federalism is not a threat]," said the MPC staff member. "They now agree that federalism is not a monster and does not lead to secessionism. There are two exceptions to the government's acceptance of federalism: first, it should not lead to the disintegration of the Union; second, it should not lead to the loss of sovereignty. So in the context of federalism, the government agrees that it can discuss power sharing and resource sharing, but this discussion can only take place when they have a political dialogue."[32]

Overall, then, the period under USDP governance revealed much greater division within the ruling elite than originally anticipated, as democratization had appeared to be well orchestrated from the outset. There is no doubt that some key members of the Thein Sein administration were strongly and genuinely committed to achieving peace. But electoral incentives, personal ambition and rivalry, and the need to cater to ethnic minorities to gain political capital began to push reforms related to democracy and ethnic rights much further than the military had originally envisioned. Conceivably, there was at least some credibility at the beginning of democratization that the new arenas could produce negotiated outcomes, and were therefore much less controlled and manipulated than under the previous regime.

The Pluralization of Actors (2011–16): Layering and Dividing the State and Ethnic Minority Groups

The partial democratization contributed to diversifying the interests within the state itself, and allowed a number of new actors to claim representation of ethnic groups. Moving from the highly centralized and streamlined authority structure of the SPDC state under Than Shwe's command, the civilian regime under Thein Sein's presidency created a number of new stakeholders within this state with differing viewpoints from the leadership. Meanwhile, ethnic minorities gained new representative positions within the state itself, including as members of the ruling USDP, while outside the state, claims to ethnic minority representation also proliferated. New ethnic political parties were formed and civilian society organizations multiplied, while EAOs sought to maintain their primary roles in representing their respective groups, especially in the peace negotiations. As a result, a number of new state actors, combined with the voices of different ethnic representatives, created pressures for a number of reforms to address some of the long-standing grievances.

Legislators in the Union Hluttaw (legislature) and newly empowered state and regional governments participated in reforms and created pressures for decentralization. Regional cabinets and assemblies where ethnic political parties held a relatively higher proportion of seats or dominated the regional legislatures (such as Chin, Kayin, and Rakhine States) most strongly voiced demands for greater decentralization. But even within the ruling USDP, some members were vocal in pressuring the central government for reforms designed to empower states and regions. Some USDP regional ministers, such as in Bago or Ayeyarwady Regions, increasingly expressed frustration with regional governments' limited autonomy.[33] Local branches and chief ministers from the USDP regularly supported further political decentralization.[34] In the Mon State regional parliament, the USDP, which held fourteen out of twenty-three seats, shared some of the same objectives as the All Mon Region Democracy Party, with seven seats. They both wanted to increase regional powers by making chief ministers an elected position, as well as by enhancing regional governments' decision-making powers.[35] In Tanintharyi, the local USDP branch allied with regional parties to ask for increased regional influence over the planned Dawei Special Economic Zone.[36]

Indirect support came from a majority of elected legislators in Bamar-dominated regional parliaments. They shared with members of ethnic political parties a desire to push for greater regional autonomy and decentralization. They criticized the overcentralized post-2011 civilian state and they supported the new Region or State Hluttaw Bill in 2013. There was broad-based support within the Union parliament for the establishment of an autonomous state/regional hluttaw office out of the central government's control, permission for the public to attend hluttaw sessions, the allocation of funds to electoral districts, and independent representative offices.[37]

Elected members exercised some pressure and also participated in the drafting of laws dealing with minority groups. For instance, ethnic affairs ministers (also called national race affairs ministers) were highly involved in drafting the law titled the Ethnic Rights Protection Law (2015).[38] The law mandated the formation of a national ethnic affairs ministerial position with its own separate budget at the Union level, and guaranteed the right of *taing yin thar* (national races) to be informed, and their consent obtained, for major development programs and extractive activities in their respective regions.³⁹ Some influential minority nationalities in the USDP also contributed to change. T. Khun Myat, a Kachin national and chair of the USDP-led Pyithu Hluttaw's Bill Committee, for instance, tabled a draft encouraging the adoption of new legislation on protecting the rights of Myanmar's national races.⁴⁰ And a USDP member of the upper house from Kachin State reportedly influenced Shwe Mann's support for the principles of federalism.⁴¹

Within the state, therefore, demands were made for more decentralization toward the states and regions. Newly empowered ethnic minorities, as representatives of ethnic political parties but even within the USDP, exercised the greatest amount of pressure and participated in legislative initiatives designed to provide more powers. But they found some allies even in Bamar-dominated regions, where USDP ministers and representatives also complained of overcentralization.

In addition, EAOs lost their monopoly over the representation of ethnic minorities. Ethnic political parties began to claim representation of ethnic minorities, although their success in elections was poor. Political parties with minority ethnic names or states constituted over half of registered political parties in the 2010 elections. Yet only fifteen of the twenty-one ethnic political parties won seats.⁴² The parties established for the 1990 elections initially joined the NLD and refused to participate in the 2010 elections, but then ran in the 2015 elections. They competed against other ethnic parties that were formed to run in the 2010 elections.

Nevertheless, both elected and unelected ethnic political parties remained vocal under Thein Sein's government. They demanded to be included in the peace negotiations and consulted on potential reforms. They made public statements, gave interviews, and asked questions in the legislature. They also raised their constituents' concerns in national addresses, which were televised and printed in newspapers.⁴³ These interventions contributed to creating new pressures on government and the legislature. Although ethnic political parties collectively gained only about 14.9 percent and 11.2 percent of the elected seats in the national parliament under the USDP and NLD governments, respectively, they expressed minority grievances and contributed to maintaining them on the political agenda.⁴⁴

Therefore, there were several sources of support for greater decentralization across the political spectrum during the 2011–16 period. Within the state, even some unlikely alliances between USDP members and representatives from state/regional governments shared the objective of obtaining more powers and resources at the regional level. Others supported the agendas of emerging ethnic political parties, which made similar demands. Yet the ultimate objectives sometimes differed markedly. Ethnic political parties even differed with respect to the degree to which their goals of federalism could be met by cooperating with the state for short-term decentralization. They competed among themselves as well as with EAOs for leadership and representation of ethnic minority groups. While their collective mobilization increased pressure on the government, their divisiveness led to weakness at the polls and difficulties crafting common strategies to obtain more concessions from the state.

In addition, the USDP government's policies tended to support only reforms that were also beneficial to the Bamar majority, such as decentralizing the national government in favor of both ethnic states and regions. They generally refrained from changes that would require altering the constitution and rejected proposals that were exclusively beneficial to ethnic minority groups.

For instance, the national parliament in 2011–16 rejected a number of initiatives that were considered too radical, as they departed from the existing constitutional framework. Although the law on the protection of the rights of national races (2015) was designed to protect ethnic minority nationalities, the fact that Bamar were included in the national races may have helped its adoption by parliament.[45] The national parliament increased the list of regional governments' jurisdictional and fiscal powers, but only in areas that were neither strategically nor financially significant. For instance, a total of thirty-four addendums were added to Schedule 2 of the constitution (which initially recognized forty-one subsectors under which regional legislatures can enact laws) and twenty addendums to Schedule 5 (taxation). These additions broadened regional legislatures' powers to enact laws and levy taxes but were limited to minor areas such as hotels and tourism, industrial zones, and wildlife protection, and the powers tended to be very specific in those sectors, rather than broad ones. Schedule 5 was extended to allow twenty new revenue streams, including levies on income, commerce, and customs, and taxation of oil and gas revenues. But the amended Schedule 5 did not include several other natural resources, such as teak, other hardwoods, and mineral deposits. Ethnic areas, especially Kachin, Shan, and Kayin States, are rich in natural resources, particularly precious stones, gold, and timber, but these resources remained strictly under the national government's control.

Chief ministers represent "older" structures of rule, as they derive their power directly from the center, but they nevertheless hold the top executive position in states and regions. There are fourteen chief ministers representing each of the fourteen states/regions. Almost half of them have names associated with minority ethnic groups, but all of them represented either the USDP in 2011–16 or the NLD in 2016–21. Under the Thein Sein government, regional chief ministers were the most powerful figures in their respective regions, partly because most of them were ex-military officers with seniority over the border affairs ministers in their respective regional government cabinets. They had the constitutional authority to form their cabinets, composed of both elected and unelected candidates. Policy implementation was top-down, but USDP chief ministers were able to maintain a certain level of de facto authority to enhance their own interests or those of their regions.

Chief ministers under the NLD government did not enjoy the same level of power and influence as under the Thein Sein government, partly because they were civilians with no prior military or senior government experience.[46] The policies and practices of the NLD chief ministers tended to reflect the positions and preferences of the NLD government rather than those of the local populations, let alone minority ethnic groups. So did the positions of the Union minister of ethnic affairs and of twenty-nine state and regional ethnic affairs ministers (nineteen of whom were NLD members), a majority of whom simply followed the NLD official line.

The layering that democratization entailed created a more diverse state institutional arena and expanded the space for new political actors to emerge among ethnic minority groups. By some measures, this constituted a pluralization of actors and interests that was reflected in some meaningful debate regarding the nature and extent of decentralization, as well as new claims to represent ethnic minority groups within and outside the state.

Recentralization and Balancing the Bamar-Ethnic Electorate (2016–20)

Aung San Suu Kyi and the NLD's landslide victory in the 2015 elections gave them legitimacy to push forward reforms and promised a new relationship with ethnic minority groups. Yet it became quickly apparent that they failed to use that legitimacy to make any significant progress on peace negotiations or on restructuring the governance of ethnic minority states toward their goal of federalism. Instead, Aung San Suu Kyi sought to recentralize the state and streamline the NLD's governance mechanisms to avoid the kinds of cracks that appeared in the USDP's leadership. Ironically, her government came across as more centralized than its predecessor, with opportunities to voice differences and make claims for accommodation even narrower than they had been. While some of this reaction could be attributed to the government's uneasy relationship to the military and the need to preserve its strength relative to the armed forces, it nevertheless contributed to preserving authoritarian legacies of the past. The NLD also relied heavily on strong support from the Bamar majority, which was mainly lukewarm on the idea of federalism and greater concessions toward ethnic minority groups.

In effect, it allowed a consolidation of the civilian side of the state, and created a new, clearly two-pronged state, with the military remaining fully united on the other side.[47] A tug-of-war would emerge that essentially squeezed out the ability of ethnic minority groups to make gains.

The NLD's decision to participate in the by-elections in 2012 and its overwhelming victory in the 2015 election initially created a more open and freer political environment. It radically transformed the democratic nature of governance with a much higher proportion of civilians in top-level executive branches and representatives who were more sensitive to the grassroots population's demands. Aung San Suu Kyi initially refused to take the oath and abide by the 2008 constitution, but after a period of working as an MP inside the parliament from 2012 to 2015, she relented and attempted to bring about incremental changes within the 2008 constitution. Like Thein Sein previously, she used the 2008 constitution to bypass the limitations on her power, in her case because the constitution prevented her from assuming the presidency. She therefore instead arranged to become foreign minister while simultaneously taking advantage of a constitutional loophole to create a position of state counselor. She legalized her power over the president and parliament, despite the military's objections.[48]

Meanwhile, the EAOs' loss of monopoly over the representation of ethnic minorities accelerated. After 2015, the number of political parties with ethnic minority names or states increased from twenty-one in 2010 to forty-nine in 2015.[49] They were not very successful, as only a dozen parties won seats in both elections. They remained highly divided, though, even within particular ethnic groups. In 2015 and 2020, several ethnic political parties tried to form alliances to reduce competition among themselves that could prevent them from gaining seats. But in the end, few managed to sufficiently bridge the gap in their respective differences to form strong competition for the major parties, particularly in the NLD in the 2015 election and more significantly the 2020 election. As a result, in 2015, only the Rakhine National Party and the Shan Nationalities League for Democracy were successful at making strong gains in regional parliaments, whereas the NLD swept almost all seats everywhere else. In 2020, ethnic parties were slightly more successful, as fifteen parties merged into six larger parties representing Chin, Kachin, Karen, Kayah, Mon, and Wa.[50]

Whether by constraint or by commitment, Aung San Suu Kyi's government showed little enthusiasm to support deep reforms and accommodate ethnic minority demands. Aung San Suu Kyi was somewhat constrained by her political base, but also by her leadership style and her convictions. She rose to power with the very strong popular support of the majority, most of which was Bamar. Therefore, this majority had a substantial indirect ability to influence the nature and structure of Myanmar's future federal system.

Aung San Suu Kyi's leadership style came across as quasi-authoritarian, closed, and lacking in consultation, with negative consequences for ethnic minorities. Her apparent desire to micromanage the entire peace process, to "recentralize" power by exercising control over NLD state/regional chief ministers and by refusing to delegate power, was reminiscent of her Bamar predecessors under the military and civilian regimes.[51] She justified her approach with the knowledge that the NLD enjoyed higher levels of legitimacy and popular support than the previous government.[52] Ultimately, while the NLD's accession to power represented a significant departure from the past authoritarian governing system, the NLD government continued to operate within the same institutional framework that had governed its predecessors and was not clearly committed to crafting a federal state.

In addition, a long history of hostility and ideological conflict between the military and the NLD hindered the development of common strategies, and ultimately led to the coup of 2021. The USDP government was composed of former high-ranking military officers who still enjoyed considerable influence over their peers in the army. As a result, they were able to bridge differences in policy with respect to negotiations with EAOs.[53] Under the NLD government, the military still retained formal authority over major political and security decision-making, yet its relations with Aung San Suu Kyi and the NLD became increasingly tense. Electoral considerations may have contributed to the military's unwillingness to cooperate with the NLD, since success in peace negotiations may well have enhanced the NLD's popularity at the expense of the USDP in the following electoral cycle.

As a result, the NLD's policies toward ethnic minorities showed little progress from the USDP period. At first, the NLD appeared to be favorable to ethnic minorities, but it became apparent that its approach was strongly favorable to the NLD primarily, and quite ambiguous in its commitment to respond to ethnic minority grievances and foster an environment conducive to building new relations.

Initially, and in contrast to the USDP government, Aung San Suu Kyi named a good number of ethnic minority representatives to high-ranking positions. For instance, Henry Van Thio, an ethnic Chin, became one of two vice presidents, while T Khun Myat, Manh Win Khaing Than, and Aye Thar Aung—all ethnic minorities—became chair and deputy chairs, respectively, of the national legislature. Shortly after its inauguration, the NLD government implemented the Ethnic Rights Protection Law (passed by the national parliament in 2015 under the previous administration). It therefore created the Ministry of Ethnic Affairs and appointed Naing Thet Lwin of the Mon National Party—an NLD ally—as minister of ethnic affairs.[54] At the regional and state legislature levels, the record was more mixed. The proportion of chief ministers who were members of ethnic minorities remained almost the same as under Thein Sein's administration. But the NLD government had fewer ethnic minority members as speakers of the regional and state legislatures (five out of fourteen, compared to seven out of fourteen under the USDP government).[55]

In her approach to many arising issues, however, Aung San Suu Kyi was relatively uncompromising and unsympathetic. Many minority groups were dismayed, for instance, by her silence on the deaths, destruction, and civilian displacement resulting from ongoing conflicts, many of which escalated after 2015. Leaders of armed groups that signed the NCA in 2015 complained of her patronizing and dismissive attitude when she met with them.[56] She also missed an opportunity to make gestures of reconciliation with ethnic political parties. In spite of appointing several ethnic minorities to key leadership positions, for example, she refused to appoint chief ministers from Rakhine and Shan parties that had won a majority of seats in their respective state assemblies. Instead she persisted in appointing chief ministers from the NLD. Also, the NLD's relationship with Mon political parties deteriorated after the NLD-dominated lower house voted in March 2017 to name a new bridge after Bogyoke Aung San, the country's independence hero and Aung San Suu Kyi's father. The bridge crosses the Thanlwin (Salween) River and links Mawlamyine with rural Chaungzon Township, known as Bilu Kyun (Ogre Island).[57] A ninety-six-member committee composed of Mon political parties, local community elders, women's groups, monks, youth leaders, and human rights and political activists organized a public rally and sent a petition with over ninety thousand signatures to the president's office. The protesters wanted the bridge to be named either the Salween or the Yamanya Bridge, names that they believed would better represent Mon regional identity. They also resented that the Union-level parliament had made the decision without consulting either local communities or the state governments and legislatures.[58] When their appeal was rejected, campaigners accused the (NLD) government of "bullying" and ignoring the principles of federalism.

A similar situation arose in Kayah State, where people protested plans to erect a statue of General Aung San. Instead of selecting local heroes for this distinction, the choice of Aung San was associated with the previous military-led governments' policies to Burmanize or assimilate them.[59] They were even further infuriated by the NLD chief minister, a Kayah national, who threatened to call in troops to quell the protests, and by charges of defamation and incitement, under Sections 505(b) and 505(c), against ten youths who participated in the protests.[60] Similarly, Karen civil society groups and political parties were outraged when the NLD government prohibited any reference to Ba U Gyi—a Karen revolutionary hero who was killed by the Myanmar Army in the independence period—as a "martyr" at a public ceremony.⁶¹ As these examples show, when issues arose, the NLD government showed little sympathy for the sensitivities of ethnic minorities.

Aung San Suu Kyi and the NLD were certainly mindful of maintaining support from the Bamar majority, which gave it its electoral success. The extent to which this majority would favor federalism or greater concessions to the ethnic minorities was unclear. In fact, a survey by the People's Alliance for Credible Elections found that respondents in regions that were mostly Bamar were generally less supportive of devolving more power to the state/regional level and more satisfied with the status quo.⁶² While they were strong supporters of changing the 2008 constitution, they were focused mainly on reducing the role of the military, rather than on building a new federation. As a Yangon-based researcher and analyst of Myanmar's politics observed, "Let's not forget, from the government's standpoint, that the only group that hasn't been consulted in all that [peace] process is the Bamar. . . . Yet they are the ones with the ultimate electoral weight."⁶³ The majority of Bamar, who were often ignorant of the plight of ethnic minorities due to the past military regime's propaganda and control of the media, increasingly expressed alarm over the armed groups' demands, which were found on social and private media. Some Bamar in core areas still could not understand why ethnic minority groups disliked and distrusted them, and why non-Bamar wanted to implement their language as a medium of communication in government, courts, and schools.⁶⁴ The war between the Tatmadaw and the Kachin Independence Organization, Arakan Army, and Kokang groups in the post-2010 periods, and the backlash against the coverage of the Rohingya crisis by foreign media, seemed to increase support for the military and Bamar Buddhist nationalists.⁶⁵ "In Kokang," one political analyst told us, "there was a backlash by the nationalists . . . who saw the Chinese behind the Myanmar National Democratic Alliance Army. It is perhaps the first time that the Burman so openly supported the army. People changed their Facebook profile pictures with military insignia."⁶⁶

Even the Bamar elite that favored complete democratization while in opposition remained ambivalent and sometimes even hostile toward federalism. Some openly supported federalism in principle, mostly because it became NLD policy. As an NLD senior member remarked at a June 2016 workshop in Yangon, "I did not accept the federal model for Burma, but I now have to accept it because of the changing times and circumstances. The NLD's current focus is on federalism, and we perceive people who oppose federalism as destructionists."⁶⁷ When asked what form of federalism he would like to see implemented in Burma, an NLD chief minister from a Bamar-dominant region reportedly said, "Any kind of arrangements instructed to me by my boss."⁶⁸ Bamar members of the NLD often rejected federalism or reacted with hostility toward proposals by minority ethnic groups to have their languages recognized as official languages and as a medium of official communication in their respective states.[69] Ko Ko Gyi, a prominent 1988 student leader, remarked with resentment regarding reverse discrimination he experienced as Bamar, "Whenever minority ethnic issues are discussed, Bamar have been excluded. I want you to remember that we are also one of the ethnic nationalities in Myanmar."[70] While somewhat anecdotal, these comments were typical and showed varying attitudes that became more apparent after the NLD gained power in 2015 and began to address minority issues.[71] Its policies became just as ambivalent as those of the preceding USDP government, reflecting a general reluctance among the Bamar to accommodate ethnic minority group demands.[72]

The most vulnerable among these minorities were Rohingya, descendants of immigrants during the British colonial period from Chittagonian Region in what is now Bangladesh. Rohingya constituted a third of the population in Buddhist-dominant Rakhine State but formed a majority in two townships in northern Rakhine. They were not accepted as one of the 135 official national groups, and faced various forms of discrimination and displacement throughout the military regime. Decades of tension and localized violence between Rakhine Buddhists and Muslim Rohingya (which were contained and localized under successive military regimes) erupted in a major outbreak of communal violence in 2012 and quickly spread to the rest of the country.[73] Newfound democratic norms also privileged the majority, whose growing prejudice against Muslims pressured elected MPs to pass anti-Islamic laws in 2015.[74] The situation of Rohingya further deteriorated after the NLD came to power in 2016.

On this issue, Aung San Suu Kyi and the NLD found themselves squeezed between two opposing sides with seemingly irreconcilable viewpoints. If Aung San Suu Kyi sided with Buddhist nationalists, the international community would blame her for failing to protect the rights of the Rohingya and other Muslim communities in Myanmar. If she sided with the international community and recognized the Rohingya's rights, she would pay a heavy domestic political price as the Myanmar public remained largely intolerant of both Muslims and Rohingya. In a bid to diffuse the tensions, in August 2016 Aung San Suu Kyi formed an advisory commission, chaired by former United Nations Secretary General Kofi Annan, to provide "rigorously impartial" assessments and recommendations to the government on solutions to the problems in Rakhine State.[75] But the night following the release of Annan's report, the Arakan Rohingya Salvation Army launched a series of coordinated attacks on government outposts in Rakhine State. This provided the Tatmadaw with the perfect excuse to launch a scorched-earth operation against the militia, leaving thousands dead and pushing more than seven hundred thousand Rohingya into Bangladesh.[76] In response, the UN sponsored an independent international fact-finding mission on Myanmar, which found evidence of gross human rights abuse by the army in its operation in Rakhine State.

The resulting international condemnation and punitive measures against the country and Aung San Suu Kyi only encouraged Burmese to get behind both the government and the army. The army's actions resulted in calls to bring those responsible before the International Court of Justice. Gambia filed a case in 2019 on behalf of the Organisation of Islamic Cooperation countries. In an unexpected turn of events, Aung San Suu Kyi, Myanmar's state counselor and a Nobel Peace Prize laureate, stood at the podium of the court and defended her country and the Tatmadaw against accusations of genocide. Whether she did that for strategic purposes, to keep the military onboard with democratic transition, or due to her own bias against the Rohingya, is unclear. What is clear, however, is that popular support for her increased after she appeared at the Hague in December 2019.[77]

By the end of their mandate, the NLD and Aung San Suu Kyi had not only failed to deliver on past promises made to ethnic minorities, but also appeared to be just as determined as their predecessors to maintain a strong centralized state, and perhaps even more so. They cast themselves as the sole defender of democracy, including in ethnic minority areas, and their electoral success in 2015 and again in 2020 reaffirmed their broad claim to legitimacy. On that basis, they seemed little inclined to compromise with ethnic political parties or armed groups, and remained focused on their primary struggle to reduce the military's power while limiting concessions to minority groups.

The partial democratization that began in 2011 and ended in 2021 opened up opportunities for reform but also subjected potential concessions on ethnic minority issues to the limitations of majority rule. While there were initial signs of new commitments for peace negotiations and concessions to ethnic minorities, the new democratic institutions also revealed a number of constraints.

The Tatmadaw strategically decided to open up the regime mostly to manage opposition internally and pressures externally, but this had profound implications for relations with ethnic minority groups. With the transition to a quasi-civilian government and partial democratization in 2011, the regime essentially opened up a new state institutional arena for ethnic minority actors to negotiate new powers and resources. A democratic state created new rules, laws, institutions, and opportunities for ethnic minorities to obtain representation and advance their interests from within the state, in addition to seeking similar gains in formal negotiations and the theater of war.

This new space was not trivial. The formal negotiation arena of the NC was less than credible and only revealed crude attempts to provide minimal concessions to particular groups in exchange for ceasefires. Thus the opening of the new state institutional arena did credibly set the stage for more significant negotiations and concessions to occur within the state. It accompanied a more credible resetting of the formal negotiation arena that began on the eve of the transition to partial civilian rule.

State actors became more diverse under the USDP. Initially, the state planned limited concessions to ethnic minority groups. But once launched, the reforms went further than the military and conservative forces within the government preferred. Democratic rules and procedures that provided minority ethnic leaders with channels to express their grievances, power struggles among the "moderate" factions within the government, and unexpected pressures among the Bamar regions contributed to deepening some reforms.

Nevertheless, the military and conservative factions within the USDP government were able to place limits on the concessions. As will be shown in more detail in the following chapters, sequencing mattered. The adoption of the 2008 constitution created the new institutions, allocated the powers and resources that ethnic states could manage, and set a very high bar for amendments to be introduced. The layering that subsequently occurred—in terms of both expanding state actors and permitting ethnic political parties and civil society actors the space to provide an alternative to armed groups—certainly did allow for some indeterminacy in outcomes and possibilities for making real gains but within the tight framework that the Tatmadaw had laid out.

After its election, the NLD had strong legitimacy to undertake a new series of reforms and placed peace negotiations as its top priority, but limited the diversity of perspectives within the state itself by recentralizing its control over different institutional levels, mostly in response to Aung San Suu Kyi's directives. While most likely a defensive response from a party that had long been in opposition, the centralization also avoided appearing unfocused and divided. With the military continuing to play a strong independent role, the NLD government was certainly cautious to avoid a conflictual approach that could invite retaliation or create paralysis. The tight control over policy ended up being surprisingly conservative, given how much legitimacy it enjoyed from the elections and its initial positive gestures toward ethnic minorities.

The following chapters describe how these institutional incentives and constraints shaped the process of negotiating peace and extending concessions to ethnic minority groups. The negotiation process under the USDP and then the NLD operated in two arenas: first in formal negotiations toward a nationwide ceasefire agreement and subsequently in the political dialogue (the 21st Century

Panglong Conference), and second, outside the institutional arena, where EAOs and the military continued war. In a third, the state institutional arena, the implementation of the 2008 constitution shows how, de facto, the state moved toward its own vision of decentralization, subject to the government's goals and constraints, including the dual-governance system with the military. Its effect was to create ever-entrenched institutional structures that reflected the 2008 constitution's model of decentralization, while increasingly penetrating areas previously held by EAOs.

4

PROCESS OVER WAR
From Ceasefire to Political Dialogue

The transitional government of Thein Sein and its successor, the National League for Democracy (NLD)-led administration, attempted to break the vicious cycle of civil war by engaging in unprecedented peace talks with armed groups. The previous regime had reached bilateral ceasefire agreements with ethnic armed organizations (EAOs). But their informal nature and thin substance revealed the state's strategic attempts to reduce the number of fronts in its civil war, rather than seeking a lasting political settlement to the conflict with ethnic minority groups. The multiparty negotiations that ultimately led to the 2015 Nationwide Ceasefire Agreement (NCA) and subsequent political dialogue represented a departure from past trends, at least in the degree to which EAOs participated in drafting the rules of engagement and in the transparency of the formal process.

Yet despite what appeared to be a messy and sometimes incoherent process, the general trend ultimately aligned with the state's limits on ethnic minority accommodation and the profoundly entrenched bias of the majority Bamar elite against extending significant concessions. State negotiators wavered in their commitments, largely reflecting important disagreements between hard-liners, mostly in the armed forces, and more moderate members of the Thein Sein and NLD administrations, often backed by advisers sincerely committed to a settlement. On the ethnic minority side, divisions and negotiating strategies were even more inconsistent, largely because of a lack of experience and strong control over substantive issues, as well as the inherent difficulties in forming a common negotiation front. EAOs jockeyed with one another for dominance over the process, with some, such as the Kachin Independence Organization (KIO), choosing to exit the formal negotiations altogether and seeking to create alternative forums (and fronts) to negotiate through a combination of military force and recasting of the agenda. Their relationship to other representatives of ethnic minority groups, such as ethnic political parties and civil society organizations, created even more obstacles to a united front, as EAOs sought to remain the principal players against the alternative forms of ethnic representation that emerged after the initiation of the transition to electoral democracy. As a result, somewhat by design but mostly from its more dominant position, the Bamar-dominated state largely succeeded in ensuring that rules of engagement and negotiation stayed within its control and that substantive issues aligned with its interests in maintaining a Bamar-centric Myanmar.

This chapter examines the formal process of negotiation leading to the NCA and subsequent political dialogue. It shows how the state—including the Tatmadaw and the NLD government—used strategies to control the process and ultimately steer the negotiations toward its goals, while ethnic minority groups faced increasing difficulties to make gains. The evidence suggests that a mix of locking in, layering, and sequencing were most effectively deployed and exploited in the formal negotiation arena, in the end creating an overwhelming ability of the state to limit concessions and thwart ethnic minority goals. Some EAOs attempted to use an outgunning strategy to gain leverage, but with few gains by the end of the NLD government's mandate.

This outcome was not a foregone conclusion. In fact, the rules of negotiation were crafted largely at the EAOs' initiative. It was ironically their concept that locked in a process that the Tatmadaw and NLD could exploit. Furthermore, layering strategies were used on both sides, as the regime's opening up of democratic space allowed a number of new ethnic minority actors to emerge (or reemerge), most significantly political parties and civil society actors. The latter created pressure on the EAOs to allow their participation in the formal arena, so the negotiation process added layers of participants that ultimately divided ethnic minority groups even more, and made a united front an even more remote possibility. Meanwhile, the rules had locked in the greater ability of the Tatmadaw and civil government representatives to control the agenda, participants, and further rules of negotiation. Finally, sequencing added to the state's advantage. With the constitution of 2008 in place, the state and Tatmadaw negotiators could continually insist on its primacy and on the need to proceed by amendment of the existing constitution, thereby creating huge obstacles ahead for change. The decision to proceed first with a civilian government under the Union Solidarity and Development Party (USDP), and a general election in 2015, also allowed the USDP-led government and the Tatmadaw to set the terms of the formal negotiations. The USDP, in particular, hoped that sealing the NCA before the election, and beginning the political dialogue under its announced structure, would increase its political capital and ensure its reelection. Ethnic minority groups engaged in the negotiating process were increasingly funneled into accepting terms largely set by the state's negotiators.

Some EAOs, as a result, opted for an outgunning strategy in an attempt to leverage the theater of war in hopes of breaking the Tatmadaw's seal on negotiations or forcing an alternative negotiation framework. The KIO and its allies contested the process, while using continued civil war as a bargaining chip. But the Tatmadaw also used war to influence the formal negotiations, by launching attacks against remaining armed groups while inviting them to accept the ceasefire, and simultaneously attempting to crush others to whom it denied the possibility of joining.

Negotiating a Nationwide Ceasefire Agreement

The Nationwide Ceasefire Agreement that was signed in October 2015 set the parameters for subsequent political dialogue. Thein Sein placed a high priority on reaching such an agreement and including as many EAOs as possible, even though only less than half ended up signing it. While the hopes that this achievement would pay off in the elections were ultimately dashed, the agreement nevertheless locked in a set of rules of engagement for political dialogue that were binding for the subsequent NLD government. War fatigue, the desire to stabilize the country to foster greater investment and development, and a political incentive to reach peace combined to unify the transitional regime behind negotiations. But internal tensions within the regime manifested themselves through ebbs and flows in the pace of negotiations and the degree of concessions that were made. After 2015, tensions between the new NLD government and the Tatmadaw created even more uncertainty and complexity as a two-pronged state became increasingly apparent.

EAOs were united in their goals of establishing a federal state, but struggled to remain united as disagreements and rivalries among larger groups in particular led to frequent coalitional realignments and somewhat divergent strategies to maximize group interests. In the end, of the major armed groups, only the Karen National Union (KNU) and Restoration Council of Shan State (RCSS) signed the NCA. The KIO and the United Wa State Army (UWSA) failed to reach agreements with the government. Smaller groups aligned on both sides, with some signing the NCA and others allying themselves with its opponents. The state moved ahead in the hopes of reducing war fronts and setting a framework to integrate the remaining outsiders subsequently.

In the late 1980s and 1990s, the junta had reached ceasefires with several EAOs, but these were mere informal agreements. There was little credibility in the negotiation process, and therefore these agreements could be better understood through classic strategies of civil war dynamics involving multiple armed groups.[1] The Tatmadaw's goal was not a political settlement but the elimination of antistate armed groups and a reduction in the number of fronts; for EAOs it was a chance to rebuild their forces while being rewarded with generous business opportunities.[2] With these bilateral ceasefires, the Tatmadaw weakened the armed groups' Democratic Alliance of Burma and triggered the gradual disintegration of the National Democratic Front.[3] This isolated the KNU, which was committed to a collective approach to ceasefire negotiation, even though there had been few signs that such a path was even possible. The KNU felt betrayed as several large armed groups that had initially committed to collective bargaining defected to gain benefits. Smaller groups within each of their spheres of influence tended to bandwagon. A few defected and signed by fear of losing out, mostly because their forces were almost nonexistent. The regime finally used some ceasefire groups, like the Democratic Karen Buddhist Army (DKBA), the UWSA, and the Karenni National People's Liberation Front, to fight against other nonceasefire groups (e.g. the KNU, the RCSS, and the Karenni National Progressive Party).[4]

Just prior to the transition to quasi-civilian rule in 2011, the state attempted some strong-arm tactics. In April 2009, it required all of the 1990s ceasefire groups to transform themselves into Border Guard Forces (BGFs) or People's Militias (PMs) for the government, following the newly adopted 2008 constitution. After most armed groups resisted, the regime imposed an ultimate deadline of September 1, 2009.[5] With such an ultimatum and no external mediators to guarantee their security, some armed groups refused. As a consequence, the government declared all ceasefire agreements with resisters null and void, including those with the UWSA, the KIO, the New Mon State Party (NMSP), and the Shan State Progressive Party.[6] In June 2011, the government attacked the KIO, thereby resuming the war against one of the most powerful armed groups. The war also expanded, particularly along the border with China, with groups such as the Arakan Army (AA), then mostly located in Kachin State and having received military training by the KIO; the Ta'ang National Liberation Army (TNLA); and the Myanmar National Democratic Alliance Army (MNDAA), which is the armed organization of the Kokang minority. What appeared to be a strong-arm tactic by the armed forces to force insurgent groups to abandon civil war actually backfired and forced the Tatmadaw to end ceasefire agreements with the EAOs to enforce the credibility of its ultimatum for them to become BGFs or PMs.

When the junta transformed itself into a quasi-civilian government in 2011, peace with armed groups was one of its top priorities, and it clearly changed its approach.⁷ The attempt to pressure armed groups to disarm and broker weak ceasefires held little promise of reaching its ultimate goal of ending civil war. The state needed to end the long-standing violent conflicts in order to achieve its economic and political goals, largely aligned with the junta's previous "road map to democracy." While an agreement with ethnic minority groups was not the main impetus for change, it was certainly clear that some degree of negotiation would be required to find a path to ending the civil war.

Therefore, at the outset, there was some genuine attempt to craft a process of negotiation that would convincingly attract EAOs. To be credible, the process had to allow for some degree of flexibility and uncertainty in its outcome, where negotiation could lead to gains on both sides. The Tatmadaw had to offer—and the civilian state to support—talks on the negotiation process itself with EAOs if they wanted to avoid the boycotts and failed strategies of the previous decade. Negotiation would no longer be only a tool of war, but a process involving multiple actors in expanding arenas to reach agreements to reduce incentives to pursue civil war. The year 2011 therefore marked the starting point of this process, initially open and relatively genuine, but one where the state—both the Tatmadaw and the civilian government—increasingly made gains, not necessarily fully but at least in part through strategy.

EAOs faced a changing landscape that required more unity if they wanted to strengthen their negotiating position, but this would prove difficult with past divisions as well as an expanding set of ethnic minority actors involved in the process. They overcame those divisions and created new alliances to raise their bargaining leverage significantly. Alliance formation and transformation were mainly political, in that most groups realized, along with the state, that military victory was not possible.

The formation of a common front was not easy. There were several obstacles to establishing a solid alliance. First, there were many groups, with some, such as the UWSA, the RCSS, the KIO, and the KNU, being large and well armed, while others were either relatively new or very small groups, sometimes with merely a few dozen soldiers. But all claimed a right to voice their demands. Second, as armed groups were used to being independent and hierarchically organized for decades, it was not easy to reach a compromise on the leadership of an alliance. Third, communication among the groups remained challenging, given physical distances within Myanmar and the fact that several group leaders remained in Thailand or even further abroad. Finally, no alliance managed to include all of the armed groups, so the potential for groups to disrupt negotiations remained high. In addition, none of these alliances included the BGFs and PMs, which were excluded from formal negotiations. In 2015, there were 23 BGFs, eight PMs (similar in structure to BGFs, but under looser control), and countless smaller state-linked militias, as well as numerous armed criminal organizations (often splinter factions from other groups).[8]

A new alliance, the Committee for the Emergence of a Federal Union (CEFU), was created in November 2010 to send strong signals that it would not yield to unilateral conditions toward peace. Most importantly, CEFU included two of the largest groups, the KIO and the KNU. It was the first time that the two had formed an alliance since 1994, when the KIO defected to a bilateral ceasefire agreement with the government. Several smaller groups bandwagoned and joined, particularly those that had previously signed ceasefires that were now nullified.[9]

In February 2011, CEFU extended the alliance from six to eleven groups and became the United Nationalities Federal Council (UNFC). On the eve of the transition to quasi-civilian rule, the new alliance declared its intention of creating a "federal army" and offered a united voice against the government.[10] It represented a proactive attempt to set new terms for negotiation in the context of uncertainty regarding the government's approach to the civil war. While difficult to achieve in the presence of multiple armed groups, such a broad negotiation alliance promised to create a united front that could overcome some of the divisive dynamics that weakened armed groups' bargaining strength relative to the state.

Some enabling factors contributed to progress in negotiations. First, sixty years of civil war created "war fatigue," including a displaced and increasingly impoverished population. External support to insurgents had declined, while, internally, the regime capitalized on previous ceasefire agreements and successful territorial operations to build roads and open up previously inaccessible areas.[11] The regime, for its part, failed to defeat armed groups in spite of growing armed forces and successive operations. "Even the Tatmadaw is fed up with [war]," one EAO leader told us. "So there is strong will to move forward with a ceasefire."[12] While past ceasefire agreements were a welcome reprieve, they were only temporary arrangements that grew increasingly untenable as the regime began its transition.[13]

Second, international donors, a handful of foreign experts, and a few key local organizations played important roles in supporting the institutions that brokered the negotiations. The Norwegian government launched an international donor support initiative and, in collaboration with the Myanmar government, created the Peace Donor Support Group, and the Myanmar Peace Support Initiative, through which donors could channel funding to the peace process.[14] It led to the creation, for instance, of the Myanmar Peace Center (MPC), which, with strong subsequent funding from the European Union and Japan, could then attract many well-educated technocrats of Burmese origin to advise on various aspects of negotiating and implementing ceasefire arrangements.[15] A number of Scandinavian and other European countries also funded EuroBurma, a nongovernmental organization formed in 1997 that first began operating from outside Myanmar. It relocated to Yangon after 2011 and played an important brokering role with armed groups in the initial stages of ceasefire negotiations, particularly the decision by the KNU and RCSS to lead a new phase of ceasefire negotiations. Finally, the promise of much larger amounts of development aid and investment if peace was implemented was a carrot, but not a decisive one.[16]

These factors mainly provided the background against which alliances shifted and armed groups repositioned themselves against a rapidly changing state. But why such shifting alliances led to the NCA depended on other factors: the regime's democratization, the state's unilateral concessions, and the decision of the KNU and RCSS to break away from others to move ahead with signing new bilateral ceasefires with the state.

Liberalization and democratization began with the inauguration of the Thein Sein government in 2011. Liberalization was clear at the outset, as the new government relaxed many restrictions against its citizens and allowed much greater freedom of association and expression, including the release of Aung San Suu Kyi in November 2010 and the NLD's ability to legally register. Once the NLD was able to participate in the by-elections for parliament in 2012, and subsequently a general election in 2015, the regime became subjected to electoral competition and accountability. The government's turnover and the election of the NLD in 2015 marked the establishment of a free and fairly elected government, but not a full electoral and liberal democracy. With the Tatmadaw still holding seats in parliament, its sphere of independent executive power, and its involvement in internal affairs, the new regime was a limited democracy. Nevertheless, the introduction of more accountability and electoral competition created new sets of incentives around negotiations for a ceasefire.[17]

Sequencing was important. Thein Sein's strategy was to reach separate ceasefires with various armed groups, and then confirm them through a nationwide ceasefire before the 2015 elections. Very soon after the new government took office, several new ceasefires were reached. Within twelve months, thirteen groups signed bilateral agreements (see table 6). Some of these reiterated those that were signed in the late 1980s and early 1990s. For instance, the UWSA, the NMSP, and the Shan State Progressive Party had long-standing ceasefires that had primarily remained stable and that were reaffirmed in 2011–12. It became clear, particularly in the persistent efforts to sign a ceasefire ahead of the 2015 elections, that Thein Sein was linking the future of the USDP to success in achieving peace with ethnic minorities. Intense electoral competition and an uncertain political outcome in the post-2015 election period forced the Thein Sein government to rush

TABLE 6 Bilateral ceasefires (2011–12)

ETHNIC ARMED ACTOR	PREVIOUS CEASEFIRE	NEW CEASEFIRE
United Wa State Army	1989	September 6, 2011
National Democratic Alliance Army (Mongla)	1989	September 7, 2011
Democratic Karen Buddhist Army	1995–2010	Transformed into a Border Guard Force in 2010
Democratic Karen Buddhist Army-5/Democratic Karen Benevolent Army (DKBA-5)	2010	November 3, 2011
Restoration Council of Shan State	None	December 2, 2011
Chin National Front	None	January 6, 2012
Karen National Union	None	January 12, 2012
Shan State Progressive Party	1989–2011	January 28, 2012
New Mon State Party	1995	February 1, 2012
Karen Peace Council	2007	February 7, 2012
Karenni National Progressive Party	1994	March 7, 2012
Arakan Liberation Party	None	April 5, 2012
National Socialist Council of Nagaland (Khaplang)	None	April 9, 2012
Pa'O National Liberation Organization	None	August 25, 2012

Source: Kim Jolliffe, *Ethnic Armed Conflict and Territorial Administration in Myanmar*, Asia Foundation, 2015, 19–20, 26–27.

to finish what it had started, after having invested a lot of time and effort in the peace process, as well as playing the "ethnic card" for electoral gain and hoping to seal the rules of negotiation before the election.[18]

Unilateral concessions were crucial to making such gains and convincing EAOs that the negotiation process would be credible. After announcing that peace was a top priority, Thein Sein's government approached armed groups for negotiations without preconditions and without requiring that they disarm. This new approach represented the first time that the government made such an offer in the context of formal negotiations. While in the past, bilateral ceasefires allowed the ethnic armed organizations to retain arms, they were informal agreements. Offers to negotiate were often accompanied by a precondition to disarm. This time, the state was willing to talk about a ceasefire leading to a structured political dialogue, without any prior agreement on disarmament. It also dropped the previous requirement that armed groups first transform themselves into BGFs or (if they were not located in the border areas) PMs, or disarm. Finally, it accepted that ceasefire negotiations would lead to political dialogue for the formation of a federal union.[19] This condition again was unprecedented. Previous administrations had refused political dialogue before complete disarmament, and discussions of federalism were off the table. Armed group leaders were willing to engage Thein Sein because of the removal of these preconditions.[20] The reforms being put into place, the greater accountability that the government was offering in terms of the peace process, and the ability to discuss it freely in the media strengthened the credibility of the government's commitment.

Several groups that had previously signed ceasefire agreements were willing to settle once again. The UWSA was the first to sign in September 2011, as signing remained consistent with protecting the extensive control it enjoyed over its territory. Others included the National Democratic Alliance Army–Mongla, close to the UWSA; the Democratic Karen Benevolent Army–Brigade 5 (DKBA-5), which defected from the DKBA that was turned into a border guard force in 2010; and the RCSS. None of these signatories belonged to the UNFC, which temporarily kept a united front and demanded that its members not sign ceasefires. The KIO, which played a strong role in the alliance, did not sign ceasefire agreements that might undermine the common objectives and its own interests.

Yet the UNFC's solidarity was fragile. The KNU, one of the largest and oldest armed groups, departed from the group's common position and signed a ceasefire agreement in January 2012. Getting the KNU onboard was strategically significant, as it had never signed a bilateral agreement but was one of the most important groups. The government's concessions were probably the most significant factor attracting it. "The KNU," said one observer of the process, "came in with a long list of demands expecting a long negotiation . . . [but] the government side said yes [right away]. The committee [KNU negotiators] was not expecting to have it all accepted, so it signed."[21] Among the KNU's demands were the establishment of a nationwide ceasefire, a stop to forced labor, the cessation of military operations in ethnic areas, transparency in the peace process and its openness to the media, and the release of political prisoners, among others. Chief negotiator Aung Min agreed to these points, even though it would later become clear that several top generals from the Tatmadaw disagreed with these concessions. The ceasefire took effect immediately.[22]

Furthermore, the state also conceded to some more indirect benefits. KNU leaders, realizing that Myanmar's economy was going to be integrated into the Southeast Asian region, wished to become stakeholders and have closer relations with business entrepreneurs, in part to protect the economic interests of the Karen, including land rights, and to secure their own interests.[23] While fighting resumed between the KIO and the state, the KNU saw an opportunity to reap a first-mover advantage and shape conditions for a bilateral ceasefire and, eventually, the Nationwide Ceasefire Agreement.

KNU leaders were also willing to break off from the UNFC as the latter was dominated by the KIO and the NMSP. Both groups had hurt the KNU in the past when they broke off from a previous alliance in the 1990s, thereby leaving the KNU alone to bear the brunt of large-scale military attacks. Furthermore, their leadership of the UNFC greatly constrained the KNU's ability to advance its organizational interests.[24]

Similarly, the RCSS moved ahead to sign an eleven-point peace agreement with the government in January 2012. Although not as broadly encompassing as that of the KNU, it nevertheless included clauses that secured the future of business interests for RCSS members, along with more standard clauses regarding security arrangements.[25] The RCSS would also have found itself isolated without KNU support and without the UNFC, which it never joined.[26]

With the KNU and RCSS signing in 2012, they created a momentum for other, smaller groups to bandwagon and also sign or renew bilateral ceasefire agreements.[27] Some were near the Kayin State, or were weak groups, such as the Karen National Union/Karen National Liberation Army Peace Council and the DKBA-5, which sought to capitalize as well on the opportunity to make some gains.[28] The Chin National Front (CNF) was very weak and saw an opportunity to gain bargaining leverage beyond what it would command by its size and strength. Other small and weak groups included a Rakhine organization (the Arakan Liberation Party), a Pa'O armed group (the Pa'O National Liberation Organization), and a Naga group (the National Socialist Council of Nagaland–Khaplang).[29] The NMSP, also in the UNFC, had been offering services and education to the population in Mon State, much of which had returned to a state of relative normalcy. So the NMSP had an interest in bandwagoning. But it did not do so at the time because it was playing a leadership role in the UNFC.

Once the government had secured a good number of bilateral agreements, it sought to convince individual groups to sign a nationwide ceasefire, which was originally drafted and proposed by EAOs. Multilateral negotiations continued alongside attempts to expand bilateral agreements with the remaining groups.

Armed groups tried once again to create a united front. There was an initial attempt, in February 2012, to create a Working Group on Ethnic Coordination (WGEC), with the UNFC playing a lead role. The WGEC had representatives from all seven ethnic states, along with technical teams and civil society groups, and included some members, such as the RCSS, that were not part of the UNFC. The KIO, which was the most influential group within the UNFC, was reluctant to provide the WGEC with the legitimacy to negotiate, as it saw the UNFC as performing that role. The KNU, conversely, saw the UNFC's attempts to negotiate on its behalf as a constraint on its own interests. The WGEC nevertheless managed to adopt a "framework for political dialogue" in March 2013 and presented it to government negotiators in May.

Aung Min, the government's chief negotiator, again took armed groups by surprise when he announced, in June 2013, that he accepted all of the concepts presented in the framework, which included a joint monitoring mechanism for the ceasefire and a structure and schedule for political dialogue that would be embedded in the NCA. This was a significant unilateral concession, again showing the government's determination to reach a deal, particularly before the 2015 elections.

The armed groups backpedaled. The KIO was concerned that the WGEC's framework accepted the 2008 constitution while not creating a new federal constitution. The WGEC collapsed in June 2013, when the UNFC, under KIO influence, withdrew. Afterward, the KIO used an outgunning strategy to balance against signatories of the nationwide ceasefire, arguably holding out to gain an agreement that would better serve its interests. The KIO's main goal was to reach an agreement to replace, rather than only modify, the 2008 constitution, and stronger guarantees that a peace dialogue would create a truly federal constitution. It also sought an agreement that would be all-inclusive. The KIO therefore insisted on reaching a ceasefire with groups such as the AA, the TNLA, and the MNDAA, which the Tatmadaw refused to include in the NCA.[30] The KIO's interests were tied to these three organizations, as the absence of a ceasefire would allow the Tatmadaw to continue attacks and operations against these groups in Kachin and Shan States.

The KNU, RCSS, and CNF took the lead, again, to secure a nationwide ceasefire agreement. They presented their version of the framework to the government in August 2013, without broad consensus. It included a process toward political dialogue and structures of negotiation. By pushing ahead with their framework for political dialogue, they thought they could define the terms of the nationwide ceasefire agreement. Their confidence in the process was enhanced by the feeling that democratization was actually proceeding, given the landslide victory in the 2012 by-elections of Aung San Suu Kyi and NLD members. The regime's acceptance of the results and commitment to general elections in 2015 made more formal negotiations and possible agreements credible.

In October 2013, the KNU and KIO once again attempted to unite and create a broad alliance to negotiate a nationwide ceasefire. The KIO had taken the initiative of calling the meeting and seeking new unity. At the Laiza Conference, held at the KIO's headquarters, seventeen armed groups managed to rebuild bridges between the RCSS/KNU and the UNFC, with the creation of a new Nationwide Ceasefire Coordinating Team (NCCT).[31] The NCCT was the broadest and most representative of alliances so far, initially representing thirteen armed groups, both those under ceasefire (such as the KNU and the RCSS) and those not (such as the KIO). Bolstered by a newfound unity, the NCCT presented in January 2014 its version of a draft ceasefire agreement to Aung Min.[32] The government recognized the NCCT as the official representative of armed groups, which gave some stability to the negotiation process.

The following year, the NCCT and the government negotiated a draft NCA. Although both parties agreed on a very large number of issues, they disagreed over the armed groups' disarmament. "The government," an expert in the peace process recalled, "wanted security issues addressed too early, whereas armed groups thought that they should be at the end of the process. Armed groups also rejected a proposal that they should become political parties. They rejected it because, until and unless the future is guaranteed, they can't lay down their arms. If they have disarmament, demobilization, and reintegration and security-sector-reform processes, they would be disarmed before there is a political accord."[33] This requirement led to the collapse of negotiations in September 2014.

The collapse partly reflected internal divisions in the government over concessions that were being offered. Up until August 2014, there had been significant progress on issues of principle, such as federalism but also a commitment to non-secession, as well as a road map toward peace that included plans for political dialogue, processes toward ratification in parliament, and constitutional changes. There had been agreement as well on disarmament at the end of the process. But hard-liners from the Tatmadaw believed that too many concessions had been offered and therefore imposed new conditions on the bargaining team.[34] As a result, the armed groups refused and negotiations ended.

The negotiations were further strained by the KIO's continued outgunning and balancing strategy against the KNU and pro-ceasefire armed groups, and the ongoing violent conflict in Kachin State. In this context, it became very difficult for the NCCT to maintain a facade of unity, while the KIO also controlled the UNFC and its less conciliatory position with the alliance. For several months during 2014, the KNU sought to reform the UNFC and proposed a rotating form of leadership to replace the KIO-dominated administrative structure. When the KIO refused, the KNU left the UNFC in August 2014. So, while the NCCT maintained its role as a broad alliance in the negotiations, the KIO and KNU balancing against each other for greater leverage widened the gap between the two major armed groups.[35]

The KIO attempted to further strengthen its position and leverage in negotiations. The state's strong push for a nationwide ceasefire, and the KNU's equally strong motivation to convince several smaller groups to seek a compromise, were tilting the balance toward a settlement. In response, the KIO convened the first meeting of the Federal Union Army, the armed wing of the UNFC. While the formation of the Federal Union Army had been an objective of the UNFC since 2010, the KIO took the initiative to strengthen its bargaining power. It also reactivated relations with three groups that were still engaged in armed conflict against the Tatmadaw—the AA, the TNLA (which the KIO had armed and supported in 2011 at the time conflict resumed with the Tatmadaw), and the MNDAA.

Nevertheless, Thein Sein's government gave new impetus to negotiations, with a formal declaration supporting federalism, again another level of unilateral concessions.[36] With negotiations stalling, and presumably to counteract adverse pressures from more hard-line factions within the Tatmadaw, Thein Sein declared an official "deed of commitment" to federalism on February 12, 2015, and hoped to attract groups to sign. Thein Sein and commander in chief Min Aung Hlaing had finally agreed that federalism did not spell disaster for Myanmar. As a senior MPC member noted, "It took us [the MPC] two years to make them understand this point.... It is the first time since independence that a government has accepted federalism as a basis of organization of the state."[37]

The deed had a provision to sign a nationwide ceasefire agreement as soon as possible, and the government requested that groups sign on. Once again the KNU and RCSS were at the forefront and supported it, while others were more reluctant. Some groups inside the NCCT (which did not include the RCSS) were more strongly keen on maintaining unity before making any strong commitment toward a nationwide ceasefire.[38]

There were three main reasons why the deed of commitment failed to gain more support. First, many armed group leaders included in the NCCT remained worried that the government ultimately sought to divide and weaken them. They pointed to the continued violent clashes with the Kachin and other small groups as evidence. Second, they thought that there was a small window of opportunity to maximize their demands, in light of the government's willingness to negotiate. Third, perhaps most importantly, they were reluctant to hand over a major accomplishment that the Thein Sein government could promote in the first elections scheduled for the fall of 2015.[39] In their own analysis, Thein Sein was using a nationwide ceasefire as an electoral strategy. Meanwhile the NLD was encouraging the armed groups not to join and promised instead a better deal after the NLD would be elected.

The armed groups' vacillation regarding the nationwide ceasefire was reflected in the events of the following months. Suspicion and the lack of enthusiasm for giving the USDP an electoral boost were superseded by the government's concessions to reach an agreement. With promises of locking in some gains, the NCCT relented and signed a draft agreement on March 31. But when the leadership convened a summit on June 2–9, 2015, to discuss and ratify the agreement with all armed groups, it failed to gain its members' support. Instead, various groups proposed a number of new amendments to the NCA text. Many of these were minor changes that seemed merely to be meant to delay the process.[40]

The most important point of disagreement concerned the desire for all-inclusiveness as a principle for signing the agreement. While armed groups had shown a strategic commitment to unity, they had more than once broken it off.

Nevertheless, likely driven by a sense of having the upper hand with elections looming, NCCT members raised the stakes by requiring not only that all NCCT members be allowed to sign the NCA, but also that all non-NCCT armed groups should be allowed to join as well.

The Tatmadaw in particular strongly opposed the inclusion of several groups. It refused to accept some small groups in the NCCT, such as the Rakhine National Council, the Lahu Democratic Union (LDU), and the Wa National Organization, which had almost no armies or combatants. While it agreed that they could participate in the political dialogue, it did not believe they needed to be part of the NCA. The Tatmadaw was even more strongly opposed to the inclusion of the three groups that had been in armed conflict with the Myanmar Army—the AA, the TNLA, and the MNDAA. It refused to include the first two, partly because the KIO trained them and gave them support in an alliance to boost its own military strategy, and partly because it reasoned that they were relatively new. The MNDAA, although an older armed group, resurfaced and engaged in new armed clashes with the Tatmadaw under a close alliance with the KIO. The Tatmadaw could not accept, other than the UWSA, a group with strong links to China.[41]

Thein Sein nevertheless pushed ahead, and showed, again, that peace with EAOs was his top priority, as he made it the cornerstone of the USDP's electoral strategy. He launched the USDP's election campaign by meeting with ethnic leaders in September 2015, symbolically reinforcing his strong commitment.[42] With two months left before the elections, armed group divisions once again reappeared. The RCSS and KNU, joined by the DKBA and Karen National Liberation Army Peace Council, announced on August 17, 2015, that they were ready to sign the NCA. Once again, on September 9, the president made concessions when meeting with representatives from armed groups. He conceded to the principle of including all groups, but would not accept the immediate inclusion of the AA, TNLA, and MNDAA, instead proposing alternative arrangements with each group but remaining open to the idea that they might eventually join the process.

The NCA was signed in October 2015, just before the election, showing how important it was for the USDP government as part of its election strategy. In reality, the ceasefire was partial, as only eight groups became signatories. They included the RCSS and KNU, which were the strongest advocates of locking in gains before a change of government, as well as several smaller groups that bandwagoned to lock in some advantages. Other groups remained less intent on giving the USDP government a boost in its electoral campaign, and remained suspicious of the military's full commitment.[43] From the state's perspective, the NCA locked in rules and a process to engage EAOs in political dialogue, with the 2008 constitution firmly in place. It would constrain any future government, and they likely foresaw the ability to use this process to their advantage.

The NLD and the Panglong Conference

After the election of the NLD government in November 2015, negotiations between EAOs and the state failed to produce concrete outcomes, and progress appeared increasingly stalled. In spite of the NLD's initial promise prior to the election that, if elected, it would offer a much better agreement than the USDP, the negotiations advanced at a snail's pace and the so-called achievements of the political dialogue were meager.

How can one interpret this outcome? One possibility may be that the increasingly two-pronged nature of the state pulled the Tatmadaw and the NLD government in different directions and prevented the latter from advancing its agenda. The evidence overwhelmingly suggests, however, that the NLD government itself was highly reluctant to make significant concessions to ethnic minorities with regard to establishing genuine federalism.[44] With respect to the political dialogue with ethnic minority groups, both the Tatmadaw and the NLD government shared the relatively common goals of maintaining a centralized state and securing the continued dominance of the Bamar majority. While tensions between the Tatmadaw and the NLD led to increasing confrontation, the NLD's attempts to amend the 2008 constitution were mostly aimed at trimming the Tatmadaw's role in politics, creating a full democracy, and removing restrictions that prevented Aung San Suu Kyi from becoming president. More decentralization and even acceptance of federalism were relegated to a secondary status in the NLD's political objectives and translated into few actual attempts to build stronger bridges with ethnic minority groups. The NLD ended its mandate having mostly alienated a majority of ethnic minority representatives, both armed groups and ethnic political parties, in spite of its broad electoral appeal.

After its defeat, the USDP government had attempted to seal the gains that had been made. In the last few weeks of the administration, in January 2016, Thein Sein presided over a Union Peace Conference (UPC), the last phase of the political dialogue that was supposed to be held only after all ethnic groups had held regional dialogues.[45] While the latter had not yet taken place, Thein Sein's government nevertheless held the first conference, with the aim of convincing the incoming NLD government to buy into the peace process.[46]

The NLD, however, wanted to create a clear split from the USDP while respecting the terms of the NCA, whose rules it was forced to accept. But the changes were mostly cosmetic. It convened the 21st Century Panglong Conference, the renamed UPC, with essentially the same framework. It sought, however, to broaden the number of armed groups participating in the dialogue, and attempted to expand the number of ceasefire signatories. The substance of the discussions over several meetings aimed at adopting broad principles for a future federal state, but never came close to developing concrete proposals. Near the end of the NLD's mandate, the discussions collapsed. With the EAOs reluctant to return to war, the power differential had shifted decidedly in favor of the state (particularly the Tatmadaw), which managed to control the process by delaying and manipulating the rules of the game.

The framework for political dialogue provided broad guidelines for negotiations (see figure 1). The state and EAOs that signed the NCA had agreed to this process. Over time, however, it became clear that the EAOs felt highly constrained by this locked-in arrangement. Tatmadaw members were able to control the agenda and use the committee structure to prevent broader engagement. As ethnic minority representatives were divided into a variety of armed groups, political parties, and other members, they ended up with little ability to leverage the process to their advantage.

The framework first defined the participants that were to be included in the dialogue. Second, it provided broad guidelines on how to address the basic issues to be discussed. Third, it established a mechanism for consulting ethnic minority communities. EAOs agreed to all of the provisions, but as the negotiations progressed, they became frustrated at the restrictions that the state imposed based on its own interpretation of these rules and the control it exercised over the proceedings.

Participants were to include representation beyond the military, the government, and EAOs. Political parties, civil society organizations, academics, and special invited guests were integrated into the negotiations, with a provision that any agreement required the approval of 75 percent (plus one) of the attendees. While this provision aimed at curtailing the power of the military and protecting the interests of smaller groups, it also required a high degree of compromise in order to move the negotiations forward.

The framework also provided for discussions to occur in a number of committees. It identified "politics," "the economy," "social issues," "land and resources," and "security" as key issue areas to be negotiated. These committees were to discuss separately the issues pertaining to each broad set of concerns. Finally, the NCA specified that EAOs were to consult their respective ethnic communities through "nationality-based dialogues." These dialogues were intended to seek input from a broad segment of the ethnic communities, including grassroots organizations as well as representatives from a wide range of socioeconomic and professional backgrounds.

A number of preparatory committees were designed to set the terms of the dialogue at the broader UPC. The dialogue steering committees assessed proposals from the grassroots-level dialogues on the range of specified topics. The Union

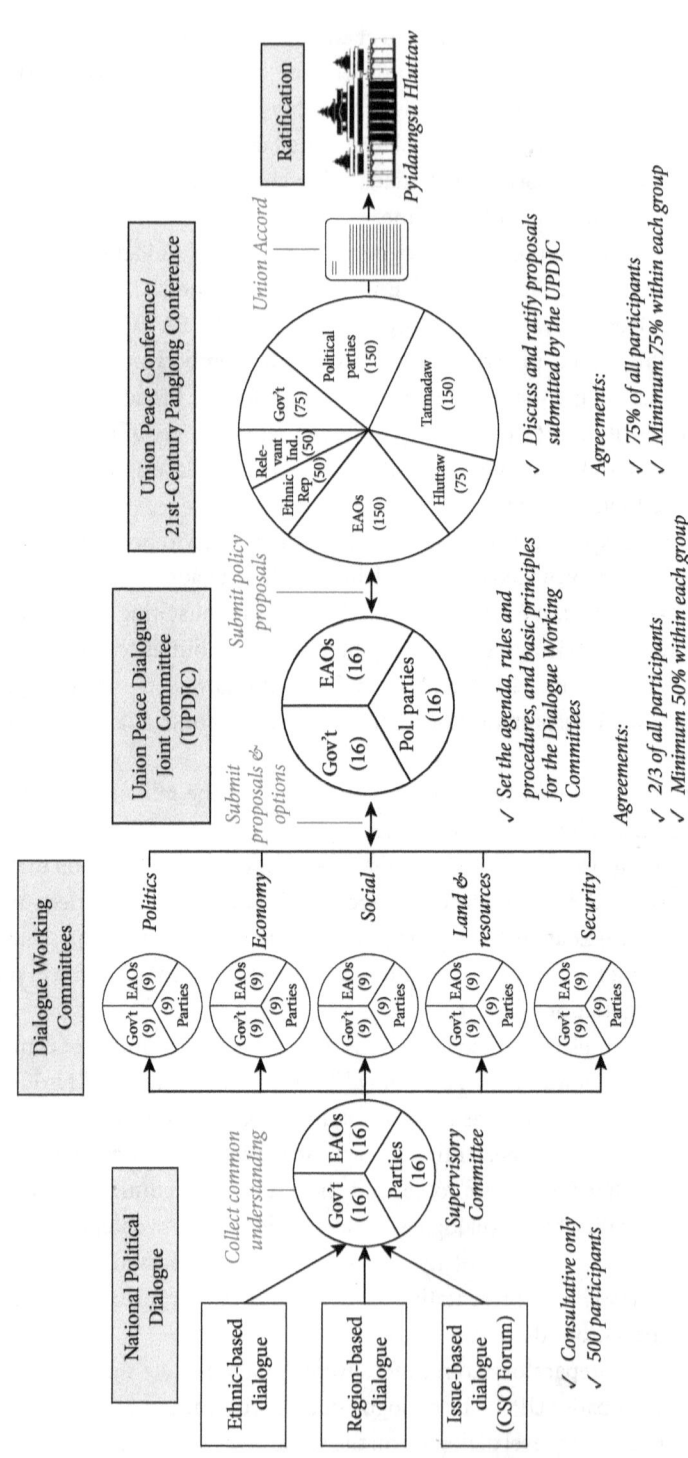

FIGURE 1. Myanmar's peace process.

Peace Dialogue Joint Committee (UPDJC) set the agenda, rules, procedures, and basic principles for various stages of the political dialogues (including the UPC), and would prepare and submit proposals to be forwarded to the formal UPC, which would debate and ratify them. The NCA provided that the UPC would meet twice a year for a period of between two and five years. Any agreements reached at the UPC would subsequently require approval by the national parliament, which would then draft accompanying legislation to enshrine various aspects of the agreements. In principle, both the dialogue steering committees and the UPDJC were to be composed of an equal number of representatives from the government (including the military and parliamentarians), political parties, and EAOs that had signed the NCA.

From the outset, the outgoing Thein Sein government already violated the framework's provisions to serve its political interests, but the framework would remain the basic structure for the negotiation process. The UPC was supposed to be held only after all the nationalities' dialogues had been concluded. Yet the government went ahead and convened the first meeting in January 2016 as a showcase designed to pressure the NLD government to honor the NCA. While no significant agreements were reached, it nevertheless provided a precedent for the incoming NLD government.

After a brief period of inaction and oscillation characterized by an assessment of what was entailed in the NCA, the NLD government ultimately renewed the commitment. It mostly preserved the broad framework for political dialogue, while making minor modifications and placing its own stamp on the process. After all, the NLD enjoyed widespread legitimacy and wanted to launch a peace process on its own terms. It formed a new government negotiating body called the National Reconciliation and Peace Center. Aung San Suu Kyi also announced the 21st Century Panglong Conference,[47] which was presented as a new initiative for peace, but in reality was a different name for the UPC that was part of the agreed-on political dialogue process under the NCA.

One difference between the former UPC and the new 21st Century Panglong Conference was the participants invited to the table. The Thein Sein administration convened past and serving military officers from the government and the eight armed groups that had signed the NCA, along with parliamentarians, experts, and representatives of elected political parties and civil society organizations. Aung San Suu Kyi broadened the list to include nonsignatories of the NCA, but only as observers. While it was a more truly inclusive process, the weight of the EAOs considerably diminished. This was mostly visible in the approval process. In the dialogue steering committees and the UPDJC, EAOs constituted one-third of the participants, sharing the table with the government and political parties. At the UPC, responsible for discussing and ratifying the UPDJC's proposals, the weight of the EAOs fell to 21 percent of the participants, just below the threshold for a form of veto. As noted above, ratification required the approval of 75 percent (plus one) of all participants.

The NLD convened the first 21st Century Panglong Conference in August–September 2016, thinking that the process could be wrapped up quickly. The government nevertheless modified the previous government's policy by inviting some non-NCA signatories to attend. The military continued to refuse the inclusion of the AA, TNLA, and MNDAA, but the UWSA, one of the most powerful armed groups and a nonsignatory, decided to attend upon invitation. But the group stormed out of the meetings on the second day when it was prevented from speaking. Its prepared speech expressed skepticism that a single agreement could include all groups. It also stated the need for a high degree of autonomy. The UWSA emphasized its own ceasefire with the state, signed in 1989, which had allowed it to build a de facto Wa State although not formally recognized. While the NLD hoped to create momentum for an all-inclusive process, the UWSA's exit reaffirmed the group's confidence in its status as the most powerful and autonomous armed group to seek leverage for an alternative agreement.[48]

The subsequent, more substantive conference was held in 2017 and showed, once again, a tendency for the NLD-governed state to disregard aspects of the framework for negotiation and employ tactics to control the negotiating process. For instance, only three nationality-based dialogues (Karen, Chin, and Pa'O), three region-based dialogues, and one theme-based dialogue were concluded before the second 21st Century Panglong Conference, which was held from May 24–29, 2017. Nevertheless, the conference went ahead.

The Tatmadaw in particular placed some restrictions on ethnic minority groups' ability to hold their nationality-based dialogues.[49] In February 2017, the UPDJC refused to allow the Arakhine Liberation Party and the CNF to hold national dialogues in preparation for the second Panglong Conference. The Chin, as well as the Pa'O, required intense negotiations with military authorities before, in the end, they allowed their respective dialogues to go ahead. Many other groups, such as the RCSS, were not granted permission to hold dialogues in their preferred locations. So only a few were able to hold their dialogues before the second conference.

Similar problems arose in preparation for the Third 21st Century Panglong Conference, held on July 11–16, 2018. Once again, several groups faced restrictions in their ability to discuss among themselves their goals and objectives. A number of Shan groups created an umbrella organization, the Committee for Shan State Unity, to hold a national dialogue of all Shan people. In December 2017, the Tatmadaw prevented the dialogue from being held, despite the fact that the committee had obtained prior permission from the UPDJC and the Shan State government.[50]

Ethnic leaders felt they were de facto negotiating with two governments: the NLD and the military. The NLD joined the peace process at a later stage, and did not seem to develop a clear common strategy with the military, yet sought to micromanage the process.[51] The military also used its power to dominate negotiation forums. The ten NCA signatories (two of which, the NMSP and LDU, signed the NCA after the NLD came to power) faced difficult obstacles with both the NLD and the military, while coping with skeptics within their own organizations and the nonsignatory armed groups.

The ten signatories had weak technical skills to negotiate, thereby further strengthening the government's side. One aspect that raised several complaints from EAOs was the NLD's tendency to exercise tight control over the flow of international funds. In effect, it meant that EAOs had difficulty obtaining support from outside organizations and specialists, as they could not obtain foreign financial assistance without the approval of Aung San Suu Kyi.[52] They were therefore limited in their ability to use outside expertise in the negotiations.

They were also concerned with future steps toward a federal union, even if significant agreements were to be reached. Since any agreements from the peace conference, for instance, required ratification by parliament, where EAOs had no representation, they were worried that parliament might modify or derail any negotiated settlement.[53] The parliament could easily dilute any emergent federal union and diverge significantly from the ideals that minority ethnic groups envisioned.

Furthermore, military representatives effectively controlled many of the negotiation committees. During the proceedings, the military prevented the discussion of sensitive topics, such as the role of armed groups in a future federal army, or minority rights. As a consequence, only an agreement on gender inclusiveness was reached in the political section at the third Panglong Conference.[54] The military continued to fear that concessions toward greater autonomy would heighten the threats of secession.[55] The military wanted clear statements by EAOs on their commitment to nonsecession. They posed this as a precondition for discussing any further progress on some of the crucial issues for EAOs, such as the right to draft their own state constitutions.[56]

The Panglong Conference itself became mostly a rubber-stamping forum, while the UPDJC was the major player in negotiating the texts of the agreements. The conference was in principle to be attended by a total of 700 delegates, drawn from the government, parliament, military, political parties, EAOs, experts (or special invited guests), and other ethnic representatives. Based on the quota assigned to each group, the NLD (with a majority of the 300 representatives from the government, parliament, and political parties) and the military (with 150 representatives) dominated the proceedings. Yet the NCA prescribed that 75 percent of the delegates plus one, in this case 526, must approve any agreement, and that 75 percent plus one were needed within each subgroup in order to ensure that agreements were not passed without the approval of any minority groups.[57] In reality, no votes were held, as the negotiations had been predetermined within the UPDJC. The UPDJC was composed of equal numbers of representatives from the government, military, and parliament; EAOs; and political parties. While a smaller working group could legitimately prepare drafts and iron out some of the differences, the expectation was that the deliberations and approvals in the Panglong Conference would be more broad based. In the end, many representatives considered the process controlled and constrained, and believed it violated the provisions of the NCA.

Finally, the agreements on "basic principles" that were reached in the first four meetings of the Panglong Conference were vague, were mostly unrelated to federalism, and, most importantly, remained consistent with the existing constitution and laws.[58] For the most part, the principles were based on values and norms that would be difficult for anyone to refute in a democratic environment, or even in any state. Some examples include (1) the idea that sovereignty is derived from citizens; (2) checks and balances between the executive, legislative, and judiciary branches of government; (3) free and fair elections; (4) gender equality; and (5) alleviation of poverty and reduction in inequality. A few principles were suggestive of a federal system while remaining so vague that their interpretation could remain consistent with a highly centralized state. For instance, negotiators agreed to the principle of setting up a federal state, but slightly more specific principles remained superficial: (1) the union should be formed by regions and states; (2) certain powers should be divided among the union, regional, and state levels; and (3) regional and state governments should be allowed to undertake development projects. All of these principles were consistent with the existing 2008 constitution, which had few elements of a genuine federal system (see table 7). Negotiations leading up to the third Panglong Conference illustrated some of the basic obstacles to progress. While gender equality and ethnic minority rights had been two subjects previously proposed for discussion under the political sector, the UPDJC rejected the inclusion of ethnic minority rights because of fundamental disagreement over its meaning, as well as the argument that democratic principles had not yet been fully agreed on. So gender equality became the only principle that could be moved forward from the July 2018 session of the Panglong Conference.[59]

TABLE 7 Agreements reached at the 21st Century Panglong Conference, 2016–20

	THEMES				
	POLITICAL	ECONOMIC	SOCIAL	SECURITY	LAND AND ENVIRONMENT
1st Panglong meeting (August 31–September 3, 2016)	0 agreements	0 agreements	0 agreements	0 agreements	0 agreements
2nd Panglong meeting (May 24–29, 2017)	12 agreements 1. Sovereignty of citizens 2. Three branches and checks and balances 3. Equality of national races 4. Union based on democracy, federalism 5. Regions/states to be units of federal state 6. Recognize SAZs 7. Three branches to each level of government 8. State Hluttaw 9. Taxes to each level of government 10. Constitutional tribunal 11. Multiparty democracy 12. Multiparty elections 13. Free and fair elections	11 agreements 1. Market economy 2. Protect market economy by laws 3. Alleviate poverty 4. Deter bad economic transactions 5. Antimonopoly law 6. Provide equal opportunities 7. Fair budget allocation 8. Share management of economy among all levels of government 9. Transparency, accountability, and responsibility 10. Regional development plan 11. Attract international investments	4 agreements 1. Forge solutions to IDPs without discrimination 2. Create conditions for IDPs return 3. Boost socioeconomic conditions for marginalized groups 4. Fight drug trafficking	0 agreements	10 agreements 1. Land policy for durable development 2. Justice in land policies 3. Reduce central control 4. Land policies informed by human rights 5. Transparency on land matters 6. Consult local people and farmers on land policies 7. Nationals' right to own and manage land 8. Women and men have equal rights to land 9. Right of government to take back land 10. Prevent environmental depletion

(Continued)

TABLE 7 (Continued)

	THEMES				
	POLITICAL	ECONOMIC	SOCIAL	SECURITY	LAND AND ENVIRONMENT
3rd Panglong meeting (July 11–16, 2018)	**4 agreements** 1. Gender equality 2. Gender quotas 3. Gender-based violence prevention 4. Empowerment of women	**1 agreement** 1. Economic projects by states, in accordance with Union policies	**7 agreements** 1. Women's participation 2. Accessible education system 3. Universal health care 4. Rights for the handicapped 5. Social cohesion in social development 6. Drug treatment and reintegration 7. Children's rights	**0 agreements**	**2 agreements** 1. Limits on foreign land ownership 2. Social and environmental assessments prior to land-use projects
4th Panglong meeting (August 19–21, 2020)	**8 agreements** 1. Democracy and federalism 2. Establish a Constitutional Tribunal 3. Separation of power between Union and state; three branches of government 4. Equality among regions and states 5. Ensure fundamental rights for citizens 6. Separation of religion and politics 7. Settle disagreements with good will 8. Implement accord and peace process with transparency, responsibility, and accountability	**0 agreements**	**1 agreement** 1. Recognize diversity of Myanmar people	**3 agreements** 1. Protect life, property, and wealth 2. Hold dialogue on NCA 3. Take steps to implement UPDJC and Joint Ceasefire Monitoring Committee accomplishments	

While the Panglong negotiations produced few concrete results, the broader context of continued civil war became another, indirect negotiating arena. The events outside the formal negotiation process continued to have a strong impact. The legitimacy of the NCA was undermined by the fact that only ten out of twenty-one armed groups signed the NCA (the NMSP and the LDU signed on February 13, 2018).[60] It was meant to be broadly inclusive, but it actually covered only around 20 to 25 percent of the total military forces controlled by nonstate armed groups. Furthermore, only four out of ten signatory groups actually had credible armed wings, so the NCA attracted mostly those with little military capability in the first place. Nonsignatory groups continued to fight in order to obtain further concessions, whether for their private interests or to claim a better negotiating framework toward a federal state.

Under the NLD government, armed conflicts between the Tatmadaw and the KIO, AA, TNLA, and MNDAA actually intensified. The military launched a number of attacks against armed groups, and EAOs retaliated in other rounds as the violence escalated in 2016–18. During 2016 and 2017, the KIO continued to arm and support the TNLA, AA, and MNDAA under a newly created "Northern Alliance." The KIO's main resource base in jade mining, alongside formal and informal taxation, helped the organization support its allies. This alternative alliance, and the intensification of attacks, clearly aimed at outgunning the military and forcing it to negotiate on different terms, although it remained unable to achieve its goals.

The escalation, along with the NLD's dismissive treatment of the Arakan National Party (which had won the largest number of seats in Rakhine State in the 2015 elections), allowed the AA to gain greater popularity and legitimacy among Rakhine Buddhists.[61] As a consequence, the AA rapidly grew its ranks with new recruits and expanded its territorial base from Kachin State (where many AA soldiers, including Rakhine who were working in jade mining, received armed training) to Rakhine State, and then to Paletwa, Chin State. It was able to mount much more significant attacks against the Tatmadaw. Massive casualties from both sides further perpetuated the cycle of conflict. In order to defuse some of the violence, the military announced in December 2018 a unilateral ceasefire against nonsignatory groups. But it continued its attacks against the AA.[62] As a consequence, in the 2020 elections, the Union Elections Commission canceled voting in many constituencies in Rakhine State for security reasons.[63]

In parallel to the mounting obstacles in the negotiations, more frequent clashes also erupted between the Tatmadaw and armed groups that had signed the NCA. Numerous skirmishes broke out between the military and the KNU's Fifth Brigade after March 2018 when the Tatmadaw violated the ceasefire agreements by building roads in the KNU's controlled territory.[64] These were also part of the broader strategy of the Tatmadaw to force the KNU to abide by the NCA on its own terms, while the Fifth Brigade used war as a reminder of the KNU's ability to continue using armed resistance and therefore gain leverage for greater concessions. Neither side could successfully outgun the other but used force as a bargaining chip.

The UWSA, the strongest armed group that had renewed its bilateral ceasefire agreement but had not yet signed the NCA, also sought greater leverage and concessions. It hosted a summit at its headquarters in Panghsang in February 2017, and proposed an alternative nationwide ceasefire agreement. Like the KIO, the UWSA had a strong resource base that allowed prolonged conflict and continued to enjoy extensive and unchallenged control over its territory.[65]

The continued ebb and flow of violent conflict, combined with the highly restricted and difficult negotiating environment in the Panglong Conference, created high incentives for signatories to seek alternatives. In spite of their strong commitment to retaining the NCA, the KNU, the RCSS, and other signatories expressed increasing frustration at the slow progress, and obstacles, in the negotiations. As the conflict remained stalled, they certainly realized the few gains that were made and increasingly believed that the Tatmadaw and the NLD were deliberately slowing down, and manipulating, the process.

As a result, the KNU announced in October 2018 that it would "temporarily" leave the peace negotiations, making it impossible for the government to host the subsequent Panglong meeting.[66] The KNU's withdrawal was a product of continued mistrust of the military's intentions, the lack of progress in negotiations, and some divisions within the KNU itself. The KNU leadership was particularly frustrated at the lack of substance in the negotiations, in part due to the large number of people involved in those negotiations. "Whenever we sit for a meeting with other EAOs," one KNU officer told us, "we don't discuss, we just block each other and discuss broad principles."[67] The withdrawal from formal negotiations was seen by some KNU members as a way to engage in possibly more fruitful one-on-one discussions with the government.[68] In an attempt to safeguard the negotiation process, the government convened a meeting of Aung San Suu Kyi, the armed forces' commander Min Aung Hlaing, and leaders of the NCA signatory EAOs. The meeting quickly deteriorated, however, when the military leader strongly reiterated the condition that the EAOs adopt a pledge of nonsecession as a precondition to having the right to draft state constitutions. He also accused the RCSS of using the NCA to continue building up its military strength. Finally, he rejected the demand of the EAOs for a federal army.[69]

While KNU leaders reluctantly agreed, in principle, to a single army, they insisted that further negotiations would need to occur. This apparent concession created strong reactions among several Karen groups, and within the KNU itself.

The KNU's Fifth Brigade in particular resented the Tatmadaw's construction of a road at Hpapun in Kayin State, in an area under KNU control. They accused the Tatmadaw of attempting to weaken the KNU's control by creating new road access and disregarding the need to consult the KNU.[70] In general, the Tatmadaw got closer to KNU-controlled areas and in some cases successfully clawed back some of the KNU's territory, all while the formal peace process was unfolding. Various strategies were used by the Tatmadaw, including mine clearance operations as well as simply visiting monasteries and making donations to monks.[71] The KNU had long been divided over the peace process and the degree to which it should accommodate the state. Factional divisions became more intense as the peace negotiations became stalled. These pressures led to the KNU's withdrawal from the peace process at the end of October 2018, and to a call for its own members to discuss an alternative approach to move the negotiations forward.

Meanwhile, the RCSS also objected to negotiations and withdrew as well from the Panglong process. On October 26, it issued a statement distancing itself from the suggestion that the RCSS might join a united Myanmar military, or that it would agree to a principle of nonsecession. It reiterated its perspective that such decisions required consultations and agreement from all Shan people, thereby reinforcing its demand for a large consultation with Shan people in Shan State. It withdrew from the Joint Monitoring Committee of the NCA on November 1, after the KNU's withdrawal.[72]

Negotiations resumed in January 2020 after a hiatus of eighteen months. The pause allowed participants to reevaluate and reformulate their positions. Consequently, they agreed to proceed by lumping all disarmament, demobilization, and reintegration/security-sector reform issues under the broad heading of "security sector integration," and hosted a mini version of the 21st Century Panglong Conference on August 18–21, 2020.[73] Participants agreed on twenty additional principles that focused on clarifying the steps toward an implementation of the NCA in the postelection period. One significant achievement of the August conference was the agreement reached on the guiding principles for a "democratic federal union," including power sharing between the Union government and the states.[74] A further landslide victory by the NLD in the general elections held on November 8, 2020, offered a reason for some cautious optimism that peace negotiations could proceed under the next term of the NLD government, although it had failed to make progress during its first term.

A close analysis of the formal negotiation process shows how strategies of locking in, layering, and sequencing effectively served the state's interests. The conflict became stalled as formal negotiations produced few concrete results, while both the Tatmadaw and several armed groups continued to launch attacks to make gains in the formal negotiation arena. Although at the outset, the negotiations reflected a credible new opportunity to reach a mutual agreement, by 2020 it was clear that the process had eroded ethnic minority power in favor of the state's.

The initial period under the USDP government essentially set the rules of negotiation, with the Tatmadaw and the civilian government mostly agreeing on steps forward. While some of the engagement between EAOs and the Tatmadaw could be understood as classic strategies of bandwagoning and the balance of alliance making in multiparty civil wars, the outcome was a negotiated nationwide ceasefire agreement with a large number of armed groups, and the establishment of bargaining rules and procedures in a formal political dialogue. Both sides could not win, and both experienced war fatigue. The opening up of the regime to a greater democratic space for the first time allowed some sort of formal negotiations to proceed in a credible form. Initial state concessions, and even some from the Tatmadaw, showed a desire to attract EAOs to the bargaining table, in a shift of strategy that departed from the Tatmadaw's attempt under the previous regime to coerce and control EAOs into negotiating, which backfired in the end. The opening up allowed EAOs to attempt to form a unified front and to reach some degree of understanding that ultimately led to the NCA and the political dialogue. Sequencing was important to the USDP government, which wanted to lock in the process and rules for negotiation before the 2015 elections.

The NLD period then showed the consequences of the rules that had been locked in, the establishment of the formal negotiation prior to the NLD's mandate, and the layering that inevitably occurred as a result of partial democratization. The format of the 21st Century Panglong Conference meetings reproduced the format that the USDP had inaugurated in its UPC only weeks before ceding power. Layering was inevitable, as a greater number of actors, including ethnic political parties and civil society organizations, claimed representation of ethnic minority groups alongside EAOs. While largely a result of pressures within ethnic minority groups to open up participation to nonarmed organizations, the layering created an advantage for state and Tatmadaw negotiators, as EAOs became only a small percentage of participants in the negotiation forum, thereby diluting their clout with regard to the agenda and the ratification of agreements. The Tatmadaw in particular could seize control of the deliberations and set the agenda and the pace of negotiations, as it prevented unified pressure for concessions, since agenda items were discussed separately in different committees. It therefore became clear that, even though the EAOs had accepted and even participated in the crafting of the process, they did not envision how the locking in of the agenda and participants, the layering that came with including more ethnic representatives, the sequencing of agreeing to the NCA, and the political dialogue framework prior to the election of the NLD could subsequently be used to reach only minimal, and somewhat innocuous, consensus points.

Outgunning strategies proved essentially ineffective. NCA participants—except some KNU factions such as the Fifth Brigade, which expressed frustration at the lack of progress in negotiations—hesitated to use war as a bargaining chip. Meanwhile, the AA, TNLA, and MNDAA sought a place at the table, as the Tatmadaw used its power over the formal negotiations to repeatedly prevent them from being included in the NCA. In the end, they joined the KIO and UWSA in the Northern Alliance, designed to leverage war and force an alternative negotiation process. The Tatmadaw launched attacks designed to punish NCA transgressions, but mostly with the aim of eliminating actors seeking negotiating power, such as the AA, or raising the costs of those not joining the NCA, such as the KIO. By the end of 2020, outgunning had failed to produce any results and mainly showed a deterioration in the stalled conflict.

While the formal negotiating arena essentially appeared to collapse, it was in conjunction with the expanding state arena that the winning strategy would become clear. The formal negotiations allowed the Tatmadaw and NLD to maintain their control, and set a path that preserved the centralized state enshrined in the 2008 constitution and created a process that set a precedent for actor inclusion, agenda setting and control, and steps for ratification. The following chapters show how the parallel strategies used in the context of implementing the 2008 constitution complemented the formal negotiations to produce the state's winning strategy.

5

NORMALIZING WEAK ETHNIC STATES
Constitutional Lock-In and Implementing Layers

The process of negotiation toward a new settlement occurred in parallel to the steady implementation of the 2008 constitution and the penetration of state institutions in areas previously at war or controlled by ethnic armed organizations (EAOs). The constitution created the institutional and legal apparatus that channeled ethnic minority engagement in the state arena. But adding new layers of governance, regulated and bounded by the constitution and subsequent laws, forced on ethnic minority states a new set of institutions, rules, and procedures that regularized and normalized the model envisioned by the Tatmadaw.

The constitutional lock-in was accepted not only as the foundation of the quasi-democratic state's evolving institutions but also as the basis against which the political dialogue and its eventual outcomes would be compared. The military made the acceptance of the 2008 constitution a sine qua non of negotiation. But the constitution also created precedents for how to conceptualize and operationalize a decentralized state. The Union Solidarity and Development Party (USDP) government forged ahead with its implementation, as its members had been part of the former junta that crafted it. More surprisingly, the National League for Democracy (NLD) and ethnic political parties changed their position from initially rejecting the constitution altogether to accepting it. Once in power, the NLD was actually involved in implementing its various aspects.

Several elements of the process of implementation strengthened the state's position toward ethnic minority groups. The new allocation of powers and resources to ethnic states, as well as the new institutions themselves, such as local parliaments, were cast by the central government as progressive measures toward an undefined goal of a "federal state." In addition, the web of procedures, institutions, and reinforced norms of conduct created a set of constraints that significantly increased the costs of eventually crafting an alternative, truly federal state. As each of these new procedures, powers, institutional processes, and methods of resource allocation required renegotiation to dismantle or modify, it became increasingly difficult to depart substantially from the existing frame, as the state institutional arena became entrenched and framed by the 2008 constitution's provisions. This process was tied to the negotiations occurring in the 21st Century Panglong Conference, where each aspect was to be negotiated under the requirement that the 2008 constitution would be amended. Since the main thrust of the existing constitution was still highly centralized, the path toward modifying it to become truly federal appeared complex, lengthy, and difficult to envision.

As a result, sequencing mattered. The longer the negotiations lasted, the more aspects of the 2008 constitution became entrenched and gained some measure of legitimacy, or at least normalization. Ethnic minority representatives gained positions within ethnic states, and conformed to the expectations of their constitutionally defined functions. They became de facto new actors that helped to confirm the Union government's and the Tatmadaw's views of a supposedly "almost federal," decentralized Myanmar.

The first section of this chapter shows how the constitution became locked in, through its gradual acceptance by initial opponents, including the NLD and EAOs. Where resistance to the constitution continued to arise, it was based mostly on the NLD's attempts to reduce the role of the military in government and expand the democratic space, but hopes for an NLD-led government's push for amendments toward a truly federal state proved elusive.

Meanwhile, as the second part of the chapter shows, the layers being put into place in ethnic states clearly solidified and perpetuated a highly centralized approach to governance. The process by which the central government could determine the limits and nature of decentralization clearly gave it greater leverage over defining the future form of so-called federalism. As shown in examples such as the management of land, natural resources, education, and culture, it was reflected in the most important areas for ethnic groups' self-determination.

The 2008 Constitution: From Rejection to Acceptance

The 2008 constitution began to be implemented mostly after the transition to civilian rule in 2011. It created new structures and defined new allocations of power and resources at the state and regional level. Though it was initially decried by both domestic and international actors, the military's biggest feat over the following decade was to slowly entrench its acceptance and even support. Once the constitution was locked in, political actors found themselves increasingly constrained in their options and had to play by the rules of the game or risk marginalization.

By accepting the 2008 constitution as a basis of governance, state and non-state actors that initially opposed it granted the Tatmadaw the leverage that it sought in negotiations. Members of the USDP government had of course been part of the process leading to its adoption prior to 2011. But the NLD came a long way from strongly opposing the constitution to forming a government that participated actively in its implementation. The NLD had boycotted the National Convention that led to the constitution's drafting and called on the people of Myanmar to vote no in the 2008 referendum that led to its adoption.[1] In a bold gamble, the NLD also boycotted the 2010 elections, largely because of its rejection of the 2008 constitution.[2] During those elections, however, a new coalition of "moderate" civil society organizations (CSOs) was formed. Often referred to as the "Third Force," this group sought to steer a path between the military regime and its opponents, represented by Aung San Suu Kyi and the NLD. It advocated for incremental changes toward greater democracy *within* the 2008 constitution and asked for a lifting of international sanctions on Myanmar. The Third Force was highly controversial, as it was somewhat complicit (or perceived as complicit) in legitimizing the junta's road map to democracy, its elections, and the 2008 constitution.

The NLD nevertheless came to espouse the Third Force's incrementalist vision. It first decided to run in the 2012 by-elections, which marked Aung San Suu Kyi and the NLD's entry into parliament and the first tacit acceptance of the new institutions. The newly elected NLD members initially refused to swear the parliamentary oath that required their loyalty to the 2008 constitution. But they eventually relented, since otherwise they would have been prevented from taking their seats. In 2015, the NLD still entertained the idea of a boycott of the elections, but not for long.[3] It won a landslide victory, and therefore gained control of both parliament and the executive, which required that it respect and abide by the constitution. Right up until the 2021 coup, Aung San Suu Kyi and the NLD continued to express their strong desire to change the constitution, but nevertheless increasingly accepted it. In 2013, the party conducted a survey of its membership, which confirmed its new pragmatic approach, showing that 80 percent of those polled wanted "to amend the constitution rather than redraft it."[4] In the 2020 elections, the NLD went as far as slamming any attempt by opposition parties and groups to boycott the polls, a quite significant change in ten years. Hence, after rejecting the constitution, the NLD gradually accepted having to play by the rules that the junta, and the USDP government, had put into place. By doing so, the NLD essentially granted the constitution legitimacy and subsequently helped change even the international community's initial reluctance to support it.

Ethnic minority groups also increasingly accepted having to abide by the constitution's rules, despite persistently rejecting it in their discourse. Like the NLD, ethnic representatives were quite unified in their boycott of the referendum and their rejection of the 2008 constitution. But as they prepared for the 2010 elections, ethnic political representation split into two broad camps: most political parties that were created in 1990 continued to reject the 2008 constitution and boycotted the 2010 elections, while new ethnic political parties that were created after the new constitution agreed to run. The 2010 ethnic political parties believed in a pragmatic approach, one in which the "Panglong Spirit" of federalism and decentralization could be achieved under the 2008 constitution.[5] By the 2015 and 2020 elections, however, in spite of a continued split between the 1990 and 2010 parties, they all participated. The elected ethnic members of parliament (MPs) then joined the Union parliament and the newly created state parliaments, while some were even appointed to local cabinet seats. They had therefore pivoted from their initial rejection and ended up tacitly accepting the new rules of the game.

The population also accepted the 2008 constitution. Surveys conducted between 2014 and 2017 found that an increasing majority of people thought that the constitution supported a democratic system, a peaceful change of government, human rights, and genuine political choices. Positive views toward the constitution increased substantially after the election of the NLD and the peaceful transfer of power.[6] In 2018, the People's Alliance for Credible Elections found that only 1 percent of respondents thought that constitutional reforms were a priority, while most believed that conflict and peace, the economy, and government services were the actual priorities. In the same survey, only 33 percent of the respondents thought that regions and states should have more power in the constitution. When asked about specific powers, regarding such areas as education, health care, and natural resources, no more than 14 percent thought that regions should have those powers exclusively, and most thought they should be shared constitutional responsibilities.[7] According to Michael Breen and Baogang He, results from a 2018 survey showed that many ethnic minority participants "no longer aspired to ethnofederalism. . . . [They] wanted to retain their ethnic identity and to have it recognized, but ethnofederalism was no longer the main objective."[8] In essence, the 2008 constitution and the model it reflected were clearly being socialized broadly among the ruling elites as well as the population.

A closer examination of the constitution reveals that most of its provisions reinforced central government power and minimized the space for ethnic states to exercise greater autonomy. It created new structures significantly different from those of previous constitutions. These included a multiparty system; separation of powers between the executive, judiciary, and legislative branches; a bicameral legislature; fourteen state/regional parliaments, governments, and chief ministers; and reserved seats for minority populations (ethnic affairs ministers).[9] Yet the president, rather than the regional parliaments, appointed state and regional chief ministers, who then formed their respective executives. The president therefore retained an enormous amount of power and leverage over state and regional governments. The military preserved extensive authority over key ministries and de facto veto power over constitutional amendments. As seen in chapter 2, the central government retained primary authority over every significant jurisdiction as well. The national parliament retained authority over defense, foreign affairs, currency making, and trade, which is common in many federal states. But it also retained jurisdiction over a large number of other areas, including health care and education.[10] Rather than allocating exclusive jurisdictions to central and regional/state governments, the constitution instead devolved very select areas of responsibility to lower levels of government, while the central government retained overarching authority. It also gave very little legislative and taxation powers to the fourteen region/state legislatures, five self-administered zones (SAZs) and one self-administered division (SAD).[11] In fact, most of the powers allocated to state/regional governments under Schedule 2 of the 2008 constitution were very specifically within broader areas of jurisdiction that remained with the Union government.

During the USDP government's mandate (2011–16), the NLD and other members of the prodemocracy camp campaigned extensively for constitutional amendments. In response, in 2013 the Union parliament established a constitutional review committee. The NLD made the following demands: identify the Union as a "federal" Union; remove the military from parliament and abolish its power to appoint the vice president and other ministerial positions; balance the president's power by requiring him or her to make certain decisions together with the speakers of the upper and lower houses; allow state parliaments to choose their chief ministers; limit cabinet positions to only elected representatives; and change the amendment procedure so that proposals could be approved by two-thirds of the civilian members of parliament.[12] Pressures to amend the constitution culminated with the "Section 436 movement" in 2014, which collected close to five million signatures, conducted high-profile constitutional amendment talks in major cities, held media interviews, and organized protests across the country.

In mid-2015, two bills were introduced in parliament to propose constitutional amendments. Most of the NLD's demands were either ignored or defeated. Only two were approved, and neither had any profound consequences for the shape of the state and regime. The first was a change to the wording of Section 59(d) on presidential requirements, which had stated that a president must be familiar with "military" affairs; this was changed to "defense." This suggested that a presidential candidate would not need to have a military background.[13] Although full approval of this provision required a referendum that was never held, it was implemented with the appointments of two successive NLD presidents who did not have any military background. The second change was the clarification and expansion of legislative and taxation powers, which was adopted.[14] The proposal clarified the ability of state governments to collect income tax, various duties (customs and stamps), and levies on services (tourism, hotels, private schools, and private hospitals) and resources (oil, gas, mining, and gems).[15] It also enabled regional governments to receive loans and international assistance. These clauses, while generous in theory, were qualified with the statement "in accordance with the law enacted by the Union." In 2018, almost none of these laws on the expansion of local legislatures' powers were passed by state and regional legislatures, most probably because the Union parliament had not revoked and amended existing laws affected by constitutional amendments. Only 19 out of 126 laws passed in 2015–20 in the Union legislature were related directly to the amendments on legislative and taxation powers of the states and regions.[16]

After this defeat, the NLD made only timid efforts to amend the constitution, even after it took office in 2016. The formal division of powers remained the same, and the NLD mostly abandoned the strategy of pursuing formal constitutional amendments because the risks of a coup were significant and the positive outcomes unlikely.[17] But in January 2019, the NLD finally pushed ahead and submitted an emergency motion to parliament aimed at setting up a constitutional amendment committee. This was its first attempt to change the constitution, but the move largely reflected its reelection ambitions in 2020.[18] The government set up a Joint Parliamentary Committee for Constitutional Amendment, comprising forty-five members representing all parties in parliament, including the Tatmadaw. Although committee members made a total of 3,765 recommendations, the committee approved only proposals presented by the NLD. Particularly significant was the fact that the committee did not approve any of the suggestions made by ethnic political parties related to federalism and the recognition of the identity groups they represented.[19] Ultimately, of the 135 amendments forwarded, parliament adopted only four minor ones.

This last-minute push by the NLD to amend the constitution rang hollow following four years of unwillingness to tackle more attainable reforms. Despite its parliamentary majority, the NLD failed to amend or repeal repressive laws that criminalized speech and peaceful assembly.[20] Under Aung San Suu Kyi, the

NLD became an increasingly centralized, top-down decision-making structure with little space for internal debate and democratic practice. Aung San Suu Kyi herself adopted a quasi-autocratic leadership style, and preferred to micromanage rather that to build up and institutionalize lower-level or regional grassroots decision-making within the party. She mostly relied on a small inner circle of advisers. As U Zaw Myint Maung, chief minister of Mandalay Region, stated, "The party is above all of us. Below the party is the parliament. Below the party is the government." This governance was, for Richard Roewer, "reminiscent of the former military-backed regime, which lacked transparency and accountability."[21]

Far from embodying a federal spirit, the NLD government actually paid little attention to regional demands. Like the USDP, the NLD refused to appoint members of other political parties as chief ministers, entrenching the power of the central government rather than local parliaments. Aung San Suu Kyi appointed NLD chief ministers in state parliaments, even where ethnic minority parties won a majority of seats, such as in Shan and Rakhine States. She even rejected a proposed constitutional amendment to allow chief ministers in ethnic minority regions to be elected.[22] The NLD even adopted a law to strengthen "cooperation" among the country's parliaments, which, in fact, increased central control over state and regional parliaments.[23]

During the NLD's first government, many ethnic leaders and CSOs doubted the sincerity of the NLD's call for federalism. In its 2015 electoral manifesto, the NLD pledged to strive for the establishment of a genuine *federal-democratic* union, while in its 2020 manifesto, it promised to fight for a *democratic-federal* union. The shift in the words' order was, for many observers, not innocent. According to Kyaw Lynn, it denoted "a policy change in terms of the party's orientation towards federalism and democratic reform."[24] Others complained that after gaining power, Aung San Suu Kyi had looked at ethnic communities as a problem rather than as partners or equals; in her view, they said, those communities had responsibilities toward the Union rather than rights. For Aung San Suu Kyi—an ethnic Bamar—ethnic minorities, as David Scott Mathieson puts it, always seemed "colourfully garbed" but also "unruly, ungrateful and uncouth, and in dire need of benevolent control."[25] Her vision of "unity," iron discipline, and vague appeals to peace became increasingly reminiscent of the military era.[26] In her 2020 electoral campaign, writes Mathieson, she "delivered messages somewhere between exhortation and warning of the need for 'Union spirit' and an end to unreasonable demands from ethnic communities who she says must buckle down and contribute to ethnic Burman-led state-building."[27]

While a generous interpretation of the NLD's record would point to constraints from the Tatmadaw, much of the evidence shows meager efforts at best. The NLD certainly had strong popular appeal and political support, as well as sufficient legislative and executive authority, and it could have much more strongly presented a vision of reform toward more genuine federalism. But instead, after its acceptance of the 2008 constitution, it showed strong resolve to use amendments in order to reduce the military's role in government, but very weak, and even counterproductive, efforts to introduce more decentralization or autonomy for ethnic states and groups.

Layering Ethnic State Powers: A Confirmation of Weak Decentralization

Aside from the NLD government's public posturing with respect to federalism and ethnic minority states, the actualization of the constitution's decentralization further reaffirmed how limited and how circumscribed it was by Union government practices. While there was some debate and disagreement about whether the constitution offered incremental steps toward greater decentralization and perhaps federalism, the evidence suggests that such an interpretation was overly optimistic.[28] Against the backdrop of the NLD government's lack of prioritization of federalism or decentralization in its late attempts at constitutional reform, combined with the little initiative to make significant progress in the political dialogue, a cursory view of the evolving powers and practices of ethnic states confirms that, in the process of crafting a democratic regime with greater political space for ethnic state governance, the NLD government nevertheless retained centralization and made increasingly costly any future ability to shift away from that path. There was no difference from the previous USDP government in this respect.

Wording in the constitution places limits on the regional governments' authority to pass laws within their designated powers. The phrase "in accordance with the law enacted by the Union" appears repeatedly in Schedule 2, in the Region or State Government and Legislative Laws, and in the 2015 constitutional amendments. Coupled with Article 198, which states that Union law takes precedence over laws passed by subnational parliaments, these safeguards strengthen the power of the Union government. A small but illustrative example was the Mon State Land Tax Law. After the Mon State legislature adopted it in December 2012, the local branch of the central government's line ministry refused to implement it. The line ministry invoked Articles 446 and 447 of the constitution, stipulating that Union laws shall prevail as long as they are not revoked by the Union parliament. It continued to apply the land tax rates that were specified in Union law, while ignoring the local legislation. The Mon State Hluttaw referred the case to the Union Constitutional Tribunal, which ruled that the president should decide which law took precedence. President Thein Sein decided to delay the implementation of the local law until all states and regions had passed their respective land tax laws, and until all of them conformed to the land registration process determined by the Union government.[29] By 2020, twelve out of fourteen regional legislatures had passed land tax or land revenue laws, but they were unable to implement them because the Union legislature did not revoke the related law that had precedence.[30]

Such problems were widespread across different regions but particularly acute in ethnic minority states. One local parliament reportedly had to amend its law on small- and medium-scale electricity after the Union passed the Union Electricity Production Law.[31] Several others wanted to pass local legislation but were prevented because the Union parliament had not yet passed related legislation. For example, Ayeyarwady's parliament was not able to adopt its Inshore Fishery Law because of the absence of the corresponding Union law.[32] Regional legislatures dominated by the Bamar majority (Sagaing, Mandalay, Bago, Ayeyarwady) faced fewer constraints and were able to pass more laws. But the problem was worse in ethnic states.[33] With the exception of Kachin and Mon, most ethnic state parliaments lagged behind regional parliaments in enacting and implementing laws in their legislative domains. While states and regions were hesitant, in some cases they were prevented from enacting laws supposedly proscribed by Union law.[34]

There was a hierarchy of legislation from the Union level that framed the ability of lower-level governments to exercise their designated powers. This top-down practice was even reflected at the state and regional level in their relationship with SAZs. As the chairman of the Pa'O SAZ in Shan State complained in 2017, "Out of all our ten areas of legislative authority, we only passed one law on municipalities, but I don't have the resources and time to draw its bylaws, so I am stuck. The Shan State passed only four out of ten of them, and I need to wait until the Shan State passes its own law; otherwise I will just be wasting my time as [the law] could be eliminated or modified after the Shan State legislature passes its corresponding law."[35]

Faced with these constraints, state and regional parliaments passed laws that would allow their respective governments to conduct daily and basic functions. For the most part, they focused on the budget and local finances, while passing a few laws that were relevant to their local contexts. By the time the NLD began its tenure in office in March 2016, subnational legislatures had adopted laws in less than half of their designated legislative areas.[36] The slow trend continued after the NLD came to power, mostly because the Union parliament failed to amend Union laws to allow local legislatures to enact their own.[37]

The state and regional parliaments were further constrained in their ability to implement the few laws that they could pass. The implementing authority resided with the central government's line ministries, whose local offices were mandated to support state and regional governments.[38] Even the areas under their jurisdiction often required some reliance, fiscally or otherwise, on the line ministries.[39] For example, the state minister for forestry was responsible for the regulation of bamboo, charcoal, and small forestry production, while large timber production remained under the Union Forestry Ministry. This created ambiguity regarding the relative roles of regional/state governments and the local offices of central government line departments. In some cases, these line department offices had one section dealing with issues that were nominally under the state/regional government's jurisdiction, while another remained directly under the authority of the central government. As with the case of forestry, the regional/state offices of the Ministry of Agriculture and Irrigation, for example, had an agricultural section that fell under the state/regional government's jurisdiction, but the irrigation department remained under the control of the central government.[40] Such ambiguous and overlapping authority was reproduced in every jurisdictional aspect of powers divided between both levels of government.

The states and regions' ability to finance their activities was also limited. Although in 2015, amendments to the constitution allowed them to raise more taxes, their independent revenue sources remained small, a tiny fraction of their total revenue. They could raise taxes from investments, insurance, and income; commercial taxes; and hotel and tourism taxes, among other sources. These were added to land, property, and transportation taxes, for instance.[41] Nevertheless, while state and regional governments were legally permitted to collect revenues from these sources, taxes were collected by twenty subnational bodies, most notably the General Administration Department (GAD), which was under the central government until 2018, and only the Development Affairs Organizations (formerly known as "municipal offices") were accountable directly to the state/regional governments.[42] In addition, the Union government determined the revenue shared between the levels of government. As a result, state and regional governments continued to rely mostly on central government transfers, which constituted by far their main source of revenue. In 2017–18, general grant transfers constituted 69 percent of total state/regional revenue nationwide.[43]

Finally, until the end of 2018, the preexisting GAD, a unit of the national Ministry of Home Affairs, further restricted the power of regional and state governments. The GAD straddled the regional/state and Union governments because it was also the bureaucratic core of Myanmar's administrative structure that operated from the center down to the township level. The GAD was the backbone of Myanmar's public administration. It acted as the administrator of state/regional governments and their chief ministers, as well as of the 16,700-plus wards and village tracts. The GAD also had a host of other functions, inherited from previous constitutions, such as the administration of excise taxes, land and property management, the resolution of boundary disputes, public land expropriation, and financial management.[44] The senior GAD administrator for each state and region served as the executive secretary of the state/regional government, and was directly accountable to the Ministry of Home Affairs.[45] The senior administrator supervised several hundred employees at the General Administration Office of the states/regions. As summarized by an influential ethnic leader with a strong role in the peace process, "It doesn't matter which party is in power . . . because it is the Ministry of Home Affairs that really controls."[46] In a move to demilitarize the administration, the GAD was transferred from the Ministry of Home Affairs, under military control, to the Ministry of the Office of the Union Government, under civilian control.

Despite this transfer, there was no sign that the NLD government intended to use its newly acquired control over the GAD administration to strengthen state/regional administrations' coordination and interaction and nudge "federalism from below." On the eve of the 2021 coup, it remained unclear whether this move was a first step toward decentralization or yet another way for the NLD government to increase central control over regional policy making. In other words, these transfers were nothing more than an affirmation of the principle of civilian control and oversight and an assertion of the civilian government's authority.[47] The GAD structure, which by its nature contradicts principles of decentralization and federalism, remained firmly in place.

Overall, while the constitution enshrined some degree of fiscal and administrative decentralization, the latter was limited and constrained. State and regional governments gained limited taxation powers that were specified in Schedule 5 of the constitution, in jurisdictions that were mostly retained at the center, or where significant overlaps in power rendered their authority almost insignificant. Coupled with very few fiscal revenues, and an administrative system that remained highly centralized, there were few opportunities for these governments to exercise even the limited autonomy that they enjoyed.

Two important areas that, among others, fell under the jurisdiction of the central government illustrate the very limited devolution of power toward state and regional governments, and the ways by which the central government retained control even when it devolved power. Land and natural resource management was crucial, as agriculture, mining, and forestry were still major sources of revenue in Myanmar's economy and the most important economic activities in ethnic minority areas. Language and culture, as part of the broader educational sector, were also key to ethnic groups' concerns. The next sections discuss these two issues, which could have the most impact on ethnic groups in any scenario for greater federalism and autonomy. The processes and practices were typical across different jurisdictional areas.

Land and Natural Resources

The management of land and natural resources was at the core of ethnic minority grievances. Myanmar is rich in natural resources, but the most lucrative ones tend to be situated in ethnic minority areas. During the State Law and Order Restoration Council (SLORC) and State Peace and Development Council (SPDC) period, the military and EAOs fought over control of the most significant resource-rich areas, and created alliances with business entrepreneurs that mostly plundered the resources with no benefits to local populations. Furthermore, as the state remained the sole owner of land, it frequently repossessed large land areas without compensation in order to foster economic development projects or, in the case of the military, its own business interests. As a consequence, ethnic minority organizations, including EAOs involved in the peace negotiations, clamored for the right to reclaim control over land and resources, both to ensure steady sources of revenue and to avoid the damaging degradation that affected ethnic minority areas.

Yet there were virtually no changes after 2011 in the control and management of land and resources, either formally under the 2008 constitution or informally, as a result of a realignment of business interests in a more open economy and ongoing peace negotiations with EAOs. In fact, the expansion of ceasefire zones and greater government presence mainly increased both the military's and the central government's ability to penetrate areas that EAOs previously controlled, and expanded both business and development interests while maintaining the practice of little consultation with local populations and ethnic minority representatives, and few benefits accruing to ethnic minority areas.

The 2008 constitution maintained strong central government control despite the core importance of land and resources for revenue generation and economic activity in ethnic states. The constitution declared the Union the "ultimate owner of all lands and all natural resources above and below the ground, above and beneath the water and in the atmosphere." It also granted the Union the sole authority to supervise the extraction and use of natural resources by economic forces and to collect and use revenues from the sale of high-value natural resources.[48]

In practice, however, weak state capacity and ongoing war limited the central state's complete control over resource revenues in peripheral areas. Kachin State, which is rich in jade, gold, and hydro sources, is a particularly strong example.

Much of the revenue from the lucrative exploitation of jade completely evaded official revenue collection. In 2014, official national jade exports were about $1 billion, whereas the UN trade data reported on Chinese imports from Myanmar showed a total of $12.3 billion in jade and gem imports. Since almost all jade is produced in Kachin State, this gap in trade data requires some explanation. Global Witness's estimate for jade and gem exports was even higher, at $31 billion in 2014.[49] David Dapice argued that Global Witness's estimate may have been a bit too high, and that even if one estimates it at $15 billion, very little went to the government ($300.8 million) or even to KIO accounts ($800 million).[50] A majority of revenues accrued to Wa or Chinese mining companies (approximately $10 billion, or 64.7 percent of revenues). So if, in the past, the military and the KIO fought over control of the jade trade, new business interests expanded in mining areas, without creating large new revenues for the state. In a similar way, private businesses and local Myanmar military officials were able to reap a significant portion of profits from gold mines and timber extraction in KNU-controlled areas, which depleted the environment and polluted the water for local populations.

As in the past, few benefits accrued to the local population. There was arguably deterioration in living conditions after the 2011 reforms, sometimes because of environmental degradation and other times because of poor working conditions worsened by a continued civil war economy. A local Kachin Christian leader described the deterioration of social conditions among the Kachin population:

> There was progress during the ceasefire between the government and KIO between 1994 and 2011, but not for the general population. The roads were built for private companies. A majority of them are owned by Chinese. In the past, individuals dug their own holes to extract jade. But private companies barricaded the area, so that nobody could come and extract precious stones. The companies took over villages and we have no voices to complain. They compensated between five hundred and twenty-five hundred in US dollars per house for the loss of our land. The local population now goes through landfills and leftover rocks to look for small pieces of jade. There was a mudslide last year and one hundred people died.... The workers are asked to work very hard, and for a long time, and they are given yaba [derivative of methamphetamine]. So now drug use has become a real problem.[51]

Similar issues were reported in Rakhine and Kayah States. Local residents complained of being rich in resources but with few benefits for local residents. "Rakhine State produces oil and gas, but our current electricity cost per unit is one of the highest in the country," said one.[52] Resources and their revenues were often grabbed in side deals. As a member of a Rakhine political party recounted, "We used to have abundant freshwater and seawater fisheries. We used to have enough rainfall but now the rainfall has fallen because of deforestation in western forests in Rakhine. Because the military government and its cronies are engaged in logging, there is deforestation and there is no replantation so it has impacted the livelihood of local people. Our oil and gas from Shwe natural gas exploitation is being exported to China. But we did not get to keep any revenue from it. Out of fourteen regions and states, we [Rakhine] are the second poorest."[53] The situation was similar in Kayah State. "[Kayah] State has supplied the rest of the country with electricity from Lawpita, but most of our towns do not have electricity," said a Kayah resident.[54] The complaints were the same in other ethnic minority states, including in Shan State, which is known for its timber, mineral resources, and large rivers.[55]

While the economy opened up to a greater number of investors, the new policies simply expanded the number of business interests that competed for Myanmar's resource-rich sector. The military continued to broker deals with foreign investors, mostly Chinese, to expand and export resources for the personal gain of officers and associated business cronies. EAOs, mostly in Wa, Kachin, and Kayin States, retained some of their previous control and revenues from resources. Most of these business ventures remained in the black-market economy.

Under Thein Sein's administration (2011–16), the government sponsored major investments in large-scale mining, logging, fisheries, and oil and gas exploration but, again, with few benefits to ethnic minority areas.[56] Plans for hydroelectric plants drew criticism in Chin and Shan States.[57] So did other large-scale projects. As a civil society activist from Chin State reported in 2015, "The government has signed an agreement to extract nickel in the area. The people protested. But the government ignored the people's request, and will go ahead with the project. Local MPs said that they could not do anything."[58] A large part of the revenues from these projects disappeared without accountability. As a leading participant in the Multi-Stakeholder Group of the Extractive Industries Transparency Initiative pointed out, the Ministry of Oil and Gas Enterprises paid only 45 percent of its net profits to the Ministry of Finance, while it failed to account for the rest.[59]

There were a few instances where coalitions of local interests succeeded in stemming the tide of large-scale resource exploitation. The most famous was the mobilization against the building of the Myitsone Dam. Chinese entrepreneurs won a lucrative contract to build the dam, which would have supplied more hydroelectricity to China. But the dam was situated at the confluence of two of the most important rivers in Kachin State, which supplies a vast irrigation network downstream in Kachin State and beyond. A large protest movement therefore allied Kachins worried about the local displacement and destruction, along with other downstream people eager to protect their source of irrigation.[60] There are other examples of some local CSOs managing to build small protest movements that halted some local large-scale projects. By January 2019, a coalition of Chin CSOs was able to prevent the implementation of nickel mining. Resistance to the building of coal factories in Mon and Kayin States led to the projects' delay or cancelation.[61] But overall these victories were few and far between, and did not significantly halt the large-scale exploitation of natural resources, which damaged local environments while failing to produce either revenue for ethnic states or benefits to local populations.

Meanwhile, state officials were unable, or unwilling, to complain or resist. Of course, under the 2008 constitution, they lacked the legal authority to approve and manage the terms and conditions of large-scale natural resource extraction. Also, chief ministers were appointed by the central government, so they had very little incentive to be critical. The NLD chief minister of Kayin State, for instance, was criticized by CSOs for her implementation of the central government's National Electrification Plan to develop a coal-generated electricity project in Kayin State.[62] State governments also had little say in the share of revenue they might eventually receive.

In some cases, local officials were complicit with corruption schemes. While the central government in principle controlled major natural resources, some state and regional chief ministers under the Thein Sein government found creative loopholes to bypass some of the central government's restrictions. For instance, some managed to break up large mining operations into smaller ones that would not require central government approval because of their smaller size.[63] They could then form "joint ventures" with business partners, and generate mostly private gains beyond government monitoring.[64]

There were few changes after the NLD came to power. The NLD government suspended the licensing of jade and gemstone mining in June 2016 while parliament drafted a new law to reassess safety, environmental, and health standards in mining, and to protect the interests of local communities.[65] But it did not have the resources or the capacity for such assessments, and therefore thousands of applications had not yet been examined by June 2017.[66] It also failed to grant state governments more significant power over the natural resource sector. In 2016, the Myanmar Investment Commission devolved power to allow state and regional investment committees to approve foreign investments up to $5 million, or 6 billion kyat, but the central government still made the decisions regarding large-scale investments in natural resources.[67] There were, therefore, few concrete ways in which the NLD government's policies created any significant changes in the management of natural resources or the revenues that they generated.

Attempts to establish more transparent and accountable procedures governing the extractive sector mostly failed.[68]

In the state institutional arena, therefore, state governments and local ministries were basically absent from the management of natural resources, and made virtually no gains under the NLD. Most of the business activity in the resource sector, and its lucrative gains, remained outside formal government control. The military retained some control over several mining activities in conjunction with foreign and domestic investors. So did a few armed groups. There were no significant signs of an ability to gain revenues or control to the benefit of ethnic states and their respective populations.

Outside the state institutional arena, struggles for control over natural resources remained relatively constant as well. Many of the mines, and other resources, were still situated in war zones, particularly in Kachin. Even when they were formally within government reach, such as in parts of Kachin State, they remained nevertheless mostly outside formal control.

The formal negotiating arena made few inroads on new proposals to manage natural resources and their revenues. EAOs in principle favored regional authorities' greater control over the resource-rich areas. The Nationwide Ceasefire Agreement signatories reportedly proposed that local regions retain 70 percent of revenues, while the army proposed 30 percent, but they did not discuss revenue redistribution to resource-poor regions, or how these revenues would be used to promote development.[69] Some members of ethnic minority groups favored the idea that producing regions should receive more, without sharing with resource-poor states, but mostly these questions had not even been fully discussed among EAOs and political parties by the end of the NLD's term in office.

Some EAOs wavered in their commitment to move beyond the status quo. In practice, many of them still funded their operations through extractive industries. They had an interest in retaining the informal economy, so the extent to which they were willing to share resource revenues and relinquish control to regional governments was not clear.[70] This problem was particularly acute in Shan, Kachin, Kayin, and Rakhine States.[71]

In spite of its importance to ethnic states, and future revenues for their development, the resource sector remained firmly outside their reach. The 2008 constitution maintained strong central government control over these resources. Revenue streams were mostly untapped, and instead disappeared in corruption and private interests. There was little evidence that state governments were able, or even willing, to exercise the limited powers they had to tax very small parts of the sector, or to push for a greater share or greater control. The Myanmar State and Chinese companies have been the major beneficiaries of the China-Myanmar Oil and Gas Pipelines, a 770-kilometer joint venture operated by the Ministry of

Oil and Gas Enterprises and the China National Petroleum Corporation, which runs from Kyuak Pyu in Rakhine State in the Bay of Bengal to Yunnan Province. Local populations have lost their lands from the construction, have suffered from adverse environmental consequences, and have not been compensated.[72] Ironically, Rakhine State's access to grid-based electricity remains the lowest of all states in Myanmar, with only approximately 10 percent of the population having access.[73] EAOs in resource-rich areas have continued to operate their own businesses, while in principle advocating for formal control of resources under state governments, when and if a federal agreement is reached.

Beyond the resource sector, the same issue arose with respect to control over land more broadly. Under the 2008 constitution, all land remained the property of the state. A series of land laws, adopted without popular consultation, changed the legal basis for land use and established a legal land market.[74] But many members of ethnic communities in the peripheral areas practiced customary land laws and did not have official land titles. Many had already lost land through civil war, infrastructural development projects, and commercial activities in mining, plantations, and timber extraction under the junta. But after 2012, they became vulnerable to land grabbing by outside private investors. Land reforms allowed the government to seize land from owners who did not have official titles and to lease it to third parties.[75] As a former state MP (2011–16) from Kayin State put it, "Land grabbing is the most frequent complaint the Karen [Kayin] State government has faced since the NLD government came to power."[76] Land grabbing occurred frequently for mining, hydroelectric projects, and other infrastructural development. Little, if any, compensation was provided.[77]

During the USDP and NLD administrations, therefore, basically no devolution of control or increased benefits from natural resources were provided to ethnic minority states. While the provisions of the 2008 constitution maintained most of the central government's control, most of the revenues even eluded the central government. Instead, the military, EAOs, and mainly private investors exploited and reaped all the gains. Most of the sector fell outside the realm of the state, in the extrainstitutional realm of the informal economy. Governments of ethnic states gained little control and did not apply much pressure to devolve power or resources to their local states. Business activities continued as in the past, with distant promises that the peace negotiations would eventually produce a new formal arrangement that would benefit ethnic minority states.

Education, Language, and Culture

Education, language, and culture were also core areas of demands and grievances among ethnic minority groups. Yet while the central government introduced a number of new policies, the 2008 constitution reaffirmed that education fell under the jurisdiction of the central government. It therefore retained the discretion to decide the extent to which the curriculum could be tailored to local circumstances, ethnic languages would be taught, and cultural content could reflect the uniqueness of each ethnic community. Over the course of the years of reform, the central government extended greater concessions on language and culture, and institutionalized a new set of practices and norms regarding the teaching of ethnic languages and culture. But overall these concessions were very minimal, and the central government maintained strong control.

Under the military regime, and into the USDP's transitional administration, ethnic minorities resented "Burmanizing" policies. In spite of recognizing "national races" in the previous constitution, and preserving ethnic states, the former military junta had actually increased assimilation policies relative to the preceding Ne Win government. Education had been highly centralized and homogenized across the country, but there was some tolerance toward the teaching of ethnic languages and culture outside the classroom. The military junta under the SLORC and SPDC tightened the rules and increased policies making Burmese the only language used in schools, alongside a curriculum that only minimally mentioned ethnic minority groups while reifying the primacy of the Bamar and its historical roots in past kingdoms that ruled over the existing territory.[78]

In June 2012, the Ministry of Education took significant steps toward implementing a new approach to ethnic languages and culture, allowing the teaching of ethnic languages and literature in elementary school (up to third grade).[79] This new measure represented a major break from the previous military regime, which recognized only Burmese as the official language and the only medium of exchange in government offices, schools, media, and the courts.[80] The ministry also formed a task force to translate and compile school textbooks for larger minority ethnic groups.

This approach was reaffirmed in a vast curriculum renewal that the USDP government initiated. In 2014, after a comprehensive review of the educational sector, the government adopted a new National Education Law. The NLD government subsequently upheld the reform law and began its implementation. The law acknowledged the role of informal, nonstate, and private education, which has often played a complementary role to the formal education system and has been the main vehicle for teaching ethnic minority languages. It also began to include some aspects of ethnic languages and culture in the formal education system. It permitted in primary education the use of ethnic languages along with Burmese, if necessary,[81] and it reaffirmed in law the ability to teach languages in the early years of primary school. Finally, later revisions went further by beginning to transfer some authority to state and regional governments. Article 39(g) of the Law Amending the National Education Law (June 25, 2015) gave state and regional governments the responsibility to develop the local content of the education curriculum.

In terms of the planning and decision-making in education, a certain amount of decentralization had occurred, but mostly as deconcentration of central government authority.[82] The authority to promote and transfer different levels of staff in education was given to districts (for middle and high school heads and township education officers) and townships (for primary and middle school teachers).[83] Township education officers could participate in planning, budgeting, and identifying the priorities and needs of their schools, which received increased financial, technological, and technical support from the central government. To a very limited degree, this measure allowed for some adaptation to local contexts, including ethnic minority areas. But overall these decisions remained within the line ministry of the central government, and did not allow much input from state governments. While in some cases the state minister of social affairs played an active role and was consulted on some important decisions, actual power continued to reside with the central government, and therefore the practice of limited, decentralized decision-making varied tremendously from one ethnic state to another, and from one chief minister or social affairs minister to another, depending on competence or personal leadership.

Furthermore, the reality of implementing the new curriculum or teaching languages in ethnic minority areas showed important limitations. The teaching of mother tongues remained difficult for most ethnic minority groups.[84] Minorities that are Christian, such as Kachin and Sgaw Karen, had more success in protecting their language, since the church provided a ready-made infrastructure with some resources. They regularly taught languages in after-school or weekend programs. When the government became more tolerant of their role, they became increasingly open. After the adoption of the new educational law, some were involved in local committees working on local language textbooks to integrate into the primary school curriculum. Buddhist monasteries in Buddhist areas, such as Rakhine, Mon, and Shan States, offered similar services, but they were decentralized and depended on individual monks. The lack of resources was a strong impediment to the teaching of ethnic languages outside the school system, and therefore relied mostly on volunteers and established religious organizations.[85] Furthermore, up until the slow implementation of educational reforms in 2019, ethnic languages continued to be taught mostly in after-school programs in most places, which made the school day longer and was sometimes a disincentive for pupils to attend.[86] Ethnic states therefore had very few resources or powers to preserve local languages and culture.

The broader curriculum and its delivery continued to reflect the dominance of the Bamar majority. While the situation varied from one ethnic state to another, most textbooks were written in Burmese and contained material that ignored the social and cultural realities of ethnic regions.[87] Most teachers were still sent by the central government, spoke Burmese, and were of Bamar origin.[88] As a result, ethnic minority groups often rejected the textbooks and were resentful at the lack of sensitivity to local needs and realities.[89]

Beyond the education system, there were no signs that the government was even considering adding any ethnic minority languages as official languages, or even accommodating them in public offices. Mon political parties and civil society groups advocated for the adoption of Mon as one of the official languages,[90] but it was likely that any such demand in peace negotiations would be rejected.[91] There were no signs of willingness to consider accommodating local languages beyond minimal acceptance of their inclusion in the educational curriculum.

The implementation of the 2008 constitution led to reforms and the creation and layering of new institutions, norms, and processes that aligned with the central government's approach to accommodating ethnic minorities. The USDP government began to implement powers and offer resources to state and regional governments, but, for the most part, the latter had very limited ability to actually exercise authority beyond very specific areas. Moreover, those governments relied on the GAD for access to fiscal resources and even for permission for certain initiatives. Given the absence of local bureaucracies, they also required the services of the local offices of central government line ministries to implement laws and programs. While amendments were made to include more areas of jurisdiction, the ambiguity in the exercise of authority, limited fiscal resources to support state governments, and the absence of bureaucracy meant that, in reality, ethnic state governments remained highly constrained in their ability to govern. Given that the central government appointed chief ministers, and that the ministers were constitutionally accountable to the central government, the leadership of state governments also had little autonomy from the central government.

Little changed under the NLD government. While the NLD had initially resisted the 2008 constitution, it continued to implement it after coming to power in 2015. As the NLD was concerned with retaining control over all levels of government, it kept even tighter control over chief ministers, most of whom were NLD members and appointed by Aung San Suu Kyi. The parliaments, similarly dominated by the NLD in most ethnic states, exercised little independent power from the central government.[92] The NLD's success in transferring the GAD from military to civilian authority was a victory in its objective of slowly reducing the military's role in governance, but did little to change its centralizing role.

The central government also retained strong control over jurisdictions and issue areas that were crucial to ethnic states. Natural resources, which were a major source of revenue and economic activity in ethnic states, remained out of reach of state governments. The military, private business interests, and EAOs continued to control most resources and reap their benefits, with the relative share of revenue eluding even central government control. Education, language, and culture remained firmly under the control of the central government. While reforms of the educational curriculum were slowly allowing for the inclusion of ethnic languages and some local content in the curriculum, these constituted very minimal accommodations to ethnic minorities to preserve their local languages and culture in an otherwise still centralized, and Bamar-centric, curriculum. With some decentralized management, more teachers were sourced locally, but the central government controlled their appointment, and their independence was highly restricted. Such patterns continued under the NLD government, and were reproduced in almost every significant issue area.

In the state institutional arena, the negotiation toward greater federalism was therefore strongly skewed in favor of the central government. Governments of ethnic states applied very little pressure to increase their independence or exercise greater authority. With constitutional lock-in, they stuck to their assigned functions and were socialized into new forms of mostly minimal decentralization, while maintaining familiar practices of deference toward and dependence on central authorities. They continued past practices of reliance on central government decisions and initiatives. De facto, the state had been changing, parliaments were created at the state level, and new powers and resources were allocated, but they mainly created the layers of institutionalization that cemented a new version of a Bamar-dominated centralized state.

With the NLD's and even some EAOs' broader acceptance of the 2008 constitution and its base for negotiation, the constitution framed the limits of possibilities in the Panglong Conference. Sequencing was key. With the Tatmadaw and the Union government (both USDP and NLD) making all parties accept that the constitution would be amended rather than replaced, over time the new practices and institutions in the state institutional area were being socialized and normalized. Every aspect of jurisdictional and fiscal power would subsequently require discussion and eventual renegotiation of divisions of authority between the central government and ethnic states. With the Panglong process forcing negotiating parties to negotiate every aspect separately, it was doomed to drag on for several years, while the new model of limited decentralization became entrenched and increasingly difficult to reverse. The 2021 coup ended this tension, but its shadow would continue in any subsequent negotiations.

6
OUTFLANKING AND THE EROSION OF DE FACTO AUTONOMY

The Nationwide Ceasefire Agreement (NCA) and political dialogue occurred against the backdrop of decades of informal arrangements that gave some ethnic armed organizations (EAOs) a certain measure of territorial control and autonomy. Ceasefires in the late 1980s and 1990s allowed EAOs to exercise varying degrees of de facto autonomy, most often through informal agreements with the state. Some even developed fairly extensive services for their local populations, particularly in the educational and health care sectors. Yet, ironically, although the nationwide ceasefire and political dialogue were more institutionalized and promised greater formal autonomy if conclusive, the uncertainty of the transitional phase opened up opportunities for the state to erode past autonomy.

The NCA locked in an agreement that the Tatmadaw and EAOs would not specify demarcation lines. EAOs had accepted this condition to secure an agreement, as they feared the consequences of failure. The Tatmadaw saw an opportunity to undermine the EAOs by expanding the state's reach into ethnic minority territories and avoid reproducing the kind of de facto autonomy it had conceded to the Wa.

The Myanmar state was subsequently able to fulfill on its own terms the local ethnic population's demand for development, social services, and education. The lack of specified territories in the ceasefire agreements and the absence of interim arrangements for local governance facilitated this process. By doing so, it sought to outflank the EAOs. It could erode the services that the EAOs had provided and gradually replace them, thereby contributing to reducing their legitimacy in the eyes of ethnic minority groups. The peace process allowed the state to expand its reach into territory previously at war and seize control over several jurisdictional areas. The longer the indeterminacy of the interim period and the absence of a final political agreement, the more the state gained significant ability to outflank grassroots ethnic organizations. This chapter illustrates this trend by briefly examining three strategic policy areas: education, health care, and land management.

State Expansion under the 1990s Ceasefires

After crushing the prodemocracy movement, the junta adopted a new way of dealing with armed rebellion. The regime initiated a "ceasefire movement" in addition to classic counterinsurgency measures. With ceasefire groups, the regime set out to use development spending, joint business ventures, and the rerouting of economic flows to strengthen national unity.[1] This new approach was meant to extend the state's authority and influence into the borderland region without achieving a political settlement.

In the 1990s, groups that agreed to a ceasefire were allowed to maintain control over some territory and continue some cross-border trading.[2] In exchange, according to Mary Callahan, the regime deployed "regional commanders, local battalions, the Ministry of Development of the Border Areas and the National Races, and other line ministries to build roads, power plants, telecommunications relay stations, Burmese-language schools, hospital and clinics, and other institutions aimed at both modernizing and pacifying former rebel-held territory."[3] Meanwhile, it intensified its symbolic presence in former rebel-held areas by setting up large propaganda billboards, holding frequent ceremonies, opening township and village offices of the Union Solidarity and Development Association, building new pagodas, and setting up road checkpoints and other taxes or levies.

Every EAO that signed a ceasefire in the 1990s was faced with state expansion, except for the Wa and the Kokang. The first two groups that signed, the United Wa State Army and the Kokang Democratic Party, obtained "special regions" with more extensive local autonomy over economic, social, and political affairs.[4] In these two special regions, the junta had limited oversight and influence, and the EAOs engaged in taxation activities, poppy cultivation (initially), and cross-border activities.

Aside from these two groups, the 1990s ceasefires allowed the government to more fully deploy its authority in regions previously inaccessible. The junta could exchange economic, political, and cultural autonomy for state expansion in its areas, particularly in strategic and resource-rich regions, such as territory that the Kachin and Pa'O controlled. The Karen experienced a similar fate after the Democratic Karen Buddhist Army (DKBA) split from the predominantly Christian-led Karen National Union (KNU). The regime signed a ceasefire with the DKBA and used it as a proxy against the KNU, while expanding state power in former KNU-held territory. Afterward, the remaining territories under KNU control became much less clearly identifiable.

The ceasefires deprived some armed groups of their revenues to finance services for their constituencies.[5] In some cases, they even incentivized rent seeking instead of service delivery by ethnic armed leaders.[6] In the past, EAOs funded their military operations, education, health care, and legal and security needs through various self-financing activities. These included taxation on local households and businesses, transit fees at checkpoints, cross-border trades, and legal businesses (gas stations, transport companies, hotels, investment in the real estate sector, and natural resource projects such as agro-industry, logging, and mining), as well as illicit businesses and trade (such as illegal logging, mining, and drug production and trafficking) and land grabbing. These resources dwindled as the Burmese military gradually extended its reach into areas controlled by armed groups after the 1990s, either through outright military takeover or through the establishment of military settlements and the creation of new towns in ceasefire areas. This allowed the state to impose and transplant its own version of education, health care, and other services in ethnic minority areas.

The regime also created webs of commercial and patron-client ties that pulled ethnic leaders toward the center. Joint ventures with local elites, particularly in the natural resource sector, allowed the state to expand its military, administrative, and economic presence where it previously had none.[7] It allocated resource concessions to local elites who brokered ceasefires and provided patronage money to regional army commanders,[8] and it also encouraged ethnic elites to invest their illegally obtained money in the national economy. Drug barons and smugglers laundered their money through state-owned banks and were allowed to invest in legitimate national businesses. Hence, while borderland development could have strengthened ceasefire groups, the regime deliberately centralized the economic flows to weaken centrifugal forces and make access dependent on loyalty to the state.[9] Myanmar's licit and illicit markets were thus all rerouted through Yangon, which at the time was Myanmar's capital.

Finally, the regime sought to cut off EAOs from autonomous sources of revenue. The Tatmadaw shut out many businesses linked to the Kachin Independence Organization (KIO) by taking control of the jade mines and redirecting timber exports away from cross-border roads to the Yangon port.[10] In agriculture, local elites were squeezed out if they did not join networks of army commanders or Chinese investors. They also allowed foreign investment in hydropower, oil, and gas, which increased revenues to the state while bypassing the borderlands altogether. "The gains from development spending and ceasefire capitalism," notes Lee Jones, "have accrued to a narrow elite, while rapacious extractive projects have alienated many."[11]

Already in the 1990s, therefore, the regime had managed to use a ceasefire strategy to expand state control. While some EAOs benefited from the decrease in violence and from expanded business activities, several also lost control over territory they had previously held. Most significantly, in the name of expanding services and development, the state could increase its presence through business networks and infrastructure while curtailing some of the EAOs' independent revenue sources. As a result, whether for war or for provision of their own services, ethnic minority groups lost some of their autonomous sources of income while the state used cooperation to increase its influence.

State Expansion under Bilateral and Nationwide Ceasefires (2012–20)

Unlike previous ceasefires, new ones under the NCA were more than economic deals, as they included the promise of political dialogue and settlement. Yet these new ceasefires were a continuation of the previous waves of ceasefires rather than a radical departure from them. After the transition to civilian rule, both bilateral ceasefires and the NCA allowed the state to once again increase its influence over territory that EAOs had previously controlled. This time, two features of the ceasefires allowed the state to expand its reach into territory previously claimed by EAOs, just as it did under previous regimes.

First, none of the new ceasefire agreements, bilateral or national, specified explicit ceasefire lines on paper. The Tatmadaw and ceasefire groups had some mutual understanding of zones of respective state and EAO influence, but large zones of joint governance ("gray zones") continued to exist. The absence of clear territorial demarcations in the ceasefire agreements opened up opportunities for informal territorial expansion, mostly favoring the state. The NCA referred to "ceasefire areas" but did not define them, and efforts to establish codes of conduct and greater mutual understanding of ceasefire zones repeatedly failed. None of the officially signed documents, according to Kim Jolliffe, "mandated any form of parallel administration or led to the official designation of areas under the exclusive armed group authority." After a decade, discussions on respective territorial control were still ongoing. Meanwhile, territorial authority continued to overlap significantly, creating vast areas where both the state and EAOs operated.[12]

The more recent ceasefires and the NCA avoided explicitly designating ceasefire areas. According to the general secretary of the KNU, "The Tatmadaw had its own agenda and policies and did not want to compromise on territorial demarcation."[13] It is likely that the Tatmadaw deliberately avoided negotiating specific zones of influence to prevent reproducing the de facto territorial autonomy it had granted the Kokang and the Wa in northern Shan State. As part of ceasefire agreements with these groups, the Tatmadaw had granted almost complete control of the territory to the Wa, allowing them to govern almost independently from the Myanmar state.[14] Other bilateral ceasefires in the 1990s allowed groups to govern "special regions" with varying degrees of autonomy. Groups such as the KIO and the New Mon State Party (NMSP) controlled exclusive areas, where the government could enter only after requesting permission. They could raise taxes and provide services to their constituents. Meanwhile, many smaller EAOs or weaker brigades from larger ones such as the KNU did not push for clearly demarcated ceasefire zones in their own bilateral ceasefires and the subsequent NCA, as they barely controlled territory anyway.[15] They probably feared that designating ceasefire zones would run against their interests and expose their vulnerability. The best that the EAOs got was a verbal agreement from the Tatmadaw to discuss demarcation lines later, but, as the KNU general secretary recalled, "it never happened."[16]

Second, recent ceasefire agreements did not specify clear provisions regarding both parties' expected conduct during the interim period—that is, the time between signing the ceasefire and reaching a final political agreement. Instead their proper conduct was to be determined in further negotiations. Without agreement on the ceasefire zones, it was unclear which areas would even be covered, and what should be specified in any transitional agreement. The government certainly aimed to extend its sovereignty over all the territory, while EAOs sought to retain their governance system until a political agreement could be reached.[17] The NCA (Chapter 6, Art. 25) recognized the role of EAOs in the fields of health care, education, development, environmental conservation and natural resource management, preservation and promotion of ethnic cultures and languages, security, the rule of law, and illicit drug eradication. The agreement stopped short, however, of defining any coordination mechanisms in these policy areas. EAOs' status was undefined, and they were not recognized as either governance structures or civil society organizations. Government officials, one group of scholars observes, seemed "to regard EAOs primarily as service delivery actors, and/or private companies, rather than legitimate governance and administrative actors."[18] Prior to the NCA, preexisting bilateral ceasefires had been more explicit regarding the role of EAOs. The 2012 agreement with the KNU, for instance, recognized its parallel governance arrangements and service delivery functions.[19]

But the Tatmadaw believed that the NCA took precedence over previous bilateral ceasefires and subsequently ignored the latter's provisions. It took two years after the 2015 signing of the NCA for the government and ceasefire groups to begin talks on interim arrangements.

This lack of clarity enabled the government to expand its reach into areas otherwise controlled or claimed by EAOs. Mutual deterrence created some local-level understandings of exclusive "areas of operation" but also left open large zones of "hybrid governance," or "gray zones," where authority was shared between the government and the EAOs. In hybrid areas, Jolliffe notes, "conflict dynamics have been transplanted into the governance domain, with various institutions of the [EAOs] and the state vying for influence at the village level."[20] The state and the EAOs were not equal players in this race, and the state had much more power to provide services to local people. By doing so, the state used the indefinite interim period to outflank ethnic leadership by extending its influence over village-level leaders, thus irremediably displacing EAO authority structures.

The varying size of gray zones created uneven and sometimes overlapping authority across different conflict areas. In Shan State, towns and major roads were under government control and gray zones were mostly confined to rural areas. The Restoration Council of Shan State (RCSS) controlled much of the Shan State–Thailand border and had varying degrees of influence in territories along the China border. In Kayin State, the government controlled all towns and major roads in lowland areas, while the KNU had a presence in seven townships and firm control over border territories, especially in northern Kayin State.[21] In the neighboring Tanintharyi Region, where the KNU previously had dominant control, much of the central and eastern parts became gray zones where villagers regularly interacted with both the KNU and the government. While the KNU maintained powerful influence through its civil administration and social service provision, many villages had both a KNU leader and a village tract administrator appointed by the government.[22] In Mon State, the territory controlled by the NMSP was much clearer, a legacy of its previous ceasefire in 1994. The NMSP controlled twelve ceasefire zones (each of them five kilometers in diameter) and had varying degrees of influence in Mon-populated mixed-administration areas in Mon and Kayin States. In northern Tanintharyi, the NMSP contested territorial authority with both the KNU and the government.

The government exploited these fuzzy lines of authority and territory to extend and consolidate its sovereignty over gray zones. As Jolliffe shows, it used small towns surrounded by EAO territories as launch pads for outward expansion. Central towns were sometimes long under government control, but in other cases, the government used "subtownship towns" that acted as administrative hubs in areas too difficult to govern from the township capitals.[23] Jolliffe found nine subtownship towns that were established in Kayin State after 2012; they varied in size from a few households to a long-established settlement, but all were close to large Tatmadaw bases. Once established, they allowed government departments to expand their reach and carry out development activities in surrounding rural communities.[24] Furthermore, the government invested heavily in road infrastructure to connect the subtownships to other towns. Finally, the General Administration Department established village tract administrations where it could, and often did, use the same chairperson that had served or continued to serve as part of the KNU administration. That way, local officials were brought into key departments as administrators.

The state expanded its reach through infrastructural development and service provision by exploiting EAOs' diminished capacity and willingness to respond.[25] After 2012, it built new roads, bridges, police stations, schools, and health centers. After being deprived for so long, many communities welcomed these new projects as they improved access to markets, other towns, and social services previously out of reach. Local communities somewhat legitimized state expansion with their enthusiastic support, thereby creating new tensions with EAOs, especially in Kayin State.[26] Building roads and bridges was a double-edged sword for EAOs. While it offered economic opportunities to their populations, it made them more vulnerable to the state. As one junior staff member for the KNU lamented, "In the past, it took several days to reach the KNU headquarters from Hpa-An, the Kayin State capital. Nowadays, it takes only three hours. . . . The Tatmadaw can attack us anytime they want."[27]

The KNU central executive committee did not set rules on how township-level officials could make decisions about cooperation with the government. Variations existed as a result. The First, Second, Third, and Fifth Brigades generally resisted government infrastructure projects, with the Second and Fifth Brigades clashing at times with the Tatmadaw.[28] Some KNU leaders also restricted international humanitarian and civil society organizations' activities under their controlled areas for fear of losing their autonomy and legitimacy. In some cases, the KNU leaders' opposition to the building of roads and bridges or international humanitarian assistance drove a wedge between the leadership and Karen villagers who welcomed these initiatives. Thus, one Karen retired government official criticized the KNU's Fifth Brigade for refusing to accept rice donated by the Nippon Foundation, while "it continued to tax its starving Karen people."[29]

In other KNU districts, such as those under the control of the Fourth, Sixth, and Seventh Brigades, KNU officials welcomed and supported development projects when the KNU benefited from taxation to fund these projects or from the involvement of KNU-affiliated companies.[30] Infrastructure projects de facto incorporated EAOs into development schemes and made them complicit in further state expansion. As was the case when the KNU refused to be part of development projects, its support of them generated tensions between the leadership and the local communities. Some villagers resented that some KNU leaders took advantage of the peace process to get rich, while not providing enough to the villagers.[31] Karen villagers told the staff of a Yangon-based health center that "the KNU only set up empty clinics, but they are nowhere to be found when we are really sick."[32] In sum, whether they resisted the state's development projects or not, the outcome seemed to be increased tensions between EAOs and their populations.

While some communities preferred EAO governance, they increasingly realized EAOs' limited capacity and resources. Since the fall of its headquarters in 1995, the KNU had lost many of its soldiers, staff, and teachers to refugee camps in Thailand and to various Western countries. Although a few came back after the ceasefire of 2012, the KNU still suffered from a "shortage of human resources," as one high-ranking KNU official put it.[33] EAOs often could not compete with the government. All teachers employed by the government were college graduates, for instance, while among the EAOs' staff, few were. The government also provided better salaries to its employees than the KNU could provide to its revolutionary members. Most of them were volunteers. Only in the late 2000s did the KNU start paying stipends to its teachers. Some KNU departments or committees paid a stipend worth between fourteen and forty US dollars per month, in addition to monthly food rations. During the interim period, the EAOs' lack of resources explained why it was difficult to attract talented people to the organization and why many were increasingly drawn to government jobs.[34]

In the past, several EAOs had their own taxation systems, but the NCA left the question of taxation unsettled, while the Tatmadaw insisted, as part of its "six principles for peace," that EAOs cease taxing civilians and collecting custom duties in border areas. In 2017, the Tatmadaw used this principle as a rationale for taking control of NMSP checkpoints and pressuring them into signing the NCA.[35] By reducing taxation capacity, the Tatmadaw sought to make it increasingly difficult for EAOs to maintain armies and deliver social services. While some EAOs continued to tax civilians, they sometimes lost local support, particularly where both the government and EAOs extracted resources. So civilians had sometimes welcomed the reduction of EAO taxation and increased government presence, as they appreciated greater security and a lower taxation burden. KNU officials recognized, for instance, that "previously 'loyal' communities [were] less easily controlled by the organization, and increasingly [came] under the influence of the government . . . , which is able to offer more services."[36] By providing new services and imposing greater limits on taxation, the central government was undermining the EAOs' capacity to deliver services, while preserving the existing state structure.

While not directly related to state strategy, ceasefires also opened previously unreachable areas to private business investments, thereby undermining EAO control. New business ventures increased, particularly in mining and agriculture. Legal loopholes and weak law enforcement, especially in gray zones, allowed many shady businesses to invest in and exploit natural resources. They bribed government, Tatmadaw, and EAO officials or included them as informal business partners.[37] Multiple actors vied for control of natural resources, often leading to overlapping rent seeking from armed actors and civilian authorities in mixed areas.[38] Many projects, according to South et al., moved ahead "before the government and EAOs [had] reached agreements on key questions of economic governance..., including resource sharing, property and land rights, and rules and regulations that form the regulatory environment for business."[39] The existing legal and regulatory framework centralized decision-making and lacked mechanisms for local input. Within EAOs themselves, decision-making on issues of natural resource exploitation remained opaque and obscure.

Even though international aid attempted to contribute to development, it often helped the central state extend its presence in many postconflict zones. Myanmar became one of the largest recipients of international aid in the world. International aid was no longer limited to health and humanitarian projects, but involved support for new infrastructure projects in the transportation and energy sectors throughout Myanmar, including in conflict-affected areas.[40] For instance, a large share of international assistance in Kayin State was channeled to the subtownship towns discussed above. Jolliffe found that Shan Ywa Thit, a town of only 531 people that did not even appear on most maps in 2010, had received nearly two hundred humanitarian and development projects.[41] More extensive projects also durably reconfigured space by binding ethnic areas to central Myanmar. In central Kayin State, the Greater Mekong Subregion East–West Corridor Program had plans to construct large-scale hydropower projects on the Salween River and in the Dawei Special Economic Zone in Tanintharyi Region.[42] In their design, aid-funded initiatives were centralizing, not federalizing, in nature: they sought to improve national-level indicators such as education and they were designed to be implemented throughout the country.[43] Foreign aid also lessened politicians' need to find domestic consensus and respond to local concerns and particularities.[44] Between 2012 and 2020, three of the five largest programs in Myanmar had extended into conflict areas.[45] These development programs all worked through the central state and did not involve state governments, although some had agreements and worked with the EAOs.

By exploiting ambiguous gray zones and inserting itself through different means in territory previously controlled by EAOs, the state expanded its influence and control. Its expansion into EAOs' territory accelerated rather than slowed down under the National League for Democracy (NLD) government. Under U Thein Sein, the government had acknowledged the existence of EAOs as alternative service providers. Under the NLD, however, the government more blatantly disregarded such coexistence. One KNU leader remarked, "We have a hard time dealing with the chief minister of Karen [Kayin] State, who is an NLD member. She publicly upholds the policy of one country, one law, one rule, one policy and does not recognize the territories and existence of the KNU. The NLD government does not want the process outside of the legislature, whereas this is what the NCA agreement is all about."[46]

Daily administration in mixed areas had contributed to changing people's perception of the central state. In health care and education, the extension of new services was particularly insidious, as they contributed to winning the hearts and minds of local populations while avoiding concessions to EAOs. In matters of land ownership, the state's extension was even more flagrant, as the central government adopted a new law that facilitated land grabbing. This trend posed a threat, particularly to larger armed organizations such as the KNU, the NMSP, the KIO, and the Karenni National Progressive Party (KNPP). These groups enjoyed high political legitimacy among their populations, and operated like states within a state by running their schools, hospitals, and clinics and offering dispute settlement mechanisms.[47] They governed and provided services tailored to their local populations' needs, using policies and practices that were different from those of the government. The broader state goal was to undermine the legitimacy of armed groups. This legitimacy was closely tied to the EAOs' ability to provide services and security to the populations living in the areas under their control, particularly since parents often preferred to send their children to better-resourced government schools with more qualified teachers. The following sections expand on these three areas.

Education

Education has been the most significant aspect of state expansion into EAO territory. The landscape of the EAOs' education services is diverse. The Chin National Front (CNF) holds only minor influence over small pockets of territory in three townships in Chin State.[48] It helps run a few community schools, at most. By comparison, other EAOs, such as the KNU, NMSP, and KIO, have run extensive educational services. The KNU, for example, supported a little over 1,500 schools in Myanmar, and fifty-five basic education schools in seven refugee camps in Thailand. The KNU's educational wing, the Karen Education Department, ran about half of them, while local communities ran the other half. The Karen Education Department also provided teacher stipends, teacher training, administrative support, and schooling materials.[49] There were approximately two hundred thousand students in the KNU educational institutions before the military coup in February 2021. In Mon State, the NMSP maintained 225 schools, of which the Mon National Education Committee directly ran 132, with the rest under mixed government-NMSP control. In Kachin State, the KIO's education system suffered greatly from the resumption of war. The KIO still ran 4 high schools, 32 middle schools, and 243 primary schools, as well as several higher-education institutions, teaching nursing, military science, education, computer sciences, arts and social sciences, and law.[50] In Kayah State, the KNPP's education department managed 460 primary schools, 33 middle schools, and 12 high schools, with 1,677 teachers and 50,351 students. In Shan State, both the RCSS and the Shan State Progressive Party (SSPP) ran separate education systems. In southern Shan State, the RCSS provided support to around 200 schools in its area of greater control, including teacher stipends, operating costs, and materials.[51]

In the 1990s, there were two main models of EAO education. First, ceasefire groups such as the KIO and the NMSP were allowed to expand their education systems in ceasefire and adjacent government-controlled areas. In their schools, the Mon Education Committee and the Kachin Education Department both adopted a hybrid system. They translated the government curriculum but added the teaching of ethnonational history and ethnic languages.[52] This system allowed children to learn Burmese and join the government education system at any time. Most importantly, it allowed children to pass the matriculation exam that is required to be admitted to university.[53] Second, and by contrast, the KNU did not agree to a ceasefire in the 1990s and developed its own separate education system. It did not implement a hybrid curriculum, as the Mon and Kachin had. Its education system produced graduates qualified to work for aid agencies and opposition groups—or possibly to seek work as exiles in third countries, but these graduates lacked the expected qualifications to work in Myanmar outside the Karen-controlled areas. Their diplomas were also not recognized, so they were unable to access Myanmar's higher-education system. They lacked proficiency in the Burmese language and in required skills, but of course this lack of recognition was also a convenient state administrative limitation to thwart Karen attempts to develop an alternative system.[54]

Under the nationwide ceasefires, the government attempted to replace the EAOs as primary education providers. Through its Ministry of Education, it extended its coverage into ceasefire zones, including the gray areas. With better resources and capacity than local EAOs, it could meet the unfulfilled needs of local communities. But state funding and changes in school "ownership" contributed to the "Burmanization" of education, and the penetration of state-controlled structures into previously semiautonomous areas.[55] Some communities welcomed the new resources, while others did not. Many were coerced and forced to accept it.

The process of state penetration was easier and more frictionless where EAOs were the weakest. Most of the Chin territory was under the control of the Myanmar government when the CNF signed a ceasefire in 2012. Afterward, the Ministry of Education (MoE) funded and staffed most community schools, with the consequence that it changed the language of instruction from Chin to Burmese.[56] The dominance of the central state in education became almost complete. The same was true in large sections of Shan State. In the KNU and DKBA ceasefire areas, especially the gray areas of mixed government and EAO control, the state also made significant inroads. It provided school grants for renovations and electronic material, "sometimes as a first step to initiate relations with the school," according to Jolliffe and Mears.[57] More importantly, the government assigned thousands of new teachers to existing KNU- and DKBA-supported schools. As a result, the Myanmar government ended up running schools that these EAOs had previously managed. Also, the number of MoE teachers in KNU and DKBA schools almost tripled (from 1,574 in 2012 to 4,718 in 2016).[58] Once these teachers were assigned to a school, they started transforming it into a full MoE school. They implemented more of the MoE curriculum, taught more Burmese language, and moved Karen culture and history to the sideline.[59] Some Karen teachers were brought onto the government's payroll, but others were deemed insufficiently qualified to teach in government schools and thus lost their employment to Bamar teachers.

The capacity of the KNU to resist state encroachment was limited. In some areas, lower-level authorities tried to obstruct government activities while waiting for subsequent gains in the peace process, but in many other areas the KNU was unwilling or unable to force local authorities to resist the state. EAOs were often overwhelmed by the state's rapid and uncoordinated expansion. In the absence of clear ceasefire territories and interim arrangements, the government could bypass the KNU and deal directly with the communities by offering funding, for example. Communities generally welcomed government teachers, mostly because they were free, while they had to pay or provide food to teachers from their ethnic community. Incorporating community schools into the MoE also offered more opportunities for students to transfer to the Myanmar education system.[60] It even became a source of tension between the KNU and the Karen communities. Communities often resented the KNU's efforts to limit state spending in their areas. Meanwhile, state spending in other areas helped strengthen the Karen communities' support for the government and desire to get a similar treatment.[61]

A similar situation existed in Mon and Shan States. Mon national schools, too, experienced similar state encroachment on their staff, curriculum, and autonomy.

Moreover, the NMSP did not prohibit schools from obtaining financial and material support from the MoE, which opened further opportunities for the government. In contrast to the Karen, however, the NMSP still enjoyed autonomy, or greater exclusivity, negotiated during its ceasefire in 1994. In Shan State, some teachers were also sent to areas controlled by the RCSS's education department and the Shan State Development Foundation.[62] The RCSS, of its own volition, apparently developed an approach to ensure coordination with the ministry.

After the ceasefire broke down in 2011, the KIO lost control over some of its territory, but still ran hundreds of schools. But the hybrid system that it had developed after the 1994 ceasefire collapsed. The ten schools that the KIO and the government jointly managed were closed down, and the government discontinued arrangements that had existed under the 1994 ceasefire for the KIO Education Department's students to take government high school diploma examinations.[63] The department continued to teach the MoE curriculum, but, given its non-NCA status, the government kept strong pressure on the schools and monitored the teaching and the staff.[64] The conflict, however, increasingly drove various Kachin groups to disengage totally from the state system and to reject Burmese as a medium of instruction. Some even began developing a new curriculum in the local Jingpaw language.

In sum, government officials neglected to coordinate their educational policies and plans with the EAOs' education departments. In the absence of interim arrangements, the central government had no obligation to recognize the EAO education system or cooperate with its education department. As a result, neither Kachin nor Karen students could pass the matriculation exams in the post-NCA era and were thus barred from access to the broader Burmese education system. Among other consequences, this posed an important obstacle for Karen people who wanted to gain employment and recognition of their credentials,[65] which in turn had the effect of attracting Karen students to pursue education outside Kayin State, in other areas of Myanmar. But it created a new dilemma by which families had to choose between the attraction of gaining recognition of one's education in the Burmese language or sending their children to school in their native language, with a curriculum more adapted to their ethnic minority group.

Health Care

The state also used health care provision, just like education, as a means to expand its sovereignty. While there was potential for collaboration and convergence on health care systems because they are less emotionally charged than education, and more technical, convergence remained confined to a few policy areas, as EAOs generally resisted collaboration.

A complex mix of community-based and EAO health organizations provided much of the health care in ethnic states. The former included the Burma Medical Association, which provided broad services, and the Backpack Health Worker Team, which served displaced people in conflict areas, particularly in Kachin and Kayin States. Among EAOs, the KNU and the KIO had the most significant health care services. In KNU areas, the Karen Department of Health and Welfare served a population of around 190,000 people through sixty-one clinics, and also provided medical services in harder-to-reach areas and refugee camps. It employed over seven hundred health workers. In KIO areas, the KIO Health Department operated twelve hospitals and sixty-one rural health centers, staffed with more than a thousand people. The KIO abandoned one hospital and twenty-one rural health centers in northern Shan State after the conflict resumed. But the KIO Health Department also extended care to more than eighty thousand internally displaced persons (IDPs) living in nineteen camps in KIO areas. The NMSP, the SSPP, the RCSS, and the CNF offered more limited services. The Mon National Health Committee operated only nineteen clinics and provided essential health care services to Mon IDPs in Mon State, Kayin State, and Tanintharyi Region. In southern Shan State, the RCSS's Shan State Development Foundation managed a clinic in each of the five Shan IDP camps in RCSS territory along the Thai-Myanmar border. In northern Shan State, the SSPP had at least one clinic for civilians. The other EAOs of Shan State, which also controlled small parts of the territory, also had some limited social services. In Chin State, the CNF operated a few mobile clinics and offered more comprehensive health services near its headquarters in Thantlang, but little else in other areas.[66]

Once the transition to civilian rule began, the Union government considerably expanded funding to the Ministry of Health, which was historically underfunded. It developed new policies to strengthen the system and expand its coverage, but it generally failed to consult EAO health care services or local communities. Government health care services often overlapped with those of the EAOs. This duplication helped the government undermine the EAOs' services, as it also had the capacity to provide better care. Furthermore, the government often looked down on the EAOs' services. One senior-level KNU leader in Bago Region, for instance, noted that "when we cooperated with government doctors, they tended to see our health care workers as their subordinates who should carry their bags."[67] And when they did attempt to streamline and cooperate, ethnic representatives felt overwhelmed by government and military negotiators who were, according to another KNU leader, "fully prepared and supported by technical experts."[68]

International nongovernmental organizations (INGOs) played an important role in health care and often made the problem worse. They built government clinics in several territories where the government had limited or no stable control, without consulting with EAO-linked health care providers.[69] These clinics were staffed mostly by Bamar doctors and nurses.[70] In some cases, the local people stayed away because of lack of trust. INGOs also helped normalize a centralized Naypyidaw-led health care system, which disregarded existing EAO-led ones. The International Red Cross, for instance, facilitated an agreement with the Ministry of Health and the Myanmar Peace Center to recognize EAO-trained Karen, Shan, Mon, and Kayah health care workers who completed a course package offered by a university in Thailand.[71] EAOs and the government saw this approach as mutually beneficial. It would help integrate EAO-trained health care workers into the government system and allow them to find employment in government-controlled areas, and it would also help the government address shortages of health care workers in the government's health care facilities. Si Thura and Tim Schroeder write that "the willingness of the Ministry of Health and Sports under the current NLD government to engage and recognize Ethnic Health Organizations has provided hope for future effective and politically sensitive health care arrangements during the interim period."[72] This arrangement, however, indirectly recognized the central government as the sole legitimate provider of health care, rather than strengthening an independent ethnic-controlled health care system.

Land Use and Ownership

Control over land management and land ownership is another area with competing, overlapping, and contradictory legal frameworks. Here, as in other policy areas, the existing practices also privileged central government policies and initiatives over those of the EAOs.

Under the 2008 constitution, all land is officially the property of the state. In 2012, however, the government adopted two new laws that created a de facto private property system. The Farmland Law allowed holders of land use certificates to exchange, inherit, lease, and use land for credit. The Virgin, Fallow, Vacant Land Management Law regulated land leasing considered "wasteland." This residual category comprised all land that had not been mapped as farmland, urban land, or reserved forest, for example. According to the government, wasteland would constitute more than 50 million hectares (around 123.5 million acres), which represented one-third of Myanmar's total land area.[73] Only about 4 million acres of that land were granted in concessions, which left the majority available to developers.[74] Under this law, domestic and foreign enterprises, government and nongovernment entities, could apply for up to a maximum of 50,000 acres, with leases of up to thirty years, plus extensions (5,000 acres at a time).

The new land ownership regime was particularly detrimental to ethnic minorities, who are often victims of land grabs. Of the 123.6 million acres of "available" land, more than 80 percent was located in the borderland ethnic states. Ethnic communities used much of this land according to customary or collective forms of land tenure that were not recognized by the law. Most farmers had no records for the land they farmed. An amendment to the 2012 law exempted "customary lands" from the law's provisions, but this category was not subsequently defined. It left decisions regarding what counted as customary land to officials. The law thus allowed authorities to take over land or let businesses and private companies claim land from communities that had, for generations, passed down land to their children through traditional or informal means.[75] The most vulnerable communities included those displaced by conflict, whose members already had problems accessing their land when they returned from hiding in nearby villages or refugee camps.

The postceasefire period was particularly conducive to land grabbing, as it happened while the national law had yet to recognize or converge with ethnic customary laws. The NCA was mostly silent on land and resource issues, except for a few points mentioning investment and environmental conservation to be conducted during the interim period. It also included some references to the protection of civilians, which included land confiscations and loss of livelihood.[76] As part of the Union Peace Dialogue Joint Committee, the NCA signatories established the Land and Environment Working Committee, which asked for a land policy and customary land recognition. In 2017–18, the second and third Union Peace Conferences reached twelve agreements on principles of land. One of the principles recognized local cultural heritage in land and another reduced central control. No mention was made, however, of decentralizing authority over the right to control, use, manage, and benefit from land and natural resources. Instead, as Kevin Woods observes, several of the principles reinforced Union-level laws and control, which worsened the situation for ethnic minority populations and EAOs.[77]

As a result, the KNU and other EAOs started to issue land titles to protect farmers under their area of control. Of these EAOs, the KNU went the furthest to enact a significant land policy and administer land tenure. The KNU policy recognized that people own the land instead of only land-use rights, as recognized by the government of Myanmar. It allowed households to own up to thirty acres with no time limit, though they would lose the right if the land was not used for more than three years. Unlike official laws in 2012 that did not recognize customary landholdings, the KNU land policy recognized local variations in customary laws and attempted to protect communal land ownership. Also, the policy tried to keep land held within a community by forbidding its sale (but allowing its lease) to outsiders, particularly during the immediate postceasefire period, in which there was great fear of an influx of new investments. The KNU policy also set much greater limits on the amounts of land that companies could own, with a maximum of fifty acres for lease periods of five, ten, or twenty years.[78] The NMSP also gave out land certificates, but it did not have a land policy or as comprehensive an administrative system. With assistance from local and foreign technical advisers to the KNU land policy, other armed groups, including the NMSP, KIO, and KNPP, started to develop their own land policies.[79]

EAOs' areas of control were only a small portion of their territory, which left communities in mixed-control areas particularly exposed to land grabbing. After 2012, the government and the Tatmadaw confiscated land for infrastructure development, natural resource exploitation, commercial agriculture, and military facilities. Land grabs were most severe in areas of mixed control, where EAOs were too weak to resist the imposition of the central government's land ownership regime. In such areas, SiuSue Mark found, the government attempted to give away much larger land concessions than elsewhere and failed to abide by the ceasefire agreements on land use management. For example, in Kaw Sa Lo village in the Hpa-An area, the government seized five hundred acres of land in 2008 from people who fled from war. The KNU issued land titles when people started to return a few years later, but the government refused to recognize these certificates and, according to Mark, "instead burned down their houses and arrested five village organizers after charging them with criminal code 447." In another case in Aseh Kaw Yin village in Hpa-An the government allegedly burned down houses and charged twenty-seven people with trespassing into forestland where the KNU had granted 8,413 acres to a community of 130 households to form a new village.[80]

Land grabbing also occurred in areas of active conflict, such as northern Rakhine State. As more than 750,000 Rohingya fled to Bangladesh and left their villages behind, numerous reports documented the Tatmadaw clearing land, destroying villages, and building new military bases on this land. Similar land grabbing took place in Shan and Kachin States, where conflict persisted. One agreement reached at the third session of the 21st Century Panglong Conference in July 2018 could possibly make things worse. This agreement recognized that "only citizens can own land in the country, and foreigners and illegal settlers must not own it directly or indirectly."[81] This was concerning, as many displaced ethnic minority populations did not have proper documents to apply for citizenship and, in the case of the Rohingya, were often considered foreigners even if they had lived in Myanmar for several generations.[82]

Finally, as in the health and education sectors, the government used land administration issues to discredit EAOs. The government prohibited INGOs from collaborating with the Karen Environment and Social Action Network, the Karen local NGO that provided technical support to the KNU on its land policy.[83] While the KNU land policy stood to protect vulnerable populations, it suffered from weak enforcement and implementation capacity due to lack of a regular budget and, in the KNU-controlled areas, the presence of Border Guard Forces that did not abide by the KNU's land policy. Within the KNU leadership, there was also growing disagreement and conflict over the maximum amount of land concessions to investors, and the reliance on extractive activities by some KNU officials to fund the group's operations.[84]

Bilateral and multilateral ceasefire agreements allowed the state to expand its presence and to present itself as an alternative, and superior, service provider in areas previously controlled by EAOs. Although the state and the EAOs were to continue to work on interim arrangements during the political dialogue, they were not equal players in this race for influence. The state used the interim period to normalize the central government's sovereignty over all the territory. With the NCA locking in the ability to do so, because of a lack of specific territorial demarcation and governance arrangements, the EAOs were undermined in their previous ability to offer services to their communities, thereby significantly reducing an important source of their legitimacy.

Beginning even prior to the transition to civilian government, the state pursued a strategy of outflanking EAOs and creating more direct linkages to local ethnic communities. EAOs lost the ability to tax their populations as part of ceasefire agreements. Although they could raise revenues through state policies that allowed them to run businesses, extract resources, and undertake development projects, the state increased its control over the terms of participating in these activities. In the end, many EAOs lost previous sources of funding, including some direct links to foreign humanitarian assistance that became channeled through the Myanmar state. Despite alternative revenue streams, these trends weakened their financial position.

Furthermore, the state sought to replace EAO services and expand its own reach, particularly in gray zones of joint control. The state built new infrastructure, such as roads and communication networks that allowed it to penetrate further into territory that EAOs had previously controlled. It then outflanked them by building state schools, hospitals, and clinics, thereby increasingly offering state services to replace those the EAOs had long established. With EAOs facing reduced revenues, shortages of human resources, and increasing challenges to ensure ethnic minority participation in the broader Myanmar economy, the state was able to attract local communities to participate in its expanded services, while facing little need to formally integrate EAO services or discuss how best to transition away from them. The longer the interim period lasted, and the longer a final settlement was discussed without agreement, the more the state could continue encroaching on ethnic minority territory and outflank the EAOs.

7
FRAGMENTATION, MARGINALIZATION, AND SUBJUGATION
Layering and Locking In Ethnic Recognition

The political liberalization of 2011–21 brought greater political freedoms but did little to deemphasize ethnicity in politics and society. In fact, in a reversal of past repression or assimilation, the state seemed to celebrate ethnic minority religion, culture, and language to a degree that was previously unthinkable. On paper, the gains for ethnic minorities were unparalleled in recent Myanmar history. This positive environment led to the revival of long-repressed identities and languages, the resurgence of Literature and Culture Committees to promote smaller and larger ethnic identities, demands for recognition and political accommodation, and the formation of new ethnic political parties.

Yet this apparent accommodation had pernicious outcomes. In previous chapters, we mostly emphasized the multiple strategies for containing, controlling, and channeling negotiations with the historically larger umbrella ethnic groups that had been fighting for greater federated power and autonomy for ethnic states. By contrast, this chapter analyzes the Myanmar state's strategy to reify and recognize a large number of smaller ethnic identities. Many of these are subgroups of the larger, historically recognized ones that have been given ethnic states.

We argue that the pluralization of ethnic claims, far from reducing Bamar hegemony, actually helped to strengthen it. The 2008 constitution both locked in and layered new institutions of representation that, combined with greater freedom of expression, led to a surge of ethnic claims by smaller groups. We examine the impact of four such changes: (1) the recognition of 135 ethnic nationalities and an attempt to use them as census categories; (2) the creation of ethnic affairs ministers; (3) the formation of self-administered zones (SAZs/SAD); and (4) the emergence of new ethnic political parties.

These new institutions perhaps did more to fragment ethnic nationalities and destroy political solidarity than decades of war. The goal remained the same—to undermine threats to political and territorial unity—but the method had changed. As groups fragmented into smaller units, they were less likely to represent a credible basis for self-government and meaningful political autonomy. They were also less likely to coordinate successfully and threaten the political dominance of the majority. Fragmentation and competition for accommodation also created interethnic tensions and conflicts, which gave greater leverage to the Tatmadaw to build new alliances with smaller groups and shift political cleavages in its favor. Although smaller groups greatly valued recognition under the 2008 constitution, they ironically made negligible gains, to the benefit of the state and the Bamar majority.

Meanwhile, the Union government ensured that questions of ethnic recognition, whether for small or large groups, were reduced to a very narrow scope of individual "rights." Despite allowing the proliferation of new ethnic claims, the Union government locked in, with the 2008 constitution and subsequent legislation, its own control over the definition of ethnic rights, whether relating to culture and language or more broadly to ethnic groups' capacity to protect their communities. It essentially deprived both ethnic states and minority groups of the levers of governance that could be used to preserve their communities and their ability to enhance their livelihoods. In essence, the government depoliticized ethnicity by reducing it to the superficial and narrow ability to teach local languages and celebrate local folklore. Finally, its border trade and economic policies created incentives for ethnic migrants to leave their states for urban centers or to seek opportunities abroad, while Bamar were largely brought to replace them, whether as state officials, workers in large businesses, or owners of small retail shops.

Layering and Locking In New Institutions of Recognition

Diversity in Myanmar is ubiquitous. Large ethnic nationalities, such as the Chin, Kachin, Shan, Karen, Kayah, Mon, and Rakhine, are more or less cohesive "imagined communities."[1] They are constructions based on deep-seated cultural cores, similar languages, and communal histories of collective suffering and struggle. They also contain important and sometimes overlooked internal diversity. Pan-ethnic *groups* are collections of clans, tribes, and dialects with more or less common affinities. And ethnic *states* have minority groups that are unrelated to the local majority. Multiculturalism as a sociological fact does not imply that ethnicity is politically mobilized. But the layering of new institutions, starting in the 1990s, created a new political environment that incentivized the political mobilization of smaller and larger minorities.

The first institutional layer, the seven ethnic minority states, has long been present. The 2008 constitution preserved the boundaries of the states created by previous ones: the Kachin, Shan, and Karenni (now Kayah) States, included in the 1947 constitution; the Karen state (now Kayin), upgraded from special division to state in 1952; and the Mon, Arakan (now Rakhine), and Chin States, created or upgraded from special divisions by the 1974 constitution. It is ambiguous, however, whether states were ever conceived as the basis of an ethnofederal state. None of the current ethnic states have boundaries that perfectly match those of the groups they are said to represent. Ethnic state borders were sometimes drawn with little understanding of the ethnic groups that inhabited the territory. In some places, it would have been simply impossible to design ethnically homogenous states, as ethnic groups are mixed, especially in transition zones. Aside from a few disputed areas, current states' boundaries form the basis of the seven major ethnic nationalities' political mobilization and aspirations.

In parallel, in the 1990s the government increasingly promoted the notion that Myanmar is composed of 135 ethnic nationalities. The origin of this number is unknown. Some have suggested that the three digits summed up equal the number nine, the military's lucky number. Perhaps more credibly, the number seems to be derived from the 1931 British census of India, which identified fifteen indigenous "race groups" and some 135 subgroups in Burma.[2] The colonial-era list, which was slightly different from the current one, was based on linguistic groupings. The 1953 census used a list adapted from previous periods but published data only for the seven main ethnic groups and four "foreign" groups.[3] A 1960 government publication listed forty-five groups and suggested that, if it was broken down, one could count 160 subgroups.[4] The government built a comprehensive list that contained 144 groups in preparation for the 1974 constitution, but it was not appended to the constitution. The 1983 census removed eight groups from the list and introduced the current number, 135 subgroups, but no official list was published until the census of 2014.[5] In sum, the number 135 appears extremely arbitrary and somewhat dubious.

The junta's intent was clear from the outset: the recognition of 135 "ethnic nationalities" provided a rationale to draft a new constitution that was not based on the "Big Seven."[6] In other words, the junta tried to recognize smaller ethnic groups that were not associated with any specific territories, while denying full recognition to those that were (i.e., the Big Seven). The junta proposed the 135 ethnic nationalities theory to curtail autonomist claims, and ethnic groups and observers widely perceived this recognition as what Mary Callahan calls "a confusing but tactical attempt to weaken non-Bamar solidarity around identity in a new game of 'divide-and-rule.'"[7]

Moreover, the 2008 constitution moved away from the "Big Seven" concept by layering within ethnic states another form of territorial autonomy for smaller nested ethnic groups: the five self-administered zones and one self-administered division (SAZs/SAD), which were absent from both the 1947 and 1974 constitutions. The 2008 constitution established the SAZs and SAD (Naga, Kokang, Danu, Palaung, Pa'O, and Wa), with limited legislative, executive, and judicial powers. The SAZs/SAD range from two to eight townships wide. Importantly, the constitution left entirely open the possibility of creating new zones, for groups that met certain conditions—namely, being one of the recognized national races, not already having a state, and forming a majority in at least two adjacent townships. Table 8 lists the SAZs in each state and region. As we can see, all SAZs and the SAD are located in Shan State, with the exception of Naga in Sagaing.

The constitution also introduced the position of ethnic affairs ministers (EAMs), another form of representation layered within ethnic states and SAZs. Unlike other members of parliament, who are elected in a single township, EAMs are elected from members of an ethnic group across the whole state or region. The goal of EAMs is unclear. At the National Convention, according to Melissa Crouch, the creation of EAMs "appeared to be a concession proposed for inclusion in the Constitution for ethnic nationalities that could not satisfy the criteria of a Zone."[8] A second hypothesis is that the government created the position of EAM as a means to ensure the representation of Bamar in most ethnic states.

TABLE 8 Layers of ethnic representation in the 2008 constitution

STATE/REGION	ETHNIC AFFAIRS MINISTER	SELF-ADMINISTERED ZONES/DIVISION
Shan	Bamar, Akha, Padaung, Lahu, Intha, Lisu, Kachin	Danu, Kokang, Pa'O, Palaung, Wa
Kachin	Bamar, Rawang, Lisu, Shan	
Kayin	Bamar, Mon, Pa'O	
Mon	Bamar, Pa'O, Karen	
Ayeyarwady	Karen, Rakhine	
Yangon	Karen, Rakhine	
Sagaing	Chin, Shan	Naga
Tanintharyi	Karen	
Bago	Karen	
Magway	Chin	
Mandalay	Shan	
Rakhine	Chin	
Kayah	Bamar	

Since they form substantial minorities in many ethnic states, Bamar have ministers in Kachin, Kayah, Kayin, Mon, and Shan States. The numbers support both hypotheses. A total of twenty-nine representatives were elected in 2010 as ethnic affairs ministers (see table 8). Shan State is the most diverse state, with seven representatives; Kachin has four; Kayin and Mon have three each; Ayeyarwady, Yangon, and Sagaing Regions have two; and Rakhine State, Kayah State, Magway Region, Mandalay Region, Bago Region, and Tanintharyi Region have one. The Kayin and the Bamar have five ethnic affairs ministers each. As with SAZs, the constitution leaves open the possibility of creating new EAM positions. Group rights and entitlements are also linked to group size: the constitution requires that, in order to obtain a minister, a group must be a national race and represent at least 0.1 percent of the total Myanmar population (roughly 51,400 people).

The electoral system is a final important layer with consequences for ethnic politics. The junta decided in early 2010 to adopt the first-past-the-post (FPTP) electoral system. FPTP is a system in which voters cast their vote for their preferred candidate in a constituency. The candidate with the highest number of votes, but not necessarily a majority, is elected. FPTP is a system that generally rewards the winning party by granting it more seats than its share of votes. Importantly, FPTP is also known to reward parties that have a geographically concentrated voter base (such as ethnic political parties) and punish parties with diffuse support across regions. In contrast to Indonesia, for example, Myanmar's constitution and lawmakers did not seek to prevent or ban the formation of local political parties, including ethnic or regional identity-based political parties. The FPTP system contributed, in 1990 and the 2010s, to the fragmentation of the party system along a multiplicity of ethnic groups, both smaller and larger ones.

Laying the Basis for Fragmentation

The state strategy to fragment and layer ethnic recognition was clear from the National Convention of the 1990s. The junta opened the door to numerous ethnic claims, and chose to include several of these in the 2008 constitution. It announced in 1994 that it was willing to provide a form of autonomy for national races at an intermediate level between townships and states while preserving a "three-step unity" (unity within unity within unity).[9] The offer, while aimed at undermining secessionism, ironically almost led to the collapse of the government's strategy. There was an explosion of demands for recognition, many of them requesting some form of territorial autonomy, such as self-administered zones.[10] Given the new recognition of 135 nationalities, notes Mary Callahan, it "almost derailed the regime's progress toward finalizing a new constitution back in 1996."[11] There were suddenly legitimate claims for having one's own territory, which the state had not foreseen.

In the end, more than twenty-five smaller ethnic nationalities made official demands or were considered for this new form of special autonomy, but the Tatmadaw and the Union government would in the end concede to only a few, adopting constraining rules for awarding them (e.g., a majority of the population in two adjacent townships). The map of Myanmar would have looked different if all of the proposals put forward in 1994 were adopted (see map 2). In Shan State, ten groups asked for an SAZ: the Lahu and Akha in the East; the Kokang, Wa, and Palaung (Ta'ang) in the North; and the Danu, Inthar, and Pa'O in the South. While some of them had led armed struggles in the past, others such as the Akha, Danu, Inthar, and Lahu had not. In addition, Kayan leaders asked for a special zone cutting across Shan, Kayah, and Kayin States and Mandalay Region, while Kachin representatives demanded an SAZ in the north of Shan State. Some other delegates also argued that a special zone for Bamar nationals should also be created. If all of these requests had been granted, twenty-nine of the fifty-five townships of Shan State (52 percent) would have been transformed into special zones for non-Shan groups.

Elsewhere, too, delegates pushed for autonomy. Ethnic representatives asked for SAZs for the Chin, Kuki-Chin, and Naga in Sagaing Division and for the Asho-Chin and Mro nationals that would cut across Magway Division and Rakhine State. In Chin State, the Khami asked for a special zone in the Paletwa Hills of the southern part of the state, while other Mro leaders asked for an SAZ that would cut across both Chin and northern Rakhine States. But a group of Shan leaders argued that if the Mro-Khami were to get their own special zone, many other groups should get one, such as Karen nationals in Ayeyarwady Region and Mon States, and Pa'O nationals in Kayin and Mon States. In Kachin State, the Tai-Leng (Shanni) asked for a special zone in the South, while the Lisu, Rawang, and Tai-hkamti (Shan) asked for a zone in the Putao area of northern Kachin. If all of these proposals had been adopted, eleven of the eighteen townships (61 percent) of Kachin State would have been transformed into special zones for non-Kachin groups.

On the ethnic minority side, the fragmentary consequences of claims to ethnic recognition and the further territorialization of these claims appeared to elude even the representatives of the larger ethnic groups. While the latter long aimed at creating strong, unified ethnic groups with claims to federated states, they nevertheless supported smaller group demands for recognition. For instance, a draft federal constitution prepared in the 2000s by ethnic armed organizations (EAOs) and civil society representatives included forms of territorial autonomy similar to the SAZs of the 2008 constitution—that is, any indigenous nationalities "that have not obtained the status of a National State [would obtain] . . . the right to

MAP 2. Proposed self-administered zones, National Convention (1994).
Note: Proposed SAZs are based on the 1994 proceedings of the National Convention, as reported in U Aung Toe, "Report to National Convention, Part I," Burma Library, 1994, https://www.burmalibrary.org/reg.burma/archives/199409/msg00064.html. The boundaries of Chin (Asho), Karen (in Ayeyarwady), Pa'O (in Kayin), and Tai-Lai (in Kachin and Sagaing) are tentative, since the townships included in these proposed SAZs were not named in the proceedings. Tentative boundaries are based on linguistic boundaries provided in Myanmar Information Management Unit, "Main Spoken Language of Myanmar, 2019," Myanmar Information Management Unit, accessed October 29, 2021, https://www.themimu.info/sites/themimu.info/files/documents/Ethnologue_Map_Main_Spoken_Languages_of_MyanmarNeighbour_MIMU1300v03_7Jan2019_A1.pdf. Today's approved self-administered zones differ slightly in shape and size from those proposed in 1994 and pictured on this map.

seek the formation of an autonomous region or a national area within the state or states where they reside" (Art. 53[c]). Whether this idea was borrowed from the National Convention is unclear, but the idea of granting autonomy below the state level was not included in the Panglong Agreement or the 1962 Shan Federal Proposal.

The idea also entered the draft state constitutions, also prepared by ethnic minority and civil society representatives in the 2000s. The Shan draft state constitution created two additional layers of territorial autonomy below the state level—a sort of federation within a federation. It created "sub-states for each dominant ethnic group" (Art. 51) and "special areas within sub-states" to protect the rights of minorities as small as five thousand people (Art 56). Wa representatives proposed that ethnic groups with more than three hundred thousand people should automatically be given a separate state, those with two hundred thousand should be given an SAD, those with one hundred thousand an SAZ, and small tribes with fewer than twenty thousand people should be granted separate townships to preserve their religion and traditions.[12] Although much less specific, the Kayah draft constitution also created substates, called provinces, which were areas "inhabited by indigenous peoples that share the same culture" (Art 40). The Mon draft constitution established "special areas" with additional powers, if a majority of the population of a township or three adjacent village tracts were not Mon (Art 56[b] and Art. 84). The Chin draft constitution required the state government to "draw local government boundaries so as to follow cultural, dialectical, and/or traditional administrative lines" (Art. 181).

From the 1990s and leading up to the adoption of the constitution of 2008, therefore, the junta had enabled ethnic minority claims to be made. Conveniently, their proposals for recognition and concessions cut across the established identities of the larger groups that already had ethnically based states.

The Escalation and Proliferation of Ethnic Claims

When the regime began to open up in 2011, a number of factors coalesced to further escalate ethnic groups' demands. While the 2008 constitution had been passed, it had barely begun to be implemented. The recognition of 135 ethnic nationalities, the creation of SAZs, and provisions for EAMs were realized at the same time that greater freedom of expression was allowed, and ethnic groups had several new channels through which to communicate their demands, including the ability to create new political parties.

Recognition as one of 135 nationalities became highly controversial once the new government announced that a planned census would use those ethnic categories to determine relative group size and location. This contentiousness was due to the fact that the 2008 constitution linked rights and privileges to group size. By doing so, it reinforced ethnic divisions and created an informal hierarchy of status and power between different groups (with different sizes), institutionalizing competition and triggering "zero-sum competition in which ethnic minorities competed for entitlements," according to a report by the International Crisis Group.[13] The list created fertile conditions for the emergence of new interethnic conflicts and cleavages.

While the junta had recognized the total number of groups in the 1990s and 2000s, it had remained silent on the exact identities of those groups. In preparation for the census, however, the government finally released the list of these 135 ethnic nationalities. As a result, larger *and* smaller ethnic groups intensified their mobilization. While ethnic leaders recognized the manipulative aspects of the list, the new categories and associated benefits became highly prized and a source of envy for recognition. Some complained that they were miscategorized, absent, or listed more than once. Others reported that they were divided into several groups or listed under a wrong name. Ironically, they also realized that the anomalies in the list and their consequences in terms of representation were part of a long-standing policy to water down the minority cause.[14]

The census and the provisions of the constitution triggered ethnic mobilization and generated two contradictory tendencies. The first was for groups to try and define their identity as broadly as possible, at times overlooking or suppressing internal diversity. "Nation building" among ethnic minorities ironically reproduced the similar homogenizing nationalism that they had fought against with their opposition to the assimilationist tendencies of Burmese nationalism. For instance, the Pwo and Buddhist Karen often criticized the domination of the Karen nationalist movement by the Sgaw and Christian Karen. They accused the Karen National Union (KNU) of promoting Sgaw culture as the "official" culture of the whole Karen nation.[15] Ashley South notes that "the Sgawization of Karen society in the borderlands and refugee camps resembles aspects of the military-dominated state's 'Burmanization' of national culture."[16] The Lisu and Rawang often condemned the Jinghpaw's ascendancy over the Kachin nationalist movement and the fact that they promoted their language, culture, and Baptist Christianity as "Kachin" culture, while excluding other groups from decision-making.[17] Local majorities pressured smaller minorities to surrender their identities and become part of larger groups in other ethnic states as well.

Against this backdrop, pan-ethnic leaders criticized the census and the constitution for threatening to "break up ethnic national identity" and to, as Joseph Schatz characterized it, "divide and dilute [ethnic groups'] political voice ahead of national elections."[18] For instance, the Chin National Action Committee urged Chin people *not* to identify with their clan or tribe when filling out the census form, but to identify themselves only through the pan-Chin category.[19] Kachin leaders contended that listing Kachin people by subgroup (Jinghpaw, Lisu, Rawang, Lhaovo, Lachid, and Zaiwa), rather than as a single group, was a strategy to foster division by creating what one group of analysts described as "ambiguities around the question of who is and is not Kachin."[20] They noted that, by contrast, Shan and Bamar were listed as single groups. The census, according to an article in the *Myanmar Times*, was thus perceived as "undermining long-standing efforts to foster a sense of pan-Kachin unity."[21] Similarly, the appointment of EAMs for the Lisu and Rawang, two Kachin subgroups, was already unpopular among Kachin nationalist leaders. According to the Transnational Institute, they considered it an attempt to "deepen fractures within the larger group," and to recognize Lisu and Rawang identities as entirely distinct. They were backed by increasing evidence that the EAM policies and their inconsistencies were applied to minority groups partly as a divisive tool. In some cases, the pan-ethnic group was used as the basis for assigning EAMs; for example, the "Chin," rather than the Mro, Khumi, Asho, or any other Chin subgroups, were given an EAM in Magway, Sagaing, and Rakhine. But elsewhere, the identity of the subgroup was used, such as the Lisu in Shan State, a group considered to be part of "Kachin."[22]

The second, opposite tendency was to define groups as narrowly as possible. Liberalization allowed ethnic minority groups to create or revive their cultures—for instance, through the formation of Literature and Culture Committees that greatly helped to enhance the teaching of local languages and histories. Liberalization also allowed ethnic minorities to revive their languages, express their cultures publicly, and hold national day celebrations and festivals. But the census offered even greater rewards for ethnic minorities that were historically marginalized. Since the threshold to obtain an EAM was particularly low (only fifty-one thousand people required), ethnic leaders from smaller groups had strong incentives to mobilize around a narrow identity in the hope of garnering enough members to be recorded in the census. Furthermore, the government opened the door to a proliferation of narrow ethnic identities. Ethnic groups that felt excluded from existing census categories were invited to pick the "Other" category, under the code 914. Khine Khine Soe, director of the Population Department of the Union government, revealed that "nearly 100 distinct ethnic groups were recorded under the 914 designation."[23] The large number of "Others" showed not only the proliferation but also the increasing politicization of identities in the context of the 2014 census.

One consequence of this quest for recognition was the proliferation of ethnic-based political parties. In part, the FPTP system created incentives for ethnic groups to form political parties, and rewarded those with geographically concentrated voter bases. The number of political parties with ethnic minority names increased from thirty-three to forty-eight between 1990 and 2020, with an all-time high in 2015 (fifty-one parties). In 2015, twenty-one parties competed under the names of the large pan-ethnic groups, or the Big Seven (see table 9). Another thirty competed under the names of smaller minority groups. Among these smaller political parties, several were hoping to represent groups that were rightly or wrongly considered "subgroups" of larger ones, such as the Zomi and Khumi in Chin State, and the Lisu and Lhaovo in Kachin. Although some parties

TABLE 9 Ethnic political parties, 1990 and 2015 elections

STATE/REGION	PAN-ETHNIC GROUPS ("BIG SEVEN")			SMALL ETHNIC OR SUBETHNIC GROUPS		
	GROUP	YEAR		GROUP	YEAR	
		1990	2015		1990	2015
Shan	Shan	2	2	Akha	0	1
				Danu	1	2
				Intha	1	2
				Kokang	2	2
				Lahu	1	1
				Pa'O	1	2
				Ta'ang	1	1
				Wa	1	2
				Shanni	0	1
Rakhine	Rakhine	5	3	Kaman	1	1
				Mro	1	3
				Daignet	0	1
				Khami	0	1
Kachin	Kachin	5	4	Lisu	1	1
				Lhaovo	0	1
				Tai Leng	0	1
Chin	Chin	1	3	Zomi	1	1
				Khumi	0	1
				Asho	0	1
Kayah	Kayah	1	1	Kayan	1	1
Kayin	Karen	3	5			
Mon	Mon	1	3			
Sagaing				Naga	1	0
Tanintharyi				Dawei	0	1
Total		18	21		14	28

Source: Khin Kyaw Han, "1990 Multi-party Democracy General Elections," *Democracy Voice of Burma*, accessed February 25, 2022, https://www.burmalibrary.org/docs4/1990_multi-party_elections.pdf; results of elections in 2015, Union Elections Commission/Myanmar, accessed January 15, 2021, http://www.uec.gov.mm; VOTE MM. 2020, "Political Parties," accessed December 6, 2020, https://www.votemm.info/parties?fbclid=IwAR2-Qj1IdIuv-Uw-ALBMr9dyFlIfJp9cy5m477DvywdsqEtpH1wtYWHr6nAwY.

Note: This table lists registered ethnic political parties in two categories (pan-ethnic and smaller/subethnic) based on the names of their political parties. There is a small possibility that a few political parties use pan-ethnic names but in fact represent a smaller or a subethnic group, or that a few parties represent particular minority groups without having an ethnically or religiously connotative name. These parties would not be included in this table.

merged in 2020, the portrait was similar; many ethnic groups still had at least one, often several, parties competing for a narrow share of votes. The table shows the multiplication of parties from the 1990 to the 2015 elections, especially in the category of small ethnic or subethnic minority parties (from fourteen to twenty-eight parties). In 2020, the numbers of both pan-ethnic parties and subethnic minority parties stayed almost the same, at twenty (-1) and twenty-eight (-2), respectively.

Another consequence of the constitution's new ethnic categories and institutions was the resurgence of identities that had never been politically mobilized or that had been suppressed for a long time. The Shanni, also known as the Red Shan or Tai-Leng, have an estimated three hundred thousand members, but the community, according to U San Pyae, a Shanni MP, is composed of groups "with little cohesion," living "in different regions [and who are generally] unaware of each other."[24] They remained quiet for most of Myanmar's recent history, especially after 1972, when the military imprisoned one of their leaders for treason. During the war, Shanni communities were often caught between the Tatmadaw and the Kachin Independence Organization (KIO), which incited Tai-Leng leaders to side with the Tatmadaw for protection. While they used the space offered by the transition to revive their language, which had almost fallen out of use, they also lobbied during the census period to have their ethnicity recognized and used on national registration cards.[25] San Pyae admitted that "identity had not been particularly important to the Shanni in the past but the impending census has brought the matter to the forefront of leaders' minds."[26] Identity building became even more of a priority during the 2015 elections, as two new parties competed for Shanni votes: the Tai-Leng (Red Shan) Nationalities Development Party and the Shanni and Northern Shan Ethnic Solidarity Party.

The political context also encouraged the Shanni to militarize. At the 21st Century Panglong Conference, Red Shan leaders asked for the creation of a Shanni State covering three districts of Kachin State and five of Sagaing Region.[27] Other, more ambitious proposals even included parts of Mandalay Region and Shan State. But with little political success, the Shanni rapidly turned to armed struggle. Shanni leaders, and an increasing number of ethnic minorities during that period, sensed that they had, as a Shanni activist from Sagaing Region puts it, "lost [their] ethnic rights because [they] did not have an armed group to represent [them]." The Shanni created the Shanni Nationalities Army in 2016 to, as a retired Shanni soldier explains, gain "a more prominent role in Burma's political dialogue" and, an ICG report points out, to get a "seat at the negotiating table in the peace process."[28]

Among the Chin, similar renegotiations of identity also emerged as a consequence of the 2008 constitution's new incentives for ethnic recognition and of the politicization of the census. The Chin are extremely diverse, a loose association of eight main groups with several hundred tribes and clans. This fragmentation became increasingly visible during the 2015 elections, in which three parties competed for pan-Chin votes while nine smaller parties competed for the votes of specific tribes. Among them, the Zomi have been among the most vocal opponents of a pan-Chin identity. During the census, Zomi leaders rejected their classification as Chin, asked for an independent census code, and urged Zomi to declare themselves "Others" rather than Chin. They also pushed to have the Zomi language more widely recognized. The Zomi's census activism was also an electoral strategy. Not one but two political parties competed for Zomi votes in the 2015 and 2020 elections. In the end, the Zomi Congress for Democracy was the only ethnic party elected in Chin State in the 2015 elections.[29] Like their Zomi counterparts, Kuki leaders criticized the census for dividing them into three tribes and urged Kuki to declare themselves "Others," "in order to protect their rights in line with the Constitution," according to one report.[30] The Kuki population, which was estimated at forty thousand in 1990, was very close to the threshold required for gaining an EAM, which they hoped to secure as a result.

The area that straddles Chin and Rakhine States has also witnessed extensive ethnic mobilization. The Khumi, who dominate the Paletwa Hills in southern Chin State, have long rejected being lumped into the Chin category, as they deny any similarity with the northern Chin communities.[31] And the northern Chin groups do not consider the Khumi part of their identity either. Khumi leaders mobilized to ensure that Khumi nationals did not identify as a subcategory of Chin in the census.[32] Political competition also played a role in census activism, as two parties vied for Khumi votes and a total of six parties (ethnic and nonethnic) competed for seats in the Paletwa Hills alone.[33] In northern Rakhine State, the Mro-Khami (closely related to the Khumi of southern Chin State) also mobilized for proper census recognition, rejecting the name "Khami" as a historical aberration. Mro leaders estimated their population to be around one hundred thousand people in Chin and Rakhine States, well above the threshold to deserve at least an EAM under the 2008 constitution, and perhaps even an SAZ.[34] Moreover, three Mro political parties ran in both the 2015 and 2020 elections.

As a result, claims for recognition and ethnic mobilization rose, and with them new tensions and potential for conflict. In Shan State, the 2008 constitution gave an SAZ to the Danu, Pa'O, Palaung, Kokang, and Wa, and an ethnic affairs minister to the Bamar, Kachin, Akha, Padaung, Lahu, Lisu, and Intha. Shan politicians feared that the creation of the SAZs was a government strategy to undermine the integrity of the Shan State. They had reason to fear this, as ethnic claims rapidly spiraled. Many of the groups that had obtained an EAM questioned the government's census and ratcheted up their demands while conducting their own population count.³⁵ The Mongla army asked the government to create an SAZ for the Akha; Intha leaders asked for an SAZ around Inle Lake; the Lahu Democratic Party requested an SAZ for the Lahu; and Kayan leaders demanded an SAZ that covered parts of Kayah and Shan States.³⁶ As one participant in the 21st Century Panglong Conference lamented, "It looks like all the 55 townships of Shan State will [soon] be gone.... There will be nothing left for the Shan people." The constitution even triggered the mobilization of smaller groups that had not yet mobilized. For instance, the Taung Yoe in southern Shan State used to identify as Shan. But in 2016, Taung Yoe leaders initiated a new census in the hope of tallying enough people to qualify for an EAM in the state government. There were fifteen thousand Taung Yoe, but its leaders claimed that there were actually sixty thousand to one hundred thousand.³⁷

In the same escalating spiral, most of the groups that were given an SAZ in the 2008 constitution began to ask for a state or the right to expand their territory into new townships. The Wa, Pa'O, and Palaung (Ta'ang) each requested to transform their SAZ into a full-blown ethnic state, which would have meant substantial territorial losses for Shan State.³⁸ The United Wa State Army (UWSA) demanded control over the region south of the Wa SAD which it claimed had been its land since at least the twelfth century. In reality, the UWSA occupied some of these areas from the late 1990s as result of a campaign of forced annexation and relocation of local populations, especially Lahu nationals.³⁹ Palaung leaders sought to expand their territory into two additional townships (from two to four).⁴⁰ Territorial disputes between Shan and Palaung armed organizations led to several clashes after 2015, the year the NCA was signed.⁴¹

In some cases, under the Tatmadaw's patronage, smaller ethnic groups formed militias that compromised larger groups' attempt to foster cohesion and more united identities. The Tatmadaw encouraged and benefited from such interethnic tensions. It had long supported and sponsored militias, whether they were based on ethnicity or created at the village or village tract level as an extension of their security apparatus. Small ethnic militias were sometimes created in response to tensions between EAOs and local ethnic minorities. In Kayin State, for instance, the Democratic Karen Buddhist Army is one of the most notorious militias and was originally a splinter group from the Karen National Union. It was formed by Buddhist, mostly Pwo-Karen officers who were dissatisfied with the dominance of Christian Sgaw-Karen within the KNU. The Tatmadaw subsequently collaborated with the Democratic Karen Buddhist Army, as it was known before its conversion into a Border Guard Force, to overrun the KNU's Mannerplaw headquarters in 1995.⁴²

In Kachin State, the Tatmadaw supported the Rawang, a Kachin tribe in the Putao area, after conflicts arose between the Rawang and the Jinghpaw, Kachin's majority group, which led to a split in the Kachin nationalist movement in the 1960s. In 2007, the Tatmadaw's active sponsorship of the Rawang led to the creation of the Rebellion Resistance Force, which was instrumental in keeping the KIO out of northern Kachin State. In subsequent years, pro-Tatmadaw militias were formed among Lisu, Shanni, and Lhaovo communities, all to oppose the KIO's dominance in Kachin State. Likewise, progovernment militias in Shan State, by engaging in business and controlling territories, assisted the Tatmadaw by serving as important sources of intelligence and armed opposition to established EAOs. Progovernment militias and splinter groups had direct violent conflict with the Shan State Progressive Party and the Restoration Council of Shan State.[43]

Other groups also tried to expand their territory. Naga leaders claimed two more townships—Khamti and Homalin—to include in their SAZ, on the basis of the high proportion of Naga among their populations. They cited historical records to prove that the two townships were part of the former Naga Hills District. Residents in Homalin, however, rapidly rejected the idea, splitting the region along ethnic lines and threatening to escalate the dispute into violent conflict.[44] Similarly, the Arakan Army (AA) claimed, as part of Rakhine State, the Paletwa Hills, a region of Chin State home to just under sixty-five thousand people. The AA asserted that the disputed territory in fact rightfully belonged to Rakhine and was included in Chin State only after independence. In January 2020, it sparked further controversy by saying that the Khumi, who are recognized as Chin, were actually a Rakhine subgroup.[45] An increasing number of Rakhine Buddhists were moving and settling in the area, a form of colonization of the region.[46] The situation became so tense that the Mro even discussed with the Tatmadaw the possibility of forming a new militia unit, while Chin people residing in Paletwa looked to the Tatmadaw for protection against the AA. This is very rare in Myanmar.[47]

Kayan leaders in Kayah State urged the government to consider them a separate ethnic group rather than Karenni.[48] Kayan people, like the Karenni (an ethnic group in Kayah State), are related to the Karen, the largest ethnic group in the region, which has its own state as well. Four of the main Kayan subgroups—the Ka Khaung, Ka Ngan, Lahta, and Gedot—asked to be joined together under the same census code, "Kayan." Their leaders sought to gain an EAM, like the Kayan in Shan State. But in Kayah State, individual Kayan groups were not sufficiently numerous to obtain automatic representation under the 2008 constitution. When united, however, they represented over sixty thousand people and became eligible.[49] After the census, Kayan leaders once more ratcheted up their demands and, as in the 1990s, asked for the creation of a new Kayan SAZ, carved out of Pekon Township in Shan State and Demawaso Township in Kayah State.[50] As Lieutenant Colonel Win Maung from the Kayan New Land Party told the

Myanmar Times, "The development of our race has to be undertaken by us," and since "there are already other SAZs in Shan State ... I don't see why we can't also have [one]."[51]

Finally, the Rohingya were also victims of the politicization of new identities, categories, and territorial claims. While the Rohingya conflict had complex causes that are beyond the scope of this chapter, the 2008 constitution certainly exacerbated the conflict. The Rohingya mostly resided in parts of northern Rakhine State. Since World War II, they had often been targeted and persecuted, but violence against them reached unprecedented levels after 2012. In May of that year, the rape and murder of a Buddhist woman by Rohingya men sparked two waves of violence in northern Rakhine State and around the provincial capital, Sittwe. Riots then spread to more than twenty different towns in central and lower Myanmar throughout 2013 and 2014. The targets were Muslims, rather than Rohingya per se.[52] After a short lull, violence against the Rohingya climaxed in 2016 and 2017 when the Tatmadaw launched a counterinsurgency operation in northern Rakhine State, allegedly to dislodge members of the Arakan Rohingya Salvation Army.[53] The attacks led to the brutal killing, rape, and beating of more than one hundred thousand Rohingya, in what the UN human rights chief, at a Council's meeting, called a "textbook example of ethnic cleansing," and forced more than seven hundred thousand Rohingya to flee to Bangladesh.[54]

While the causes and consequences of the violence are much broader, the census nevertheless was extremely controversial in Rakhine State and became a catalyst for the violence against the Rohingya.[55] Rohingya, the ethnicity claimed by northern Rakhine Muslims, is not among the official 135 national races. Since the 1970s, the Rohingya have been gradually deprived of citizenship, even its lesser forms (naturalized and associated), through subsequent state-sponsored citizenship and identity documentation verifications. The 1982 citizenship law officialized this marginalization by requiring membership in an officially recognized national race a *sine qua non* for full citizenship, even though the government had issued no list of national races prior to 2014. In the lead-up to the 2015 elections, the prospect that Muslims in Rakhine State could self-identify as Rohingya in the census stirred up concerns in Rakhine political circles and the broader Rakhine community. They worried that if the Rohingya gained recognition as a national race, they would claim an SAZ, or worse, an autonomous state.[56] Rohingya represented a third of the state's population, thus potentially qualifying for such representation.

Furthermore, given their numbers, the Rohingya represented a genuine electoral threat to Rakhine nationalist parties. In the months leading up to the census, therefore, Rakhine politicians became increasingly worried that the Muslims of Rakhine State would use the code 914 to self-identify as Rohingya. As a result, Rakhine leaders organized numerous protests against the Rohingya and threatened a boycott of the census. The government eventually barred Muslims in Rakhine from using the code 914, and removed voting privileges from most of them while banning Rohingya political parties. They also denied the existence of a Rohingya ethnicity and considered them instead as foreigners, as Bengali. Although they were not the only cause, these perceived threats contributed to Rakhine nationalists' hatred of the Rohingya and their role in the deadly religious feud and eventual ethnic cleansing.

As groups fragment into smaller units, the risks of interethnic conflict increase. Ever-smaller groups are also less likely to represent a credible basis for self-government and meaningful political autonomy. Studies from around the world have shown that the usefulness of territorial autonomy is conditional on striking the right balance in terms of unit size. Had the smaller ethnic minority groups achieved their goals, their push to obtain their own state or SAZs might have undermined their capacity to protect and enhance the status of their group. Federated units with populations that are too small might not be sustainable: they might not be able to tax, generate enough revenue, or have the capacity to offer services. With little capacity, territorial autonomy can fail, or worse, lead to local units' greater dependency on the center.[57] The same is true of several of Myanmar's SAZs, and could certainly have been the case had they multiplied. In the end, the multiplying calls for territorial autonomy served the Union government's broader goal of rendering political autonomy meaningless and reinforcing, in the process, its own leverage and power.

Depoliticizing and Subjugating Ethnic Power

The mobilization surrounding ethnic recognition and territorial accommodation produced very few concrete results. Even though groups made strong claims to obtain EAMs, SAZs, or other benefits, none of these new forms of accommodation of ethnic minorities produced meaningful powers or resources to protect group culture and language, or enhance their livelihoods. In fact, beyond mostly symbolic and superficial gains, the reality on the ground showed dramatic transformation with lasting adverse consequences for the long-term viability and sustainability of ethnic minority groups. With the implementation of the 2008 constitution, as the political dialogue dragged on with few concrete results, Myanmar's economic and political liberalization intensified migration, with many ethnic minorities fleeing continued poverty to cities or mostly abroad, while Bamar in quest of new opportunities (and sometimes employment) moved into newly opened ethnic minority areas. With discrimination in hiring and other areas, Bamar often moved in while ethnic minorities fled. Realities on the ground therefore showed that, even if gains were eventually made in protecting group culture and language, and providing new powers and resources for development, the rapid demographic changes may make some of these accommodations obsolete.

The 2008 constitution recognized Burmese as the only official language and the main medium of education, government, and justice (Art. 450). It gave states and SAZs neither the power to adopt and implement an official language policy nor the power to manage their culture or education. Schedule 1 of the constitution gave all powers in education to the Union government (Arts. 9[a] to 9[e]), and no digressions from these provisions were made during the Union Solidarity and Development Party and National League for Democracy (NLD) mandates.[58] The constitution also mandated that the Union, not the states, "assist to develop language, literature, fine arts and culture of the National races" and "promote socio-economic development including education . . . of less-developed National races" (Arts. 22[a] and 22[d]). The Ethnic *Rights Protection Law* (2015) was presumably designed to safeguard the rights, privileges, and distinct cultural identities of "indigenous populations," but it was essentially symbolic, as it defined "rights" narrowly. It gave no additional powers to ethnic states and merely required the government to "inform, coordinate, and perform with the relevant ethnic groups in cases of development works, major projects, businesses and extraction of natural resources."[59]

The law also undermined the state-level EAMs by creating a Union-level Ministry of Ethnic Affairs (see chapter 3), even though the pressure to create the ministry came from the newly created twenty-nine EAMs. The 2008 constitution had created EAMs, but EAMs appointed under the Thein Sein government lacked their own designated budget and ministry. Rather than decentralize power, however, the ministry, according to the *Myanmar Times*, decided "to bring all official activity relating to ethnic issues under the jurisdiction of a *Union*-level . . . ministry" (emphasis added).[60] Therefore the Union, rather than state governments, was granted the responsibility to protect ethnic minority cultures.

Furthermore, by reducing language and cultural preservation to a narrow scope, and then failing to offer additional levers of governance to enhance groups' abilities to manage their affairs, the Union government essentially subjugated ethnic powers and depoliticized them to a degree that rendered them almost meaningless. As explained in chapter 5, the government's new education policy, adopted in 2014 and amended in 2015, allowed the teaching of ethnic languages as subjects and as classroom languages (not to be confused with languages of instruction). The law provided a limited role for local governments to develop the curriculum in their region, working from a single unique national curriculum but adjusting part of it to the local context (Art. 39[g]). But the constitution did not grant local governments the right to adopt policies to protect language, such as state official languages, quotas, affirmative action, and residency requirements for minorities in the civil service, education, or labor sectors. As Joshua Fishman observes, "Nowhere in the world have major programs of language maintenance, revival, or revitalization succeeded if their major thrust was on the school rather than other, more primary social processes."[61] There was no provision to allow local governments to compel or reward their residents to speak the local language, and nothing to curb the use of the Burmese language either. The constitution therefore failed to create the conditions that would keep minority culture and language alive. As shown in many other parts of the world, in multilingual contexts one language will invariably offer more opportunities and a higher status than other languages, which may drive weaker languages into attrition and extinction as they gradually or rapidly lose their speakers.[62] Members of minority groups always consider the trade-off between speaking their language to enhance their identity and speaking the dominant language to obtain jobs and social mobility. The Union government's policies, from education and employment to the use and teaching of local languages, reaffirmed the primacy of the Burmese language and the essential need for ethnic minority groups to learn and master it for any advancement, while relegating local languages to a cultural niche.

In response, ethnic minorities offered little resistance. Neither language nor culture featured in any of the first four rounds of the Panglong Conference. And of the fifty-two principles agreed to at the conference, education and languages were nowhere to be found. In fact, ethnic minority representatives increasingly embraced a more narrow, depoliticized conception of ethnic recognition and rights, and played into the Union government's hands. They adopted the concept of mother tongue–based multilingual education (MTB MLE), summarized in the Naypyidaw Principles of 2014 and promoted by international actors such as UNESCO.[63] MTB MLE was conceived as a transitional program in which children would learn their mother tongue in primary school and switch to the Burmese language as they enter secondary school.[64] Shan, Mon, Karen, and Kachin representatives, the National Network for Education Reform, and the Ethnic Nationalities Affairs Center, among others, pushed hard for the adoption of MTB MLE to break the model and move beyond the Bamar-dominated education system. But MTB MLE conceived of cultural preservation as an individual, rather than collective, right, and stopped short of questioning central government control over education, language, and culture.

Meanwhile, other institutions created to enhance ethnic minority powers and representation were also largely ineffective. Although many groups fought for an EAM, which was seen as second best (after getting a state or an SAZ), they too, achieved little. The 2008 constitution recognized the EAMs as state-level ministers, but most regional cabinets treated them as simple elected members of parliament. The Thein Sein government gave them lower salaries and privileges, and they were unable to attend cabinet meetings and lacked their own designated budget. In response to their poor treatment, the EAMs brought their case to the Constitutional Tribunal, which confirmed their status as regional ministers and helped them obtain slightly more influence. The Union government initially ignored the ruling but eventually conceded. As a result, EAMs gained the status, salaries, and privileges given to other state cabinet ministers, including their own separate budget at the Union level and guarantees that they would be consulted for major development programs and extractive activities in their respective areas. After that, EAMs slightly increased their power, and some were able to work toward the preservation of their ethnic group's culture, literature, and identity; promote their group's welfare and development; advocate for their constituents; and help mediate between armed groups and the government.[65] Aside from successfully pressuring the government to create a Union-level Ministry of Ethnic Affairs, the EAMs' achievements remained largely limited, and their Union ministry understaffed, underfunded, and lacking in autonomy.

A by-product of more liberalization and the new electoral system, ethnic political parties created greater representation but achieved little to advance ethnic interests. Ethnic parties that target small groups tend to have weak organizational and few material resources. Among larger groups, the FPTP system not only diluted ethnic political voices but also created coordination problems that further undermined their capacity to gain leverage. In both 2015 and 2020, ethnic political parties failed to win more than 15 percent of the seats in the national legislature. An FPTP electoral system forces coordination between parties, which is difficult with over forty different ethnic parties. Ethnic alliances generally failed to minimize vote splitting, as they were unsuccessful at reaching "noncompete" agreements between parties from the same ethnic group. Nor were they able to agree on mergers with parties from the same ethnic group, with some exceptions in 2020. They also failed to reach a noncompete agreement with the NLD, which decided to run for every seat in the country, to the disadvantage of ethnic parties. Voters supported the NLD for strategic reasons (the "bandwagon effect"—that is, the desire to vote for the perceived winning party) or because they felt the NLD offered a more compelling program in comparison to ethnic parties, which tend not to be comprehensive.[66] Moreover, Myanmar's constituency structure also prevented ethnic parties from winning. Constituencies are based on townships, which give 60 percent of the seats to regions in central Myanmar, where Bamar are a majority. In these Bamar-majority regions, it is virtually impossible for ethnic minority parties to win seats. In the seven ethnic states, ethnic minorities are a majority but constituencies are often so multiethnic that it is difficult for one ethnic party to win a plurality of votes, even with strong support from the party's community. So, even with parties, ethnic minority groups have been unable to exercise much leverage to gain more power and resources.

Beyond mostly symbolic and superficial gains, the reality on the ground showed dramatic transformation with lasting negative consequences for the long-term viability and sustainability of ethnic minority groups. States failed to generate local development to the benefit of the groups they were "meant" to represent, with important consequences for population movements. The 2014 Myanmar Population and Housing Census revealed that more than 9.2 million people, almost 20 percent of the total population, had migrated during their lifetime (see figure 2). The most important driver of migration was the wide gap between the economic development of central Myanmar and its periphery, a development that overwhelmingly favored urban areas located in Bamar-majority areas. Yangon and Mandalay had booming industry and service sectors, which attracted migrants. Ethnic minority states' GDP per capita remained, with the exception of Mon State, much lower than the national average.[67]

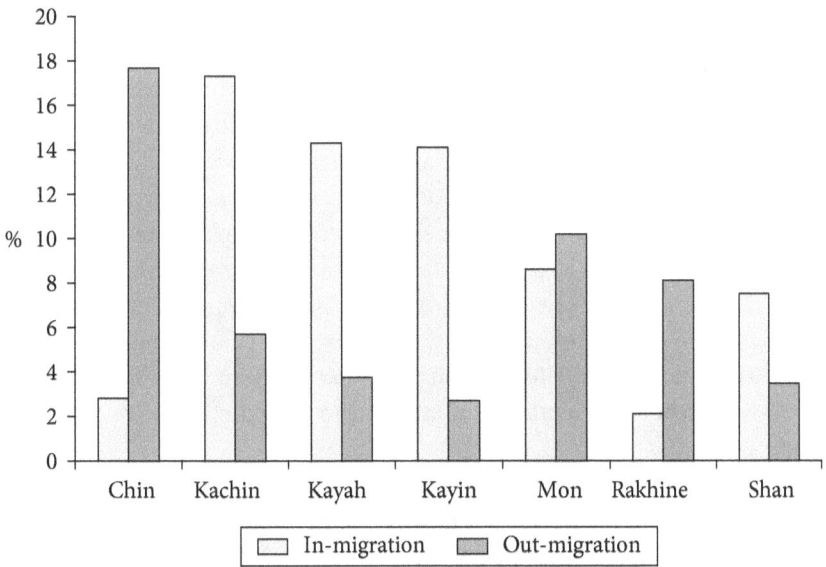

FIGURE 2. In- and out-migration in Myanmar's ethnic states.
Note: **In-migration**: percentage of the state population born outside the state at the time of the census. **Out-migration**: percentage of the state-born population who lived outside their state at the time of the census.
Source: Department of Population, *2014 Myanmar Population and Housing Census*.

Migration not only transformed the demographic makeup of ethnic states, but also contributed to cultural erosion. At least one million people born in an ethnic state lived elsewhere, mostly in the Bamar areas of Mandalay, Sagaing, and Yangon. Chin, Mon, and Kayah states had been "emptying" at a much faster pace than other states, and lost about a third of their state-born residents to out-migration. Yangon received the bulk of that ethnic migration. When not leaving the country, ethnic migrants joined highly heterogeneous communities, often in informal settlements on the outskirts of those cities. In these areas, people tended to converge toward Burmese as a lingua franca. Over time, more than government polices alone, a more open economy also fostered ethnic minority assimilation into the Burmese majority, mostly through the need to adopt the majority's language while gradually losing their own.

Ceasefires in ethnic areas also allowed greater migration of mostly Bamar-majority people into resource-rich ethnic areas, with negative consequences for ethnic minority languages and culture. According to the 2014 census, approximately one million people born in a Bamar-majority state lived in one of the seven ethnic states. Kachin, Kayin, and Kayah States were the largest recipients of out-of-state migrants, with 13 percent of the 2014 population born outside their state. The census did not provide data on ethnicity, so we cannot know for sure whether these migrants were actually ethnically Bamar, but ample evidence suggests that a significant proportion were. The conflict and lack of employment opportunities in Shan State, for example, drove many ethnic Shan away from the state, leaving their land behind. Afterward, according to a Shan journalist we spoke with, "a growing number of Bamar [reportedly] moved to Shan State near the China border, like in Namkhan or Muse, for example. There are so many Bamar people there that you do not see indigenous people anymore; it is like new colonies."[68] In central Shan State, the population is predominantly Bamar. "Bamar are shameless, they would do any jobs," said a Shan MP. "It is a form of internal colonialism. When they come, they bring their culture, their beliefs, and destroy local traditions."[69] Towns along the Myanmar-China and Thailand borders have also become multicultural hubs due to the influx of Bamar and other ethnic minorities.

Migration was facilitated, if not encouraged, by the government in a subtle policy that overwhelmed ethnic minorities. The government generally staffed its schools and hospitals with Bamar, who came and settled (some temporarily) in the state with their families. Sometimes a lack of graduates among ethnic minority populations motivated these hires, but other times it was a policy to send Bamar to ethnic states, informally called a "punishment policy." Bamar civil servants had to accept a posting in one of the ethnic states if they wanted a promotion or if they performed badly.[70] Towns under government control also attracted migrants from other parts of the country—even if surrounding areas remained under the influence of EAOs.[71] The construction of new long-distance roads opened up areas to outsiders and helped bring migrants who then competed for land and business opportunities.[72] Recently arrived migrants from other parts of the country generally owned businesses along new roads, and outsiders tended to monopolize new commercial opportunities.[73]

Private companies, especially when owned by Bamar, mostly employed nonlocals. In Kachin State, the numbers were astonishing. Thousands of migrants were brought in from central Myanmar and Rakhine State to work in Chinese-owned banana plantations around Myitkyina, and one hundred thousand to work in the jade mining industry.[74] Ahead of the 2015 elections, many were apparently given residency permits to officialize their status with the hope that they would support the Union Solidarity and Development Party.[75] In Mon State, a large number of workers came from the central dry zone and the delta area to work in paddy fields and rubber and palm oil plantations to replace native Mon labor that migrated to Thailand. In Kayin State, Hpa-An's outskirts were swamped with daily-wage laborers, many of whom were Bamar, to replace Karen labor that migrated to Thailand.[76]

As a consequence, migration contributed to the erosion of minority languages and cultures over and above other threats. A survey conducted in 2018 by two of this book's authors in Chin, Kachin, Kayin, and Magway showed that ethnic languages have a lower status, a situation prone to language shift in favor of the dominant language (i.e., Bamar). Most respondents spoke their mother tongue at home, but, with the exception of Bamar, few spoke it exclusively outside their home, at the market or with state officials such as police officers, government employees, and school or hospital workers. As table 10 shows, less than a third of Chin, Karen, and Kachin could speak their mother tongue alone at the market in "their" own state. Some spoke other ethnic languages, but this most likely indicates the dominance of the Burmese language in the life of ethnic minority groups. Even fewer members of ethnic minority groups could speak their language with state officials.

The majority of respondents said that they valued learning their language (table 11). But aside from Bamar, few people thought that learning their language would be a source of social promotion, mobility, or career advancement. Many smaller minorities, according to Marie Lall, believe "that Burmese is the essential language for their children to be able to get good jobs and bring their families and communities out of poverty."[77] This mismatch between attachment to a language and its objective value is what eroded many languages over time. The survey was conducted in ethnic minority states, but it is reasonable to assume that speakers of minority languages in Bamar areas would find their language to be an even

TABLE 10 Mother tongue use in four states/regions of Myanmar

	"I SPEAK MY MOTHER TONGUE EXCLUSIVELY . . .		
	AT HOME." (%)	AT THE MARKET." (%)	WITH STATE OFFICIALS." (%)**
Bamar*	97.5	96.3	97.3
Chin in Chin State	96.6	30.6	23.5
Karen in Kayin State	88.1	17.8	10.7
Kachin in Kachin State	95.0	3.5	2.5

* In every state covered by the survey—i.e., Chin, Kachin, Kayin, and Magway.
** State officials include police officers, health care professionals, school staff (including teachers), and other front-line state officers.
Source: University of Toronto–MIPS Survey on the Delivery of Public Services in Chin, Kachin, Kayin, and Magway, 2019.

TABLE 11 Mother tongue and social promotion in Myanmar

	"MY MOTHER TONGUE IS . . .	
	IMPORTANT TO ME."	A SOURCE OF SOCIAL PROMOTION."
Bamar	80.6	62.1
Chin	86.9	21.8
Kachin	87.4	42.1
Karen	84.0	40.3

Source: University of Toronto–MIPS Survey on the Delivery of Public Services in Chin, Kachin, Kayin, and Magway 2019.

lesser source of social promotion. Minority languages, even those with larger number of speakers, have low status and are spoken in very limited areas.

Migration therefore contributed to reducing the power of numbers in ethnic states, while policies gave few tools to counter such large demographic effects. With states, SAZs, EAMs, and obtaining recognition contributing little to preserving language, culture, and even local abilities to protect communities and their rights, the influx of largely Bamar-majority people into ethnic states exacerbated the already clear decline in local languages and the erosion of local cultures.

This chapter has argued that the layering of new institutions of recognition, combined with the political liberalization of 2011–21, did more to neutralize ethnic minority groups than decades of war. The state partially reversed decades of repression and assimilation of ethnic minority identities by allowing them instead to celebrate and express their culture, religion, and language publicly. The constitution even created new layers of recognition and rights for ethnic minorities in the form of ethnic affairs ministers, self-administered zones, and ethnic minority states.

But this seemingly positive turn had pernicious effects. These new institutions recognized but also reified ethnicity and led to the explosion of demands for recognition and accommodation by both larger and smaller groups. Membership in an ethnic nationality, Nick Cheesman observes, came to precede and surpass citizenship as "the primary basis for determining the rights of someone claiming to be a member of the political community that [is] 'Myanmar.'"[78] As identity fragments into smaller, increasingly mutually exclusive groups, the articulation of broader, more inclusive and plural subnational identities such as Kachin or Shan seems increasingly fragile. First, as groups fragment into smaller units, the risk of interethnic conflict and violence increases. And smaller groups also represent a less plausible basis for self-government and meaningful political autonomy. As groups mobilize politically to preserve their identity, the logic set in motion by the 2008 constitution may, ironically, undermine their capacity to preserve that identity over time. Second, ethnic mobilization and institutions put into place by the constitution brought little concrete benefits. Instead, the opening of the economy triggered increased migration in and outside ethnic states and created new pressures on the preservation of ethnic identities and languages. Free markets may, over time, contribute more to Burmanizing ethnic minorities than the junta's past strong-arm tactics. Before the coup, the state seemed therefore to have succeeded in generating hope by providing symbolic recognition at best, while never truly altering the political and territorial dominance of the Bamar majority.

CONCLUSION

Myanmar is at a crossroads. The transition that began in 2011 and ended in 2021 showed initial promise that decades of war, military rule, and economic stagnation would yield to peace with ethnic armed organizations (EAOs), democracy, and greater economic opportunities, from integration to regional and global markets. Yet under five years of governance by Aung San Suu Kyi's National League for Democracy (NLD), Myanmar's long-standing opposition party, as well as four years of the Union Solidarity and Development Party (USDP)-led transitional government, little was achieved. Economic growth first took off but slowed down significantly by the end of the decade.[1] In spite of retaining much popularity, Aung San Suu Kyi and the NLD's governance showed mixed results and lost some of their democratic credentials.[2] When the armed forces unleashed unprecedented violence in 2017 against the Rohingya, who fled by hundreds of thousands across the border, a new spate of violence, displacement, and atrocities arose, while Aung San Suu Kyi's government remained initially silent and later defended the military at the International Court of Justice.[3] In spite of rapidly losing her image abroad and a poor governance record, Aung San Suu Kyi nevertheless retained huge popularity domestically and led the NLD to a landslide majority in the November 2020 elections. On February 1, 2021, when parliament was scheduled to inaugurate a second mandate for the NLD, the armed forces launched a coup and ended its decade-long experiment with democracy.

Against this backdrop, the slow-moving and almost moribund political dialogue with ethnic minority groups also ended. It triggered new cycles of violence with some armed groups, while leaving huge uncertainty regarding the future course of the civil war. But the coup was unrelated to either the course of the civil war or the state of these discussions. Ethnic minorities fell victim to a tug-of-war between the armed forces and the NLD. Ironically, the state—whether the Tatmadaw or the Union government—had been mostly achieving its goals relative to ethnic minorities, while reducing the costs of civil war. The coup instead created huge setbacks and made either peace or victory by war even more elusive.

In this book, we have argued that, on the eve of the 2021 coup, the state was "winning by process." Partly by design, partly semicoordinated, the state manipulated the process of negotiation to its advantage, almost neutralizing ethnic minority groups. For the casual observer, the conflict appeared largely stalled, with neither side able to win by war and the two sides unable to reach a peace agreement. But stalled conflicts are not static outcomes between war and peace, waiting for a disruptive event to propel the civil war toward either of these endpoints. Instead, we have shown that a stalled conflict can be a dynamic equilibrium that warring parties strategically use to advance their goals, as was the case with the Myanmar state.

After sixty years of civil war, the USDP's and NLD's stated resolve for peace produced few results. Initially, bilateral ceasefires with large EAOs, such as the Karen National Union (KNU) and the Restoration Council of Shan State (RCSS), were celebrated with great fanfare.[4] Even the partial, yet symbolically important, Nationwide Ceasefire Agreement (NCA) appeared to be an important milestone, particularly given its level of detail and commitment to political dialogue. Yet subsequent negotiations progressed slowly, stalled several times, and produced only vague commitments. Meanwhile, violent conflict continued against the Arakan Army (AA), the Kachin Independence Organization (KIO), and other armed groups, including some that had signed the ceasefire.[5]

The process of negotiation, both formal and informal, reflected a mostly coherent strategy to weaken ethnic minority groups and retain Bamar-centric state control over Myanmar's future political structure. In order to explain this outcome, it is important to consider not only the negotiations themselves, but the various points of engagement between ethnic minority groups in the state, from continued civil war to representation in existing state institutions. The state was progressively reaching its objectives of reducing violent conflict, limiting concessions to ethnic minorities, and reaffirming a centralized state under Bamar dominance.[6] While war had long been its chosen method to achieve these goals, it turned to process as a more powerful, ultimately stronger one. Ethnic minorities increasingly accepted the 2008 constitution, whose institutions at the national and state level provided more representation than before. State decentralization, while minimal, raised the quality of public services in ethnic minority areas. Meanwhile, few concessions were made in formal negotiations. The state penetrated ethnic areas as never before, and spread its own services and institutions to replace those formerly controlled by EAOs. It introduced new forms of ethnic representation that contributed to dividing large ethnic groups and rendering them weaker.

Democratic Change and Making the Process Credible

The decade of quasi-democracy and political liberalization created a genuine possibility that the civil war could end and a peace agreement could be reached. The Tatmadaw and the USDP government had initiated and supported negotiations for a nationwide ceasefire agreement, which, even though partial, was nevertheless an unprecedented achievement. They had agreed to include a framework for political dialogue that EAOs suggested and mostly crafted. The process was not a sham; it was enough to have EAOs support it, and it clearly departed from past attempts to appease EAOs through ceasefires and sideline deals.

The NLD initially created strong expectations for peace to be achieved. It came to power with an unprecedented amount of legitimacy. Aung San Suu Kyi enjoyed outstanding popular support, mostly because of her status as the daughter of the "father" of independence, Aung San, as well as her decades-long resistance to the military regime.[7] The NLD and Aung San Suu Kyi's electoral victory in 1990 consolidated the party and Aung San Suu Kyi as Myanmar's democratic leader. Relegated to the opposition, and with Aung San Suu Kyi sentenced to house arrest when the junta rejected the results, the NLD remained the unofficial opposition to the regime. As a Nobel Peace Prize winner, and with solid democratic credentials, Aung San Suu Kyi led the NLD to an overwhelming victory in 2015. Since the NLD had nurtured close links with ethnic minority groups and political parties in the 1990s, it was largely expected that it would prioritize the peace agreement and move decisively toward a peace settlement.[8]

In conceptual terms, the democratic opening therefore increased the likelihood that a negotiated agreement could be reached. Although the regime was only partially democratic, the fact of allowing an opposition party to run in elections and form a civilian government with significant power in a broad array of jurisdictions elevated expectations that negotiations could be genuine.[9] Moreover, both EAOs and the state agreed on and helped to shape the formal negotiation process.

It may seem surprising, therefore, that by the end of its first term, the NLD faced a stalled conflict, with a suspended peace dialogue, persistent war, and policies designed to more strongly implement the 2008 constitution. After five years of political dialogue, the 21st Century Panglong Conference produced only general principles, most of which had little to do with federalism. Several EAOs complained of being increasingly frustrated at the slow pace of negotiations and the repeated ability of the Tatmadaw and government representatives to control the agenda and prevent meaningful progress. Yet despite little to no progress in the formal negotiation arena, few EAOs had any appetite to go back to war, thus implicitly accepting the status quo. When the KNU stopped participating in the official peace talks in 2018, the political dialogue was paused.

In spite of the NLD's initial rejection of the 2008 constitution, when it came to power it introduced very few, mostly symbolic modifications to the constitution, while mostly continuing in the same vein as its USDP predecessor to implement the constitution's decentralization features.[10] Decentralization remained highly limited, with the central government continuing to control most levers of decision-making and budgetary allocation. In some respects, there were even indications of greater centralization of decision-making and less space for discussion than had occurred under the later years of the USDP government.

Winning by Process: How and Why the State Was Reaching Its Goals

The state was attaining its long-standing historical goals mostly through process rather than war or peaceful agreement. This book has shown that powerful actors can strategically manipulate process to make gains not only in formal negotiations but also in other arenas of engagement between parties in a civil war. The state in Myanmar, even if evolving into a two-pronged competition for power between the Tatmadaw and the NLD government, remained capable of controlling and directing this process, especially since unity among ethnic minority groups, and EAOs in particular, proved elusive.

Myanmar's civil war has some specific characteristics that are relatively common in other settings. First, it involves multiple insurgent groups, which creates difficulties in reaching peace agreements because of alliance shifting. Second, it appears to be "protracted," which we call "stalled." In comparative terms, with a duration of more than sixty years, it is one of the longest-lasting civil wars. In combination with the presence of multiple insurgent groups, other structural factors have contributed to the inability of any party to win by war or all sides to win by agreement. This in-between status, a period of dynamic engagement in multiple arenas, however, can be used strategically. Myanmar in this respect is representative of several other types of civil wars, particularly where multiple insurgent groups are involved.

While the strategic use of process is clear even in classic civil war bargaining contexts, it becomes even more evident when a state arena becomes part of the broader negotiation environment, as in the case of Myanmar. Many civil wars occur in either dysfunctional or failed states, or insurgent groups fall outside state institutions. But in some cases, such as Myanmar or other quasi-democratic contexts, state institutions also operate as a locus of representation and governance, and sometimes include aggrieved groups, while civil war continues. These institutions, parallel to traditional civil war arenas, constrain or provide broader opportunities to pursue different goals and strategies simultaneously. The pace and degree of negotiations, while occurring outside state institutions, have an impact on how groups represented in these negotiations position themselves within the state. Governments seeking to co-opt, control, divide, or repress their civil war opponents similarly use existing state institutions as tools in a broader strategy that connects both formal negotiations and the exercise of power relative to groups that armed organizations claim to represent.[11]

Outside Myanmar, such linkages between the arenas of formal negotiation, state institutions, and war are frequent. The Free Aceh Movement in Indonesia remobilized strongly in the late 1990s, largely in response to the state's attempts to co-opt a moderate Acehnese elite and impose a version of autonomy for Aceh that diluted what the Acehnese had sought through insurgency. Subsequent attempts were again pursued while the state negotiated with the Free Aceh Movement for a peace settlement.[12] In the Philippines, the state exploited fragmentation among armed groups by negotiating with one major group, the Moro National Liberation Front (MNLF), extending benefits and including the group within renewed state institutions. Once disarmed and included in transitional autonomy institutions, however, the MNLF lost leverage to force the state to deliver on its promised enhanced autonomy, both in territorial claims as well as in powers and resources. The MNLF's subsequent mobilization and positioning with respect to its own negotiations with the Philippine state were directly linked with changes occurring in the Autonomous Region of Muslim Mindanao under the MNLF's leadership.[13]

In Spain, after the fall of Franco, Basque Homeland and Liberty (ETA) lost its quasi-monopoly over representation of the Basques, as democratization and a new constitution recognized historical nationalities and provided new opportunities for representative organizations to reemerge. The Basque Nationalist Party, which had long been the principal Basque party, lost much of its role and ability to mobilize during the Franco regime. Many of its youth migrated to ETA and supported its resistance to the authoritarian regime. After democratization in 1976, the Basque Nationalist Party reemerged as a significant force, while ETA divided into those continuing to support violence and moderates who joined other organizations. Over time, the availability of alternative channels of representation, and a credible constitutional process, significantly eroded the support that ETA received from the Basque population, while the state counted on its courts and central government policies to reduce the Basque's capacity to gain further autonomy. By the time ETA negotiated formally with the Spanish state, it had almost completely lost support, as the vast majority of Basques supported mobilization within the state arena, in spite of frustrations resulting from the Spanish state's centralizing tendencies.[14]

The outcome can sometimes be the neutralization of opponents. In Myanmar's case, the state was winning, increasingly able to shape the country's future toward its own version of a so-called federal state, while effectively neutralizing ethnic minority groups. By "neutralizing," we mean that ethnic minority groups were unable to make gains either through politics or through war. In essence, an apparently stalled conflict can reflect one side's ability to render ineffective the others' attempts to reach their goals. We therefore require closer analysis of situations where civil war might have shed its worst violence, remained at low levels, or been seen as stuck in between a full-scale war and a peace agreement. As the case of Myanmar has shown, fluctuations in violence levels, or even ceasefires with some groups, were far from conflict resolution or more than simply an in-between stage. The conditions leading and sustaining violence are often clearly distinct from the grievances that underlie conflict or that are addressed in negotiation.[15] While, over time, slow integration and socialization into new institutional structures may indeed transform group interests and reduce grievances, even if demands are not met, it is a bet rather than a path to conflict resolution. But as we have shown, the study of the process by which groups may become institutionally constrained to participate, accept greatly diluted concessions, and lose some of their ability to pursue violent strategies is a promising area of inquiry to better understand the conditions under which armed groups may lose their support and raison d'être, and where the diffusion of interests may prevent a cohesive strategy for previously aggrieved groups to meet their objectives.

How the State Was Winning: Five Strategies

In the various arenas, actors can use a number of strategies to make gains through process. In the case of Myanmar, we have identified five such strategies: locking in, sequencing, layering, outflanking, and outgunning. While there are no specific, predictive outcomes to any of these strategies, they nevertheless represent a sample tool kit of strategies that powerful actors in civil war settings use to control and manipulate process. When successful, as was the case in Myanmar, these actors can attain their goals without resorting to the costlier options of continuing warfare or providing large political concessions.

The Myanmar state locked in a set of rules regulating the formal negotiating arena and was able to use its greater cohesion and strength to control much of the proceedings. EAOs had themselves agreed to the framework that gave many other ethnic representatives access to the proceedings of the political dialogue. They failed to anticipate that their numbers would be diluted as a result, and state representatives would be sufficiently powerful that EAO priorities would be difficult to advance. Even the Union Peace Dialogue Joint Committee, which was the preparatory committee for negotiations, gave greater voice to EAOs but remained strongly under state control.[16] Some of the slowness in the proceedings, as well as the narrow outcomes, directly resulted from fundamental disagreements over the path to bringing nonsignatory armed groups into the nationwide ceasefire and political dialogue. With NCA members insisting on an all-inclusive dialogue and the Tatmadaw refusing to accept many nonsignatory armed groups, several aspects of negotiations were delayed.[17] Skirmishes with the Tatmadaw involving NCA members, such as the KNU and RCSS, and between NCA and non-NCA signatories, also had an impact on negotiations, thereby clearly showing how the theater of war had a direct influence on the formal negotiating arena.

Furthermore, and more significantly, the locked-in negotiating structure allowed state negotiators, particularly from the military, to control the agenda. As the political dialogue forum was divided into several committees to discuss issue areas separately, such as social or economic issues, the committee chairs were able to curtail items for discussion and limit the agreement only to principles and items that resulted in little real weakening of state power or resources. In the end, the KNU and other EAOs that had joined the NCA and negotiated with the NLD government became increasingly frustrated that the negotiations failed to produce concrete concessions toward federalism and, instead, led to a large number of principles that were unrelated to aspirations for a federal state and sufficiently vague that they felt no gains were made. While the KNU most strongly voiced its disillusion by suspending its participation, others also felt the same disappointment. Splits also grew between larger NCA signatories like the KNU or RCSS, which pushed for a federal state, and smaller groups that were more willing to compromise on solutions far short of a federal state.

The stalled negotiations, and few concrete outcomes by the end of the NLD government's term, were less a result of failed compromises than of difficulties in agreeing even to very basic items. As we have shown, while divisions among ethnic minority groups and their inability to channel concrete demands may have reduced the scope of dialogue, military representatives and committee chairs often limited attempts to raise more substantive issues. The state may not have deliberately attempted to hijack the negotiations, but it certainly contributed in large part to the very slow pace of their progress. When looking at the sum of what was agreed to, basically nothing had been conceded in concrete terms. Furthermore, with the military preventing some of the ethnic minority groups from holding their national dialogue, which had been accepted as part of the process, those groups were even more constrained in their ability to articulate strong negotiating positions.

The state arena most significantly shows how layering was effective at advancing the state's model through process. It shaped power and resources for ethnic minority groups, while de facto creating more support for its views and dividing ethnic loyalties. The constitution of 2008, which the military adopted before the transition, recognized existing ethnic states and further enshrined the concept of "national races" contained in the citizenship law of 1982; in the context of the census, it then provided a list of 135 national races that it officially recognized. By codifying and institutionalizing ethnicity in this dual way, the state preserved the idea of ethnic states but also diluted their effectiveness by providing new powers, and even claims to autonomous regions within states, to groups that were sufficiently concentrated and numerous to meet the constitutionally established criteria. While the constitution perpetuated and even intensified ethnicity as a main political marker, it also created new ways of dividing large umbrella groups, in the name of empowering national races.

Democratization added a significant institutional layer by expanding the field of representation and rendering parliamentary roles more credible and meaningful, creating different levels of government with greater decentralized executive power, allowing a greater array of political parties to participate more freely and actively, and expanding the space for civil society organizations to voice grievances and exert pressure on state institutions.[18] More broadly, in most cases, democratization greatly diluted insurgent groups' claims to exclusive representation of their supporters, thereby increasing their incentive to strike a bargain in negotiations, disband, and claim leadership through state institutions, or conversely become increasingly marginalized.[19] The more functional and representative state institutions become in a transition, particularly with respect to groups from which insurgents are drawn, the more armed groups end up negotiating terms of their dissolution rather than the transformation of state institutions. A dilemma becomes greater, however, when state institutions provide benefits and resources to the group while falling short of the initial demands that armed groups made. As with the case of Myanmar, to join state institutions runs the risk of never achieving the goals, even remotely, that initially motivated civil war. In the context of stalled formal negotiations, an incomplete ceasefire, and continued implementation of state institutional reforms, such a dilemma can become quite large.

Sequencing is another strategy that the Myanmar state used effectively. In addition to layering, the timing of the 2008 constitution was crucial. Having adopted it before the democratic opening, the military imposed its framework as a sine qua non against which any negotiated agreement would be compared. It insisted that the constitution could be amended as a result of the political dialogue, but not replaced. Furthermore, its subsequent normalization solidified the maintenance of a centralized Myanmar over ethnic accommodation. While in opposition and in its early days, the NLD had taken a firm position against the 2008 constitution, which it considered illegitimate on the basis of its origins under the military junta. Over time, it appeared to shift its position, when faced with strong military signals that drafting a new constitution was out of the question and that any change would need to proceed by amendment. The NLD's most forceful opposition had been related to clauses preventing Aung San Suu Kyi from becoming president, as well as the military's strong representation and veto power in state institutions.[20] But it came to tacitly accept the constitution and propose instead some amendments, mostly on these issues. After October 2015, when it gained power, the NLD continued to push for these changes while nevertheless largely continuing with the full implementation of the 2008 constitution, including all aspects relating to ethnic minorities.

The NLD's approach to ethnic minorities suggested that it supported clauses on divisions of power and allocation of resources to ethnic states, as well as the recognition of 135 national races. It sponsored amendments to Schedule 2 that defined ethnic states' powers,[21] but these powers were highly restricted, subsumed under jurisdictional issue areas that remained under the central government's control, and ambiguous at best regarding the degree of actual authority devolved to the state level.[22] While in theory more powers and opportunities for increased resources through taxation were extended to states, we found little evidence to suggest that any of them exercised a significant degree of autonomy. Instead, most officials at the state level emphasized how even small decisions and any significant funding required the central government's approval, and there were tendencies for even greater centralization than what they had experienced under the USDP government. One observer, for instance, remarked about the constitutional amendment committee formed by the NLD in 2019 that ethnic political parties "particularly resent[ed] the fact that the NLD [had] gone 'quiet' about their aspirations for federalism, to which the NLD [had] responded by saying that the party now prioritize[d] democratization over federalism."[23] Finally, in its daily interactions with ethnic minority states and parties, the NLD failed to govern in a way that reflected a federal spirit.

The NLD's approach to negotiations, combined with an apparent acceptance of, and even strengthening of support for, the 2008 constitution, solidified the link between the state and formal negotiating arenas. With an absence of progress in negotiations, commitments only to vague principles, and the solidifying of a minimal decentralized model, over time the institutions became increasingly normalized and new practices routinized. While EAOs continued to ask for federalism, several other representative groups of ethnic minorities, within and outside government, focused on smaller gains such as the election of chief ministers or the securing of more powers under Schedule 2 of the constitution. The military's position that no change would occur without proceeding through amendments to the 2008 constitution ensured that negotiating efforts and lobbying remained focused on incremental changes, while new powers, positions, and institutional practices were being normalized at the state level.

When analyzing all three arenas together, the pattern of state control over process and the expansion of its power becomes clear. In sequence, ceasefires and negotiations allowed the military to use outgunning and concentrate its resources against remaining groups in the theater of war, while the state expanded its control in territories formerly under the control of EAOs. The costs of returning to civil war became much greater, in particular as the state arena became more functional in ethnic states. State institutions integrated some ethnic minorities into parliament and state governments. The central government expanded some services and infrastructure and continued to implement the 2008 constitution. Meanwhile, EAOs remained divided between ceasefire and nonceasefire groups, those in negotiations lost much of their prior influence as more ethnic representatives were included in negotiations, and ethnic political parties and officials provided alternative representation. Combined with new forms of mobilization prompted by the rights allocated to the 135 national races, the large umbrella ethnic minority groups became increasingly divided, and the established ethnic states came under increasing challenge as claims were made for smaller autonomous zones to be carved out.

Time was also on the state's side, another by-product of sequencing. Without presuming that the stalled negotiations were a deliberate strategy, it is clear that slow progress allowed the state to increase its leverage. Weakened armed groups, the normalization of the 2008 constitution, the continued expansion of government services in gray zones, and the building of roads and infrastructure all contributed to increasing the state's reach into territories that had been more solidly in EAOs' control. We call this strategy "outflanking." It is significant that the military refrained from waging war against the more powerful Wa, which de facto control their own territory but do not expand beyond those borders. Instead, the military continued to fight against groups that they could weaken and whose territorial control they could compete with, in terms of either military control or expansion of state services and infrastructure. With respect to territories associated with ceasefire groups, again the rapid infrastructural expansion made a return to civil war increasingly costly and strategically difficult.[24] While the KNU had internal disagreements over continued support for the peace process, and despite skirmishes that took place between the Tatmadaw and the KNU's Third and Fifth Brigades, none of its brigades actually returned to civil war prior to the coup.[25] Where nonceasefire groups held out the hope of obtaining new terms or a better formal negotiation process before joining a ceasefire, as the creation of the Northern Alliance suggested, the military and the state more broadly continued to cooperate in formal negotiations while reducing both territorial control and the effective ability of ceasefire groups to return to civil war.

Finally, controlling much of the process of negotiations, gaining advantage in the theater of war, and using outgunning allowed the state to significantly contain the degree of concessions while crafting a path consistent with its objectives. The impact of the process was evident not just in the way state negotiators skillfully used the rules of negotiation that ceasefire EAOs actually proposed and agreed to, but also in the overall effect of balancing negotiation and concessions with sustained civil war against some of the other groups. The Tatmadaw continued violent campaigns against the AA and the KIO, but much more forcefully against the first, to which it denied access to join the nationwide ceasefire.[26] The KIO was weakened after the KNU and RCSS signed ceasefire agreements, as the military could more effectively redirect its resources to combat it. While the military continued to fight against the nonceasefire armed groups in the theater of war, the latter attempted several times to leverage the violence to negotiate an alternative to the nationwide ceasefire agreement. The military sought to sideline some groups from the possibility of joining the formal negotiation arena, while increasing its repression in the theater of war. Having signed a ceasefire with a number of groups, it could deploy greater military resources against the remaining EAOs, which found themselves weaker in relative terms.

While many of these strategies can be attributed to war tactics to divide armed opponents, fragmentation in itself does not explain why the state came so far in achieving the goals of reducing violent civil war, weakening most armed groups, and avoiding concessions for a strongly decentralized federal state. Myanmar was locked into sixty years of civil war that pitted the Tatmadaw against several EAOs. In spite of perpetual fragmentation among these armed groups, and even within them, the military could not win. Conversely, EAOs, many of which were actually weak militarily but enjoyed strong popular support, nevertheless gained merely private concessions over natural resources in resource-rich areas or illicit business operations, and very few concessions even for the preservation of their language and culture.

Process, as we have argued, created institutional structures that moved the conflict away from a bipolar confrontation, to multiple arenas where rules and procedures constrained both the state and ethnic minority groups. Yet the state could deploy its power in all three arenas and, through step-by-step manipulation, stalling, and making small concessions, slowly craft an outcome that favored it. It was winning, as there were few plausible scenarios in which progress in negotiations would lead to the federal model that ethnic minority groups long aspired to achieve through civil war.

Our argument likely overstates the degree of coherence of state strategy, but the apparent unity of the state relative to ethnic minority groups is a by-product of both calculated statecraft and a high degree of elite convergence over the normative values of Bamar dominance and concepts of "state unity." Certainly, despite some degree of reformist and conservative divisions within the military itself, the institution as a whole maintained a great deal of influence in the negotiations as well as the insistence on retaining the 2008 constitution. While Thein Sein may have pushed the transition further than originally anticipated, with respect to ethnic minority groups, few concessions were actually made. The nationwide ceasefire achieved a reduction in violence among some groups, which was the military's main goal, but little else. The USDP and NLD both made strong statements in support for peace negotiations with ethnic groups, but little progress was made in subsequent negotiations, which stalled at the end of the NLD's mandate. While the NLD government may have been seen to be cornered by the military's position on concessions to EAOs, its own implementation of the 2008 constitution and its approach to negotiations showed surprisingly little political resolve to strongly accommodate ethnic minority demands. Whether for political and electoral reasons or due to policy, the NLD appeared much more reluctant to move decisively toward meaningful federalism, and therefore differed little from the military's more overt position against it. Underlying its position was certainly the consideration of political calculations to maintain the support of the Bamar majority, but also a deeply seated historical reinforcement of Bamar dominance and strong state centralization to maintain unity and stability. Against a weak and fragmented opposition, there was little reason to believe that the state would offer greater concessions.[27]

The End of Process: The 2021 Coup

At the end of the NLD's first government, the outcome was clear: stalled negotiations, continued civil war in some areas, and steady implementation of the 2008 constitution. We have argued that, in itself, this was an outcome worthy of analysis, as it also showed that the state had gained ascendancy and, through a multipronged strategy in several arenas, was giving few concessions to ethnic minorities' historical demands for federalism while gaining ground on expanding territorial control, weakening EAOs, greater fractionalizing of ethnic minorities generally, and molding Myanmar's institutions according to long-standing state views of a mostly centralized polity under Bamar-majority dominance. At that juncture, of course, the military continued to exercise power over and above the civilian government, and mostly provided a check on concessions to ethnic minority groups. While some military reformers emerged, the overall path certainly seemed to remain closer to the centralized vision that the military espoused under its own road map to democracy.

Where the NLD government had opportunities to exercise more autonomy and take new initiative, it showed very little resolve or clear policies that articulated a much different view from the military. Although it took small steps to challenge the 2008 constitution, it nevertheless mostly proceeded with its implementation and accepted that future change had to occur through its amendment. Overall, then, the path set at the end of the NLD's first government was clearly one where the state was making major gains in its long quest to quell ethnic minority demands and reinforce its vision of Myanmar over the ethnic groups' view of federalism. It was winning through this multipronged process, and making greater gains than it ever had through war.

The coup on February 1, 2021, ended the process, even though the state had been winning. Formal negotiations and the nationwide ceasefire collapsed. The state arena was suspended. Only the theater of war remained. While full-fledged civil war did not return on all fronts against ethnic minorities, significant combat resumed against former ceasefire, nonceasefire, and new armed groups led by Bamar protesters.

The military coup specifically targeted the NLD. The junta accused it of voter fraud, promised to hold elections within a year, and hinted at changing the electoral system to proportional representation.[28] The military prevented the NLD from beginning its second mandate with a stronger majority, most likely as a preemptive attempt to thwart its ability to use greater political leverage and strengthen its confrontational approach against the military's dominance and position in formal state institutions. It was surprising given that, on many fronts, the military still mostly held the upper hand, particularly against ethnic minorities. But it likely saw a longer, and perhaps thorny, path toward a return to power for its civilian wing, the USDP. And it ran out of patience.

Following the coup, the Tatmadaw's relations with ethnic minority groups backfired. There is little evidence that the status of the political dialogue or of the conflict with ethnic minorities in any way influenced the military's decision to stage a coup. The overwhelming resistance against the coup, including from those who opposed or did not care much about the NLD, took the military by surprise, and fighting between the Tatmadaw and anticoup forces rapidly transformed the political landscape. A majority of EAOs publicly denounced the Tatmadaw's brutal and arbitrary repression of protesters. The KIO and KNU offered shelter and training to protesters, defectors, and members of a broad civil disobedience movement, while intensifying war against the military. Battlefields expanded beyond what the Tatmadaw had been covering—from Kachin, Kayin, and Kayah States to new frontiers such as Magway Region, Sagaing Region, and Chin State. The Tatmadaw faced not just conventional EAOs, but also hundreds of localized People's Defense Forces, which resorted to explosives and handmade guns; targeted police, collaborators, and administrators; and engaged in urban guerrilla war across different cities.

The coup also created new links between ethnic minority groups and the Bamar majority, now jointly allied in their quest to resist the military. The Tatmadaw's brutal repression against protesters led to public acknowledgments and apologies from Bamar people regarding their ignorance about the suffering of minority groups (including Rohingya), and increased the support among the Bamar population for federalism and EAOs that had fought against the Myanmar military.[29] When the NLD led the creation of a National Unity Government (NUG), it gained support from some ethnic minority groups while it also softened its prior stance toward them. The NUG adopted policies and practices that were more favorable to minorities, and that departed significantly from those of Aung San Suu Kyi's government between 2015 and 2020. These included changing its objective from democratic federalism back to federal democracy, which was perceived to be an important conceptual shift supporting stronger acceptance of the principles of federalism. It also appointed ethnic minorities in more than 50 percent of its governing body (though they were overwhelmingly NLD members). It also appointed as a Union minister Dr. Lian Hmung Sakong, a Chin national and second vice chairman of the Chin National Front. He was also given the responsibility of overseeing the drafting of the federal constitution, which therefore appeared to concede unprecedented power to ethnic minority groups to advance their own conception of a future federal state.

But many of these newly created alliances also raised old suspicions, as concessions were made out of weakness and promises could not readily be fulfilled while the junta remained in power. Efforts by the NUG to lead the opposition movement (composed of strike committees, worker/student unions, and minority ethnic groups) were reminiscent of similar alliances during the aftermath of the military coup of 1988 and the failed election of 1990. At that time, students and elected members of parliament fled to EAOs' controlled areas and formed a student-led armed resistance group called the All Burma Students' Democratic

Front and an NLD-led exile government called the National Coalition Government of the Union of Burma. Aung San Suu Kyi built bridges and made many promises to ethnic minorities regarding a future democratic state. She later reneged, as it became clear that none of these promises became a reality during the NLD's mandate.

Unlike the situation that immediately followed the 1988 coup, the military was not able to run the country after the 2021 coup. The significant difference was that, following the latter, EAOs and People's Defense Forces organized widespread armed resistance. A civil disobedience movement deprived the military government of teachers and health care professionals. The Myanmar diaspora provided strong support. The local population boycotted businesses. And finally, the internet and cell phone technology allowed citizens to share information and expose military atrocities.

Nevertheless, even with the common sense of purpose to remove the military from power, several ethnic minority organizations were ambivalent regarding their support for the junta and their hesitation to create strong bonds with the NUG. Many perceived the coup as Bamar fighting Bamar, and therefore sought to balance their interests between both political forces. Some ethnic political parties (such as Mon, Karen, and Rakhine) who felt marginalized by the NLD joined the military's administrative council. As a prominent Rakhine politician told us, "We do not trust the military but we dislike Aung San Suu Kyi and the NLD more. They have mistreated us. The NLD officially praised and acknowledged the Tatmadaw's fight against the AA and delegated responsibility to the Tatmadaw to take necessary actions against the AA."[30] The NCA signatories, including the KNU, that engaged in war against the military in the postcoup period also kept open the option for international mediation, while their counterparts representing political parties contemplated joining the military's orchestrated elections or joined the opposition movement. The Tatmadaw also attempted to appease the AA by removing it from a list of terrorist organizations, releasing Rakhine political prisoners, and lifting restrictions on internet access in Rakhine State, while intensifying its fight against the KIA and KNU. It also made symbolic gestures, such as renaming the controversial General Aung San Bridge in Mon State as Thanlwin Bridge (Chaungzon), a more acceptable name for the local population. The KIO and KNU accepted the NLD-led NUG not as a legitimate parallel government but only as an antimilitary alliance partner. The Shan National League for Democracy felt alienated by the NLD's continued top-down, Bamar-dominated decision-making, and considered forming an alternative anticoup alliance. Thus, minority ethnic groups remained fragmented and divided into the camps led by the Bamar-dominated military and the NUG, the two major entities they distrusted, but hedged their bets in order to reach their ever-elusive goal of crafting a genuine federal union.

Whatever scenario follows the military's end of democracy in 2021, the experience of a decade of negotiations, continued conflict, and implementation of the 2008 constitution remains relevant to the future. The long-standing historical trend of Bamar dominance and state centralization will continue to cast a shadow over any resumption of negotiations to end the civil war and to reestablish inclusive democratic governance. While ethnic minority groups could be potential powerbrokers in any resumption or deepening of democracy, where the military would withdraw from politics, the state's strategies to reduce ethnic minority power, manipulate process, and reach its goals of a loosely decentralized but still Bamar-dominated Union are likely to reemerge as well. While a new chapter may begin, this book's main story will remain the same.

Notes

INTRODUCTION

1. Silverstein, "Fifty Years of Failure"; Smith, *Burma*; South, *Ethnic Politics in Burma*; Thawnghmung, "Dilemmas of Burma's Multinational Society."

2. Aung San, the founder of the Anti-Fascist People's Freedom League, Burma's nationalist front, is widely considered the father of the nation, the first nationalist leader who led Burma to independence, although he was assassinated six months before the official handover of power.

3. See Callahan, *Making Enemies*.

4. For a similar argument about how "Burman-ness" permeates the Myanmar state and society and constitutes a system of institutionalized dominance, see Walton, "'Wages of Burman-ness.'"

5. Horowitz, *Ethnic Groups in Conflict*, 55–92.

6. In this book, we use the term "ethnic nationalities" to avoid making assumptions about the biological and inborn nature of ethnic identities and to describe groups that have played a major political role (including Bamar) in Myanmar. We are conscious that in Myanmar, as elsewhere, terms such as this one are charged and controversial. In Myanmar, ethnic identity is usually categorized in terms of *lumyo*, which literally means "kind or race of people(s) or person(s)." *Lumyo* is often used together with *taing yin thar*, another term that is close to the English concept of "indigenous." *Taing yin thar lumyo* thus connotes the biological, native, verifiable, fixed, and blood-borne nature of identity (see Callahan, "Distorted, Dangerous Data?," 459). The Myanmar government has officially recognized 135 *taing yin thar lumyo*, or "original inhabitants," who lived in Myanmar before the British first annexed the country in 1824, but scholars, experts, and ethnic organizations have challenged these categories based on their arbitrary and exclusive nature. We use "ethnic nationalities" because, like many scholars, we agree that identities are socially constructed, and their meanings and implications have evolved depending on specific political contexts and changing times. Some minority ethnic leaders have refused to use the term "minorities" because they argue that the term denigrates their status and makes it politically insignificant. We often refer to non-Bamar populations as "ethnic minorities," however, to differentiate them from the majority Bamar populations without making any political statement about their role and status.

7. Callahan, "Distorted, Dangerous Data?"; Transnational Institute, "Ethnicity without Meaning"; Thawnghmung, "Politics of Indigeneity." We use "Bamar" as the name for the majority ethnic group. Some scholars also refer to the majority group as "Burman."

8. The existing official identification of ethnic groups is based on a very large number, and therefore reduces the power of any single one. At the same time, the state has not been able to move away from the long recognition of seven "umbrella" groups.

9. Thawnghmung, "Contending Approaches."

10. Smith, *Burma*, 77–80; Walton, "Ethnicity, Conflict, and History."

11. Smith, *Burma*, 98.

12. Smith, *Burma*, 80.

13. Smith, *Burma*, 304.

14. Zaw Oo and Win Min, *Assessing Burma's Ceasefire Accords*.

15. Aung San Suu Kyi was officially "state councilor," a special position created after the 2015 election to give her de facto leadership of the government. She became a popular and charismatic leader of the democratic movement against the entrenched military rule in 1988, and was placed under house arrest at various times between 1989 and 2011. The 2008 constitution still barred her from the position of president, which is Myanmar's official head of state and government, as it denies that office to those citizens with foreign spouses and children.

16. Luttwak, "Give War a Chance"; Licklider, *Stopping the Killing*; Licklider, "Consequences of Negotiated Settlements."

17. Cunningham, Gleditsch, and Salehyan, "It Takes Two."

18. Kreutz, "How and When Armed Conflicts End."

19. Findley, "Bargaining and the Interdependent Stages."

20. Findley, "Bargaining and the Interdependent Stages"; Cunningham, "Veto Players"; Pillar, *Negotiating Peace*.

21. See for example, Choudhry, ed., *Constitutional Design*; Simeon and Conway, "Federalism and the Management of Conflict"; Lustick, "Stability in Deeply Divided Societies"; Lijphart, *Democracy in Plural Societies*; Chandra, "Ethnic Parties."

22. Walter, "Critical Barrier"; Bertrand, *Democracy and Nationalism*. For an analysis of how democratization can also fuel more violent mobilization, see Snyder, *From Voting to Violence*.

23. Callahan, *Making Enemies*.

24. Smith, *Burma*; Smith, *Burma*, 2nd ed. Similarly, the journalist Bertil Lintner provided one of the first and most extensive accounts of the connection between the drug economy and insurgencies in Burma's borderland in the pretransition period, but was again focused on the authoritarian period. Lintner, *Burma in Revolt*.

25. There was a move away from this strategy after Khin Nyunt was fired. See Selth, "Myanmar's Intelligence Apparatus."

26. Nongovernmental organizations like the Asia Foundation and the Transnational Institute have published extensive descriptive and categorical analyses of armed groups and ethnic political parties, as well as of the emerging structures and practices of provincial governments, but many of them tend to analyze minority groups separately in their distinctive categories rather than as part of interactive and dynamic relationships within a broader political context. See, for example, Nixon et al., *State and Region Governments*; Transnational Institute, "Ethnic Politics"; Joliffe, *Ethnic Armed Conflict*.

27. Crouch, *Constitution of Myanmar*, 30.

28. Cheesman, *Opposing the Rule of Law*. See also Crouch and Lindsey, *Law, Society and Transition*, for a broad analysis of law in Myanmar since 2011. A number of edited volumes focus on certain aspects of the transition, such as constitutionalism, democracy, social change, and conflicts. See Harding and Khin, *Constitutionalism and Legal Change*; Egreteau and Robinne, *Metamorphosis*; Cheesman and Farrelly, *Conflict in Myanmar*.

29. For an analysis of the ceasefire, see, for example, Bertrand, Pelletier, and Thawnghmung, "First Movers"; Thawnghmung, "Signs of Life." On policies toward language and education, see South and Lall, "Language, Education and the Peace Process."

30. Ye Htut, *Myanmar's Political Transition*; Thant Myint-U, *Hidden History of Burma*; Soe Thane, *Myanmar's Transformation*; Aung Naing Oo, *Pathway to Peace*.

31. See, for example, Brand, "Achieving 'Genuine Federalism'?" Mael Raynaud has also written a number of reports taking a similar position. Finally, the Asia Foundation and the Myanmar Development Resource Institute have published a number of reports on Myanmar's current state of decentralization under the 2008 constitution.

32. Thawnghmung, *Karen Revolution in Burma*; Thawnghmung, *"Other" Karen in Myanmar*.

33. Brenner, *Rebel Politics*; Kyed, *Everyday Justice in Myanmar*; South and Lall, "Language, Education and the Peace Process"; Si Thura and Schroeder, "Health Service Delivery."
34. On particular ethnic groups, see, for example, South, *Mon Nationalism*; Sadan, *War and Peace*; Sadan, *Being & Becoming Kachin*.
35. Bertrand and Pelletier, "Violent Monks in Myanmar"; Walton and Hayward, *Contesting Buddhist Narratives*; Gravers, "Anti-Muslim Buddhist Nationalism"; Thawnghmung, "Politics of Indigeneity."

1. WINNING BY PROCESS

1. Kreutz, "How and When Armed Conflicts End"; Fearon and Laitin, "Civil War Termination"; Walter, "Critical Barrier."
2. Wagner, "Causes of Peace." See also Luttwak, "Give War a Chance."
3. Toft, "Ending Civil Wars," 20. For a response to Toft, see Nathan, "Civil War Settlements."
4. Licklider, "Consequences of Negotiated Settlements."
5. Zartman, "Ripeness."
6. On the prevalence of ethnic civil wars, see Fearon and Laitin, "Ethnicity, Insurgency, and Civil War"; Fearon and Laitin, "Sons of the Soil"; and Sambanis, "Ethnic and Nonethnic Civil Wars."
7. For an excellent overview, see Choudhry, *Constitutional Design*.
8. Lijphart, *Democracy in Plural Societies*.
9. Leff, "Democratization and Disintegration"; Cornell, "Autonomy as a Source of Conflict"; Brancati, "Decentralization"; Erk and Anderson, "Paradox of Federalism."
10. Horowitz, *Ethnic Groups in Conflict*, part 5; Reilly, *Democracy in Divided Societies*; Bogaards, "Favourable Factors"; Andeweg, "Consociational Democracy."
11. Horowitz, "Constitutional Design," 29.
12. See Bertrand, *Nationalism and Ethnic Conflict*, 188–91; Horowitz, *Constitutional Change*, 58; and Schiller, *Formation of Federal Indonesia*.
13. Pillar, *Negotiating Peace*; Doyle and Hegele, "Talks before the Talks."
14. Lederach, *Sustainable Reconciliation*, 39.
15. Jupille, *Procedural Politics*, 24.
16. See Mac Ginty, *No War, No Peace*, chap 1.
17. Stedman, "Spoiler Problems"; Zahar, "Reframing the Spoiler Debate"; Christia, *Alliance Formation*; Akcinaroglu, "Rebel Interdependencies."
18. See Zartman, "Ripeness," 227.
19. Collier and Hoeffler, "Greed and Grievance"; Berdal and Malone, *Greed and Grievance*; Ross, "Natural Resources."
20. Zartman, "Ripeness," 228.
21. Walter, "Critical Barrier"; Hoddie and Hartzell, "Civil War Settlements."
22. See Stein, "Getting to the Table," 490–91; Doyle and Hegele, "Talks before the Talks," 233; Zartman, *Ripe for Resolution*, 246.
23. Walter, "Critical Barrier," 340.
24. Stedman, "Spoiler Problems."
25. Scharpf, "Joint-Decision Trap."
26. Jupille, *Procedural Politics*, 24.
27. Riker, *Art of Political Manipulation*.
28. Jupille, *Procedural Politics*, 25–26.
29. Jupille, *Procedural Politics*, 16.
30. Cunningham, *Barriers to Peace*. 32–33, 68.
31. Cunningham, *Barriers to Peace*, 48.

32. Cunningham, *Barriers to Peace*, 5.
33. Langer and Brown, *Building Sustainable Peace*, 429.
34. Walter, "Designing Transitions."
35. Tsebelis, *Veto Players*, 3–6; Weiss, "Trajectories toward Peace"; Mac Ginty, "Issue Hierarchies."
36. Brancati and Snyder, "Time to Kill," 822.
37. Joshi, Melander, and Quinn, "Sequencing the Peace."
38. Gurr, *Peoples versus States*.
39. In Aceh, Turkey, and Columbia, for instance, state institutions remained in place and still functioned during the civil conflict. These cases contrast with civil war in other theaters such as Afghanistan, Sudan, Lybia, and Iraq, where the civil wars led to the collapse of the state. Aspinall, *Islam and Nation*; Rotberg, "Failed States"; Ünal, "Is It Ripe Yet?"
40. Lake and Rothchild, "Territorial Decentralization"; Hartzell and Hoddie, "Institutionalizing Peace."
41. This was the case in the Basque Country, for example, where electoral competition brought new political parties other than the ETA.
42. The literature on federalism and ethnic representation shows that new institutions provide new resources and create new bases for mobilization. See, for example, Bunce, *Subversive Institutions*; Brancati, "Decentralization."
43. Mampilly and Stewart, "Typology."
44. Stewart, "Civil War as State-Making," 210; Arjona, Kasfir, and Mampilly, *Rebel Governance*, 3; Weinstein, *Inside Rebellion*.
45. Arjona, "Civilian Resistance."
46. Bueno de Mesquita et al., *Logic of Political Survival*.
47. Azam, "How to Pay for the Peace?"; Gandhi and Przeworski, "Cooperation, Cooptation and Rebellion."
48. Fjelde and De Soysa, "Coercion, Co-optation, or Cooperation?"; Acemoglu et al., "Revisiting the Determinants"; Bratton and van de Walle, *Democratic Experiments in Africa*.
49. Cunningham, *Barriers to Peace*, 212, 215.
50. Snyder, *From Voting to Violence*; Carothers, "How Democracies Emerge"; Miall, *Emergent Conflict*.
51. Cunningham, *Barriers to Peace*, 56.
52. Cunningham, *Barriers to Peace*, 55.
53. Christia, *Alliance Formation*, 34. Christia analyzes multiple groups fighting one another for political control, some of which fear that they will be excluded from the postwar political order. In that context, balancing is driven by each group's assessment of the distribution of relative power, its chances of winning, and its goals of maximizing its share of power. Small groups avoid being subsumed into alliances that are too large. In Myanmar, the context is different. Groups are not fighting for postwar political control to the exclusion of other groups; they are fighting for decentralization and increased control in their own state. The logic of balancing applies nevertheless. Groups seek to increase concessions from the state and do so by assessing each alliance's likely chance of success.
54. Christia, *Alliance Formation*, 50.
55. For a classic argument on bandwagoning and balancing, see Walt, *Origins of Alliance*, 24; Kupchan, "After Pax Americana."

2. THE FAILURE TO WIN BY WAR

1. Anderson, *Imagined Communities*, 85–114; Bertrand, *Nationalism and Ethnic Conflict*.
2. Walton, "'Wages of Burman-ness,'" 8.

3. See, for example, Transnational Institute, "Ethnicity without Meaning"; Callahan, "Distorted, Dangerous Data?"

4. These figures are based on information compiled in the 1983 census conducted by the Burmese government. See Silverstein, "Fifty Years of Failure," 169. Slightly different census data are available on the US Central Intelligence Agency website as well. See CIA, "World Factbook."

5. Republic of the Union of Myanmar, *2014 Myanmar Population and Housing Census*, 3.

6. Taylor, "Perceptions of Ethnicity," 10.

7. Robinne, "Making Ethnonyms," 59–60.

8. South, *Ethnic Politics in Burma*, 4.

9. Silverstein, "Fifty Years of Failure," 169.

10. Smith, *Burma*, 2nd ed., 42.

11. Smith, *Burma*, 2nd ed., 42.

12. Smith, *Burma*, 2nd ed., 43.

13. Selth, "Race and Resistance," 489.

14. Smith, *Burma*, 2nd ed., 46.

15. Sidel, "Fate of Nationalism," 129.

16. See Pelletier, "Identity Formation."

17. For example, Christian missionaries codified the S'gaw and Eastern Pwo-Karen alphabets and grammars in the 1830s and translated the Bible into these languages from the 1850s to the 1880s. Similarly, Christian missionaries codified Jinghpaw Kachin around 1890 and translated the Bible in the 1920s. Languages and literature helped create an educated elite and a nascent public sphere, both ingredients in the rise of pan-ethnic nationalism. See Pelletier, "Identity Formation."

18. Thawnghmung, *"Other" Karen in Myanmar*, 140.

19. Sakhong, "Christianity and Chin Identity," 216.

20. Sidel, "Fate of Nationalism," 130.

21. Smith, *Burma*, 2nd ed., 78.

22. Silverstein, *Burmese Politics*, 185–205.

23. Smith, *Burma*, 2nd ed., 79.

24. Thawnghmung, *"Other" Karen in Myanmar*, 142.

25. Thawnghmung, *"Other" Karen in Myanmar*, 142.

26. Brown, *State and Ethnic Politics*, 34.

27. Brown, *State and Ethnic Politics*, 34.

28. See Yegar, *Between Integration and Secession*, 40.

29. Thawnghmung, *"Other" Karen in Myanmar*, 143–44.

30. Keenan, *By Force of Arms*, 123.

31. Taylor, "Perceptions of Ethnicity," 19.

32. Smith, *Burma*, 2nd ed., 198.

33. Zaw Oo and Win Min, *Assessing Burma's Ceasefire Accords*, 7–9.

34. Smith, *State of Strife*, 34–35.

35. Thawnghmung, *"Other" Karen in Myanmar*, 147.

36. See, for example, Callahan, "Making Myanmars"; Callahan, "Language Policy"; Centre for Peace and Conflict Studies, *Listening to Voices*. For a more comprehensive view of official policies on Karen people, see Thawnghmung, *"Other" Karen in Myanmar*.

37. Thawnghmung, *"Other" Karen in Myanmar*, 149.

38. Zaw Oo and Win Min, *Assessing Burma's Ceasefire Accords*, 14.

39. Smith, *State of Strife*, 39.

40. Callahan, "Making Myanmars," 100.

41. Callahan, "Making Myanmars," 101, 117.

42. Buchanan, Kramer, and Woods, *Developing Disparity*.

43. Most Western countries refused to recognize the SLORC regime after it refused to recognize Aung San Suu Kyi and the NLD's victory in the 1990 elections.
44. Taylor, "Evolving Military Rule"; Taylor, *Armed Forces*; Taylor, "Myanmar."
45. Lintner, *Rise and Fall*, 39–45.
46. Smith, *Burma*, 2nd ed., 379.
47. Smith, *Burma*, 2nd ed., 441.
48. Thawnghmung, *Karen Revolution in Burma*, 32.
49. Callahan, *Political Authority*, 2–3.
50. South et al., *Between Ceasefire and Federalism*, 29.
51. Smith, "Ethnic Participation," 64.
52. Interview by the authors, July 2017, Taunggyi, Myanmar.
53. Smith, "Ethnic Participation," 63.
54. Smith, "Ethnic Participation," 45.
55. Smith, "Ethnic Participation," 45.
56. Smith, "Ethnic Participation," 64.
57. Interview by the authors, June 29, 2017, Yangon, Myanmar.
58. Interview by the authors, June 13, 2016, Yangon, Myanmar.
59. Smith, "Ethnic Participation," 65.
60. Smith, "Ethnic Participation," 63–66.
61. Interview by the authors, July 2017, Taunggyi, Myanmar.
62. "Burma 'Approves New Constitution.'" By all accounts, the population was intimidated into voting in favor of the constitution.
63. Jolliffe, *Ethnic Armed Conflict*, vi.
64. On average, there were nine ministerial portfolios in each state and region.
65. For the self-administered zones, these powers relate to markets, pastures, forest protection, environmental protection, electricity and water supply, fire prevention, and other areas such as local roads and bridges already administered at that level.
66. Jolliffe, *Ethnic Armed Conflict*, iv.
67. Kyi Pyar Chit Saw and Arnold, *Administering the State*, 26–40.

3. DEMOCRATIZATION

1. Head of a major NGO involved in the peace process, interviewed by the authors, February 2015, Yangon, Myanmar. Two other interviews confirmed this view, with one subject speaking of the reform to avoid state disintegration (senior official of the Myanmar Peace Center, interviewed by the authors, February 2015, Yangon, Myanmar). Another spoke of the military and the elite's realization that Myanmar's state was failing (senior analyst of Myanmar's political developments, interviewed by the authors, June 2015, Yangon, Myanmar). Also see Thant Myint-U, *Hidden History of Burma*.
2. Kyaw Yin Hlaing, "Reassessing the Economic Sanctions"; Lall, *Understanding Reform*.
3. Huang, "Re-thinking Myanmar's Political Regime," *Contemporary Politics*; Egreteau, *Caretaking Democratization*, 22; Taylor, "Evolving Military Role"; Taylor, *Armed Forces*; Taylor, "Myanmar."
4. Transnational Institute, "Changing Ethnic Landscape," 3–4.
5. Saw, "Tokyo Support."
6. See also Lall, *Understanding Reform*, 75, on the role of civil society; Huang, "Rethinking Myanmar's Political Regime"; Taylor, *Armed Forces*.
7. Head of a major NGO involved in the peace process, interviewed by the authors, February 21, 2015, Yangon, Myanmar. Also see Ye Htut, *Myanmar's Political Transition*, 217.
8. Senior analyst of Myanmar's political developments, interviewed by the authors, June 12, 2015, and June 25, 2016, Yangon, Myanmar.

9. See Su Mon Thazin Aung, whose analysis captures tensions that existed between conservative and reformist groups within the Thein Sein government between 2011 and 2015. Su Mon Thazin Aung, "Governing the Transition."

10. Head of a major NGO involved in the peace process, interviewed by the authors, June 11, 2015, Yangon, Myanmar.

11. Ye Htut, *Myanmar's Political Transition*, 104.

12. Journalist who covered Myanmar politics since 2011, Burma observers inside Myanmar, and two scholars who work for the government and/or have close connections with the reformists within the government, interviewed by the authors, summer 2014, 2015, 2016, Yangon, Myanmar; head of a major NGO involved in the peace process, interviewed by the authors, June 11, 2015, Yangon, Myanmar. Shwe Mann was nevertheless removed from the top position of the USDP after he called for a drastic constitutional amendment that included a diminished role for the military in politics. See Sithu, "Why Was Thura Shwe Mann Fired."

13. Tha Lun Zaung Htet, "Thein Sein, Shwe Mann Rivalry"; also see Sithu Aung Myint, "Whither Shwe Mann?"

14. Hnin Yadana Zaw, "Ruling Party Chief Sacked."

15. Senior member of the Myanmar Peace Center, interviewed by the authors, February 15, 2015, Yangon, Myanmar.

16. Close adviser to the Chin National Front, interviewed by the authors, June 24, 2015, Yangon, Myanmar.

17. Asia Foundation, *State and Region Governments*, 21.

18. Kyi and Arnold, "Administering the State"; Matthew Arnold of the Asia Foundation, interviewed by the authors, January 6, 2016, Yangon, Myanmar.

19. Egreteau, *Parliamentary Development in Myanmar*, 30.

20. Some of these included Pyidaungsu Hluttaw Law No. 57/2014—Law Amending the Emoluments, Allowances, and Decorations of State and Region Level Personnel Law, December 10, 2014; Pyidaungsu Hluttaw Law No. 41/2014—National Education Law, October 5, 2014; Pydaungsu Hluttaw Law No. 22/2013—Procedures of the State and Region Hluttaw Law, August 6, 2013; Pyidaungsu Hluttaw Law No. 8/2015—Law Protecting Ethnic Rights, February 24, 2015; Pyidaungsu Hluttaw Law No. 44/2015—Second Law Amending the Development of Border Areas and National Races, July 22, 2015; Pyidaungsu Hluttaw Law No. 45/2015—Law Amending the 2008 Constitution of the Union of Myanmar, July 22, 2015.

21. Su Mon Thazin Aung, "Governing the Transition," 132, 191, 208.

22. Su Mon Thazin Aung, "Governing the Transition," 219.

23. Su Mon Thazin Aung, "Governing the Transition," 211. Su Mon Thazin Aung, who conducted extensive interviews with USDP ministers and civil servants, interviewed by the authors by telephone, May 7, 2021; people in the inner circles of government or participants in NCA negotiations, interviewed informally by the authors, 2015–16, Yangon, Myanmar; close adviser to the Chin National Front, interviewed by the authors, June 2015, Yangon, Myanmar.

24. Su Mon Thazin Aung, "Governing the Transition," 201.

25. Myanmar researcher, interviewed by the authors, June 2016, Yangon, Myanmar. Also see Tha Lun Zaung Htet, "Shwe Mann."

26. Su Mon Thazin Aung, interviewed online by one of the authors, November 8, 2021. This insight is also corroborated by informal conversations with people within the inner circles of the government.

27. Su Mon Thazin Aung, "Governing the Transition," 200.

28. Ei Ei Toe Lwin, "U Shwe Mann."

29. Martin, "Burma's Parliament."

30. Senior member of the Myanmar Peace Center, interviewed by the authors, February 15, 2015, Yangon, Myanmar. The MPC was a quasi-governmental think tank formed by Thein Sein and generously funded by the Japanese and EU governments, to spearhead ceasefire negotiations with EAOs. It was perceived as a "progressive" force closely allied with Thein Sein.

31. Three MPC staffers, with KNU leaders and participants in NCA negotiation processes, interviewed by the authors, 2014 and 2016, Yangon and Naypyitaw, Myanmar. One Yangon-based Burma expert, for instance, mentioned how the MPC first convinced Minister Aung Min, who then convinced the president, who then convinced the commander in chief, to accept the principles of federalism. A Myanmar researcher and analyst, interviewed by the authors, June 2016, Yangon, Myanmar; close adviser to the Chin National Front, interviewed by the authors, February 2015, Yangon, Myanmar. The adviser said, "[The] commander in chief of the Tatmadaw is always respectful of the president, and in the end always tries to comply with orders."

32. Senior member of the Myanmar Peace Center, interviewed by the authors, February 15, 2015, Yangon, Myanmar.

33. The USDP held the majority in all seven Bamar-dominated state legislatures, but shared seats with ethnic parties in ethnic state legislatures. See Transnational Institute, "Changing Ethnic Landscape," 6.

34. Ethnic affairs minister from Bago Region, interviewed by the authors, June 28, 2015, Yangon, Myanmar. These views were also confirmed in numerous interviews and conversations with USDP party members.

35. Mon state MP from the All Mon Region Democracy Party, interviewed by the authors, June 2015, Mawlamyine, Myanmar.

36. Asia Foundation, *State and Region Governments*, 67.

37. Asia Foundation, *State and Region Governments*, 67.

38. Yadana, director of the Braveheart Foundation, Myanmar, and a Bamar national who is the main impetus behind this initiative, worked with ethnic affairs ministers to arrange a meeting with the president to promote their constitutionally recognized rights and to coordinate a workshop where they collectively made input and crafted the law, interviewed by the authors, June 21, 2015, Yangon, Myanmar; two ethnic affairs ministers, interviewed by the authors, August 15, 2015, Yangon, Myanmar. Also see Thawnghmung and Yadana, "Citizenship and Minority Rights."

39. Thawnghmung and Yadana, "Citizenship and Minority Rights," 120; Pyidaungsu Hluttaw Law No. 8/2015—*Ethnic Rights Protection Law*.

40. Egreteau, *Parliamentary Development in Myanmar*, 32.

41. Close adviser to the Chin National Front, interviewed by the authors, June 24, 2015, Yangon, Myanmar.

42. Transnational Institute, "Changing Ethnic Landscape," 3–4.

43. Egreteau, *Parliamentary Development in Myanmar*, 28; members of ethnic political parties and civil societal groups, interviewed by the authors, 2012–16, Yangon, Myanmar.

44. Stokke, "Political Representation," 318; Egreteau, *Parliamentary Development in Myanmar*, 27; Transnational Institute, "Changing Ethnic Landscape," 2; Transnational Institute, "2015 General Election," 6.

45. Yadana, interviewed by the authors, July 2014, Yangon, Myanmar.

46. Politicians, interviewed by the authors, June 2016, Hakha, Mawlamyine, and Hpa-An, Myanmar.

47. Thawnghmung and Saw Eh Htoo, "Fractured Centre."

48. Htoo Thant, "State Counselor Bill."

49. Transnational Institute, "2020 General Election," 12.

50. Transnational Institute, "Myanmar," 9.

51. She chaired almost all important committees, required strict party loyalty and discipline, and imposed a top-down and authoritarian decision-making style. Foreign journalist covering the issue, staffers at a Yangon-based think tank, and staffers within the inner circle of the NLD government, interviewed informally by the authors, 2016–18, Yangon, Myanmar.

52. This was made clear in Aung San Suu Kyi's conversations with ethnic leaders. Leaders of ethnic armed groups that signed nationwide ceasefire agreements, interviewed by the authors, February 2017, Yangon, Myanmar; Thawnghmung, "Signs of Life."

53. INGO staff and a government staffer interviewed by the authors, July 2015, Yangon, Myanmar; close adviser to the Chin National Front, interviewed by the authors, February 15, 2015, Yangon, Myanmar.

54. Yadana, interviewed by the authors, January 15, 2017, Yangon, Myanmar. The Ministry of Ethnic Affairs subsequently served as a coordinating body for the twenty-nine ethnic affairs ministers at the state/regional parliaments.

55. Analysis based on data in the *Myanmar Gazetteer*. Six of the fourteen chief ministers initially appointed by the USDP and NLD governments were members of minority ethnic groups. The number of chief ministers who were members of minority ethnic groups, however, went down to five during the Thein Sein administration after the Rakhine state chief minister was replaced by U Maung Maung Ohn, a Bamar.

56. Foreign journalist who has covered the Myanmar transition since 2011, interviewed by the authors, January 18, 2017, Yangon, Myanmar; individuals with close connections to Aung San Suu Kyi's or the NLD's inner circle, interviewed by the authors, January 22, 2017, Yangon, Myanmar.

57. "Controversial Bogyoke Aung San Bridge"; Nyan Hlaing Lynn, "Union Minister Criticises Own Daughter."

58. Hintharnee, "Protesters Submit Petition." The 5,203-foot bridge was built in February 2015 and was originally given the name Salween Bridge, Chaungzon. The bridge cost 59 billion kyats ($4.4 million). Also see Nyan Hlaing Lynn, "Union Minister Criticizes Own Daughter."

59. Aung Theinkha, Nay Rein Kyaw, and Thinn Thiri, "Myanmar's NLD Cautions Protesters."

60. "Army Slaps Down Karenni State Chief"; Chan Thar, "Bogyoke Statue Protesters."

61. Nyein Nyein, "Karen Martyrs' Day Case."

62. People's Alliance for Credible Elections, *Public Opinions*.

63. Senior analyst of Myanmar's political developments, interviewed by the authors, June 22, 2016, Yangon, Myanmar.

64. Informal conversations with Bamar political elites, 2014–16, Yangon and Mawlamyine, Myanmar; comment made by a Bamar representative at the International Conference on Language Policy in Multicultural and Multilingual Settings, February 8–11, 2016, University of Mandalay University.

65. Myanmar researcher and analyst interviewed by the authors, June 17, 2016, Yangon, Myanmar; senior analyst of Myanmar's political developments, interviewed by the authors, June 22, 2016, Yangon, Myanmar.

66. Senior analyst of Myanmar's political developments, interviewed by the authors, June 22, 2016, Yangon, Myanmar.

67. Comment made by a participant at a workshop with the Danish Multiparty Democracy Organization, June 25, 2016, Yangon, Myanmar.

68. Head of a major NGO involved in the peace process, interviewed by the authors, February 21, 2015, Yangon, Myanmar.

69. Workshops and conferences hosted by various INGOs and attended by one of the authors, 2014–16, Yangon and Naypyidaw, Myanmar.

70. A remark made at the Union Peace Conference, January 12–15, 2016, Naypyitaw, Myanmar.

71. Signs of the NLD's ambiguity and hostility are reflected in its silence regarding the military's continued attack against several ethnic armed groups, and its inability or unwillingness to implement and strengthen the NCA. Many interviewees particularly made reference to Aung San Suu Kyi's patronizing tone toward minority ethnic groups and her tendency to micromanage and control the NCA process, which are counterproductive. Members and staffers with the NLD, leaders of NCA signatories, and experts, interviewed by the authors, February 13, 2019, Yangon, Myanmar.

72. Walton, "'Wages of Burman-ness.'"

73. See Wade, *Myanmar's Enemy Within*, 98–122; Bertrand and Pelletier, "Violent Monks in Myanmar"; Thawnghmung, "Politics of Indigeneity"; Leider, "Transmutations of Rohingya Movement."

74. Global Legal Monitor, "Burma."

75. "Kofi Annan's Contribution."

76. See UNHCR, "Rohingya Emergency."

77. Yun, "Aung San Suu Kyi Comes Out on Top."

4. PROCESS OVER WAR

1. Christia, *Alliance Formation*.

2. Zaw Oo and Win Min, *Assessing Burma's Ceasefire Accords*, 27–29.

3. The Democratic Alliance of Burma was an alliance between the National Democratic Front, a coalition of ethnic rebel groups, and prodemocracy groups, especially former 1988 and Burma Communist Party activists.

4. Zaw Oo and Win Min, *Assessing Burma's Ceasefire Accords*, 42–43.

5. Several groups, including the DKBA, agreed to transform themselves into BGFs or PMs under the Myanmar Army's command and support structures. Buchanan, *Militias in Myanmar*, 18.

6. International Crisis Group, "Myanmar's Peace Process."

7. Euro-Burma Office, "Myanmar Peace Process," 3–4.

8. Jolliffe, *Ethnic Conflict*, 11; Buchanan, *Militias in Myanmar*, v–vi.

9. They included the NMSP, the KIO, and the Shan State Progressive Party (which had voided ceasefires), and the KNU, Karenni National Progressive Party, and CNF.

10. International Crisis Group, "Myanmar's Peace Process," 21–22.

11. EAO leader, interviewed by the authors, June 19, 2015, Yangon, Myanmar.

12. EAO leader, interviewed by the authors, February 15, 2015, Yangon, Myanmar.

13. Callahan, *Political Authority*, 50.

14. Myanmar Peace Monitor, "Myanmar Peace Support Initiative."

15. Min Zaw Oo, "Understanding Myanmar's Peace Process," 19.

16. Pedersen, "Myanmar in 2014."

17. Su Mon Thazin Aung notes that Min Aung Hlaing, the armed forces commander, might have had such incentives for his own presidential ambition. While this ambition did not seem to materialize for the 2015 elections, certainly the USDP saw its chance to use peace as leverage against the otherwise strongly popular NLD in the parliamentary elections. See Su Mon Thazin Aung, "Burma's Top General."

18. Su Mon Thazin Aung, "Myanmar Ethnic Peace Process," 356–64. See the USDP campaign pledge in the 2015 elections, which emphasized that the government had dialogue with all ethnic organizations about internal peace and national reconciliation. It specified two achievements it had made: finding a political solution to armed conflict,

and establishing a federal union for equality. See People's Alliance for Credible Elections, "Campaign Pledges."

19. International Crisis Group, "Myanmar's Peace Process," 20.

20. Chin adviser to armed group leaders and negotiations, interviewed by the authors, June 24, 2015, Yangon, Myanmar.

21. Close observer of the peace process, interviewed by the authors, June 19, 2015, Yangon, Myanmar. See also Saw Yan Naing, "KNU Divided"; Jolliffe, *Ceasefires, Governance, and Development*, 42.

22. See Jolliffe, *Ceasefires, Governance, and Development*, 42; Karen National Union, "Preliminary Ceasefire Talks."

23. Jolliffe, *Ceasefires, Governance, and Development*, 41.

24. Saw Yan Naing, "Why Did the KNU Withdraw?"

25. Myanmar Peace Monitor, "SSA-S Government."

26. Former member of the Myanmar Peace Center, interviewed by the authors, March 5, 2018, Yangon, Myanmar.

27. Min Zaw Oo, "Understanding Myanmar's Peace Process," 17.

28. Despite the Karen National Union/Karen National Liberation Army Peace Council's name, it is neither part of nor sponsored by the KNU or the Karen National Liberation Army.

29. Jolliffe, *Ethnic Armed Conflict*, 25–26.

30. Dau Kha Dumsa, the KIO's Technical Advisory Team's spokesperson, interviewed by the authors, February 27, 2018, Myitkyina, Myanmar.

31. Euro-Burma Office, "Ethnic Armed Organizations Conference"; Euro-Burma Office, "Laiza Agreement."

32. Burma Centre for Ethnic Studies, *Report*; leading expert in the peace process, interviewed by the authors, February 17 2015, Yangon, Myanmar.

33. Leading expert in the peace process, interviewed by the authors, February 17, 2015, Yangon, Myanmar.

34. Su Mon Thazin Aung, "Governing the Transition," 204.

35. Euro-Burma Office, "Karen National Union."

36. "Putting Pen to Paper."

37. Senior MPC member, interviewed by the authors, February 15, 2015, Yangon, Myanmar.

38. Leading expert in the peace process, interviewed by the authors, February 17, 2015, Yangon, Myanmar.

39. Close observer of the peace process, interviewed by the authors, June 19, 2015, Yangon, Myanmar.

40. International Crisis Group, "Myanmar," 6.

41. These views were confirmed by conversations with ethnic armed groups' negotiators, government negotiators, and Myanmar analysts, and by email correspondence with an analyst on the Tatmadaw, conducted by the authors, November 3, 2016.

42. Aye Win Myint and Hnin Yadana Zaw, "President Meets Ethnic Rebel Groups"; "President Thein Sein."

43. Slodkowski, "Myanmar Signs Ceasefire."

44. Thawnghmung and Saw Eh Htoo, "Fractured Centre."

45. Dinmore, "Government Dissolves MPC."

46. Conference convenor, interviewed by one of the authors who attended the Union Peace Conference in 2016, Naypyidaw, Myanmar.

47. The name was a reference to the 1947 Panglong Conference, which is seen by many armed groups as a foundational meeting where the state of Burma was to be created on

the principle of federalism. For armed groups, as well as the NLD, the Panglong agreement was never implemented.

48. "Powerful Militia Storms Out."
49. Thawnghmung, "Signs of Life."
50. Nyein Nyein, "Shan National Dialogue."
51. Nyein Nyein, "Shan National Dialogue"; participants in the peace process, interviewed by the authors, June 2015 and June 2016, Yangon, Myanmar.
52. Key negotiators (both government and EAO) and participants in the NCA, a foreign journalist, and insiders within the NLD government, interviewed by the authors, June 2017, Yangon, Myanmar.
53. KNU leaders and participants at the 21st Century Panglong Conference, interviewed by the authors, June 2017 and February 2018, Yangon, Myanmar.
54. KNU leaders and participants at the 21st Century Panglong Conference, interviewed by the authors, June 2017 and February 2018, Yangon, Myanmar.
55. "Secession Fears Cloud Myanmar Peace Talks."
56. "Secession Fears Cloud Myanmar Peace Talks."
57. 21st Century Panglong Conference participants from the Karen government, interviewed by the authors, June 27, 2017, Yangon, Myanmar.
58. Reassessment of the thirty-seven principles at the KNU headquarters, participant-observed by the authors, 2017, Lay Wah, Myanmar.
59. "Ethnic Minority Rights."
60. Kunbun, "UNFC."
61. The Rakhine crisis involving the Rohingya also had a significant impact on the AA's strength.
62. Kunbun, "Unilateral Ceasefire."
63. Transnational Institute, "2020 General Election," 6–11.
64. Naw Betty Han, "Military, KNU Clashes Erupt."
65. Officially, the Wa have a Special Region under Shan State, a status they gained well before the 2008 constitution. De facto, however, they exercise a high degree of control and autonomy, operating almost independently from both the Shan State and the Union government.
66. Nyein Nyein, "Analysis."
67. KNU liaison officer, interviewed by the authors, February 12, 2019, Hpa-An, Myanmar.
68. Member of the Joint Ceasefire Monitoring Committee, interviewed by the authors, February 12, 2019, Hpa-An, Myanmar.
69. Sai Wansai, "Burma's Peace Process."
70. Ye Mon, "Karen National Union."
71. Member of the Joint Ceasefire Monitoring Committee, interviewed by the authors, February 15, 2019, Hpa-An, Myanmar.
72. "KNU Central Committee."
73. National Reconciliation and Peace Center staff member, interviewed by the authors, March 4, 2020.
74. Nyein Nyein, "Myanmar Peace Conference"; Thawnghmung and Saw Eh Htoo, "Fractured Centre," 27.

5. NORMALIZING WEAK ETHNIC STATES

1. Human Rights Watch, *Vote to Nowhere*, 5, 17.
2. "Aung San Suu Kuy's Myanmar Opposition Party."
3. Marshall and Webb, "Boycott of Myanmar Election."
4. Ei Ei Toe Lwin, "Public Prefers to Amend Constitution."

5. See Raynaud, "'Panglong Spirit'"; Raynaud, "'Panglong Spirit' (Part II)."
6. David and Holliday, *Liberalism and Democracy*, 56.
7. People's Alliance for Credible Elections, *Citizens' Mid-term Perceptions*, 113.
8. Breen and He, "Do People Really Want Ethnofederalism Anymore?," 290.
9. Regional parliaments are each made up of two constituencies in each township, with a quarter of the seats reserved for military appointees. Ethnic affairs ministers are elected by minority populations of more than about 51,400 in a region or state.
10. 2008 Constitution of the Union of the Republic of Myanmar.
11. SAZs and SADs are formed in areas occupied by national minorities that constitute at least a majority in two adjacent towns.
12. Crouch, "Vehicle for Democratic Transition," 271.
13. Crouch, "Vehicle for Democratic Transition," 271.
14. The constitutional amendments in 2015 added the following areas to regional/state governments' legislative prerogatives: investment; insurance; income tax; commercial tax; domestic and internal loans; acquisition of goods; international assistance; the management industrial zones; the clearing of vacant, fallow, and wild lands; contract registration; agricultural research; shoreline fishing rights; agriculture and meteorology; hotels, tourism, and transport; the sharing of resources; small-scale mining operations; protection of mining workers; environmental preservation; small-scale gemstone operations; all timbers except for teak and other hardwood (such as thit yar, in kyin, pyin kadoe, pidauk, tha gan net, tama lan); wild animals; small ships and yacht building and maintenance; airways and air transport; housing and building; private schools and training; nonprofit and private clinics and hospitals; literature, arts, music, painting, film, and video making; the management of basic education; prevention of the production of artificial foods, drugs, and cosmetics; taking care of children, youths, women, the disabled, the elderly, and dependents; and rescue and rehabilitation.
15. Crouch, "Vehicle for Democratic Transition," 272.
16. This number is based on the titles of these amendments, and whether they, in their wording, make explicit reference to the legislative and taxation powers of states and regional governments. It is possible that Union laws that did not specifically mention these topics could still have dealt with amendments on the legislative and taxation powers of the state.
17. Crouch, "Vehicle for Democratic Transition," 279–80.
18. Nitta, "NLD Moves to Amend Myanmar Constitution."
19. Harding & Nyi Nyi Kyaw, "Myanmar's Constitutional Impasse."
20. Bauchner, "In Myanmar, Democracy's Dead End."
21. U Zaw Myint Maung, quoted in Roewer, "Three Faces," 292; Roewer, *Myanmar's National League*, 2.
22. Thiha Tun and Thet Su Aung, "Ruling NLD Votes Down Bill."
23. Sithu Aung Myint, "National League for Democracy."
24. Kyaw Lynn, "National League for Democracy."
25. Mathieson, "Suu Kyi Stirs Ethnic Pot."
26. Mathieson, "Suu Kyi Stirs Ethnic Pot."
27. Mathieson, "Suu Kyi Stirs Ethnic Pot."
28. Among such optimistic accounts, see, for instance, Raynaud, "'Panglong Spirit'"; Tinzar Htun and Raynaud, *Schedule Two*.
29. Enlightened Myanmar Research Foundation, *Performance Analysis*, 33; Brand, "Achieving 'Genuine Federalism'?"
30. Staff of Enlightened Myanmar Research Foundation, who worked on state/regional parliamentary performances in 2011–20, interviewed by the authors, May 25, 2021, Lowell, MA, United States.

31. Tinzar Htun and Raynaud, *Schedule Two*, 36.
32. Tinzar Htun and Raynaud, *Schedule Two*, 36.
33. See a list of bylaws that have been enacted at the regional and state legislatures, at Myanmar Law Information System, "Laws in Relation to Regions"; staff of Chin CSO in Chin State, Yangon-based local researcher on state and regional governments, and chairman of Rakhine State parliament, interviewed by the authors, July/August 2018, Yangon, Myanmar.
34. Tinzar Htun and Raynaud, *Schedule Two*, 34–36.
35. Chairman of the Pa'O SAZ, interviewed by the authors, July 2017, Taunggyi Myanmar.
36. Myanmar Political Information: Linking Analytical Resources, "Brief Analysis," 5. Out of the forty-one subsectors designated for state/regional governments, the Ayeyarwaddy legislature passed laws on seventeen subsectors, Shan on fourteen, Yangon on eight, Rakhine on thirteen, Mon twenty, Mandalay twenty-three, Magway fifteen, Bago nineteen, Tanintharyi twelve, Sagaing twenty-seven, Chin eighteen, Kayin eleven, Kayah eleven, and Kachin twenty-four. None of them adopted laws under the Economic Sector.
37. U Ye Htut, former minister of information, "Political Game," [in Burmese], Facebook, January 30, 2019, https://www.facebook.com/ye.htut.988/posts/2035953876518204. Also see "Laws Passed in State/Region Hluttaws," 104–9. According to a list of total laws passed in state/regional hluttaws (as of December 30, 2018) provided on the Myanmar Law Information website at https://mlis.gov.mm, only one law related to the 2015 new regional legislative list was passed. See Kachin State Hluttaw Law No. 5/2017—Kachin State Law on Senior Age Groups, July 12, 2017, http://www.mlis.gov.mm/lsScPop.do?laword ListId=6720.
38. Bissinger and Linn Maung Maung, "Subnational Governments"; Yadana, executive director of Braveheart, interviewed by the authors, January 2016, Yangon, Myanmar.
39. Tinzar Htun and Raynaud, *Schedule Two*, 30.
40. Tinzar Htun and Raynaud, *Schedule Two*, 26.
41. Bissinger and Linn Maung Maung, "Subnational Governments," 24. Schedule 5 of the constitution (Annex C) and the 2015 constitutional amendment (Annex D), which supplements Schedule 5, outline the taxes that state/regional governments are permitted to collect, and other sources of revenue. These include taxes on areas under the legislative authority of the state/region, including land, property, roads, bridges, ports, electricity use, dams, motor vehicles and boats, entertainment, and extractives (salt, all woods except teak and other restricted hardwoods); consumption in the form of excise taxes; royalties on fresh and marine fisheries; rents, revenues, and other profits from properties owned by a region or a state and from cottage industries; revenue from the Union Fund Account (money received from the central government); service enterprises; fines imposed by judicial courts in a region or a state; registration fees; contributions by development affairs organizations in a concerned region or state; and unclaimed cash and property. The constitutional amendments of 2015 added the following taxes that can be imposed by states/regions: investment tax, insurance tax, income tax, commercial tax, custom tax, hotel and tourism tax, transportation tax, contract registration tax, shoreline fisheries tax, oil and gas tax, metal and metal mining tax, gems tax, and taxes on all timber except teak and other hardwoods such as thit yar, inn kyin, pyin kadoe, pidauk, thagan net, and tamalann. Taxes, however, account for only 15 percent of total own-source revenue. See Nixon et al., *State and Region Governments*, 83, 101–4.
42. Nixon et al., *State and Region Governments*, 83.
43. The Asia Foundation reports that state and regional governments' budgets come from fiscal transfers from the Union government (through general grant transfers, tax revenue sharing, and development funds), and own-source revenue such as taxes and fees. The proportion of state/regional revenue funded by the general grant transfer and the

amounts and the sources of revenues received by own-source taxes and fees vary greatly across the states and regions. Nixon et al., *State and Region Governments*, 79.

44. Kyi Pyar Chit Saw and Arnold, "Administering the State," 3–4.

45. Nixon et al., *State and Region Governments* in Myanmar, 19.

46. Head of major NGO involved in the peace process, interviewed by the authors, June 11, 2015, Yangon, Myanmar.

47. "Now for the Hard Work."

48. Burma Environmental Working Group, *Resource Federalism*, 8.

49. Global Witness, "Jade."

50. Dapice, *Kachin State Development Prospects*, 8, 13.

51. Kachin Christian leaders from Kachin State, interviewed by the authors, June 2015, Yangon, Myanmar. Residents of Kachin State also suffer some of the worst resource degradation in Myanmar in the areas where industrial mining, logging, and commercial agriculture by non-Kachin companies expanded after the ceasefire agreement was signed between the KIO and the Myanmar army in 1994. Mudslides that sweep away homes are not uncommon. Martov, "World's Largest Tiger Reserve."

52. Intervention by a Rakhine national, member of a Rakhine political party, during a focus group discussion moderated by the authors, June 2015, Yangon, Myanmar.

53. Intervention by a Rakhine national, member of a Rakhine political party, during a focus group discussion moderated by the authors, June 2015, Yangon, Myanmar.

54. Intervention by a participant at a workshop hosted by the Danish Institute for Parties and Democracy: Myanmar, attended by the authors, June 2016, Yangon, Myanmar.

55. Several participants from all of these states echoed the examples provided. Focus group discussion moderated by the authors, June 2015, Yangon, Myanmar.

56. General sentiments expressed by participants in a focus group discussion moderated by the authors, June 2015, Yangon, Myanmar. Also see Buchanan, Kramer, and Woods, *Developing Disparity*; Ethnic Peace Resource Project, "Natural Resources and Land Issues."

57. Chin and Shan nationals during a focus group discussion moderated by the authors, June 2015, Yangon, Myanmar. Also see Suhardiman, Rutherford, and Bright, "Violent Armed Conflict."

58. Intervention by an activist from Chin State during a focus group discussion moderated by the authors, June 2015, Yangon, Myanmar.

59. Staff of an INGO, who is also a leading participant in the Multi-Stakeholder Group of the Extractive Industries Transparency Initiative, interviewed by the authors, January 2016, Yangon, Myanmar. Also see Chan Myat Htwe, "MOGE to Reveal Other Account Details."

60. Fuller, "Myanmar Backs Down."

61. Einzenberger, "Frontier Capitalism"; comment made by an activist from Mon State during a focus group discussion moderated by the authors, June 2015, Yangon, Myanmar.

62. Macleod, "Kayin State Struggles."

63. Director of an INGO, who is also a leading participant in the Multi-Stakeholder Group of Extractive Industry Transparency Initiatives, interviewed by the authors, February 7, 2017, Yangon, Myanmar.

64. Nine out of twenty-two respondents who attended our focus group discussion in June 2015 in Yangon, Myanmar, said the local government "did not participate" in resource management. Yet seven spoke of such arrangements between the local and central governments and mining entrepreneurs. It is clear that local corruption gives local governments little incentive to challenge existing arrangements in resource-rich areas.

65. Oxford Business Group, *Report*, 188. The mining sector is divided into two subsectors: minerals and precious stones. The mineral segment is governed by the 2015 Mines Law, with jade and gemstone mining regulated by the Gemstone Law of 1995.

66. Researchers from the Enlightened Myanmar Research Institute, interviewed by the authors, June 2017, Yangon, Myanmar; director of an ethnic INGO, interviewed by the authors, July 2017, Yangon, Myanmar.

67. See Pyidaungsu Hluttaw Law No. 40/2016—Myanmar Investment Law, October 18, 2016. Also see "Myanmar Surpasses FDI Target."

68. Director of INGO, who is also a leading participant in the Multi-Stakeholder Group of Extractive Industry Transparency Initiatives, and local researchers from EMReF, interviewed by the authors, June and December 2017, Yangon, Myanmar.

69. Director of Yangon-based INGO, interviewed by the authors, January 6, 2016, Yangon, Myanmar.

70. Mon, Karen, Shan, and Kachin civil society organizations in their respective states, interviewed by the authors, 2015–18.

71. Former state minister in Shan State, interviewed by the authors, June 2016, Yangon, Myanmar; civil society groups and political parties from Shan, Kachin, Kayin, and Rakhine States, and a staff member from the Pyidaungsu Institute, interviewed by the authors, June 2016, Yangon, Myanmar.

72. Thiri Shwesin Aung, Fischer, and Buchanan, "Land Use and Land Cover Changes."

73. World Bank, "Myanmar."

74. Franco et al., *Meaning of Land*, 9.

75. Mark, "Land Tenure Reform," 23–26.

76. Conversation between the authors and a former Karen MP, June 2016, Hpa-An, Myanmar.

77. The participants in our focus group discussion in June 2015 in Yangon, Myanmar, also made this point. The practice continued under the NLD government.

78. Callahan, "Making Myanmars."

79. UNICEF worked with the government, civil society organizations, and nonstate armed groups to promote "mother tongue" education throughout the country. Staff from UNICEF and Pyoe Pin International, interviewed by the authors, July 2015, Yangon, Myanmar.

80. Two staff members from Pyoe Pin International, interviewed by the authors, January 8, 2014, February 21, 2015, Yangon, Myanmar; Karen CSOs working on Karen language and literature, interviewed by the authors, January 14, 2014, Yangon, Myanmar.

81. See Pyidaungsu Hluttaw Law No. 38/2015—Law Amending the National Education Law, June 25, 2015.

82. Deconcentration, by which central government ministries delegate some implementing powers and some autonomy to lower levels of bureaucracy in the line ministry offices at the regional level, is the weakest form of decentralization. Schneider, "Decentralization."

83. Nixon et al., *State and Region Governments*, 5.

84. Twelve out of twenty-two participants who attended our focus group discussion in June 2015 in Yangon, Myanmar, said that they had not seen the teaching of minority languages in school in their areas. Three said that the teaching of minority languages had been offered "at government primary schools but outside school hours," and one said the teaching of minority languages had not been offered "at government schools," only at "nongovernment organizations."

85. Mon civil society activist, interviewed by the authors, June 18, 2015, Yangon, Myanmar.

86. Mon, Karen, and Chin civil society activists, interviewed by the authors, June 18, 2015, Yangon, Myanmar; comments made by participants from Karen areas in Bago Region in a focus group discussion moderated by the authors, June 2015, Bago, Myanmar.

87. Chin, Karen, and Naga community leaders, interviewed by the authors, February 17, 2015, June 18, 2015, February 2016, Yangon and Mandalay, Myanmar; observation

of participants in a focus group discussion moderated by the authors, June 13, 2015, Yangon, Myanmar.

88. Shan community leader, interviewed by the authors, June 18, 2015, Yangon, Myanmar; Karen community leader, interviewed by the authors, June 18, 2015, Yangon, Myanmar; members of Pa'O political party and civil society organizations, interviewed by the authors, June 2017, Shan State, Myanmar.

89. Karen community leader, interviewed by the authors, June 18, 2015, Yangon, Myanmar; comments made by participants who attended panels on education and languages in minority ethnic areas at the International Conference on Language Policy in Multicultural and Multilingual Settings, February 8–11, 2016, Mandalay, Myanmar.

90. Mon community leaders, residents, and U Aung Naing Oo, a representative in the Mon State Hluttaw, interviewed by the authors, June 2015, Mon State, Myanmar.

91. A Bamar lecturer publicly challenged Mon's initiative to have the Mon language recognized as an official language in Mon State at the UNICEF-sponsored International Conference on Language Policy in Multicultural and Multilingual Settings, February 8–11, 2016, Mandalay, Myanmar; Bamar and non-Mon residents, conversation with the authors, January 2016, Mon State, Myanmar.

92. NCA signatories, members of the government's peace negotiation team, ethnic civil society organizations, and Burma watchers, interviewed by the authors, 2016–19, Myanmar.

6. OUTFLANKING AND THE EROSION OF DE FACTO AUTONOMY

1. Jones, "Explaining Myanmar's Regime Transition," 792.
2. Jones, "Explaining Myanmar's Regime Transition," 793.
3. Callahan, *Political Authority*, 17.
4. Callahan, *Political Authority*, 13.
5. Two medical doctors who worked in areas under the control of Mon and Karen armed groups, interviewed by the authors, January 2015, Yangon, Myanmar.
6. Brenner, "Authority in Rebel Groups," 420.
7. Jones, "Explaining Myanmar's Regime Transition," 793.
8. Jones, "Explaining Myanmar's Regime Transition," 793.
9. Jones, "Explaining Myanmar's Regime Transition," 793.
10. Jones, "Explaining Myanmar's Regime Transition," 794.
11. Jones, "Explaining Myanmar's Regime Transition," 794.
12. Jolliffe, *Ceasefires, Governance, and Development*, 42.
13. General secretary of the KNU, interviewed online by the authors, April 1, 2021.
14. South et al., *Between Ceasefire and Federalism*, 26.
15. International expert on Myanmar ethnic politics, interviewed by the authors, May 9, 2021, Boston, MA.
16. General secretary of the KNU, interviewed online by the authors, April 1, 2021.
17. KNU stakeholder, interviewed by the authors, February 19, 2019, Hpa-An, Kayin State, Myanmar.
18. South et al., *Between Ceasefire and Federalism*, 6.
19. South et al., *Between Ceasefire and Federalism*, 17.
20. Jolliffe, *Ceasefires, Governance, and Development*, 44.
21. Burke et al., *Contested Areas of Myanmar*, 37.
22. Burke et al., *Contested Areas of Myanmar*, 46.
23. Jolliffe, *Ceasefires, Governance, and Development*, 45.
24. Jolliffe, *Ceasefires, Governance, and Development*, 45.
25. Jolliffe, *Ceasefires, Governance, and Development*, 48.

26. Two members of the Karen Joint Monitoring Committee, interviewed by the authors, February 21, 2019, Kayin State, Myanmar.

27. KNU junior staff member, interviewed by the authors, January 7, 2016.

28. Member of the Karen Joint Monitoring Committee, interviewed by the authors, February 21, 2019, Hpa-An, Myanmar.

29. Retired Kayin government official, interviewed by the authors, June 6, 2017, Yangon, Myanmar.

30. Member of the Karen Joint Monitoring Committee, interviewed by the authors, February 21, 2019, Hpa-An, Myanmar.

31. South et al., *Between Ceasefire and Federalism*, 48.

32. Yangon-based health staff member, interviewed by the authors, June 13, 2015, Yangon, Myanmar.

33. High-ranking KNU official, interviewed by the authors, June 24, 2015, Chiang Mai, Thailand.

34. High-ranking KNU official, interviewed by the authors, June 24, 2015, Chiang Mai, Thailand.

35. South et al., *Between Ceasefire and Federalism*, 44.

36. KNU officials, quoted in South et al., *Between Ceasefire and Federalism*, 48.

37. South et al., *Between Ceasefire and Federalism*, 66.

38. South et al., *Between Ceasefire and Federalism*, 66.

39. South et al., *Between Ceasefire and Federalism*, 65.

40. South et al., *Between Ceasefire and Federalism*, 60.

41. Jolliffe, *Ceasefires, Governance, and Development*, 47.

42. Jolliffe, *Ceasefires, Governance, and Development*, 47.

43. Burke et al., *Contested Areas of Myanmar*, 53.

44. Burke et al., *Contested Areas of Myanmar*, 54.

45. These projects are the Myanmar National Community Driven Development Project (2012–21) (World Bank and Italy), the National Electrification Project (2015–21) (World Bank), and the Livelihoods and Food Security Trust Fund (LIFT) (2010–18) (thirteen OECD countries). See Burke et al., *Contested Areas of Myanmar*, 54.

46. Top KNU central leader, interviewed by the authors, January 2018, Hpa-An, Myanmar.

47. Jolliffe, *Ethnic Conflict*; Harrisson and Kyed, "Ceasefire State-Making"; two medical doctors working in areas controlled by Karen and Mon armed groups, interviewed by the authors, June 14, 2015, Mon State, Myanmar; staff of the Committee for Internally Displaced Karen People, interviewed by the authors, July 2015, Chiang Mai, Thailand.

48. Jolliffe, *Ethnic Conflict*, 15.

49. South et al., *Between Ceasefire and Federalism*, 58.

50. Head of a higher-education institution in KIO areas, interviewed by the authors, June 2019, Yangon, Myanmar. Also see Ei Ei Toe Lwin, "In KIO Territory."

51. Jolliffe, *Ethnic Conflict*, 21.

52. South and Lall, "Language, Education and the Peace Process."

53. South and Lall, "Language, Education and the Peace Process," 137.

54. South and Lall, "Language, Education and the Peace Process," 139.

55. South et al., *Between Ceasefire and Federalism*, 59.

56. Jolliffe, *Ethnic Conflict*, 15.

57. Jolliffe and Mears, *Strength in Diversity*, 13.

58. Jolliffe and Mears, *Strength in Diversity*, 64.

59. KNU education stakeholder, interviewed by the authors, February 19, 2019, Hpa-An, Kayin State, Myanmar; South et al., *Between Ceasefire and Federalism*, 58–59.

60. Jolliffe and Mears, *Strength in Diversity*, 66–67.

61. Jolliffe and Mears, *Strength in Diversity*, 65.

62. Jolliffe and Mears, *Strength in Diversity*, 63.
63. Jolliffe, *Ethnic Conflict*, 5.
64. Representatives of the Shalom Foundation, interviewed by the authors, February 13, 2019, Kachin State, Myanmar.
65. Representatives of the Shalom Foundation, interviewed by the authors, February 13, 2019, Kachin State, Myanmar.
66. Jolliffe, *Ethnic Conflict*, 15.
67. High-ranking KNU leader, interviewed by the authors, June 2017, Bago Region, Myanmar.
68. High-ranking KNU leader, interviewed by the authors, January 2018, Yangon, Myanmar.
69. Jolliffe, *Ethnic Conflict*, 82.
70. Representative of the Kachin Baptist Church, interviewed by the authors, February 12, 2019, Myitkyina, Myanmar.
71. Medical doctors who participated in this project, interviewed by the authors, June 2015, Yangon, Myanmar. Also see Si Thura and Schroeder, "Health Service Delivery."
72. Si Thura and Schroeder, "Health Service Delivery," 103.
73. "Myanmar: Halt Land Law Implementation."
74. "One Giant Land Grab."
75. "Myanmar: Halt Land Law Implementation."
76. Woods, *Conflict Resource Economy*, 24.
77. Woods, *Conflict Resource Economy*, 24.
78. Mark, "Land Tenure Reform," 245–46.
79. Mark, "Land Tenure Reform," 105.
80. Mark, "Land Tenure Reform," 246.
81. See "14 Points Signed"; head of INGO working on land and environmental issues in Myanmar, interviewed by the authors, June 2018, Bago, Myanmar.
82. Head of INGO who participated in the third session of the 21st Century Panglong Conference, interviewed by the authors, August 2018, Yangon, Myanmar.
83. Staffer from INGO that used to operate in border areas but now operates inside Myanmar, interviewed by the authors, July 8, 2018, Yangon, Myanmar.
84. Mark, "Land Tenure Reform," 247.

7. FRAGMENTATION, MARGINALIZATION, AND SUBJUGATION

1. Imagined communities are groups of people who self-identify under a shared community of identity. See Anderson, *Imagined Communities*.
2. Transnational Institute, "Ethnicity without Meaning," 7–8.
3. Cheesman, "'National Races,'" 468.
4. Cheesman, "'National Races,'" 468.
5. Ferguson, "Who's Counting?," 15.
6. Lintner, "Question of Race"; Callahan, "Distorted, Dangerous Data?," 459.
7. Callahan, "Making Myanmars," 112; Transnational Institute, "Ethnicity without Meaning," 6.
8. Crouch, "Ethnic Rights," 7.
9. Diller, "Constitutional Reform," 402.
10. Callahan, "Making Myanmars," 112.
11. Callahan, "Making Myanmars," 112.
12. "Wa Group Proposes Political Autonomy."
13. International Crisis Group, "Identity Crisis," 10.
14. International Crisis Group, "Identity Crisis," 10.

15. South, "Karen Nationalist Communities," 61.
16. South, "Karen Nationalist Communities," 61.
17. Jaquet, "Kachin Conflict," 18; also see Pelletier, "Identity Formation."
18. Quoted in Ferguson, "Who's Counting?"; Schatz, "Protest over Myanmar Census."
19. Khin Su Wai, "More Ethnic Groups Express Concern."
20. Clarke, Seng Aung Sein Myint, and Zabra Yu Siwa, *Re-examining Ethnic Identity*, 68.
21. Khin Su Wai, "More Ethnic Groups Express Concern Over Minority Codes."
22. Transnational Institute, "Myanmar," 12.
23. Moe Myint, "Kuki Call for Full Disclosure."
24. Quoted in Khin Su Wai, "Red Shan Rally."
25. Khin Su Wai, "Red Shan Seek to Build Unity."
26. Quoted in Khin Su Wai, "Red Shan Seek to Build Unity."
27. Khin Su Wai, "Red Shan Rally."
28. "'Red Shan' Form Army"; International Crisis Group, "Identity Crisis," 21.
29. Hein Ko Soe, "Ethnic Parties' Dilemma."
30. "Kuki Minority Asks for Census Data."
31. Boutry, "How Far from National Identity?," 109.
32. Khin Su Wai, "Ethnic Groups Express Concern."
33. Aung Nyein Chan, "Myanmar Military."
34. Chan Thar, "Ethnic Mro."
35. Yen Saning, "Wary of Official Census."
36. "Mongla to Call for Self Administered Status"; Khin Su Wai, "Ethnic Intha Party Seeks Self-Administration"; "LDU Will Make Every Effort."
37. Maung Zaw, "Taung Yoe Survey."
38. Sai Wansai, "Demand of New National States."
39. On this operation, see Lahu National Development Organisation, *Unsettling Moves*.
40. "TNLA and RCSS Clashes Continue"; "Civilians Missing"; Kyaw Thu, "Two Rival Ethnic Militias."
41. Bynum, "Understanding Ethnic Conflict."
42. South, "Karen Nationalist Communities," 61.
43. Buchanan, *Militias in Myanmar*, 34.
44. Lun Min Mang, "Naga Zone Expansion Plan."
45. International Crisis Group, "Identity Crisis," 26.
46. Chin Christian minister, interviewed by the authors, June 2016, Hakha, Myanmar.
47. Yangon-based Chin who works for INGO, in conversation with the authors, July 20, 2019, Yangon, Myanmar; International Crisis Group, "Identity Crisis," 27.
48. Kyal Pyar, "Kayan Object to Designation."
49. "Ethnic Kayan Demand Representation."
50. Maung Zaw, "Kayan Leaders Push for Autonomy."
51. Maung Zaw, "Kayan Leaders Push for Autonomy."
52. According to government figures, 192 people were killed, 265 were injured, 8,614 homes were destroyed, and more than 100,000 were displaced. Most of the victims were Rakhine Muslims. See Bertrand and Pelletier, "Violent Monks in Myanmar."
53. See "Myanmar: What Sparked Latest Violence in Rakhine?" For background information on the Arakan Rohingya Salvation Army's insurgency in Rakhine State, see International Crisis Group. "Myanmar: A New Muslim Insurgency."
54. "UN Human Rights Chief Points to 'Textbook Example of Ethnic Cleansing' in Myanmar," UN News, September 11, 2017. Also see the UN Human Rights Council's report, *Report of the Detailed Findings*.
55. Jolliffe, *Ethnic Armed Conflict*, 37.
56. Jolliffe, *Ethnic Armed Conflict*, 37; Rohingya political leader, interviewed by the authors, June 2014, Yangon, Myanmar.

57. Northeastern India, for instance, is replete with small tribal states in many ways similar to the self-administered zones and division. As the economist Gulshan Sachdeva observes, tribal states were created from Assam in the 1960s, sometimes with little consideration for whether these territories had the population and resources to meet their administrative and other nondevelopmental expenditures. These small states were first and foremost "gentlemen's agreements" and were not meant to be self-sufficient, and evidence shows that they are often not. Most of them are now "special category states" and are dependent on central government assistance. According to Sanjid Baruah, this situation has encouraged fiscal irresponsibility and has created incentives for local politicians to engage in rent seeking. The irony, however, is that although they enjoy territorial autonomy, ethnic minorities are also highly dependent on the central state for most development projects, designed and funded from the center. See Sachdeva, *Economy of the North East*, 60; Dholakia and Karan, "Consistent Measurement"; Baruah, "Nationalizing Space," 924.

58. In 2014, the Union blocked the Mon State parliament from passing a bill on education. See Raynaud, "Education."

59. Morton, "Indigenous Peoples," 7; Thawnghmung and Yadana, "Citizenship and Minority Rights."

60. Htoo Thant, "Ethnic Affairs Ministry Planned."

61. Fishman, "Minority Language Maintenance," 171.

62. Hornberger, "Language Shift," 413.

63. South and Lall, "Language, Education and the Peace Process"; South and Lall, *Schooling and Conflict*.

64. UNESCO, "MTB MLE Resource Kit."

65. Thawnghmung and Yadana, "Citizenship and Minority Rights."

66. See Stokke, "Political Representation," 325.

67. CSO, UNDP, and World Bank, *Myanmar Living Conditions Survey 2017*, 9.

68. Shan journalist, interviewed by the authors, December 11, 2019, Taunggyi, Myanmar.

69. Shan MP, interviewed by the authors, December 12, 2019, Taunggyi, Myanmar.

70. Civil society activist observer, interviewed by the authors, February 28, 2018, Myitkyina, Kachin State, Myanmar.

71. Jolliffe, *Ceasefires, Governance and Development*, 56.

72. Jolliffe, *Ceasefires, Governance and Development*, 34.

73. Jolliffe, *Ceasefires, Governance and Development*, 69.

74. Civil society activist, interviewed by the authors, February 28, 2018, Myitkyina, Kachin State Myanmar; Hein Ko Soe and Dunant, "Kachin's Plantation Curse."

75. Civil society activist, interviewed by the authors, February 28, 2018, Myitkyina, Kachin State Myanmar.

76. Saferworld, *Justice Provision*, 9.

77. Lall, "Value of Bama-saga," 220.

78. Cheesman, "'National Races,'" 471.

CONCLUSION

1. Myanmar's economic growth slowed down for a number of reasons, including chronic instability in its exchange rate, in particular the depreciation of the kyat to the US dollar; the overall fragility of the legal system and banking sector; and the Rakhine conflict. By the end of the decade, inflation rates rose rapidly, affecting imports and increasing fuel and transportation costs and overall consumer costs in the country. Chau, "Myanmar Economy Losing Momentum"; Nan Lwin, "World Bank's Economic Outlook."

2. Aung San Suu Kyi and the NLD achieved mixed results in a number of areas, including civil liberties and the peace process, both of which seemed to stall by the end of

her first term. She adopted a centralizing approach to governance, and made little to no concrete realization on releasing political prisoners, repealing repressive laws, creating a free press, or addressing key environmental issues.

3. UN Human Rights Council, *Report of the Detailed Findings*. Aung San Suu Kyi's image abroad was profoundly affected by her inability to condemn the brutal violence against Rohingya Muslims in Rakhine State and the jailing of two Reuters journalists (Wa Lone and Kyaw Soe Oo). As a result, Aung San Suu Kyi was stripped of numerous awards, including the prestigious Elie Wiesel Award from the US Holocaust Memorial Museum, the Freedom of Edinburgh Award, and the Amnesty International Award. See International Crisis Group, "Myanmar's Stalled Transition"; Ellis-Petersen, "From Peace Icon to Pariah"; Marston, "Two Journalists Are Free."

4. Saw Yan Naing, "KNU, Govt Reach Historic Agreement"; McElroy, "Burma Ends One of World's Longest Running Insurgencies."

5. Davis, "Myanmar Is Losing"; "Arakan Army"; Hogan, "'Slow Genocide'"; O'Connell, "Myanmar's 'Forgotten War.'"

6. See Callahan, *Making Enemies*.

7. Silverstein, "Aung San Suu Kyi"; Popham, *Lady and the Generals*; Pederson, *Burma Spring*.

8. Transnational Institute, "2015 General Election"; Beech, "Burma's Ethnic Minorities"; Lawi Weng, "Ethnic Groups."

9. See Bertrand, Pelletier, and Thawnghmung, "First Movers."

10. See Nyi Nyi Kyaw, "Democracy First, Federalism Next?"

11. See, for example, Fjelde and De Soysa, "Coercion, Co-optation, or Cooperation?"

12. Bertrand, *Nationalism and Ethnic Conflict*.

13. Bertrand, *Democracy and Nationalism*, 145–62.

14. Bertrand and Jeram, "Democratization and Determinants."

15. Sambanis, "Ethnic and Nonethnic Civil Wars."

16. The Union Peace Dialogue Joint Committee, a key player in the peace process, was responsible for submitting proposals to the Union Peace Conference. In the UPDJC, EAOs represented only a third of the participants. The other two-thirds were composed of members of the government and of the political parties, of which a majority were from the NLD. Since agreements required two-thirds of the participants, EAOs maintained a de facto veto over decisions in the UPDJC. At the Union Peace Conference, however, EAOs represented only a fifth of the participants. Since agreements must be reached by 75 percent of the participants, EAOs were short of de facto veto power in the final decision body.

17. See Keenan, "All-Inclusiveness"; Johanson, "Inclusive Burmese Peace Process."

18. For a more general argument along these lines, see Cederman, Hug, and Krebs, "Democratization and Civil War"; Cederman, Gleditsch, and Hug, "Elections and Ethnic Civil War."

19. Brancati and Snyder, "Time to Kill"; Mansfield and Snyder, "Pathways to War"; Carothers, "How Democracies Emerge."

20. In 2014, the NLD launched a petition calling for changes to section 436, which gives the military a veto power over constitutional changes, and section 59(f), which forbids Aung San Suu Kyi from becoming president. Htoo Thant, "NLD Leader." In 2019, Aung San Suu Kyi came back with a similar proposal to gradually cut the number of military MPs over fifteen years and scrap a clause that prevented her from becoming president. The military MPs have boycotted the parliamentary debates. Shoon Naing, "Myanmar Lawmakers Debate Proposals."

21. The NLD tried twice to amend the constitution within parliament but failed both times, either ignored by parliament or blocked by the military MPs. Sithu Aung Myint, "NLD Duped Again." The NLD did not try, however, to write a new constitution, which

is not prohibited by the 2008 constitution. See Ei Ei Toe Lwin, "NLD Could Draft New Constitution."

22. Here, we disagree with those who believe that small incremental changes can lead to substantial changes in Myanmar. See, for example, Tinzar Htun and Raynaud, *Schedule Two*. By contrast, we contend that incremental changes, while perhaps decentralizing the state, will fall short of reorganizing the state into a true federal system. We argue that each constitutional amendment actually reinforces the 2008 constitution and its nonfederal aspects.

23. Nyi Nyi Kyaw, "Democracy First, Federalism Next?," 7–8.

24. After 2012, the central government invested heavily in extending government administration, social services, and development projects to communities in ceasefire areas. It deepened relations with community leaders and allowed EAOs' leaders to be involved in business. It thus gained increasing control over ceasefire areas, while raising the costs of a return to war for the EAOs. See Jolliffe, *Ceasefires, Governance, and Development*.

25. While the KNU did not return to war, there were nevertheless several armed clashes following the ceasefire of 2012. See, for instance, Naw Betty Han, "Military, KNU Clashes."

26. Nyein Nyein, "Tatmadaw Says It Has Clashed with AA."

27. Cunningham, "Actor Fragmentation."

28. Thawnghmung, "Myanmar."

29. Thawnghmung, and Khun Noah, "Myanmar's Military Coup."

30. Rakhine politician, interviewed by the authors by telephone, May 28, 2021.

Bibliography

Acemoglu, Daron, Simon Johnson, James A. Robinson, and Pierre Yared. "Revisiting the Determinants of Democracy." Unpublished manuscript, 2004. https://papers.ssrn.com/sol3/papers.cfm?abstract_id=596222.

Akcinaroglu, Seden. "Rebel Interdependencies and Civil War Outcomes." *Journal of Conflict Resolution* 56, no. 5 (2012): 879–903.

Anderson, Benedict. *Imagined Communities: Reflections on the Origin and Spread of Nationalism*. London: Verso Books, 2006.

Andeweg, Rudy B. "Consociational Democracy." *Annual Review of Political Science* 3 (2000): 509–36.

"Arakan Army: Current Conflict Due to Tatmadaw's Uninclusive Peace Approach." BNI, August 20, 2019. https://www.bnionline.net/en/news/Rakhine-army-current-conflict-due-tatmadaws-uninclusive-peace-approach.

Arjona, Ana. "Civilian Resistance to Rebel Governance." In *Rebel Governance in Civil War*, edited by Ana Arjona, Nelson Kasfir, and Zachariah Mampilly, 180–202. Cambridge: Cambridge University Press, 2015.

Arjona, Ana, Nelson Kasfir, and Zachariah Mampilly, eds. *Rebel Governance in Civil War*. Cambridge: Cambridge University Press, 2015.

"Army Slaps Down Karenni State Chief over Threat to Use Troops against Statue Riots." Irrawaddy, July 24, 2018. https://www.irrawaddy.com/news/army-slaps-Karenni-state-chief-threat-use-troops-statue-riots.html.

Aspinall, Edward. *Islam and Nation: Separatist Rebellion in Aceh, Indonesia*. Stanford, CA: Stanford University Press, 2009.

Aung Naing Oo. "Myanmar's Frozen Conflicts and the Threat to Peace." *Frontier Myanmar*, June 10, 2019. https://frontiermyanmar.net/en/myanmars-frozen-conflicts-and-the-threat-to-peace.

Aung Naing Oo. *Pathway to Peace: An Insider's Account of the Myanmar Peace Process*. Yangon: Mizzima Media Group, 2016.

Aung Nyein Chan. "Myanmar Military and Arakan Army Urged to Halt Fighting in Chin State During Election." Myanmar Now, September 8, 2020. https://www.myanmar-now.org/en/news/myanmar-military-and-arakan-army-urged-to-halt-fighting-in-chin-state-during-election.

"Aung San Suu Kuy's Myanmar Opposition Party to Boycott Elections, Pledges Democracy Struggle." Associated Press, March 29, 2010.

Aung Theinkha, Nay Rein Kyaw, and Thinn Thiri. "Myanmar's NLD Cautions Protesters Who Oppose Aung San Statue in Karenni State." Radio Free Asia, July 6, 2018. https://www.rfa.org/english/news/myanmar/myanmars-nld-cautions-protesters-07062018165754.html.

Aye Win Myint, and Hnin Yadana Zaw. "Myanmar President Meets Ethnic Rebel Groups for Peace Talks." Reuters, September 9, 2015. https://www.reuters.com/article/us-myanmar-rebels/myanmar-president-meets-ethnic-rebel-groups-for-peace-talks-idUSKCN0R90EO20150909.

Azam, Jean-Paul. "How to Pay for the Peace? A Theoretical Framework with Reference to African Countries." *Public Choice* 83, no. 1/2 (1995): 173–84.

Azar, Edward E. *The Management of Protracted Social Conflict: Theory and Cases.* Aldershot, UK: Dartmouth, 1990.

Balch-Lindsay, Dylan, Andrew J. Enterline, and Kyle A. Joyce. "Third-Party Intervention and the Civil War Process." *Journal of Peace Research* 45, no. 3 (2008): 345–63.

Barter, Shane Joshua. "'Second-Order' Ethnic Minorities in Asian Secessionist Conflicts: Problems and Prospects." *Asian Ethnicity* 16, no. 2 (2015): 123–35.

Baruah, Sanjib. "Nationalizing Space: Cosmetic Federalism and the Politics of Development in Northeast India." *Development and Change* 34, no. 5 (2003): 915–39.

Batcheler, Richard. *State and Region Governments in Myanmar.* Asia Foundation, 2018.

Bauchner, Shayna. "In Myanmar, Democracy's Dead End." Human Rights Watch, March 10, 2020. https://www.hrw.org/news/2020/03/10/myanmar-democracys-dead-end.

Beech, Hannah. "Burma's Ethnic Minorities Seek Equality and Greater Autonomy in Landmark Elections." *Time,* November 7, 2015. https://time.com/4103734/burma-myanmar-shan-ethnic-groups-elections-nld-aung-san-suu-kyi/.

Beissinger, Mark R. *Nationalist Mobilization and the Collapse of the Soviet State.* Cambridge: Cambridge University Press, 2002.

Berdal, Mats, and David M. Malone, eds. *Greed and Grievance: Economic Agendas in Civil Wars.* Boulder, CO: Lynne Rienner, 2000.

Bertrand, Jacques. "Autonomy and Stability: The Perils of Implementation and 'Divide-and-Rule' Tactics in Papua, Indonesia." *Nationalism and Ethnic Politics* 20, no. 2 (2014): 174–99.

Bertrand, Jacques. *Democracy and Nationalism in Southeast Asia: From Secessionist Mobilization to Conflict Resolution.* Cambridge: Cambridge University Press, 2021.

Bertrand, Jacques. *Nationalism and Ethnic Conflict in Indonesia.* Cambridge: Cambridge University Press, 2004.

Bertrand, Jacques, and Oded Haklai, "Democratization and Ethnic Minorities." In *Democratization and Ethnic Minorities: Conflict or Compromise?*, edited by Jacques Bertrand and Oded Haklai, 1–17. London: Routledge, 2013.

Bertrand, Jacques, and Sanjay Jeram. "Democratization and Determinants of Ethnic Violence: The Rebel-Moderate Organizational Nexus." In *Democratization and Ethnic Minorities: Conflict or Compromise?*, edited by Jacques Bertrand and Oded Haklai, 117–43. London: Routledge, 2013.

Bertrand, Jacques, Min Zaw Oo, and Alexandre Pelletier. *Delivery of Public Services in Ethnic Minority States.* Ottawa: IDRC, forthcoming.

Bertrand, Jacques, and Alexandre Pelletier. "Violent Monks in Myanmar: Scapegoating and the Contest for Power." *Nationalism and Ethnic Politics* 23, no. 3 (2017): 257–79.

Bertrand, Jacques, Alexandre Pelletier, and Ardeth Maung Thawnghmung. "First Movers, Democratization and Unilateral Concessions: Overcoming Commitment Problems and Negotiating a 'Nationwide Cease-Fire' in Myanmar." *Asian Security* 16, no. 1 (2020): 15–34.

Bissinger, Jared, and Linn Maung. "Subnational Governments and Business in Myanmar." Subnational Governance in Myanmar Discussion Paper Series no. 2. Myanmar Development Resource Institute's Centre for Economic and Social Development and Asia Foundation, 2014.

Bogaards, Matthijs. "The Favourable Factors for Consociational Democracy: A Review." *European Journal of Political Research* 33, no. 4 (1998): 475–96.

Boutry, Maxime. "How Far from National Identity? Dealing with the Concealed Diversity of Myanmar." In *Metamorphosis: Studies in Social and Political Change in Myanmar*, edited by Renaud Egreteau and François Robinne, 103–27. Singapore: NUS Press, 2015.
Brancati, Dawn. "Decentralization: Fueling the Fire or Dampening the Flames of Ethnic Conflict and Secessionism?" *International Organization* 60, no. 3 (2006): 651–85.
Brancati, Dawn, and Jack L. Snyder. "Time to Kill: The Impact of Election Timing on Postconflict Stability." *Journal of Conflict Resolution* 57, no. 5 (2013): 822–53.
Brand, Marcus. "Achieving 'Genuine Federalism'?—Myanmar's Inexorable Path towards Constitutional Devolution and Decentralized Governance." In *Constitutionalism and Legal Change in Myanmar*, edited by Andrew Harding and Khin Oo, 135–56. London: Bloomsbury, 2017.
Bratton, Michael, and Nicholas van de Walle. *Democratic Experiments in Africa: Regime Transitions in Comparative Perspective*. Cambridge: Cambridge University Press, 1997.
Breen, Michael G., and Baogang He. "Do People Really Want Ethnofederalism Anymore? Findings from Deliberative Surveys on the Role of Ethnic Identity in Federalism in Myanmar." In *Living with Myanmar*, edited by Justine Chambers, Charlotte Galloway, and Jonathan Liljeblad, 289–314. Singapore: ISEAS, 2020.
Brenner, David. "Authority in Rebel Groups: Identity, Recognition and the Struggle over Legitimacy." *Contemporary Politics* 23, no. 4 (2017): 408–26.
Brenner, David. *Rebel Politics: A Political Sociology of Armed Struggle in Myanmar's Borderlands*. Ithaca, NY: Cornell University Press, 2019.
Brown, David. *The State and Ethnic Politics in Southeast Asia*. London: Routledge, 2003.
Buchanan, John. *Militias in Myanmar*. Asia Foundation, 2016.
Buchanan, John, Tom Kramer, and Kevin Woods. *Developing Disparity: Regional Investment in Burma Borderlands*. Amsterdam: Transnational Institute—Burma Center Netherlands, 2013.
Bueno de Mesquita, Bruce, Alastair Smith, Randolph M. Siverson, and James D. Morrow. *The Logic of Political Survival*. Cambridge, MA: MIT Press, 2003.
Bunce, Valerie. *Subversive Institutions: The Design and the Destruction of Socialism and the State*. Cambridge: Cambridge University Press, 1999.
Burke, Adam, Nicola Williams, Patrick Barron, Kim Jolliffe, and Thomas Carr. *The Contested Areas of Myanmar: Subnational Conflict, Aid, and Development*. Asia Foundation, 2017.
"Burma 'Approves New Constitution.'" BBC News, May 15, 2008. http://news.bbc.co.uk/2/hi/asia-pacific/7402105.stm.
Burma Centre for Ethnic Studies. *Report: March 2012–March 2014*. Chiang Mai: Wanida, 2014.
Burma Environmental Working Group. *Resource Federalism: Roadmap for Decentralised Governance of Burma's Natural Heritage*. Burma Environmental Working Group, 2017.
Bynum, Elliot. "Understanding Ethnic Conflict in Myanmar." Armed Conflict Location & Event Data Project (ACLED), September 28, 2018. https://acleddata.com/2018/09/28/understanding-inter-ethnic-conflict-in-myanmar.
Callahan, Mary P. "Distorted, Dangerous Data? *Lumyo* in the 2014 Myanmar Population and Housing Census." *Sojourn: Journal of Social Issues in Southeast Asia* 32, no. 2 (July 2017): 452–78.

Callahan, Mary P. "Language Policy in Modern Burma." In *Fighting Words: Language Policy and Ethnic Relations in Asia*, edited by Michael Brown and Sumit Ganguly, 143–76. Cambridge, MA: MIT Press, 2003.

Callahan, Mary P. *Making Enemies: War and State Building in Burma*. Ithaca, NY: Cornell University Press, 2005.

Callahan, Mary P. "Making Myanmars: Language, Territory, and Belonging in Post-Socialist Burma." In *Boundaries and Belonging: State, Society, and the Formation of Identity*, edited by Joel Migdal, 99–120. Cambridge: Cambridge University Press, 2004.

Callahan, Mary P. *Political Authority in Burma's Ethnic Minority States: Devolution, Occupation and Coexistence*. Washington, DC: East-West Center, 2007.

Carothers, Thomas. "How Democracies Emerge: The 'Sequencing' Fallacy." *Journal of Democracy* 18, no. 1 (2007): 12–27.

Cederman, Lars-Erik, Kristian Skrede Gleditsch, and Simon Hug. "Elections and Ethnic Civil War." *Comparative Political Studies* 46, no. 3 (2013): 387–417.

Cederman, Lars-Erik, Simon Hug, and Lutz F. Krebs. "Democratization and Civil War: Empirical Evidence." *Journal of Peace Research* 47, no. 4 (2010): 377–94.

Centre for Peace and Conflict Studies. *Listening to Voices from Inside: Ethnic People Speak*. 2010. http://www.centrepeaceconflictstudies.org/wp-content/uploads/Ethnic_People_Speak.pdf.

Chambers, Justine. "Buddhist Extremism, despite a Clampdown, Spreads in Myanmar." Asia Times, August 13, 2017. http://www.atimes.com/article/buddhist-extremism-despite-clampdown-spreads-myanmar.

Chan Myat Htwe. "MOGE to Reveal Other Account Details in EITI Second Report." *Myanmar Times*, October 4, 2017. https://www.mmtimes.com/news/moge-reveal-other-account-details-second-eiti-report.html.

Chan Thar. "Bogyoke Statue Protesters to Appear in Court." *Myanmar Times*, July 5, 2018. https://www.mmtimes.com/news/bogyoke-statue-protesters-appear-court.html.

Chan Thar. "Ethnic Mro Urge Correction of ID Cards." *Myanmar Times*, July 3, 2018. https://www.mmtimes.com/news/ethnic-mro-urge-correction-id-cards.html.

Chandra, Kanchan. "Ethnic Parties and Democratic Stability." *Perspectives on Politics* 3, no. 2 (2005): 235–52.

Chau, Thompson. "Myanmar Economy Losing Momentum, IMF Warns." *Myanmar Times*, April 21, 2019. https://www.mmtimes.com/news/myanmar-economy-losing-momentum-imf-warns.html.

Cheesman, Nick. "How in Myanmar 'National Races' Came to Surpass Citizenship and Exclude Rohingya." *Journal of Contemporary Asia* 47, no. 3 (2017): 461–83.

Cheesman, Nick. *Opposing the Rule of Law: How Myanmar's Courts Make Law and Order*. Cambridge: Cambridge University Press, 2015.

Cheesman, Nick, and Nicholas Farrelly, eds. *Conflict in Myanmar: War, Politics, Religion*. Singapore: ISEAS–Yusof Ishak Institute, 2016.

Choudhry, Sujit, ed. *Constitutional Design for Divided Societies: Integration or Accommodation?* Oxford: Oxford University Press, 2008.

Christensen, Darin, Mai Nguyen, and Renard Sexton. "Strategic Violence during Democratization: Evidence from Myanmar." *World Politics* 71, no. 2 (2019): 332–66.

Christia, Fotini. *Alliance Formation in Civil Wars*. Cambridge: Cambridge University Press, 2012.

CIA (Central Intelligence Agency). "The World Factbook." Accessed May 5, 2013. https://www.cia.gov/library/publications/the-world-factbook/geos/bm.html.

"Civilians Missing as Shan and Ta'ang Forces Clash." BNI, December 9, 2015. https://www.bnionline.net/en/news/shan-state/item/1295-civilians-missing-as-shan-and-ta-ang-forces-clash.html.

Clarke, Sarah L., Seng Aung Sein Myint, and Zabra Yu Siwa. *Re-examining Ethnic Identity in Myanmar*. Centre for Peace and Conflict Studies, 2019.

Collier, Paul, and Anke Hoeffler. "Greed and Grievance in Civil War." *Oxford Economic Papers* 56, no. 4 (2004): 563–95.

"Controversial Bogyoke Aung San Bridge Opens Today." *Eleven*, April 27, 2017.

Cornell, Svante E. "Autonomy as a Source of Conflict: Caucasian Conflict in Theoretical Perspective." *World Politics* 54, no. 2 (2002): 245–76.

Crouch, Melissa. *The Constitution of Myanmar: A Contextual Analysis*. Oxford: Hart, 2019.

Crouch, Melissa. "Ethnic Rights and Constitutional Change: The Constitutional Recognition of Ethnic Nationalities in Myanmar/Burma." Unpublished manuscript. Last revised April 15, 2015. https://papers.ssrn.com/sol3/papers.cfm?abstract_id=2592474.

Crouch, Melissa. "Myanmar's Muslim Mosaic and the Politics of Belonging." New Mandala, November 4, 2014. http://www.newmandala.org/myanmars-muslim-mosaic-and-the-politics-of-belonging/.

Crouch, Melissa. "Vehicle for Democratic Transition or Authoritarian Straightjacket? Constitutional Regression and Risks in the Struggle to Change Myanmar's Constitution." In *From Parchment to Practice: Implementing New Constitutions*, edited by Tom Ginsburg and Aziz Z. Huq, 263–80. Cambridge: Cambridge University Press, 2019.

Crouch, Melissa, and Tim Lindsey, eds. *Law, Society and Transition in Myanmar*. London: Bloomsbury, 2014.

CSO (Central Statistical Organization), UNDP (United Nations Development Programme), and World Bank. *Myanmar Living Conditions Survey 2017: Socio-Economic Report*. Nay Pyi Taw and Yangon, Myanmar: Ministry of Planning, Finance and Industry; UNDP; and World Bank, 2017.

Cunningham, David E. *Barriers to Peace in Civil War*. Cambridge: Cambridge University Press, 2011.

Cunningham, David E. "Veto Players and Civil War Duration." *American Journal of Political Science* 50, no. 4 (2006): 875–92.

Cunningham, David E., Skrede K. Gleditsch, and Idean Salehyan. "It Takes Two: A Dyadic Analysis of Civil War Duration and Outcome." *Journal of Conflict Resolution* 53, no. 4 (2009): 570–97.

Cunningham, Kathleen G. "Actor Fragmentation and Civil War Bargaining: How Internal Divisions Generate Civil Conflict." *American Journal of Political Science* 57, no. 3 (2013): 659–72.

Dapice, David. *Kachin State Development Prospects and Priorities*. Boston: Harvard Kennedy School Center Ash Center, 2016.

David, Roman, and Ian Holliday. *Liberalism and Democracy in Myanmar*. Oxford: Oxford University Press, 2018.

Davis, Anthony. "Why Myanmar Is Losing the Rakhine War." Asia Times, July 2, 2019. https://www.asiatimes.com/2019/07/article/why-myanmar-is-losing-the-rakhine-war/.

De Nevers, Renee. "Democratization and Ethnic Conflict." *Survival* 35, no. 2 (1993): 31–48.

Department of Population. *The 2014 Myanmar Population and Housing Census (The Union Report: Census Report)*. Vol. 1. Yangon: Ministry of Labour, Immigration and Population, 2015.

Dholakia, Ravindra H., and Navendu Karan. "Consistent Measurement of Fiscal Deficit and Debt of States in India." *Economic and Political Weekly* 40, no. 25 (2005): 2577–86.

Diller, Janelle M. "Constitutional Reform in a Repressive State: The Case of Burma." *Asian Survey* 33, no. 4 (1993): 393–407.

Dinmore, Guy. "Government Dissolves MPC, Transfers Assets." *Myanmar Times*, March 25, 2016. http://www.mmtimes.com/index.php/national-news/yangon/19648-govt-dissolves-mpc-transfers-assets.html.

Dittmer, Lowell, ed. *Burma or Myanmar? The Struggle for National Identity*. Hackensack, NJ: World Scientific, 2010.

Dixon, Jeffrey. "What Causes Civil Wars? Integrating Quantitative Research Findings." *International Studies Review* 11, no. 4 (2009): 707–35.

Doyle, Lindsey, and Lukas Hegele. "Talks before the Talks: Effects of Pre-negotiation on Reaching Peace Agreements in Intrastate Armed Conflicts, 2005–15." *Journal of Peace Research* 58, no. 2 (2021): 231–47.

Egreteau, Renaud. *Caretaking Democratization: The Military and Democracy in Myanmar*. Oxford: Oxford University Press, 2016.

Egreteau, Renaud. *Parliamentary Development in Myanmar: An Overview of the Union Parliament, 2011–16*. Asia Foundation, 2017.

Egreteau, Renaud, and François Robinne, eds. *Metamorphosis: Studies in Social and Political Change in Myanmar*. Singapore: NUS Press, 2015.

Ei Ei Toe Lwin. "In KIO Territory, Old Casino Gets New Life as College for Kachin." *Myanmar Times*, June 22, 2016. https://www.mmtimes.com/national-news/20974-in-KIO-territory-old-casino-gets-new-life-as-college-for-kachin.html.

Ei Ei Toe Lwin. "NLD Could Draft New Constitution." *Myanmar Times*, April 22, 2016. https://www.mmtimes.com/national-news/nay-pyi-taw/19910-nld-could-draft-new-constitution.html.

Ei Ei Toe Lwin. "NLD Says Survey Shows Public Prefers to Amend Constitution." *Myanmar Times*, October 21, 2013. https://www.mmtimes.com/national-news/8581-nld-says-survey-shows-public-prefers-to-amend-constitution.html.

Ei Ei Toe Lwin. "U Shwe Mann Dismisses NLD 436 Campaign." *Myanmar Times*, July 7, 2014. https://www.mmtimes.com/national-news/10935-u-shwe-mann-dismisses-nld-436-campaign.html.

Einzenberger, Rainer. "Frontier Capitalism and Politics of Dispossession in Myanmar: The Case of the Mwetaung (Gullu Mual) Nickel Mine in Chin State." *Austrian Journal of South-East Asian Studies* 11, no. 1 (2018): 13–34.

Ellis-Petersen, Hannah. "From Peace Icon to Pariah: Aung San Suu Kyi's Fall from Grace." *Guardian*, November 23, 2018. https://www.theguardian.com/world/2018/nov/23/aung-san-suu-kyi-fall-from-grace-myanmar.

Enlightened Myanmar Research Foundation. *Performance Analysis: State & Region Hluttaws of Myanmar (2010–2015)*. 2017.

Erk, Jan, and Lawrence Anderson. "The Paradox of Federalism: Does Self-Rule Accommodate or Exacerbate Ethnic Divisions?" *Regional & Federal Studies* 19, no. 2 (2009): 191–202.

"Ethnic Kayan Demand Representation." Democratic Voice of Burma, March 14, 2018. http://www.dvb.no/news/ethnic-kayan-demand-representation/80148.

"Ethnic Minority Rights Will Not Be on Third Panglong Conference Agenda." BNI, July 5, 2018. https://www.bnionline.net/en/news/ethnic-minority-rights-will-not-be-third-panglong-conference-agenda.

Ethnic Peace Resource Project. "Natural Resources and Land Issues in Myanmar." Accessed May 28, 2021. http://www.eprpinformation.org/en/category/peace-resources-section/land-and-natural-resources-issues-in-myanmar/.

Euro-Burma Office. "Ethnic Armed Organizations Conference: Laiza, Kachin State—30 October to 2 November 2013." Euro-Burma Office Briefing Paper, October 2013.

Euro-Burma Office. "The Kachins' Dilemma: Become a Border Guard Force or Return to Warfare." EBO Analysis Paper no. 2, 2010. http://www.burmalibrary.org/docs13/EBO_Analysis_Paper_No_2_2010_-_The_Kachins%27_Dilemma.pdf.

Euro-Burma Office. "Karen National Union & the United Nationalities Federal Council (UNFC)." Euro-Burma Office Briefing Paper, September 2014.

Euro-Burma Office. "The Laiza Agreement." Euro-Burma Office Briefing Paper, November 2013. http://www.burmalibrary.org/docs16/BCES-BP-19-Laiza-en-red.pdf.

Euro-Burma Office. "Myanmar Peace Process." Euro-Burma Office Briefing Paper, January 2013.

Farrelly, Nicholas. "More on the Rebellion Resistance Force." New Mandala, September 27, 2007. http://www.newmandala.org/more-on-the-rebellion-resistance-force/.

Fearon, James D., and David D. Laitin. "Civil War Termination." Unpublished paper, Stanford University, 2007.

Fearon, James D., and David D. Laitin. "Ethnicity, Insurgency, and Civil War." *American Political Science Review* 97, no. 1 (2003): 75–90.

Fearon, James D., and David D. Laitin. "Sons of the Soil, Migrants, and Civil War." *World Development* 39, no. 2 (2011): 199–211.

Ferguson, Jane M. "Who's Counting? Ethnicity, Belonging, and the National Census in Burma/Myanmar." *Bijdragen Tot de Taal-, Land-en Volkenkunde/Journal of the Humanities and Social Sciences of Southeast Asia* 171 (2015): 1–28.

Findley, Michael G. "Bargaining and the Interdependent Stages of Civil War Resolution." *Journal of Conflict Resolution* 57, no. 5 (2013): 905–32.

Fishman, Joshua A. "Minority Language Maintenance and the Ethnic Mother Tongue School." *Modern Language Journal* 64, no. 2 (1980): 167–72.

Fjelde, Hanne, and Indra De Soysa. "Coercion, Co-optation, or Cooperation? State Capacity and the Risk of Civil War, 1961–2004." *Conflict Management and Peace Science* 26, no. 1 (2009): 5–25.

Fortna, Virginia Page." Scraps of Paper? Agreements and the Durability of Peace." *International Organization* 57, no. 2 (2003): 337–72.

"14 Points Signed as Part II of Union Accord." *Global New Light of Myanmar*, July 17, 2018. https://www.gnlm.com.mm/14-points-signed-as-part-ii-of-union-accord/.

Franco, Jennifer, Hannah Twomey, Khu Khu Ju, Pietje Vervest, and Tom Kramer. *The Meaning of Land in Myanmar: A Primer*. Amsterdam: Transnational Institute, 2015.

Fuller, Thomas. "Myanmar Backs Down, Suspending Dam Project." *New York Times*, September 30, 2011. https://www.nytimes.com/2011/10/01/world/asia/myanmar-suspends-construction-of-controversial-dam.html.

Gandhi, Jennifer, and Adam Przeworski. "Cooperation, Cooptation, and Rebellion under Dictatorships." *Economics and Politics* 18, no. 1 (2006): 1–26.

Gleditsch, Nils Petter, Peter Wallensteen, Mikael Eriksson, Margareta Sollenberg, and Havard Strand. "Armed Conflict 1946–2001: A New Dataset." *Journal of Peace Research* 39, no. 5 (2002): 615–37.

Global Witness. "Jade: A Global Witness Investigation into Myanmar's 'Big State Secret.'" October 2015. https://www.globalwitness.org/jade-story/.

Gravers, Mikael. "Anti-Muslim Buddhist Nationalism in Burma and Sri Lanka: Religious Violence and Globalized Imaginaries of Endangered Identities." *Contemporary Buddhism* 16, no. 1 (2015): 1–27.

"Guerrillas with Attitude: An Ethnic Militia with Daring Tactics Is Humiliating Myanmar's Army." *Economist*, April 16, 2020. https://www.economist.com/asia2020/04/16/an-ethnic-militia-with-daring-tactics-is-humiliating-myanmars-army.

Gurr, Ted. *Peoples versus States*. Washington, DC: United States Institute of Peace Press, 2000.

Haklai, Oded. *Palestinian Ethnonationalism in Israel*. Philadelphia: University of Pennsylvania Press, 2011.

Harding, Andrew, and Khin Oo, eds. *Constitutionalism and Legal Change in Myanmar*. London: Bloomsbury, 2017.

Harding, Andrew, and Nyi Nyi Kyaw. "Myanmar's Constitutional Impasse: The Constitutional Amendment Process in 2020." *I·CONnect: The Blog of the International Journal of Constitutional Law*, November 12, 2020. http://www.iconnectblog.com/2020/11/myanmars-constitutional-impasse-the-constitutional-amendment-process-in-2020/.

Harriden, Jessica. "'Making a Name for Themselves': Karen Identity and the Politicization of Ethnicity in Burma." *Journal of Burma Studies* 7, no. 1 (2002): 84–144.

Harrisson, Annika Pohl, and Helene Maria Kyed. "Ceasefire State-Making and Justice Provision by Ethnic Armed Groups in Southeast Myanmar." *SOJOURN: Journal of Social Issues in Southeast Asia* 34, no. 2 (July 2019): 290–326.

Hart, Michael. "Myanmar's Peace Process on Life Support." Geopolitical Monitor, January 10, 2019. https://www.geopoliticalmonitor.com/myanmars-peace-process-on-life-support/.

Hartzell, Caroline A. "Explaining the Stability of Negotiated Settlements to Intrastate Wars." *Journal of Conflict Resolution* 43, no. 1 (1999): 3–22.

Hartzell, Caroline A., and Matthew Hoddie. "Institutionalizing Peace: Power Sharing and Post-Civil War Conflict Management." *American Journal of Political Science* 47, no. 2 (2003): 318–32.

Hartzell, Caroline A., Matthew Hoddie, and Donald Rothchild. "Stabilizing the Peace after Civil War: An Investigation of Some Key Variables." *International Organization* 55, no. 1 (2001): 183–208.

Hein Ko Soe. "The Ethnic Parties' Dilemma: Merger or Strategic Alliance?" *Frontier Myanmar*, April 18, 2018. https://frontiermyanmar.net/en/the-ethnic-parties-dilemma-merger-or-strategic-alliance.

Hein Ko Soe, and Ben Dunant. "Kachin's Plantation Curse." *Frontier Myanmar*, January 17, 2019. https://www.frontiermyanmar.net/en/kachins-plantation-curse.

Hintharnee. "Protesters Submit Petition against Naming of Gen Aung San Bridge in Mon State." Irrawaddy, May 2, 2017. https://www.irrawaddy.com/news/burma/protesters-submit-petition-naming-gen-aung-san-bridge-mon-state.html.

Hnin Yadana Zaw. "Myanmar Ruling Party Chief Sacked in Power Struggle with President." Reuters, August 12, 2015. https://www.reuters.com/article/us-myanmar-politics/myanmar-ruling-party-chief-sacked-in-power-struggle-with-president-idUSKCN0QI05E20150813.

Hoddie, Matthew, and Caroline Hartzell. "Civil War Settlements and the Implementation of Military Power-Sharing Arrangements." *Journal of Peace Research* 40, no. 3 (2003): 303–20.

Hogan, Libby. "'Slow Genocide': Myanmar's Invisible War on the Kachin Christian Minority." *Guardian*, May 14, 2018. https://www.theguardian.com/world/2018/may/14/slow-genocide-myanmars-invisible-war-on-the-kachin-christian-minority.

Hornberger, Nancy H. "Language Shift and Language Revitalization." In *The Oxford Handbook of Applied Linguistics*, edited by Robert B. Kaplan, William Grabe, Merrill Swain, and G. Richard Tucker, 413–20. Oxford: Oxford University Press, 2010.

Horowitz, Donald L. *Constitutional Change and Democracy in Indonesia*. Cambridge: Cambridge University Press, 2013.

Horowitz, Donald L. "Constitutional Design: Proposals versus Processes." In *The Architecture of Democracy: Constitutional Design, Conflict Management, and Democracy*, edited by Andrew Reynolds, 15–35. Oxford: Oxford University Press, 2002.

Horowitz, Donald L. *Ethnic Groups in Conflict*. Berkeley: University of California Press, 1985.

Horowitz, Donald L. *Ethnic Groups in Conflict*. 2nd ed. Berkeley: University of California Press, 2001.

Htet Naing Zaw. "Lawmakers Call for End to Disciplinary Transfers of Corrupt, Incompetent Officials." Irrawaddy, September 20, 2018. https://www.irrawaddy.com/news/burma/lawmakers-call-end-disciplinary-transfers-corrupt-incompetent-officials.html.

Htoo Thant. "Ethnic Affairs Ministry Planned." *Myanmar Times*, July 27, 2015. https://www.mmtimes.com/national-news/15680-ethnic-affairs-ministry-planned.html.

Htoo Thant. "NLD Leader Hails Constitution Petition's Five Million Signatures." *Myanmar Times*, August 9, 2014. https://www.mmtimes.com/national-news/11278-nld-leader-hails-petition-result-as-unprecedented-in-myanmar.html.

Htoo Thant. "State Counselor Bill Passed despite Military Voting Boycott." *Myanmar Times*, April 5, 2016. https://www.mmtimes.com/national-news/19844-military-protests-but-parliament-passes-state-counsellor-bill.html.

Htun Htun. "Karen State Ma Ba Tha Chapter Keeps Name despite State Sangha Ban." Irrawaddy, June 12, 2017. https://www.irrawaddy.com/news/burma/karen-state-ma-ba-tha-chapter-keeps-name-despite-state-sangha-ban.html.

Huang, Roger Lee. "Re-thinking Myanmar's Political Regime: Military Rule in Myanmar and Implications for Current Reforms." Working Paper Series 136, Southeast Asia Research Centre (SEARC) of the City University of Hong Kong, December 2012.

Huang, Roger Lee. "Re-thinking Myanmar's Political Regime: Military Rule in Myanmar and Implications for Current Reforms." *Contemporary Politics* 19, no. 3 (2013): 247–61.

Human Rights Watch. *Vote to Nowhere: The May 2008 Constitutional Referendum in Burma*. 2008.

Huntington, Samuel P. *The Clash of Civilizations and the Remaking of World Order*. New York: Touchstone, 1997.

Institute for Security and Development Policy and the European Union. *A Return to War: Militarized Conflicts in Northern Shan State*. Lithuania: Institute for Security and Development Policy and the European Union, May 2018.

International Crisis Group. "Counting the Costs: Myanmar's Problematic Census." Asia Briefing no. 144, May 15, 2014.

International Crisis Group. "Fire and Ice: Conflict and Drugs in Myanmar's Shan State." Asia Report no. 299, January 8, 2019.

International Crisis Group. "Identity Crisis: Ethnicity and Conflict in Myanmar." Asia Report no. 312, August 28, 2020.

International Crisis Group. "Myanmar: A New Muslim Insurgency in Rakhine State." Asia Report no. 283, December 15, 2016.

International Crisis Group. "Myanmar: A New Peace Initiative." Asia Report no. 214, 2015.

International Crisis Group. "Myanmar's Peace Process: A Nationwide Ceasefire Remains Elusive." Asia Briefing no. 146, September 16, 2015.

International Crisis Group. "Myanmar's Stalled Transition." Asia Briefing no. 151, August 28, 2018.

Jaquet, Carine. "The Kachin Conflict: Search for Common Narratives." International Management Group, 2014. https://themimu.info/sites/themimu.info/files/assessment_file_attachments/The_Kachin_Conflict_-_EU_2014.pdf.

Johanson, Vanessa. "Creating an Inclusive Burmese Peace Process." Peace Brief no. 223, United States Institute of Peace, May 2017.

Jolliffe, Kim. *Ceasefires, Governance, and Development: The Karen National Union in Times of Change*. Asia Foundation, 2016.

Jolliffe, Kim. *Ethnic Armed Conflict and Territorial Administration in Myanmar*. Asia Foundation, 2015.

Jolliffe, Kim, and Emily Speers Mears. *Strength in Diversity: Towards Universal Education in Myanmar's Ethnic Areas*. Asia Foundation, 2016.

Jones, Lee. "Explaining Myanmar's Regime Transition: The Periphery is Central." *Democratization* 21, no. 5 (2014): 780–802.

Joshi, Madhav, Erik Melander, and Jason Michael Quinn. "Sequencing the Peace: How the Order of Peace Agreement Implementation Can Reduce the Destabilizing Effects of Post-accord Elections." *Journal of Conflict Resolution* 61, no. 1 (2017): 4–28.

Jupille, Joseph. *Procedural Politics: Issues, Influence, and Institutional Choice in the European Union*. Cambridge: Cambridge University Press, 2004.

Kalyvas, Stathis N. *The Logic of Violence in Civil War*. Cambridge: Cambridge University Press, 2006.

Karen National Union. "Preliminary Ceasefire Talks—2012." [In Burmese.] Accessed March 28, 2021. https://www.knuhq.org/public/user/pdf/agreements/2012_Preliminary_Ceasefire_Union_Agreement.pdf.

Kaufmann, Eric, and Oded Haklai. "Dominant Ethnicity: From Minority to Majority." *Nations and Nationalism* 14, no. 4 (2008): 743–67.

Keenan, Paul. "All-Inclusiveness in an Ethnic Context." EBO Background Paper no. 4, Euro-Burma Office, August 2015.

Keenan, Paul. *By Force of Arms: Armed Ethnic Groups in Burma*. New Delhi: VIJ Books, 2014.

Khin Su Wai. "Ethnic Intha Party Seeks Self-Administration for Inle Lake." *Myanmar Times*, December 12, 2017. https://www.mmtimes.com/news/ethnic-intha-party-seeks-self-administration-inle-lake.html.

Khin Su Wai. "More Ethnic Groups Express Concern over Minority Codes." *Myanmar Times*, February 17, 2014. https://www.mmtimes.com/national-news/9595-more-ethnic-groups-express-concern-over-minority-codes.html.

Khin Su Wai. "Red Shan Rally for an Ethnic State." *Myanmar Times*, October 10, 2016. https://www.mmtimes.com/national-news/22982-red-shan-rally-for-an-ethnic-state.html.

Khin Su Wai. "Red Shan Seek to Build Unity Ahead of Next Year's Census." *Myanmar Times*, August 4, 2013. https://www.mmtimes.com/national-news/7702-red-shan-seek-to-build-unity-ahead-of-next-year-s-census.html.

"KNU Central Committee Holds an Emergency Meeting." Mizzima, November 7, 2018. http://mizzima.com/article/knu-central-committee-holds-emergency-meeting.

"Kofi Annan's Contribution to Myanmar's Pressing Rakhine Crisis." Irrawaddy, August 21, 2018. https://www.irrawaddy.com/news/burma/kofi-annans-contribution-to-myanmars-pressing-rakhine-crisis.html.

Kreutz, Joakim. "How and When Armed Conflicts End: Introducing the UCDP Conflict Termination Dataset." *Journal of Peace Research* 47, no. 2 (2010): 243–50.

"Kuki Minority Asks for Census Data about Exact Numbers." *Nation Thailand*, January 1, 2016. https://www.nationthailand.com/ann/30276455.

Kunbun, Joe. "The UNFC: Reasons behind Signing and Not Signing the NCA." Irrawaddy, February 14, 2018. https://www.irrawaddy.com/opinion/guest-column/unfc-reasons-behind-signing-not-signing-nca.html.

Kunbun, Joe. "Why the Military Has Declared a Unilateral Ceasefire." Irrawaddy, December 25, 2018. https://www.irrawaddy.com/opinion/guest-column/military-declared-unilateral-ceasefire.html.

Kupchan, Charles A. "After Pax Americana: Benign Power, Regional Integration, and the Sources of a Stable Multipolarity." *International Security* 23, no. 2 (1998): 40–79.

Kyal Pyar. "Kayan Object to Designation in Planned Census." Mizzima, January 13, 2014.

Kyaw Lynn. "The National League for Democracy: A Party for Democracy or Federalism?" TNI Commentary, October 2, 2020. https://www.tni.org/en/article/the-national-league-for-democracy-a-party-for-democracy-or-federalism.

Kyaw Thu. "Two Rival Ethnic Militias Clash in Myanmar's War-Torn Shan State." Radio Free Asia, January 12, 2014. https://www.rfa.org/english/news/myanmar/two-rival-ethnic-militias-clash-in-myanmars-war-torn-shan-state-12192016151800.html.

Kyaw Yin Hlaing. "Reassessing the Economic Sanctions Imposed by Western Governments on Myanmar." In *Prisms on the Golden Pagoda: Perspectives on National Reconciliation in Myanmar*, edited by Kyaw Yin Hlaing, 173–201. Singapore: NUS Press, 2014.

Kyed, Helene M. *Everyday Justice in Myanmar*. Copenhagen: NIAS Press, 2020.

Kyi Pyar Chit Saw, and Matthew Arnold. *Administering the State in Myanmar: An Overview of the General Administration Department*. Yangon: MDRI and Asia Foundation, 2010.

Kyi Pyar Chit Saw and Matthew Arnold. "Administering the State in Myanmar: An Overview of the General Administration Department." Policy Dialogue Brief Series no. 6, Asia Foundation, March 2015. https://asiafoundation.org/wp-content/uploads/2016/09/Administering-the-State-in-Myanmar_Policy-Brief_ENG.pdf.

Lahu National Development Organisation. *Unsettling Moves: The Wa Forced Resettlement Program in Eastern Shan State (1999–2001)*. Chiang Mai: Lahu National Development Organization, 2002.

Lake, David A., and Donald Rothchild. "Territorial Decentralization and Civil War Settlements." In *Sustainable Peace: Power and Democracy after Civil Wars*, edited by Philip G. Roeder and Donald Rothchild, 109–32. Ithaca, NY: Cornell University Press, 2005.

Lall, Marie. *Understanding Reform in Myanmar: People and Society in the Wake of Military Rule*. London: Hurst, 2016.

Lall, Marie. "The Value of Bama-saga: Minorities within Minorities' Views in Shan and Rakhine States." *Language and Education* 35, no. 3 (2020): 204–25.

Langer, Arnim, and Graham K. Brown, eds. *Building Sustainable Peace: Timing and Sequencing of Post-conflict Reconstruction and Peacebuilding*. Oxford: Oxford University Press, 2016.

Lawi Weng, "Ethnic Groups Have Lost Faith in the NLD." Irrawaddy, April 27, 2018. https://www.irrawaddy.com/opinion/ethnic-groups-lost-faith-nld.html.

"Laws Passed in State/Region Hluttaws—Second Term, February 2, 2016 to April 24, 2018 Regional Legislatures." Asia Foundation.

"LDU Will Make Every Effort for Establishment of Self-Administered Zone." BNI, March 22, 2018. https://www.bnionline.net/en/news/ldu-will-make-every-effort-establishment-self-administered-zone.

Leach, Edmund R. *Political Systems of Highland Burma*. Boston: Beacon, 1965.

Lederach, John Paul. *Sustainable Reconciliation in Divided Societies*. Washington, DC: United States Institute of Peace Press, 1997.

Leff, Carol Skalnik. "Democratization and Disintegration: The Breakup of the Communist Federal States." *World Politics* 51, no. 2 (1999): 205–35.

Leider, Jacques P. "History and Victimhood: Engaging with Rohingya Issue." *Insight Turkey* 20, no. 1 (2018): 99–118.

Leider, Jacques P. "Transmutations of Rohingya Movement in Post-2010 Rakhine State Crisis." In *Ethnic and Religious Identities and Integration in Southeast Asia*, edited by Oi Keat Gin and Volker Grabowsky, 191–239. Chiang Mai: Silkworm Books, 2017.

Library of Congress. "Burma: Four 'Race and Religion Protection Laws' Adopted." September 14, 2015. https://www.loc.gov/item/global-legal-monitor/2015-09-14/burma-four-race-and-religion-protection-laws-adopted.

Licklider, Roy. "The Consequences of Negotiated Settlements in Civil Wars, 1945–1993." *American Political Science Review* 89, no. 3 (1995): 681–90.

Licklider, Roy. "Democracy and the Renewal of Civil Wars." In *Approaches, Levels and Methods of Analysis in International Politics: Crossing Boundaries*, edited by Harvey Starr, 95–116. New York: Palgrave Macmillan, 2006.

Licklider, Roy, ed. *Stopping the Killing: How Civil Wars End*. New York: NYU Press, 1993.

Lieberman, Victor B. "Reinterpreting Burmese History." *Comparative Studies in Society and History* 29, no. 1 (January 1987): 162–94.

Lijphart, Arendt. *Democracy in Plural Societies: A Comparative Exploration*. New Haven, CT: Yale University Press, 1977.

Lintner, Bertil. *Burma in Revolt: Opium and Insurgency since 1948*. Chiang Mai: Silkworm Books, 1999.

Lintner, Bertil. "A Question of Race in Myanmar." Asia Times, June 3, 2017. http://www.atimes.com/article/question-race-myanmar/.

Lintner, Bertil. *The Rise and Fall of the Communist Party of Burma (CPB)*. Singapore: SEAP, 1990.

Lun Min Mang. "Naga Zone Expansion Plan Sparks Protests, Petitions." *Myanmar Times*, February 2, 2015. https://www.mmtimes.com/national-news/12977-naga-zone-expansion-plan-sparks-protests-petitions.html.

Lustick, Ian. "Stability in Deeply Divided Societies: Consociationalism versus Control." *World Politics* 31, no. 3 (1979): 325–44.

Luttwak, Edward N. "Give War a Chance." *Foreign Affairs* 78, no. 4 (July–August 1999): 36–44.

Mac Ginty, Roger. "Issue Hierarchies in Peace Processes: The Decommissioning of Paramilitary Arms and the Northern Ireland Peace Process; Lessons for Ending Conflicts." *Civil Wars* 1, no. 3 (1998): 24–45.

Mac Ginty, Roger. *No War, No Peace: The Rejuvenation of Stalled Peace Processes and Peace Accords*. New York: Palgrave Macmillan, 2016.

MacGregor, Fiona, and Nyan Lynn Aung. "Rakhine's Divided Minorities." *Myanmar Times*, July 15, 2016. https://www.mmtimes.com/national-news/21413-rakhines-divided-minorities.html.

Macleod, Alexander. "Kayin State Struggles Expose Myanmar's Energy Dilemma." *Global Risk Insights*, July 29, 2017. https://globalriskinsights.com/2017/07/myanmar-energy-dilemma/.

Mampilly, Zachariah, and Megan A. Stewart. "A Typology of Rebel Political Institutional Arrangements." *Journal of Conflict Resolution* 65, no. 1 (2021): 15–45.

Mansfield, Edward D., and Jack L. Snyder. "Pathways to War in Democratic Transitions." *International Organization* 63, no. 2 (2009): 381–90.

Mark, SiuSue. "Land Tenure Reform in Myanmar's Regime Transition: Political Legitimacy vs Capital Accumulation." PhD diss., International Institute of Social Studies, 2017.

Marshall, Andrew R. C., and Simon Webb. "Suu Kyi Says Boycott of Myanmar Election an Option." Reuters, April 3, 2015. https://www.reuters.com/article/us-myanmar-suukyi-idUSKBN0MU19R20150403.

Marston, Hunter. "Two Journalists Are Free. But Democracy in Myanmar Is Deteriorating." *Washington Post*, May 11, 2019. https://www.washingtonpost.com/opinions/2019/05/11/two-journalists-are-free-democracy-myanmar-is-deteriorating/.

Martin, Michael F. "Burma's Parliament Defeats Constitutional Amendments." *CRS Insights*, June 30, 2015.

Martov, Seamus. "World's Largest Tiger Reserve 'Bereft of Cats.'" Irrawaddy, November 16, 2012. http://www.irrawaddy.org/z_environment/worlds-largest-tiger-reserve-bereft-of-cats.html.

Mason, T. David, and Patrick J. Fett. "How Civil Wars End: A Rational Choice Approach." *Journal of Conflict Resolution* 40, no. 4 (1996): 546–68.

Mathieson, David Scott. "Suu Kyi Stirs Ethnic Pot Ahead of Myanmar Elections." Asia Times, February 12, 2020. https://asiatimes.com/2020/02/suu-kyi-stirs-ethnic-pot-ahead-of-myanmar-elections/.

Maung Zaw. "Kayan Leaders Push for Autonomy." *Myanmar Times*, April 22, 2015. https://www.mmtimes.com/national-news/1054-kayan-leaders-push-for-autonomy.html.

Maung Zaw. "Taung Yoe Survey Aims to Boost Lobby for Ethnic Affairs Minister." *Myanmar Times*, July 15, 2016. https://www.mmtimes.com/national-news/mandalay-upper-myanmar/21417-taung-yoe-survey-aims-to-boost-lobby-for-ethnic-affairs-minister.html.

McElroy, Damien. "Burma Ends One of World's Longest Running Insurgencies." *Telegraph*, January 12, 2012. https://www.telegraph.co.uk/news/worldnews/asia/burmamyanmar/9010848/Burma-Myanmar-ends-one-of-worlds-longest-running-insurgencies-after-peace-deal-with-Karen-rebels.html.

Miall, Hugh. *Emergent Conflict and Peaceful Change*. London: Palgrave Macmillan, 2007.

Min Zaw Oo. "Understanding Myanmar's Peace Process: Ceasefire Agreements." Catalyzing Reflection Series no. 2, Swiss Peace, 2014.

Moe Myint. "Kuki Call for Full Disclosure Ahead of Ethnic Census Data's Release." Irrawaddy, January 7, 2014. https://www.irrawaddy.com/news/burma/kuki-call-for-full-disclosure-ahead-of-ethnic-census-datas-release.html.

"Mongla to Call for Self-Administered Status." BNI, March 20, 2014. https://www.bnionline.net/en/shan-herald-agency-for-news/item/16839-mongla-to-call-for-self-administered-status.html.

Morton, Micah F. "Indigenous Peoples Work to Raise Their Status in a Reforming Myanmar." Perspective no. 33, ISEAS–Yusof Ishak Institute, May 22, 2017.

"Myanmar: Halt Land Law Implementation." Human Rights Watch, March 9, 2019. https://www.hrw.org/news/2019/03/09/myanmar-halt-land-law-implementation.

Myanmar Institute for Peace and Security. *Annual Peace and Security Review*. 2018.

Myanmar Law Information System. "Laws in Relation to the Greater Administrative Region." [In Burmese.] Accessed May 28, 2021. https://www.mlis.gov.mm/mLsSc.do;jsessionid=3B53F7B42ECEAF054F6BE07A0D3DB5E2?menuSeq=5&upperLawordKndCode=0400&selFont=Z1

Myanmar Peace Monitor. "Myanmar Peace Support Initiative." Accessed November 1, 2021. https://www.mmpeacemonitor.org/1444.

Myanmar Peace Monitor. "SSA-S Government 11-Point Peace Agreement." January 16, 2012. http://www.mmpeacemonitor.org/images/pdf/SSA-S-Government-16jan2012.pdf.

Myanmar Political Information: Linking Analytical Resources. "Brief Analysis of Laws Issued by the First Regional and State Parliaments." [In Burmese.] June 17, 2016. https://www.mypilar.org/sites/mypilar.org/files/publication-files/laws_passed_brief_analysis_.pdf.

"Myanmar Surpasses FDI Target of $6b in Fiscal Year 2016–2017." *Nation*, March 18, 2017.

"Myanmar: What Sparked Latest Violence in Rakhine?" BBC News, September 19, 2017. https://www.bbc.com/news/world-asia-41082689.

Nan Lwin, "World Bank's Economic Outlook for Myanmar in 6 Points." Irrawaddy, June 18, 2019. https://www.irrawaddy.com/business/economy/world-banks-economic-outlook-myanmar-6-points.html.

Nathan, Laurie. "Civil War Settlements and the Prospects for Peace." *International Security* 36, no. 1 (2011): 202–10.

Naw Betty Han. "Military, KNU Clashes Erupt in Hpapun." *Myanmar Times*, August 30, 2018. https://www.mmtimes.com/news/military-knu-clashes-erupt-hpapun.html.

Nitta, Yuichi. "Suu Kyi's NLD Moves to Amend Myanmar Constitution to Curb Military." *Nikkei Asian Review*, January 30, 2019. https://asia.nikkei.com/Politics/Suu-Kyi-s-NLD-moves-to-amend-Myanmar-constitution-to-curb-military.

Nixon, Hamish, Cindy Joelene, Thet Aung Lynn, Kyi Pyar Chit Saw, and Matthew Arnold. *State and Region Governments in Myanmar*. Asia Foundation and Myanmar Development Research Institute—Centre for Economic and Social Development, 2018.

"Now for the Hard Work." *Frontier Myanmar*, January 7, 2019. https://frontiermyanmar.net/en/now-for-the-hard-work.

Nyan Hlaing Lynn. "Union Minister Criticises Own Daughter, NLD over Mon Bridge Name Dispute." *Frontier Myanmar*, March 16, 2017. https://www.frontiermyanmar.net/en/union-minister-criticises-own-daughter-nld-over-mon-bridge-name-dispute/.

Nyein Nyein. "Analysis: Why Did the KNU Temporarily Leave Peace Talks?" Irrawaddy, October 29, 2018. https://www.irrawaddy.com/factiva/analysis-knu-temporarily-leave-peace-talks.html.

Nyein Nyein. "Karen Martyrs' Day Case Shows Ethnic Rights in Retreat under Present Myanmar Govt." Irrawaddy, September 19, 2019. https://www.irrawaddy.com/opinion/commentary/karen-martyrs-day-case-shows-ethnic-rights-retreat-present-myanmar-govt.html.

Nyein Nyein. "Myanmar Peace Conference Ends with Participants Praising 'Meaningful' Principles, Post-election Plan." Irrawaddy, August 21, 2020. https://www.irrawaddy.com/news/burma/myanmar-peace-conference-ends-participants-praising-meaningful-principles-post-election-plan.html.

Nyein Nyein. "Shan National Dialogue to Continue despite Myanmar Army Obstruction." Irrawaddy, December 19, 2017. https://www.irrawaddy.com/news/burma/shan-national-dialogue-continue-despite-myanmar-army-obstruction.html.

Nyein Nyein. "Tatmadaw Says It Has Clashed with AA Nearly 100 Times This Year." Irrawaddy, March 25, 2019. https://www.irrawaddy.com/news/burma/tatmadaw-says-clashed-aa-nearly-100-times-year.html.

Nyi Nyi Kyaw. "Democracy First, Federalism Next? The Constitutional Reform Process in Myanmar." Perspective no. 93, ISEAS–Yusof Ishak Institute, November 8, 2019.

O'Connell, Tom. "Myanmar's 'Forgotten War.'" Southeast Asia Globe, June 29, 2018. https://southeastasiaglobe.com/myanmars-forgotten-war-kachin-state-forces-battle-over-resources/.

"One Giant Land Grab." *Frontier Myanmar*, March 12, 2019. https://www.farmlandgrab.org/post/view/28809-one-giant-land-grab.

Oxford Business Group. *The Report: Myanmar 2018*. 2018.

Pedersen, Morten B. "Myanmar in 2014: 'Tacking against the Wind.'" *Southeast Asian Affairs* (2015): 223–45.

Pederson, Rena. *The Burma Spring: Aung San Suu Kyi and the New Struggle for the Soul of a Nation*. New York: Pegasus Books, 2016.

People's Alliance for Credible Elections. "Campaign Pledges by Political Parties in 2015 Elections." Accessed May 27, 2021. https://www.pacemyanmar.org/2015-promises-mm/?fbclid=IwAR19VkxwqFY2gF0Cs9UXg70GRBHfi6Y-RyUXFxiR-j26pz8yz7Z5xuhYS4E.

People's Alliance for Credible Elections. *Citizens' Mid-term Perceptions of Government Performance*. 2018. https://www.pacemyanmar.org/2018-survey/.

People's Alliance for Credible Elections. *Public Opinions on Citizens' Democratic Aspirations*. 2018. https://www.pacemyanmar.org/2017-survey-report/.

Pelletier, Alexandre. "Identity Formation, Christian Networks, and the Peripheries of Kachin Ethnonational Identity." *Asian Politics & Policy* 13, no. 1 (2021): 72–89.

Pillar, Paul R. *Negotiating Peace: War Termination as a Bargaining Process*. Princeton, NJ: Princeton University Press, 2014.

Popham, Peter. *The Lady and the Generals: Aung San Suu Kyi and Burma's Struggle for Freedom*. London: Rider Books, 2017.

"Powerful Militia Storms Out of Myanmar Peace Talks." Mizzima, September 2, 2016. http://www.mizzima.com/news-domestic/powerful-militia-storms-out-myanmar-peace-talks.

"President Thein Sein Willing to Serve a Second Presidential Term." Mizzima, July 31, 2015. http://www.mizzima.com/news-domestic/president-thein-sein-willing-serve-second-presidential-term.

"Putting Pen to Paper—and Making History." *Myanmar Times*, February 16, 2015.

Quinn, J. Michael, T. David Marston, and Mehmet Gurses. "Sustaining the Peace: Determinants of Civil War Recurrence." *International Interactions* 33, no. 2 (2007): 167–93.

Raynaud, Mael. "Education, and the Local Parliaments' Legislative Competence." Tea Circle, June 14, 2017. https://teacircleoxford.com/2017/06/14/education-and-the-local-parliaments-legislative-competence/.

Raynaud, Mael. "'Panglong Spirit' under the 2008 Constitution." Tea Circle, July 22, 2016. https://teacircleoxford.com/2016/07/22/panglong-spirit-under-the-2008-constitution/.

Raynaud, Mael. "'Panglong Spirit' under the 2008 Constitution (Part II)." Tea Circle, August 16, 2016. https://teacircleoxford.com/2016/08/16/panglong-spirit-under-the-2008-constitution-part-ii/.

"'Red Shan' Form Army in Northern Burma after Demand for New State." Shan Herald Agency for News, January 25, 2016. http://english.panglong.org/2016/01/25/red-shan-form-army-in-northern-burma-after-demand-for-new-state/.

Reilly, Ben. *Democracy in Divided Societies: Electoral Engineering for Conflict Management*. Cambridge: Cambridge University Press, 2001.

Republic of the Union of Myanmar. *The 2014 Myanmar Population and Housing Census: The Union Report, Religion*. Census Report Volume 2-C, 2016.

Riker, William H. *The Art of Political Manipulation*. New Haven, CT: Yale University Press, 1986.

Robinne, François. "Making Ethnonyms in a Clan Social Organization: The Case of the So-Called Kachin Subgroups (Burma)." In *Inter-ethnic Dynamics in Asia: Considering the Other through Ethnonyms, Territories and Rituals*, edited by Christian Culas and François Robinne, 57–78. London: Routledge, 2009.

Roewer, Richard. *Myanmar's National League for Democracy at a Crossroads*. GIGA Focus Asia. Hamburg: German Institute of Global and Area Studies.

Roewer, Richard. "Three Faces of Party Organization in the National League for Democracy." *Journal of Current Southeast Asian Affairs* 38, no. 3 (2019): 286–306.

Romano, David. *The Kurdish Nationalist Movement: Opportunity, Mobilization and Identity*. Cambridge: Cambridge University Press, 2006.

Ross, Michael. "How Do Natural Resources Influence Civil Wars? Evidence from Thirteen Cases." *International Organization* 58, no. 1 (2004): 35–67.

Rotberg, Robert I. "Failed States, Collapsed States, Weak States: Causes and Indicators." In *State Failure and State Weakness in a Time of Terror*, edited by Robert I. Rotberg, 1–25. Washington, DC: Brookings Institution Press, 2004.

Rotberg, Robert I. "Failed States in a World of Terror." *Foreign Affairs* 81, no. 4 (2002): 127–40.

Rothchild, Donald. "Liberalism, Democracy, and Conflict Management: The African Experience." In *Facing Ethnic Conflicts: Toward a New Realism*, edited by Andreas Wimmer, Richard J. Goldstone, Donald L. Horowitz, Conrad J. Schetter, and Ulrike Joras, 226–44. New York: Rowman & Littlefield, 2004.

Sachdeva, Gulshan. *Economy of the North East: Policy, Present Conditions, and Future Possibilities*. New Delhi: Centre for Policy Research, 2000.

Sadan, Mandy. *Being & Becoming Kachin: Histories beyond the State in the Borderworlds of Burma*. Oxford: Oxford University Press, 2013.

Sadan, Mandy, ed. *War and Peace in the Borderlands of Myanmar: The Kachin Ceasefire, 1994–2011*. Copenhagen: NIAS Press, 2016.

Saferworld. *Justice Provision in South East Myanmar: Experiences from Conflict-Affected Areas with Multiple Governing Authorities*. 2019.

Sai Wansai. "Burma's Peace Process: From Stagnation to Drawback?" Shan Herald Agency for News, November 12, 2018. https://english.shannews.org/archives/18326.

Sai Wansai. "Demand of New National States: A Challenge That Is Unavoidable." BNI, September 8, 2016. https://www.bnionline.net/en/opinion/op-ed/item/2271-demand-of-new-national-states-a-challenge-that-is-unavoidable.html.

Sai Wansai. "Jump-Starting the Stalled Peace Process: Is Revitalization of the 1961 Federal Amendment Proposal the Way to Go?" Transnational Institute, May 4, 2017. https://www.tni.org/en/article/jump-starting-the-stalled-peace-process.

Sai Wansai. "To Hopeland and Back: The 21st Trip for the 21st Century Panglong (Day 12 and 13)." Shan Herald Agency for News, September 21, 2016. https://english.shannews.org/archives/14987.

Saito, Ayako. "The Formation of the Concept of Myanmar Muslims as Indigenous Citizens: Their History and Current Situation." *Journal of Sophia Asian Studies* 32 (2014): 25–40.

Sakhong, Lian H. "Christianity and Chin Identity." In *Exploring Ethnic Diversity in Burma*, edited by Michael Gravers, 200–226. Copenhagen: NIAS Press, 2007.

Sambanis, Nicholas. "Do Ethnic and Nonethnic Civil Wars Have the Same Causes? A Theoretical and Empirical Inquiry (Part 1)." *Journal of Conflict Resolution* 45, no. 3 (2001): 259–82.

Sambanis, Nicholas. "A Review of Recent Advances and Future Directions in the Quantitative Literature on Civil War." *Defence and Peace Economics* 13, no. 3 (2002): 215–43.

Saning, Yen. "Wary of Official Census, Burma's Ethnic Minorities Count Their Own." Irrawaddy, December 4, 2013. https://www.irrawaddy.com/news/burma/wary-official-census-burmas-ethnic-minorities-count.html.

Saw Yan Naing. "KNU Divided over Peace Treaty." Irrawaddy, February 9, 2012. http://www2.irrawaddy.com/article.php?art_id=23004.

Saw Yan Naing, "KNU, Govt Reach Historic Agreement." Irrawaddy, January 12, 2012. https://www2.irrawaddy.com/article.php?art_id=22826.

Saw Yan Naing. "Tokyo Support for NLD Stand on 2010 Election." Irrawaddy, November 23, 2009. https://www2.irrawaddy.com/article.php?art_id=17273.

Saw Yan Naing. "Why Did the KNU Withdraw from the UNFC?" Irrawaddy, September 3, 2014. https://www.irrawaddy.com/opinion/knu-withdraw-unfc.html.

Scharpf, Fritz W. "The Joint-Decision Trap: Lessons from German Federalism and European Integration." *Public Administration* 66, no. 3 (1988): 239–78.

Schatz, Joseph. "Protest over Myanmar Census Brings Ethnic Tensions to the Fore." *Christian Science Monitor*, March 27, 2014. https://www.csmonitor.com/World/Asia-Pacific/2014/0327/Protest-over-Myanmar-census-brings-ethnic-tensions-to-the-fore.

Schiller, A. Arthur. *The Formation of Federal Indonesia, 1945–1949*. The Hague/Bandung: W. Van Hoeve, 1955.

Schneider, Aaron. "Decentralization: Conceptualization and Measurement." *Studies in Comparative International Development* 38, no. 3 (2003): 32–56.

"Secession Fears Cloud Myanmar Peace Talks: Government." Mizzima, May 29, 2017. http://www.mizzima.com/news-domestic/secession-fears-cloud-myanmar-peace-talks-government.

Selth, Andrew. "Myanmar's Intelligence Apparatus and the Fall of General Khin Nyunt." *Intelligence and National Security* 34, no. 5 (2019): 619–36.

Selth, Andrew. "Race and Resistance in Burma, 1942–1945." *Modern Asian Studies* 20, no. 3 (1986): 483–507.

Shoon Naing. "Myanmar Lawmakers Debate Proposals to Curb Military Political Power." Reuters, July 30, 2019. https://www.reuters.com/article/us-myanmar-constitution/myanmar-lawmakers-debate-proposals-to-curb-military-political-power-idUSKCN1UP18Z?il=0.

Si Thura, and Tim Schroeder. "Health Service Delivery and Peacebuilding in Southeast Myanmar." In *Myanmar Transformed? People, Places and Politics*, edited by Justine Chambers, Gerard McCarthy, Nicholas Farrelly, and Chit Win, 85–108. Singapore: ISEAS–Yusof Ishak Institute, 2018.

Sidel, John T. "The Fate of Nationalism in the New States: Southeast Asia in Comparative Historical Perspective." *Comparative Studies in Society and History* 54, no. 1 (2012): 114–44.

Silverstein, Josef. "Aung San Suu Kyi: Is She Burma's Woman of Destiny?" *Asian Survey* 30, no. 10 (1990): 1007–19.

Silverstein, Josef. "The Civil War, the Minorities and Burma's New Politics." In *Burma: The Challenge of Change in a Divided Society*, edited by Peter Carey, 129–56. London: Palgrave Macmillan, 1997.

Silverstein, Josef. "Fifty Years of Failure in Burma." In *Government Policies and Ethnic Relations in Asia and the Pacific*, edited by Michael Brown and Sumit Ganguly, 157–96. Cambridge, MA: MIT Press, 1997.

Simeon, Richard, and Daniel-Patrick Conway. "Federalism and the Management of Conflict in Multinational Societies." In *Multinational Democracies*, edited by Alain G. Gagnon and James Tully, 338–65. Cambridge: Cambridge University Press, 2001.

Sithu Aung Myint. "Does the National League for Democracy Really Want a Federal System?" *Frontier Myanmar*, November 26, 2017. https://www.frontiermyanmar.net/en/does-the-national-league-for-democracy-really-want-a-federal-system/.

Sithu Aung Myint. "The NLD Duped Again on Constitution." *Myanmar Times*, June 24, 2015. https://www.mmtimes.com/opinion/15181-the-nld-duped-again-on-constitution.html.

Sithu Aung Myint. "Whither Shwe Mann?" *Frontier Myanmar*, February 14, 2016. https://frontiermyanmar.net/en/whither-shwe-mann.

Sithu Aung Myint. "Why Was Thura Shwe Mann Fired?" *Myanmar Times*, August 26, 2015. https://www.mmtimes.com/opinion/16150-why-was-thura-u-shwe-mann-fired.html.

Slodkowski, Antoni. "Myanmar Signs Ceasefire with Eight Armed Groups." Reuters, October 15, 2015. http://www.reuters.com/article/us-myanmar-politics-idUSKCN0S82MR20151015.

Small, Melvin, and J. David Singer. *Resort to Arms: International and Civil Wars, 1816–1980*. Beverly Hills, CA: Sage, 1982.

Smith, Martin J. *Burma: Insurgency and the Politics of Ethnicity*. London: Zed Books, 1991.

Smith, Martin J. *Burma: Insurgency and the Politics of Ethnicity*. 2nd ed. London: Zed Books, 1999.

Smith, Martin J. "Ethnic Participation and National Reconciliation." In *Myanmar's Long Road to National Reconciliation*, edited by Trevor Wilson, 38–74. Singapore: ISEAS–Yusof Ishak Institute, 2006.

Smith, Martin J. *State of Strife: The Dynamics of Ethnic Conflict in Burma*. Singapore: ISEAS, 2007.

Snyder, Jack L. *From Voting to Violence: Democratization and Nationalist Conflict*. New York: W. W. Norton, 2000.

Soe Thane. *Myanmar's Transformation & U Thein Sein: An Insider's Account*. Yangon: Tun Foundation Literature Committee, 2018.

South, Ashley. *Ethnic Politics in Burma: States of Conflict*. London: Routledge, 2008.

South, Ashley. "Karen Nationalist Communities: The 'Problem' of Diversity." *Contemporary Southeast Asia* 29, no. 1 (2007): 55–76.

South, Ashley. *Mon Nationalism and Civil War in Burma: The Golden Sheldrake*. London: Routledge, 2013.

South, Ashley. "Myanmar's Stalled Peace Process." Asia Dialogue, April 3, 2019. https://theasiadialogue.com/2019/04/03/myanmars-stalled-peace-process/.

South, Ashley, and Marie Lall. "Language, Education and the Peace Process in Myanmar." *Contemporary Southeast Asia* 38, no. 1 (2016): 128–53.
South, Ashley, and Marie Lall. *Schooling and Conflict: Ethnic Education and Mother Tongue–Based Teaching in Myanmar*. USAID and Asia Foundation, 2016.
South, Ashley, Tim Schroeder, Kim Jolliffe, Mi Kun Chan Non, Sa Shine, Susanne Kempel, Axel Schroeder, and Naw Wa Shee Mu. *Between Ceasefire and Federalism: Exploring Interim Arrangements in the Myanmar Peace Process*. Covenant Consultancy, 2018.
Stedman, Stephen J. "Spoiler Problems in Peace Processes." *International Security* 22, no. 2 (1997): 5–53.
Stein, Janice Gross. "Getting to the Table: The Triggers, Stages, Functions, and Consequences of Pre-negotiation." *International Journal* 44, no. 2 (1989): 475–504.
Stewart, Megan A. "Civil War as State-Making: Strategic Governance in Civil War." *International Organization* 72, no. 1 (2018): 205–26.
Stokke, Kristian. "Political Representation by Ethnic Parties? Electoral Performance and Party-Building Processes among Ethnic Parties in Myanmar." *Journal of Current Southeast Asian Affairs* 38, no. 3 (2019): 307–36.
Su Mon Thazin Aung. "Governing the Transition: Policy Coordination Mechanisms in the Myanmar Core Executive, 2011–2016." PhD diss., University of Hong Kong, 2017.
Su Mon Thazin Aung. "Myanmar Ethnic Peace Process: Strategy of the Myanmar Government in the Ongoing Democratic Transition." In *Myanmar: Reintegrating into the International Community*, edited by Chenyang Li, Chaw Chaw Sein, and Xianghui Zhu, 349–68. Hackensack, NJ: World Scientific, 2016.
Su Mon Thazin Aung. "Why Burma's Top General Is Playing Peacemaker." *Foreign Policy*, May 15, 2014. http://foreignpolicy.com/2014/05/15/why-burmas-top-general-is-playing-peacemaker/.
Suhardiman, Diana, Jeff Rutherford, and Saw John Bright. "Putting Violent Armed Conflict in the Center of the Salween Hydropower Debates." *Critical Asian Studies* 49, no. 3 (2017): 349–64.
Taylor, Robert H. *The Armed Forces in Myanmar's Politics: A Terminating Role?* Singapore: ISEAS, 2015.
Taylor, Robert H. "British Policy towards Myanmar and the Creation of the 'Burma Problem.'" In *Myanmar: State, Society and Ethnicity*, edited by Narayanan Ganesan and Kyaw Yin Hlaing, 70–95. Singapore: Institute of Southeast Asian Studies, 2007.
Taylor, Robert H. "Do States Make Nations? The Politics of Identity in Myanmar Revisited." *South East Asia Research* 13, no. 3 (2005): 261–86.
Taylor, Robert H. "The Evolving Military Role in Burma." *Current History* 89, no. 545 (1990): 105–8, 134–35.
Taylor, Robert H. "Myanmar: From Army Rule to Constitution Rule?" *Asian Affairs* 43, no. 2 (2012): 221–36.
Taylor, Robert H. "Perceptions of Ethnicity in the Politics of Burma." *Southeast Asian Journal of Social Science* 10, no. 1 (1982): 7–22.
Tha Lun Zaung Htet. "Shwe Mann Demands Parliament's Involvement in Burma's Peace Process." Irrawaddy, July 3, 2013. https://www.irrawaddy.com/news/burma/shwe-mann-demands-parliaments-involvement-in-burmas-peace-process.html.
Tha Lun Zaung Htet. "Thein Sein, Shwe Mann Rivalry Ripples through Parliament." Irrawaddy, August 28, 2013. https://www.irrawaddy.com/news/burma/thein-sein-shwe-mann-rivalry-ripples-through-parliament.html.

Thant Myint-U. *The Hidden History of Burma: Race, Capitalism, and the Crisis of Democracy in the 21st Century*. New York: W. W. Norton, 2020.

Thawnghmung, Ardeth Maung. "Contending Approaches to Communal Violence in Rakhine State." In *Burma Myanmar: Where Now?*, edited by Mikael Gravers and Flemming Ytzen, 323–38. Copenhagen: Nordic Institute of Asian Studies, 2014.

Thawnghmung, Ardeth Maung. "The Dilemmas of Burma's Multinational Society." In *Multination States in Asia: Accommodation or Resistance*, edited by Jacques Bertrand and André Laliberté, 136–63. Cambridge: Cambridge University Press, 2010.

Thawnghmung, Ardeth Maung. *The Karen Revolution in Burma: Diverse Voices, Uncertain Ends*. Singapore: Institute of Southeast Asian Studies, 2008.

Thawnghmung, Ardeth Maung. "Myanmar: Why the Military Took Over." *Critical Asian Studies*, February 22, 2021. https://criticalasianstudies.org/commentary/2021/2/21/commentary-ardeth-thawnghmung.

Thawnghmung, Ardeth Maung. *The "Other" Karen in Myanmar: Ethnic Minorities and the Struggle without Arms*. Lanham, MD: Lexington Books, 2011.

Thawnghmung, Ardeth Maung. "The Politics of Indigeneity in Myanmar: Competing Narratives in Rakhine State." *Asian Ethnicity* 17, no. 4 (2016): 527–47.

Thawnghmung, Ardeth Maung. "Signs of Life in Myanmar's Nationwide Ceasefire Agreement? Finding a Way Forward." *Critical Asian Studies* 49, no. 3 (2017): 379–95.

Thawnghmung, Ardeth Maung, and Khun Noah. "Myanmar's Military Coup and the Elevation of Minority Agenda?" *Critical Asian Studies* 53, no. 2 (2021): 297–309.

Thawnghmung, Ardeth Maung, and Saw Eh Htoo. "The Fractured Centre: 'Two-Headed Government' and Threats to the Peace Process in Myanmar." *Modern Asian Studies* (January 14, 2021): 1–29. https://doi.org/10.1017/S0026749X20000372.

Thawnghmung, Ardeth Maung, and Yadana. "Citizenship and Minority Rights: The Role of National Race Affairs Ministers in Myanmar's 2008 Constitution." In *Citizenship in Myanmar: Ways of Being in and from Burma*, edited by Ashley South and Marie Lall, 113–39. Singapore: ISEAS–Yusof Ishak Institute, 2018.

Thiha Tun, and Thet Su Aung. "Myanmar's Ruling NLD Votes Down Bill on Ethnic Chief Ministers." Translated by Ye Kaung Myint Maung. Written in English by Roseanne Gerin. Radio Free Asia, March 17, 2020. https://www.rfa.org/english/news/myanmar/chief-ministers-03172020183612.html.

Thiri Shwesin Aung, Thomas B. Fischer, and John Buchanan. "Land Use and Land Cover Changes along the China-Myanmar Oil and Gas Pipelines—Monitoring Infrastructure Development in Remote Conflict-Prone Regions." *PLoS ONE* 15, no. 8 (2020): 1–23.

Thyne, Clayton L. "Information, Commitment, and Intra-war Bargaining: The Effect of Governmental Constraints on Civil War Duration." *International Studies Quarterly* 56, no. 2 (2012): 307–21.

Tinzar Htun, and Mael Raynaud. *Schedule Two of the 2008 Constitution: Avenues for Reform and Decentralization and Steps towards a Federal System*. Yangon: Konrad-Adenauer Stiftung, 2018.

"TNLA and RCSS Clashes Continue as Talks Stall." BNI, May 9, 2016. https://www.bnionline.net/en/news/shan-state/item/1662-clashes-between-tnla-and-rcss-continue-as-talks-stall.html.

Toft, Monica Duffy. "Ending Civil Wars: A Case for Rebel Victory?" *International Security* 34, no. 4 (2010): 7–36.

Transnational Institute. "A Changing Ethnic Landscape: Analysis of Burma's 2010 Polls." Burma Policy Briefing no. 4, December 2010.
Transnational Institute. "Ethnic Politics and the 2015 Elections in Myanmar." Myanmar Policy Briefing, September 2015.
Transnational Institute. "Ethnicity without Meaning, Data without Context." Burma Policy Briefing no. 13, February 24, 2014.
Transnational Institute. "Myanmar: Ethnic Politics and the 2020 General Election." Myanmar Policy Briefing no. 23, September 2020.
Transnational Institute. "The 2015 General Election in Myanmar: What Now for Ethnic Politics?" Myanmar Policy Briefing no. 17, December 2015.
Transnational Institute. "The 2020 General Election in Myanmar: A Time for Ethnic Reflection." Myanmar Policy Briefing no. 24, December 2020.
Tsebelis, George. *Veto Players: How Political Institutions Work*. Princeton, NJ: Princeton University Press, 2002.
Tun Lin. "Govt Schools Start to Teach Karen Language in Pago Division." *Karen News*, May 23, 2014.
UN Human Rights Council. *Report of the Detailed Findings of the Independent International Fact-Finding Mission on Myanmar (A/HRC/39/CRP.2)*. September 18, 2018.
"UN Human Rights Chief Points to 'Textbook Example of Ethnic Cleansing' in Myanmar." UN News, September 11, 2017. https://news.un.org/en/story/2017/09/564622-un-human-rights-chief-points-textbook-example-ethnic-cleansing-myanmar.
Ünal, Mustafa Coşar. "Is It Ripe Yet? Resolving Turkey's 30 Years of Conflict with the PKK." *Turkish Studies* 17, no. 1 (2016): 91–125.
UNESCO (United Nations Educational, Scientific and Cultural Organization). "MTB MLE Resource Kit—Including the Excluded: Promoting Multilingual Education (Available in Russian, Chinese and English Versions)." Last modified May 17, 2019. https://bangkok.unesco.org/content/mtb-mle-resource-kit-including-excluded-promoting-multilingual-education.
UNHCR (UN High Commissioner for Refugees). "Rohingya Emergency." Accessed May 29, 2021. https://www.unhcr.org/en-us/rohingya-emergency.html.
"Wa Group Proposes Political Autonomy for Ethnic Minorities." *Eleven*, September 5, 2016. http://www.elevenmyanmar.com/local/5860.
Wade, Francis. *Myanmar's Enemy Within: Buddhist Violence and the Making of a Muslim "Other."* London: Zed Books, 2019.
Wagner, R. Harrison. "Bargaining and War." *American Journal of Political Science* 44, no. 3 (2000): 469–84.
Wagner, Robert Harrison. "Causes of Peace." In *Stopping the Killing: How Civil Wars End*, edited by Roy Licklider, 235–68. New York: NYU Press, 1993.
Walt, Stephen M. *The Origins of Alliance*. Ithaca, NY: Cornell University Press, 1990.
Walter, Barbara F. "Bargaining Failures and Civil War." *Annual Review of Political Science* 12 (2009): 243–61.
Walter, Barbara F. "The Critical Barrier to Civil War Settlement." *International Organization* 51, no. 3 (1997): 335–64.
Walter, Barbara F. "Designing Transitions from Civil War: Demobilization, Democratization, and Commitments to Peace." *International Security* 24, no. 1 (1999): 127–55.
Walton, Matthew J. "Ethnicity, Conflict, and History in Burma: The Myths of Panglong." *Asian Survey* 48, no. 6 (2008): 889–910.

Walton, Matthew J. "The 'Wages of Burman-ness': Ethnicity and Burman Privilege in Contemporary Myanmar." *Journal of Contemporary Asia* 43, no. 1 (2013): 1–27.

Walton, Matthew J., and Susan Hayward. *Contesting Buddhist Narratives: Democratization, Nationalism, and Communal Violence in Myanmar*. Honolulu, HI: East-West Center, 2014.

Weinstein, Jeremy M. *Inside Rebellion: The Politics of Insurgent Violence*. New York: Cambridge University Press, 2007.

Weiss, Joshua N. "Trajectories toward Peace: Mediator Sequencing Strategies in Intractable Communal Conflicts." *Negotiation Journal* 19, no. 2 (2003): 109–15.

Woods, Kevin M. *The Conflict Resource Economy and Pathways to Peace in Burma*. Washington, DC: United States Institute of Peace Press, 2018.

World Bank. "Myanmar: Development of a Myanmar National Electrification Plan towards Universal Access, 2015–2030 (English)." World Bank Group, January 1, 2014.

Ye Htut. *Myanmar's Political Transition and Lost Opportunities (2010–2016)*. Singapore: ISEAS–Yusof Ishak Institute Publishing, 2019.

Ye Mon. "Karen National Union Suspends Participation in Peace Talks." *Frontier Myanmar*, October 29, 2018. https://frontiermyanmar.net/en/karen-national-union-suspends-participation-in-peace-talks.

Yegar, Moshe. *Between Integration and Secession: The Muslim Communities of the Southern Philippines, Southern Thailand, and Western Burma/Myanmar*. Lanham, MD: Lexington Books, 2002.

Yun Sun. "Aung San Suu Kyi Comes Out on Top in ICJ Rohingya Ruling." *Nikkei Asian Review*, February 8, 2020. https://asia.nikkei.com/Opinion/Aung-San-Suu-Kyi-comes-out-on-top-in-ICJ-Rohingya-ruling.

Zahar, Marie-Joëlle "Reframing the Spoiler Debate in Peace Processes." In *Contemporary Peacemaking: Conflict, Peace Processes and Post-war Reconstruction*, edited by John Darby and Roger Mac Ginty, 159–77. London: Palgrave Macmillan, 2008.

Zartman, I. William. *Ripe for Resolution: Conflict and Intervention in Africa*. Oxford: Oxford University Press, 1989.

Zartman, I. William. "Ripeness: The Hurting Stalemate and Beyond." In *International Conflict Resolution after the Cold War*, edited by Paul C. Stern and Daniel Druckman, 225–50. Washington, DC: National Academy Press, 2000.

Zaw Oo, and Win Min. *Assessing Burma's Ceasefire Accords*. Washington, DC: East-West Center, 2007.

Index

Page references in *italics* indicate illustrative materials.

accountability, 88, 89–90, 115–16, 119–20, 123, 124–25, 129
agenda setting and control: in Bamar dominance and ethnic repression, 40, 55; in ceasefire negotiations and political dialogue, 82–84, 96, 97–99, 107–9, 176–77; locking-in rules in, 4–5; in winning by process, 27, 180
agriculture, 118–19, 133–34
All Burma Students' Democratic Front, 187–88
alliances: in the 1988 uprising, 49, 50–51, 53–55; in Bamar dominance and minority repression, 46–47; Bamar-EAO and the 2021 coup, 2–3, 187–89; in ceasefire negotiations and political dialogue, 86–88, 90–91, 92–93, 105, 107–8; democratization in changes in, 70–72, 74; layering and locking-in ethnic recognition in, 150, 168–69; in winning by process, 29, 36–37, 177
All Mon Region Democracy Party, 70
anticolonial movement, 40, 43–44
anti-Communist National Democratic Front, 50
Anti-fascist People's Freedom League, 44, 45–46
appeasement, 40, 50, 176, 188–89
AA (Arakan Army), 85, 92, 105, 109, 163, 184, 188
Arakan ethnic group and State. *See also* Rakhine/Arakan ethnic group and State
Arakan National Party, 105
Arakan Rohingya Salvation Army, 78–79, 164
assimilation, 12–13, 39–40, 49, 127, 170. *See also* Burmanization
Aung Min, 67–68, 90, 91–92
Aung San, 1, 44, 76
Aung San Suu Kyi: 1990 election of, 49; in ceasefire negotiations and political dialogue, 88, 92, 96, 99, 101, 106; centralization of power by, 63–64; in constitutional lock-in, 112–13, 115–17, 129; and the coup of 2021, 2, 174, 187–88; in democratization, 176; election of, in hopes for peace, 1–2, 176; as emerging democratic force, 59–60; leadership style of, 63–64, 74–75, 76–77, 115–16; official title of, 192n15; and the Panglong Conference, 99–100; recentralization and electoral balancing by, 73–80. *See also* NLD (National League for Democracy)
authoritarianism, 24, 39–40, 63, 73–74, 75
authority: democratization in layering of, 69–70, 72–73, 75; in NLD amendments to the constitution, 182; in normalizing ethnic state weakness, 113–14, 116–19, 120, 121, 127–28, 129, 130; in outflanking, 35, 132–33, 134–35, 136–37, 146
autonomy: under British colonialism, 41–42, 44; ceasefires in erosion of, 132–48; in the constitution of 2008, 57–58, 113–14, 152; and the Panglong Conference, 101–2; and the politicization of ethnicity, 6; regional, 70–73; of the Tatmadaw within the state, 4; territorial, and proliferation of ethnic claims, 165; in winning by process, 21, 33–34
Aye Thar Aung, 75–76

Backpack Health Worker Team, 144
balance of power, 5–6, 11–12, 19, 27–28, 32–33, 194n53
Bamar majority: and the 1988 uprising, 48–55; and the 2008 constitution, 55–59; under British colonial rule, 39, 41–44, 59; dominance of, in normalizing ethnic states, 129; gains of, from the 2021 coup, 2–3; in layering and locking-in ethnic recognition, 150, 152–53, 154, 165–66, 168–70, 173; limited dominance of, in failure to win by war, 44–48; and the NLD government, 63–64, 73–79, 96, 185–86; in post-coup resistance with minority groups, 2–3, 187; in USDP policy, 72
bandwagoning, 36–37, 85, 87, 91, 95, 107–8, 168–69
Basque Homeland and Liberty, Spain, 178–79

237

INDEX

Basque National Party, Spain, 178–79
Ba U Gyi, 76–77
BGFs (Border Guard Forces), 85, 86–87
Brancati, Dawn, 31
Buddhism/Buddhists: Buddha Sasana Organization, 45; in the escalation of ethnic claims, 162, 163, 164; in ethnic conflict and Bamar dominance, 45, 46, 47–48; as percentage of population, 41; in the Rohingya crisis, 77, 78–79, 164
Burma Independence Army, 43–44
Burma Medical Association, 144
Burmanization: in Bamar dominance and minority repression, 39–40, 47–48, 49, 59; of education, language, and culture, 127, 130, 141–42; layering and locking-in ethnic recognition in, 165–73; in politicizing ethnicity, 7–8. *See also* assimilation
BSPP (Burma Socialist Program Party), 47, 48
business interests, 91, 121–23, 129–30, 132–34, 139, 171
bypassing of negotiation partners. *See* outflanking

Callahan, Mary, 12–13, 49, 51
ceasefire groups: and the creation of SAZs, 56–57; in negotiating the NCA, 85; outflanking of, 132–33, 134, 135–36, 141, 183–84; in outgunning, 37; skirmishes with, 24
ceasefires: bilateral, 36–37, 50–52, 59, 85, 88–91, 134–36, 148, 175; ceasefire zones, 121, 134–36, 141–42; democratization in negotiation of, 83–84, 107–8; formal negotiations for, 80–81, 82, 83–95; informal, 50–52, 55, 82, 85, 87–89, 131, 132–34; in layering and locking-in ethnic recognition, 170, 171; in leveraging negotiation, 23; negotiations frameworks in constraint of ethnic groups, 5–6; in outflanking and erosion of autonomy, 132–48; in shifting strategies on the 1988 uprising, 48, 50–52, 59; in state expansion, 132–48; unilateral, during the Panglong Conference, 106
censuses, 17–18, 149–50, 151, 156–58, 160–61, 164–65, 169–70
centralization/decentralization: in the 2008 constitution, 14, 58, 113, 115–16, 177; in Bamar strategy, 175–76; in ceasefire negotiations and political dialogue, 96, 107–8; democratization in, 63, 66, 69–79, 80–81, 181–83; of the economy, outflanking in, 133; in ethnic conflict and Bamar dominance, 45, 46, 47, 48, 49; layering in, 117–29, 182–83; post-coup, in negotiations, 189; of power, in the 1947 constitution, 6, 8; recentralization (2016–2020), 73–79, 80; in winning by process, 33
change, institutional, 4–5, 13, 22, 30–32
Cheesman, Nick, 13, 173
chief ministers, state and regional: in the 1974 constitution, 55–56; and democratization, 9, 70, 72–73, 74–76, 199n55; in normalizing ethnic state weakness, 113–14, 116, 124, 129
China, 49–50, 121–24, 125–26
China-Myanmar Oil and Gas Pipelines, 125–26
Chin ethnic group/State: Chin rebellion, 46; exploitation of natural resources in, 123–24; layering and locking-in ethnic recognition, 154, 156, 157–58, 163, 171–72; migration in and out of, *169*; outflanking and erosion of autonomy in, 140–42, 144; and the Panglong Conference, 100; in the Union of Burma, 6–8
Chin National Action Committee, 157–58
CNF (Chin National Front), 91, 92, 100, 140–41, 142, 144
Christia, Fontini, 36–37, 194n53
Christianity/Christians, 41, 43, 47–48, 128, 157
citizenship, 147, 164, 173, 181
civil disobedience movement, 186–87, 188
CSOs (Civil Society Organizations), 17–18, 69–70, 76–77, 80, 108, 112–13, 123–24, 181–82
civil war: characteristics of, in winning by process, 177; ethnic, negotiated agreements as resolution of, 21; stalled peace process in, 1–3
colonialism, British, 39, 40–44, 59
CPB (Communist Party of Burma), 45–47, 50–51
communities, local: natural resources and land of, 124–25; in outflanking, 35, 137–38, 142, 144, 148
concessions: in the coup of 2021, 185–87; and democratization, 63–64, 68–69, 79–81; on education language and culture, 126–27; in NCA negotiations, 83, 89–92, 93, 94, 95, 107–8; in outflanking, 133, 140, 146–48; and the Panglong Conference, 96, 101–2, 106; in winning by process, 3, 23–24, 30, 36, 175–76, 179–80, 184–85
conflict, ethnic: active, land grabbing in areas of, 147; and Bamar dominance, 44–48; layering and locking-in ethnic recognition

in, 150, 156–57, 164–65, 173; under the NLD government, 105; origins of, 40–44
conflict, stalled: and credibility of democratic change, 176–77; defined, 11–12; strategic use of, 3, 4, 175; in winning by process, 11–12, 19, 25–26, 38, 179
Constitutional Amendment Implementation Committee, 68
constitution of 2008: acceptance of, 111–17, 175–76, 182, 186; amendments and amending process, 68, 72, 113–18, 129, 177, 182–83, 203n14; autonomy in, 57–58, 113–14, 152; in Bamar dominance and minority repression, 40, 52–59; and centralization, 14, 58, 74, 80, 113, 115–16, 177; in the coup of 2021, 186; land use and ownership in, 145–46; in layering and locking-in ethnic recognition, 149–50, 151–54, 156–57, 165–66, 167–68; in layering ethnic state powers, 117–29; minority representation in legitimation and consolidation of, 5–6; and the negotiation process, 13–15; in normalizing ethnic state weakness, 110–13, 114–17, 126, 129–30; and the Panglong Conference, 101–2; in winning by process, 19–20, 25, 33
constitutions: of 1947, 6–7, 8, 44–45, 152; of 1974, 47, 59, 151–52; state, 102, 106, 156
constraints: in Bamar dominance and ethnic conflict, 49–50; in ceasefire negotiations and political dialogue, 90–91, 95, 97, 101; democracy in, 9–10, 74–75, 79, 80–81; in ethnic state weakness, 110–12, 116–17, 118–19, 120, 129; layering and ethnic recognition in, 154; locked-in, 180–81; process as, 5, 9–11; in reaching state goals, 178, 179, 180–81, 185; representation in, 5–6; in winning by process, 20, 21–22, 23–26, 27, 28, 29–30, 31–32, 34
coups, military: of 1962, 46; of 1988, 49–50; of 2021, 1–3, 13–14, 174–75, 185–89
culture: Bamar, reification of, 59; cultural heritage in land use and ownership, 146–47; in layering and locking-in ethnic recognition, 158, 166–67, 170, 171–73; in normalizing ethnic state weakness, 120–21, 126–29, 130. *See also* Burmanization
Culture and Mass Education, Ministry of, 45
Cunningham, David E., 30
curriculum, 47–48, 127–28, 141–43, 166–67. *See also* education

Dapice, David, 122
Dawei Special Economic Zone, 70, 139

decentralization. *See* centralization/decentralization
demarcation lines, 55–56, 131, 134–36, 148
demobilization, 30–31, 93
democracy/democratization: balancing of the Bamar-ethnic electorate in, 73–80; in ceasefire negotiations, 83–84, 88–89, 92, 107–8; in constraints, 9–10, 74–75, 79, 80–81; in credibility, 61, 69, 80, 176–77, 181–82; in electoral balancing and recentralization, 73–79; in fragmenting interests and opportunities for reform, 64–69; in layering of the state institutional arena, 69–73, 181–82; and the politicization of ethnicity, 9–10; in winning by process, 30–33, 62–63. *See also* institutional arena, state
Democratic Alliance of Burma, 85
DKBA (Democratic Karen Buddhist Army), 52, 85, 90, 91, 95, 142, 162
development, economic: in ceasefires and political dialogue, 87–88, 101–2; in the Ethnic Rights Protection Law, 70–71; in layering and locking-in ethnic recognition, 165–66, 167–68, 170; in outflanking and erosion of autonomy, 131–34, 136–38, 139, 148; in state control of natural resources, 121, 125–26
dialogue, political: in ceasefire negotiations, 83–84, 87–88, 89–90, 91–92, 101–2, 107–8; in constitutional lock-in and ethnic state weakness, 110, 117; in credibility of democratic change, 176–77; democratization in, 8–9, 62–63; EAO participation in, 82; framework for, in the NCA, 176; in layering and locking-in ethnic recognition, 160, 98, 174–75; in outflanking the erosion of EAO autonomy, 131–32, 148; and the Panglong Conference, 96–108; in winning by process, 23, 29–30, 31–32. *See also* Panglong Conference, 21st Century
disarmament, 30–31, 85–86, 89–90, 93
diversity of ethnic nationalities, 40, 47–48, 150–51, 157, 160–61
divide-and-rule strategies, 2, 39–40, 94, 151–52
divisions: in Bamar dominance and minority repression, 39; in ceasefire negotiations, 82–84, 86, 95, 106; ceasefires in, 37, 50–51, 183; democratization in, 61, 64–69, 74; ethnic, 9–10, 21, 82–84, 156–58, 180–81, 188–89; between and within ethnic political parties, 29–30, 74; in NCA negotiations,

INDEX

divisions (*continued*)
82–83, 93, 95; in opportunities for reform, 64–69. *See also* fragmentation of ethnic minorities
dominance, Bamar: and the 1988 uprising, 48–55; in the constitution of 2008, 40, 55–59; in depoliticizing ethnic power, 167; in ethnic conflict, 40–48; in ethnic state weakness, 129; in negotiations, 175–76; origins of, 39, 40–44; post-coup, 188–89; in winning by process, 185

economy: in the 2021 coup, 174, 212n1; informal, 125, 126; in minority assimilation, 169, 173; natural resources in, 120–21, 122, 123, 126; in negotiating the NCA, 90; in outflanking and erosion of autonomy, 132–34, 148; SLORC in opening of, 49–50
education: in Bamar dominance and minority repression, 45, 47–48, 51–52; in layering and locking-in ethnic recognition, 166–67; Ministry of, 127, 140–43; in normalizing ethnic state weakness, 120–21, 126–29, 130; in outflanking and erosion of autonomy, 131–32, 133, 140–43
elections: of 1990, 49; of 2010, 61–62; of 2015, 65–68, 73–74, 83–84, 88–89, 95, 96, 113, 176; of 2020, 74, 105, 107, 112–13, 174; electoral politics, 71–72, 83–84, 88–89, 94–95, 161; electoral system, 153, 158, 168–69; in leveraging negotiations, 31–32, 33; local, elite fragmentation in reform of, 66
Ethnic Affairs, Ministry of, Union-level, 75–76, 166
EAMs (ethnic affairs ministers): and democratization, 70–71, 73; in layering and locking-in ethnic recognition, 149–50, 152–53, 157–58, 161–62, 163–64, 166, 167–68; in the politicization of ethnicity, 9–10
EAOs (ethnic armed organizations): and the 2021 coup, 186–87, 188–89; in ceasefire negotiations, 82–83, 84–85, 86–87; and democratization, 1–2, 61, 63–64, 74, 80; in the failure to win by war, 39–40, 46–47, 49, 50–51, 53–54; in land use and ownership, 146–48; in normalizing ethnic state weakness, 125, 126, 130; outflanking of, 35, 131–32, 133–34, 137–38, 139–40, 146–48; policy areas of, in the NCA, 135–36; in the politicization of ethnicity, 9; relative power of, in analysis of the civil war, 13; services offered by, 51–52, 140–45; in winning by process, 29–30, 35, 37. *See also under EAO name*; militias
Ethnic Health Organization, 144–45
ethnicity/ethnic nationalities, 6–11, 39, 41, 53–54, 149–53, 154, 156–73, 191n6. *See also* recognition, ethnic
Ethnic Rights Protection Law (2015), 70–71, 72, 75–76, 166
EuroBurma, 87–88
expansion of state reach: 1990s ceasefires in, 132–34; bilateral and nationwide ceasefires in, 134–48; outflanking in, 131–48

Farmland Law, 145
federalism: and the 1947 constitution, 44–45; and the 2008 constitution, 33–34, 113, 115, 116–17, 130; in the 2021 coup, 187; Bamar dominance in prevention of, 54–55, 77–78; in ceasefire negotiations and political dialogue, 89–90, 94, 96, 101–2, 176–77; and democratization, 62, 63, 68–69, 70–72, 73–74, 77–78, 182–83, 185–86; as EAO goal, 5–6; and layering of ethnic state powers, 120–21; meanings of, 21–22; post-coup Bamar support for, 187; as self-determination, 9
federal union, 89–90, 107, 114, 116, 188–89
Federal Union, Committee for the Emergence of (CEFU), 87
Federal Union Army, 93. *See also* UNFC (United Nationalities Federal Council)
Federal Union Republic, 47
first/last mover advantage, 30, 36, 90
Fishman, Joshua, 166–67
foreign aid. *See* international aid
fragmentation of ethnic minorities: economic policy in, 150, 165–66, 169–70, 171–72; layering and locking-in ethnic recognition in, 4–5, 149–50, 153–57, 160–61, 165, 173; and policy reversals, 66–67, 68–69; post-coup, 188–89; in winning by process, 178, 180–81, 184. *See also* divisions
Framework on Economic and Social Reforms, The, 66
Free Aceh Movement, Indonesia, 178
frontier areas, 41–43, 44–45

gender inclusiveness, 102
GAD (General Administration Department), 58, 119–20, 129, 137
gold mines, 121–22
governance, joint, 134–35, 136

INDEX   241

governance, local: ceasefires in, 51–52; in the constitution of 2008, 55–58, 113–14; democratization in power of, 63–64, 70–73; gray zones, 134, 135–37, 139–40, 142, 148, 183–84; layering and centralization in weakness of, 117–29; in leveraging negotiations, 34, 35
governments, state and regional: in the constitution of 2008, 113–15, 116, 118–19; democratization in layering of, 71–72, 75–77; in normalizing ethnic state weakness, 127–28, 129
Greater Mekong Subregion East-West Corridor Program, 139
groups, pan-ethnic, 150–51, 157–60

Health, Ministry of, 144
Health and Sports, Ministry of, 144–45
health care, 143–45. *See also* services/service provision
Home Affairs, Ministry of, 119–20
Horowitz, Donald, 21
humanitarian projects and assistance, 137, 139, 148
human rights abuses, 49–50, 78–79, 164

inclusion/exclusion of actors: in British colonialism, 42; in ceasefire negotiations and political dialogue, 99, 102, 107–8; in the constitution of 1947, 45; in legitimation of the constitution of 2008, 58–59; locking-in rules in, 4–5, 27–28; in winning by process, 27–28, 29–30, 37
India, tribal states in, 211n57
Indonesia, 178
influence maximization hypothesis, 28
infrastructure, 35, 126, 136–38, 139, 148, 171, 183–84
institutional arena, state: in Bamar dominance and minority repression, 40, 55–59; constraint of ethnic minorities in, 10–11; defined, 4, 5, 24–25; democratization in, 63, 66, 80; in fragmentation and opportunity, 64–69; layering of, 61, 62–64, 69–73, 181–82; leveraging of, 19–20, 24–25, 29, 30–33; in locking-in ethnic recognition, 149–73; in normalizing ethnic state weakness, 110–11, 112–13, 125, 129–30; in winning by process, 21, 24, 30–31, 32–34, 178, 179, 181–82. *See also* democracy/democratization
institutions of recognition, new: in fragmentation, 149–50, 153–56;

proliferation of claims in, 156–65; in subjugation of ethnic power, 149–50, 165–73
insurgents/insurgent groups, 8, 34–35, 53, 177. *See also* EAOs (ethnic armed organizations)
international aid, 139, 148
INGOs (international nongovernmental organizations), 144–45, 147–48
investment, foreign, 123–24, 126, 133–34

Japan, 43–44
Joint Parliamentary Committee for Constitutional Amendment, 115–16
Jolliffe, Kim, 134, 136–37, 139
junta. *See* military regime/junta
Jupille, Joseph, 28

KIO (Kachin Independence Organization): in ceasefire negotiations and political dialogue, 82–83, 84, 85, 87, 91–93, 105, 109; and the coup of 2021, 186–87, 188–89; and the failure to win by war, 46–47, 51, 52; outflanking of, in erosion of autonomy, 133–34, 135, 140–41, 142–43, 144; outgunning in weakening of, 184
Kachin State: Bamar dominance and ethnic conflict in, 41–42, 43–45, 46–47, 50–51, 52, 53–54; creation of, 6–8, 44–45; and democratization, 66–67, 70–71, 72; education, language, and culture in, 128, 140–41, 143, 171–72; exploitation of natural resources in, 121–22, 123–24, 125, 133–34, 171; Kachin rebellion, 46; layering and locking-in ethnic recognition in, 152–53, 154, 157–60, 162–63, 171–72, 173; migration in and out of, *169*; Myitsone Dam project in, 66–67; and the NCA, 85, 92, 93, 94; outflanking and erosion of autonomy in, 132–33, 140–41, 143, 144, 147; in the Union of Burma, 6–8
Karen Department of Health and Welfare, 144
Karen Education Department, 140–41
Karen Environment and Social Action Network, 147–48
Karen ethnic group, 6–8, 41–42, 43–44, 45–46, 132–33, 157, 163–64, 171–72
Karen/Kayin State: in the 1947 constitution, 45–46; and the Aung San Suu Kyi government, 76–77; constitutional lock-in and layers in weakness of, 126; insurgency over boundaries of, 8; layering and locking-in ethnic recognition in, 151, 162, 171–72; migration in and out of, *169*;

242   INDEX

Karen/Kayin State (*continued*)
  outflanking and erosion of autonomy in, 132–33, 136–38, 139–41, 142, 143, 144–45, 147–48
Karen National Liberation Army Peace Council, 95
KNU (Karen National Union): and the 2008 constitution, 14; in ceasefire negotiations and political dialogue, 84–85, 87, 90–91, 92, 93, 94, 95, 105–6; and the coup of 2021, 186–87, 188–89; and the failure to win by war, 50–51; outflanking of, in erosion of autonomy, 132–33, 136, 137–38, 140–41, 142, 144, 146–48
Karenni ethnic group, 41–42, 163–64
Karenni National People's Liberation Front, 85
Karenni States, 44–45, 151
Kayah State, 76–77, 122–23, 140–41, 156, 161–62, 163–64
Kayan ethnic group, 41, 154, 161–62, 163–64
Khine Khine Soe, 158
Khin Nyunt, 13, 50–51, 53, 61
Khun Myat, T., 70–71, 75–76
KIO Health Department, 144
Kokang Democratic Party, 132–33
Kokang ethnic group and SAZ, 6, 50–51, 53–55, 77, 132, 135
Ko Ko Gyi, 77–78

Laiza Conference, 92
Land and Environment Working Committee, 146
land use and ownership, 120–26, 140, 145–48
language: Burmese, 45, 142, 166–67; in ethnic conflict and Bamar dominance, 43, 45, 47–48, 49; in layering and locking-in ethnic recognition, 149, 151, 158, 166–67, 170, 171–73; in normalizing ethnic state weakness, 120–21, 126–29, 130; in outflanking and erosion of authority, 141, 142; in rejection of federalism by the Bamar majority, 77–78
layering: in ceasefire negotiations and political dialogue, 83–84, 107, 108; democratization in, 61, 62–64, 69–73, 181–82; in diffusion of minority power, 58–59; in new institutions of recognition, 149–52, 153–65, 168–69; in normalizing ethnic state weakness, 110–11, 117–30; in winning by process, 4–5, 26, 32–34, 181–82
legitimacy/legitimation: of the 2008 constitution, 5–6, 58–59, 112–13; of EAOs, outflanking in reduction of, 131, 140; of the NLD government, 73–74, 79, 80, 99–100; of the SLORC National Convention, 53; of state expansion by local communities, 137–38; in winning by process, 27–28, 35
leverage: arenas for exercise of, 22–24; ceasefires and political dialogue in, 52, 83–84, 86, 91, 93, 99, 105, 109; and democratization, 63; in the formal negotiation arena, 11–12, 19–20, 22–23, 25, 33, 178; interethnic fragmentation in, 150, 165, 168–69, 178; layering and constitutional lock-in in, 111, 112, 113–14; politicization of ethnicity in, 9–10; process in loss of, 2–3; and stalemates, 11–12; in winning by process, 25–38, 183–84
Lian Hmung Sakong, 187
liberalization: in ceasefire negotiations and political dialogue, 88; in ethnic gains, 12; in hopes for peace, 1–2, 176; in layering and locking-in ethnic recognition, 149–50, 158, 165–66, 168–69, 173; in leveraging state institutions, 33. *See also* democracy/democratization
Licklider, Roy, 20
line ministries, 55–56, 117–19, 128, 129, 132
Literature and Culture Communities, 149, 158
locking-in of ethnic recognition: in fragmentation, 149–50, 153–56; proliferation of claims in, 156–65; in subjugation of ethnic power, 149–50, 165–73
locking-in strategy: in ceasefire negotiations and political dialogue, 22, 27–30, 83–84, 88–89, 95, 97–99, 107–8, 180–81; constitutional lock-in, in normalizing ethnic state weakness, 110, 112–13, 114–17, 126, 129, 130; and the constitution of 2008, 58–59, 110, 111–17; in controlling process, 4–5; in democratization, 68–69; at the National Convention of 2003, 55; in outflanking and erosion of autonomy, 148; in winning by process, 22–23, 26, 27–30, 180–81, 185
loyalty, 34–35, 41, 43–44, 112–13, 133, 181

Magwe Region, 171–72
Manh Win Khaing Than, 75–76
marginalization, 32, 42, 47–48, 149–50, 158, 164–65, 181–82, 188–89
Mark, Siu Sue, 147
Mathieson, David Scott, 116
mediation/mediators, third party, 22–23, 27–28, 167–68

INDEX

methodology, 15–18
migration, 42–43, *169*, 165–66, 169–73, 178–79
militarism/militarization, 12–13, 59–60, 160
military regime/junta: 1988 uprising and shifting strategy of, 48–55; bilateral ceasefires by, 50–52, 85, 86–87, 132–34; and the coup of 2021, 186–89; democratization by, 25, 31–32, 33, 40, 61–63, 64; discrimination against the Rohingya by, 78; in layering and locking-in ethnic recognition, 151–52, 153–56; in normalizing ethnic state weakness, 127; in outflanking and erosion of autonomy, 132–34; in the politicization of ethnicity, 8–9. *See also* Tatmadaw
militias, 24, 78–79, 85, 86–87, 162–63. *See also* EAOs (ethnic armed organizations)
Min Aung Hlaing, 94, 106, 200n17
"Ministerial" Burma, 41–42, 44
ministers, regional, 56, 70, 167–68
MoE (Ministry of Education), 127, 141–43. *See also* education
Min Maung, 163–64
mixed-control areas, 147
mobilization, political, 150–51, 157, 161–62, 165–66, 173, 183
Mon ethnic group and State: and democratization, 70, 76; ethnic conflict and repression in, 41, 43–44, 45; layering and locking-in ethnic recognition in, 152–53, 156, 171; migration in and out of, *169*; normalizing weakness of, 117–18, 123–24, 129; outflanking and erosion of autonomy in, 136, 140–41, 142–43, 144–45; in the Union of Burma, 6–8
Mongla ethnic group, 53–55
Mon National Health Committee, 144
MNLF (Moro National Liberation Front), Philippines, 178
Muslims/Muslim communities, 6, 78–79, 147, 164–65, 174
Mutu Say Poe, 67–68
Myanmar Investment Commission, 124–25
MNDAA (Myanmar National Democratic Alliance Army). *See also* Kokang ethnic group and SAZ
MNDAA (Myanmar National Democratic Alliance Army), 85, 92, 93, 95, 100, 105, 109
MPC (Myanmar Peace Center), 68–69, 87–88
Myanmar Peace Support Initiative, 87–88
Myitsone Dam project, 66–67, 123–24

Naga ethnic group, 163
Naing Thet Lwin, 75–76

National Coalition Government of the Union of Burma, 49, 187–88
NC (National Convention), 40, 52–55, 58–59, 80, 153–56
National Council of the Union of Burma, 49
NDSC (National Defense and Security Council), 67–68
National Democratic Alliance—Mongla, 90
National Democratic Front, 85
National Education Law, 127–28
National Electrification Plan, 124
nationalism, 40–41, 42, 43–44, 77, 78–79, 157–58, 164–65
NLD (National League for Democracy) and government: and the 21st Century Panglong Conference, 8–9, 23, 32, 96–107; 1990 election of, 49; approach of, to ethnic minorities, 10–11, 182; and the Bamar majority, 63–64, 73–79, 96, 185–86; in ceasefire negotiations and political dialogue, 82, 83, 84, 96–107, 109, 180–81; in constitutional lock-in, 110, 111–17, 182, 185, 186; constitutional reform efforts by, 111–17; continued popularity amid mixed results of, 174; and the coup of 2021, 2–3, 186, 187–88; in democratization, 62, 63–64, 73, 80–81; in expectations for peace, 1–2, 176; in layering and locking-in ethnic recognition, 168–69; layering and weak decentralization by, 117–20, 124–26, 127–28, 129–30; in normalizing ethnic state weakness, 129, 130; in outflanking and erosion of autonomy, 139–41; in politicization of ethnicity, 9, 10–11; in recentralization and electoral balancing, 73–80; at the SLORC national convention, 52–53
National Reconciliation and Peace Center, 99
National United Liberation Front, 46–47
National Unity Government, 187–89
NCA (Nationwide Ceasefire Agreement): and the 2008 constitution, 14–15; collapse of, in the coup of 2021, 186; democratization in opportunity for, 68–69, 176; in land grabbing, 146–47; limited results of, 175; locked-in negotiating structure in, 180; negotiations for, 82, 83–95, 100–101; in normalizing weak ethnic states, 125; in outflanking and erosion of autonomy, 131–32, 134–36, 138, 141–43; and the Panglong Conference, 96–108; in reduction of violence, 185; in winning by process, 23, 29–30, 185

NCCT (Nationwide Ceasefire Coordinating Team), 92–93, 94
natural resources, 72, 120–26, 130, 132–34, 139, 205n64
negotiating arena, formal: 2008 constitution in credibility of, 40, 183; in ceasefire negotiations, 83–84, 95, 97–99, 107–8; collapse of, 108–9, 186; in the constitution of 2008, 55–59; constraint of ethnic minorities in, 10–11; defined, 5; democratization in, 62–63; layering of, 32–34; leveraging of, 11–12, 19–20, 22–23, 25, 33, 178; locking-in strategy in, 22, 83–84, 95, 97–99, 107–8, 180–81; and the NCA, 84–95; in normalizing weak ethnic states, 125; in political dialogue, 96–107; in shifting strategies on the 1988 uprising, 48; in weakening minority groups and continued Bamar control, 175–76
neutralization of opponents, 3, 4, 18, 173, 175, 179
New Democratic Army-Kachin, 50–51
Ne Win, 46, 47–48
NMSP (New Mon State Party), 51–52, 90–91, 135, 136, 138, 140–41, 142–43, 146–47
NGOs (nongovernmental organizations), 17–18, 147–48, 192n26
nonstate actors, 5, 29–30, 59, 65–66, 105, 112. *See also* EAOs (ethnic armed organizations)
Northern Alliance, 105, 109
Nu, U and U Nu's government, 45–47

officials, state-level, 16–18, 123–24, 171–72
organization, territorial, 6–11
"original inhabitants" *(taing yin thar lumyo)*, 191n6
"other" census declaration, 17–18, 158, 160–61, 164–65
outflanking: ceasefires in, 51, 131–48; in controlling process, 4–5; of EAOs, 35, 131–32, 133–34, 137–38, 139–40, 146–48; penetration of ethnic minority areas in, 110, 121, 141–43, 148, 175–76, 183–84; in winning by process, 26, 34–35, 183–84
outgunning: in ceasefire negotiations and political dialogue, 83, 84, 92, 93, 105, 109, 184; as strategy in controlling process, 4–5; in winning by process, 26, 36–37, 183, 184

pan-ethnic groups, 150–51, 157–60
Panglong agreement of 1947, 1
Panglong Conference, 21st Century: agreement on land use and ownership in, 147; in ceasefire negotiations and political dialogue, 96–107, 108; in constraint of ethnic groups, 5–6; in layering and locking-in ethnic recognition, 167; limited results of, 176–77; in normalization of ethnic state weakness, 110–11, 130; in the politicization of ethnicity, 8–9, 10–11; unity as purpose of, 44; in winning by process, 23, 34. *See also* dialogue, political; UPC (Union Peace Conference)
Pa'O insurgents, 91, 100
Pa'O National Organization, 52
Peace Donor Support Group, 87–88
peace settlements: democratization in sequencing of, 30–31; negotiated, as alternative to process, 11
penetration by the state, of ethnic minority areas. *See* outflanking
People's Alliance for Credible Elections, 113
People's Defense Forces, 186–87, 188
PMs (People's Militias), 24, 85, 86–87
peripheralization. *See* marginalization
Philippines, 178
pluralization of actors: democratization in, 61, 62, 63–64, 65, 69–73, 79, 80; layering in, 4–5, 33; in NCA negotiations, 86; new institutions of ethnic recognition in, 153; in winning by process, 19–20, 21, 27–28, 29–30
political parties, local/ethnic: and the 2021 coup, 188–89; in ceasefires and political dialogue, 82–84, 96, 97–99, 101–2, 108; in layering and locking-in ethnic recognition, 149–50, 153, 157–61, 164–65, 168–69; in layering and sequencing of the state, 61–62, 69–70, 71–72, 74, 76–77, 80, 181; in normalizing ethnic state weakness, 110, 113, 115, 116, 122–23; and the politicization of ethnicity, 9–10; at the SLORC national convention, 52, 53; in winning by process, 19–20, 32–33, 181–82, 183
political parties, opposition, 52–53, 112–13, 174, 176. *See also* NLD (National League for Democracy)
politicization/depoliticization of ethnicity, 6–11, 150, 158–61, 164–73
power/empowerment: allocation of, in weakening ethnic states, 110–12, 113–14, 116, 117–18, 119–21, 124–25, 129; balance of, 5–6, 11–12, 19, 27–28, 32–33, 194n53; in ceasefire negotiations and political dialogue, 96–99, 100–101, 107, 108; coercive, and the transition to civilian rule, 13; democratization in, 62–64, 69–72, 73, 74–75; distribution of, in the constitution of

2008, 56, 57, 58–59, 111–12, 156–57; ethnic, depoliticizing and subjugation of, 165–73; in ethnic conflict, 47–48; layering in, 4–5, 181; in leverage, 19–20, 22–24, 26, 27–30, 32–34, 36–37, 194n53; outflanking in, 132–33, 136; political, ceasefires in, 51–52; in politicization of ethnicity, 6, 7–8; relative, of EAOs, 12–13

procedures: in layering and sequencing of the state, 80; in normalizing weak ethnic states, 110–11, 114, 124–25; in political dialogue, 107–8; in the transition to civilian rule and democracy, 8–10; in winning by process, 22–23, 28, 185. *See also* locking-in strategy

process: control of, 11–12, 180, 183–84; defined, 4–5; manipulation of, in gains, 177

prodemocracy uprisings of 1988, 48–55

races, national, 41, 72, 152–54, 164, 166, 181, 182

Rakhine/Arakan ethnic group and State: in the 1947 constitution, 45; in ceasefires and political dialogue, 91, 95, 105; constitutional lock-in and layers in, 116, 122–23, 125–26; and the coup of 2021, 188–89; and ethnic conflict, 41–42, 44, 45–46; land grabbing in, 147; layering and locking-in ethnic recognition of, 154, 157–58, 161, 163, 164–65, 171; migration in and out of, *169*; and the politicization of ethnicity, 6–8; and the Rohingya, 6, 78–79, 164–65. *See also* Arakan ethnic group and State

Rakhine National Party, 74

recognition, ethnic: in Bamar dominance and ethnic repression, 45; constitution of 2008 in, 149–50, 151–54, 156–57, 165–66, 167–68; in depoliticizing and subjugating ethnic power, 165–73; electoral system in, 153, 158, 168–69; ethnic claims in, 149–50, 153–54, 156–65; in fragmentation, 153–56; as minority goal, 1; in the politicization of ethnicity, 6, 8

reintegration, 30–31, 93, 107

religion, 41, 43, 128. *See also* Buddhism/Buddhists; Christianity/Christians; Muslims/Muslim communities

rent seeking, 133, 139, 211n57

representation: in Bamar dominance and minority repression, 40, 42, 44–45, 47–48, 52–54, 59; in ceasefire negotiations and political dialogue, 82–83, 91, 92, 97–99, 101–2, 108; in the coup of 2021, 186; democratization in, 5, 61, 62, 63–64, 69–73, 74, 75–76, 176–77; framework for, 5–6, 180; in layering and locking-in ethnic recognition, 149–50, 151–56, 158–59, 163–64, 167–69; of minorities within the state, 4–5, 175–76; in normalizing weak ethnic states, 111, 113, 115; and politicization of ethnicity, 6, 8; in winning by process, 19–20, 23–24, 32–33, 178–79, 180, 181–82, 183

repression of ethnic minority groups: in Bamar-minority conflict, 39–40, 44–48, 59; failure of the NLD to change, 115–16; outcomes of apparent reversal of, 148–49, 173; post-coup, in Bamar-minority relations, 186–87; in the theater of war, 24; in winning by process, 178, 184

resistance: and the 1988 uprising, 49; by ceasefire groups to NCA terms, 85; and the coup of 2021, 186–88; divisive strategies in weakening of, 39–40; to exploitation of natural resources, 123–24; in the failure to win by war, 45–47; to state expansion and erosion of autonomy, 137–38, 142, 147; to subjugation of ethnic power, 167

resources/resource allocation: in Bamar dominance and minority repression, 51, 55; democratization in, 62–64, 181–82; layering in, 4–5, 32–33, 181–82; in outflanking and erosion of autonomy, 133, 138–39, 141–42, 148, 182, 183; in subjugating ethnic power, 165–66, 168–69; in weakening ethnic states, 110–12, 128, 129; in winning by process, 19–20, 24, 25, 26, 32–34, 178, 181–82. *See also* natural resources

RCSS (Restoration Council of Shan State): in ceasefire agreements and political dialogue, 84, 87–88, 90–91, 92, 94, 95, 107; outflanking of and erosion of autonomy, 136, 140–41, 142–43, 144

revenue: in Bamar dominance and ethnic repression, 48, 56, 57–58; ceasefires in deprivation of, for EAOs, 133; in ethnic state weakness, 119; in fragmentation of ethnic groups, 165; in normalizing ethnic state weakness, 117–18, 119, 120–26, 130, 204n41; in outflanking and erosion of autonomy, 133–34, 148; state and local government's right to, 72. *See also* taxes/taxation

Revolutionary Council (1962–74), 46

rights, ethnic, 69, 70–71, 75–76, 102, 150, 152–53, 160, 166

Riker, William, 28–29

Rohingya, 6, 78–79, 147, 164–65, 174

sanctions, international, 49–50, 61–62, 112

Schroeder, Tim, 144–45
secession, right of, 45–46, 101, 107
"Section 436 movement," 114, 212n20
security sector integration and reform, 93, 107
SAZs/SADs (self-administered zones/divisions), 54–55, 56–57, 114, 118, 149–50, 152–56, 165
self-autonomous regions, 6, 53–55
self-determination, 1, 5–6, 9, 47–48
self-governance proposals, 54–55
sequencing: in ceasefire negotiations and political dialogue, 83–84, 88–89, 107, 108–9; in constitutional amendments, 182–83; of institutional change, 4–5, 22, 30–32; in normalizing ethnic state weakness, 111, 130; outgunning in, 183; in the state institutional arena, 63, 80 (See also democracy/democratization); in winning by process, 12, 26, 30–32, 182–84
services/service provision: in Bamar strategy, 175–76; ceasefires in, 51–52; in the constitution of 2008, 56; in leveraging negotiations, 34, 35; in outflanking and erosion of autonomy, 131–33, 134, 135–36, 137–38, 140–45, 148, 183–84
Shan ethnic group/State: Bamar dominance and ethnic repression of, 41–42, 43–45, 46–47, 50–51, 53–54; layering and locking-in ethnic recognition in, 152–53, 154, 155–56, 157–58, 161–64, 170, 171; migration in and out of, 169; normalization of weakness in, 118, 123, 128; outflanking and erosion of autonomy of, 135, 136, 140–41, 142–45, 147; in the Panglong Conference, 100, 107; in the Union of Burma, 6–8
Shan National League for Democracy, 74, 188–89
Shanni ethnic group (Red Shan/Tai-Leng), 160
Shan State Development Foundation health services, 143–44
SSPP (Shan State Progressive Party), 50–51, 85, 88–89, 140–41, 144
Shan State Unity, Committee for, 100
Shan Ywa Thit, 139
Shwegondaing Declaration, April 2010 (NLD), 62
Shwe Mann, Thura, 64–69
signatories/nonsignatories, NCA: last mover advantage for, 30; and locked-in negotiations, 180; outgunning used against, 92; and the Panglong Conference, 95, 96–97, 99, 100, 102, 105–6; post-coup ambivalence of, 188

Si Thura, 144–45
Smith, Martin, 13, 50–51, 53
Snyder, Jack L., 31
South, Ashley, 13, 16
Spain, 178–79
SPDC (State Peace and Development Council), 55, 121, 127
"spoilers," 23–24, 27–28
stalemate, conflict, stalled
SLORC (State Law and Order Restoration Council), 49, 50–55, 121, 127
states, ethnic minority: constitution of 2008 in weakening of, 110–17, 126, 129–30; defined, 24–25; and implementation of the 2008 constitution, 9; layering and locking-in ethnic recognition in, 150–51, 153, 158, 168–69; layering and weak decentralization in, 110–11, 117–29; outflanking and erosion of autonomy of, 143–44, 145–48. See also under *name of state*
strategies, 4–5, 11–12, 26–38, 48–55, 63–64, 178, 179–85
subjugation of ethnic power, 165–73
Su Mon Thazin Aung, 67–68

TNLA (Ta'ang National Liberation Army), 85, 92, 93, 95, 105, 109
taing yin thar lumyo ("original inhabitants"), 191n6
Tanintharyi Region, 70, 136, 139
Tatmadaw: 2021 coup by, 1–3, 185–89; in Bamar dominance and minority repression, 39–40, 59–60; in ceasefires and political dialogue, 83–86, 92, 93–95, 96–97, 100, 101, 105–9; in constitutional lock-in and ethnic state weakness, 112, 113–14, 121–22, 125, 126; dominance of, in the state structure, 3–4; in layering and locking-in ethnic recognition, 162–64; and the NLD government, 75; outflanking by, 131, 133–37, 138–39, 147, 183–84; in shifting strategies on the 1988 uprising, 49–50; strategies in state domination of, 12–15; in the theater of war, 24; uprisings of 1988 in shifting strategy of, 48–55; in violence against the Rohingya, 78–79. See also military regime/junta
Taung Yoe, 161–62
taxes/taxation: authority over, in ethnic state weakness, 114–15, 117–18, 119–20; in the constitution of 2008, 57–58, 72, 114–15, 120, 203n16, 204n41; in outflanking and erosion of autonomy, 132, 133, 135, 137–38, 148. See also resources/resource allocation; revenue

INDEX

territory, control of, 131, 134–35, 162, 163, 165–66, 183–84, 185–86
Thailand, 49–50, 171
Than Shwe, 64
Thein Sein, U, 8–9, 64–73, 88–89, 95, 117–18. *See also* USDP (Union Solidarity Development Party)
Thein Zaw, 67–68
Third Force CSO coalition, 112–13. *See also* CSOs (Civil Society Organizations)
"three-step unity," 153–54
Toft, Monica, 20
transitional government. *See* USDP (Union Solidarity Development Party) and government

Union Electricity Production Law, 118
Union Government, Ministry of the Office of, 119–20
UPC (Union Peace Conference), 9, 23, 31–32, 96–99, 108. *See also* Panglong Conference, 21st Century
UPDJC (Union Peace Dialogue Joint Committee), 97–99, 100, 101–2, 146, 212n16
UNFC (United Nationalities Federal Council), 87, 90–92, 93
UWSA (United Wa State Army), 52, 85, 95, 100, 106, 109, 132–33, 162
USDP (Union Solidarity Development Party) and government: in ceasefire negotiations and political dialogue, 80–81, 82–84, 88–89, 94–95, 97–99, 107–8; in democratization, 61–62, 64–73, 75–76, 80–81; in layering and locking-in ethnic recognition, 167–68; in normalizing ethnic state weakness, 110, 114–15, 117–18, 123, 124, 127–28; in the politicization of ethnicity, 8–9; in winning by process, 31–32

Van Thio, Henry, 75–76
veto power, 21, 31, 100, 113–14, 182
violence: in the 1988 uprising, 49; ceasefires in reduction of, 52, 185; coup of 2021 in new cycle of, 174–75; and ethnic conflict in British colonialism, 42–43; layering and locking-in ethnic recognition in, 173; in leveraging negotiations, 23–24, 36–37; in outgunning strategy, 4–5; during the Panglong Conference, 105; and the politicization of ethnicity, 9–10; against the Rohingya, 78, 164–65, 174; Tatmadaw, in outgunning, 184; in winning by process, 179
Virgin, Fallow, Vacant Land Management Law, 145

Wa ethnic group and SAZ, 6, 50–51, 53–55, 132, 135, 156, 161–62
Wagner, Robert H., 20
Wa mining companies, 121–22
war, theater of: ceasefire negotiations in, 44–48, 50–55, 84, 85, 183, 184; defined, 5; leveraging of, in negotiations, 19–20, 23–25, 29, 30, 84, 183; as means of winning, 20; outgunning in, 36, 37, 84, 184; return to, 180, 186; in stalled conflict, 11–12; in Tatmadaw dominance and autonomy, 4; in the USDP negotiation process, 80–81
Ward and Village Tract Administration Law, 66
"war fatigue," 1–2, 84, 87, 107–8
"wasteland," 145–46
Win Min, 48
WGEC (Working Group on Ethnic Coordination), 91–92

Zartman, L. William, 21, 25
Zaw Myint Maung, U, 115–16
Zaw Oo, 48

www.ingramcontent.com/pod-product-compliance
Lightning Source LLC
Chambersburg PA
CBHW032146230426
43672CB00011B/2462